D0609357

ADMINISTRATIVE LAW IN ACTION

This book investigates and analyses how administrative law works in practice through a detailed case-study and evaluation of one of the UK's largest and most important administrative agencies, the immigration department. In doing so, the book broadens the conversation of administrative law beyond the courts to include how administrative agencies themselves make, apply and enforce the law. Blending theoretical and empirical administrative-legal analysis, the book demonstrates why we need to pay closer attention to what government agencies actually do, how they do it, how they are organised, and how they are held to account. Taking a contextual approach, the book provides a detailed analysis of how the immigration department performs its core functions of making policy and law, taking mass casework decisions and enforcing immigration law.

The book considers major recent episodes of immigration administration including the development of the hostile environment policy and the treatment of the Windrush generation. By examining a diverse range of material, the book presents a model of administrative law based upon the organisational competence and capacity of administration and its institutional design. Alongside diagnosing the immigration department's failings, the book advances positive proposals for its reform.

Administrative Law in Action

Immigration Administration

Robert Thomas

·HART·

OXFORD · LONDON · NEW YORK · NEW DELHI · SYDNEY

HART PUBLISHING

Bloomsbury Publishing Plc

Kemp House, Chawley Park, Cumnor Hill, Oxford, OX2 9PH, UK

1385 Broadway, New York, NY 10018, USA

29 Earlsfort Terrace, Dublin 2, Ireland

HART PUBLISHING, the Hart/Stag logo, BLOOMSBURY and the Diana logo are
trademarks of Bloomsbury Publishing Plc

First published in Great Britain 2022

Copyright © Robert Thomas, 2022

Robert Thomas has asserted his right under the Copyright, Designs and
Patents Act 1988 to be identified as Author of this work.

All rights reserved. No part of this publication may be reproduced or transmitted in any form or by any
means, electronic or mechanical, including photocopying, recording, or any information storage
or retrieval system, without prior permission in writing from the publishers.

While every care has been taken to ensure the accuracy of this work, no responsibility for
loss or damage occasioned to any person acting or refraining from action as a result of any
statement in it can be accepted by the authors, editors or publishers.

All UK Government legislation and other public sector information used in the work is
Crown Copyright ©. All House of Lords and House of Commons information used in
the work is Parliamentary Copyright ©. This information is reused under the terms
of the Open Government Licence v3.0 (http://www.nationalarchives.gov.uk/doc/
open-government-licence/version/3) except where otherwise stated.

All Eur-lex material used in the work is © European Union,
http://eur-lex.europa.eu/, 1998–2022.

A catalogue record for this book is available from the British Library.

Library of Congress Cataloging-in-Publication data

Names: Thomas, Robert, 1974- author.

Title: Administrative law in action : immigration administration / Robert Thomas.

Description: Oxford, UK ; New York, NY : Hart Publishing, an imprint of Bloomsbury Publishing, 2022. |
Includes bibliographical references and index.

Identifiers: LCCN 2021053499 (print) | LCCN 2021053500 (ebook) |
ISBN 9781509953110 (hardback) | ISBN 9781509953158 (paperback) |
ISBN 9781509953134 (pdf) | ISBN 9781509953127 (Epub)

Subjects: LCSH: Emigration and immigration law—England. | Immigrants—Legal status, laws, etc.—
England. | Immigrants—Government policy—England. | Administrative law—England.

Classification: LCC KD4134 .T49 2022 (print) | LCC KD4134 (ebook) |
DDC 342.4208/2—dc23/eng/20211109

LC record available at https://lccn.loc.gov/2021053499

LC ebook record available at https://lccn.loc.gov/2021053500

ISBN: HB: 978-1-50995-311-0
        ePDF: 978-1-50995-313-4
        ePub: 978-1-50995-312-7

Typeset by Compuscript Ltd, Shannon

To find out more about our authors and books visit www.hartpublishing.co.uk.
Here you will find extracts, author information, details of forthcoming events
and the option to sign up for our newsletters.

PREFACE

This book is about the UK's immigration department and the administrative law that governs its organisation and activities. The aim is to give an overall analysis of the immigration department, what it does, how it does it, and the problems and difficulties involved. To this end, the analysis adopts a 'law and administration' approach, that is, it approaches the problems of administrative law by investigating administrative action and views administrative law as inseparable from the political and organisational forces that impact upon administration and how it makes and implements law and policy. In this way, the book contributes to the wider endeavour of broadening the conversation about administrative law away from its traditional focus on judicial review toward analysing and evaluating how administrative agencies and administrative law works and operates in practice.

This way of understanding administrative law involves building from the ground up by examining the functions and roles of a particular administrative institution, considering that institution's history and substantive mission, and then working through how it performs its functions in practice and how it is scrutinised and held to account. This involves deep immersion in the work and behaviours of a particular administrative institution. What arises from this type of approach is that administrative law is not at all separate from matters of policy and administrative implementation, as conventional court-based administrative law would tend to assume. On the contrary, governmental policy and substance and administrative functions and structures are closely intertwined with how administrative law operates. Through an examination of what a particular government department does and how it does it, the book seeks to highlight and explore the value of a more governmental approach to administrative law and the often problematic and seemingly intractable issues that arise.

Trying to produce administrative law scholarship that embodies and reflects administrative behaviours and practices and to keep within a reasonable word length is challenging, and even more so in a complex and fast-changing area of government such as immigration. The real-world of administrative law in action is enormous, complex, intricate, dynamic, and constantly shifting and fluctuating. There are difficult decisions about what to include and exclude and how much detail to go into. I have therefore sought to give an overall analysis and evaluation, to travel down the principal stream, to examine the accompanying whirlpools and eddies, and to identify and consider the various tributaries, but without necessarily navigating each of them in full detail. My personal instinct is to examine matters in as much detail as possible, but had I sought to do this exhaustively and also take into account current developments, then the book would have been too long and it would never have been finished.

Another potentially constraining factor when producing this type of scholarship is the traditional governmental reluctance to allow researchers to venture inside government. An administrative law scholar taking an 'inside-out' perspective on the workings of a particular government department will often get the feeling that they are missing out something important, that there is more going on internally they need to know about, but which they have to piece together from the outside as best they can. There are, of course, legitimate reasons why government does not want researchers examining the inner workings of administration, such as not distracting officials from doing their jobs and protecting the privacy and confidentiality of people subject to the immigration system. However, another influential factor may well be the unstated fear that an outsider may well uncover yet more piles of dirty linen that senior officials do not want being washed in public.

Nonetheless, this feeling of not being as well-informed as possible can be significantly moderated in various ways. There is a considerable amount of material about administrative behaviour that is readily publicly available, such as parliamentary debates, select committee evidence sessions and reports, inspection reports, departmental reviews, and so on, which have been heavily drawn upon here. Internal guidance and policy documents that are not publicly available can be acquired through Freedom of Information (FOI) requests. Despite the obvious sensitivities around immigration administration, it has been possible to have interactions with some officials.

There is also personal experience. This includes having once been seconded from academia to the Home Office for some months to undertake research on immigration appeals and judicial review. This gave me the opportunity to see one aspect of government from the inside. I have also undertaken various research projects in the area on asylum appeals and immigration judicial reviews, and sat on various working parties. I am also a member of the Administrative Justice Council and co-chair its academic panel. Overall, these experiences have suggested that what is publicly known about government pretty much reflects the basic contours of what happens inside of it. Further, it is important to note that there are important knowledge gaps within government about what happens in practice within it. Given the scale of administration, there is often an asymmetry of knowledge about operations within government between officials and the different levels they work at. It is also important to note that some types of information will always be off-limits, such as official advice to ministers and sensitive personal and other information.

Another point is that the great mass of detailed information available within government is often more likely to overload than enlighten. The intricate minutiae of administrative practices are important when looking at matters very close up. But, when taking an overall 'big picture' perspective, such details are often ephemeral and of relatively marginal significance when placed in the wider scheme of things. A final point is that often the issue is not just one of accessing information, but also interpreting its significance. Government departments inevitably have their own political and presentational self-interests; as regards the immigration department, these self-interests are often quite transparent.

I have then drawn extensively upon various materials and the experience and knowledge of others. I have used my own best and informed judgement when interpreting the importance of these materials and weaving them together into an overall framework. I have also sought to develop a conceptual framework for analysing and evaluating administration and administrative law in action.

In undertaking this project, I have incurred various debts. I would like to thank many colleagues in academia, government, legal and judicial practice, and the wider immigration system for discussions. Thanks also go to Richard Rawlings, Tony Prosser and Richard Kirkham for reading drafts and for their perceptive comments. Of course, they are not responsible for the views and errors contained herein, but they have provided considerable expert scholarly guidance and support. I would also like to thank the excellent team at Hart Publishing – Kate Whetter, Rosie Mearns, and Peter Warren – for their guidance and assistance. I would also like to recognise the enormous benefits of my friendship with Charles Blake, a Manchester law graduate, former government lawyer, and immigration tribunal judge, who passed away in 2020. Finally, I would like to thank my wife and children for their support.

Robert Thomas
Hartford

CONTENTS

ABBREVIATIONS

AAR	Adults at risk
ARU	UKVI Administrative Review Unit
CAO	Chief Adjudication Officer
CCU	UKVI Chief Caseworker Unit
CFMT	Charter Flight Monitoring Team
COAT	UKVI Central Operations Assurance Team
DHSC	Department of Health and Social Care
DQF	Decision quality framework
DWP	Department for Work and Pensions
DVLA	Driver and Vehicle Licensing Agency
ECAA	European Communities Association Agreement
ECHR	European Convention on Human Rights
EEA	European Economic Area
EHRC	Equality and Human Rights Commission
FNPs	Foreign national prisoners
FOI	Freedom of Information
Ft-TIAC	First-tier Tribunal (Immigration and Asylum Chamber)
GLD	Government legal department
HAC	House of Commons Home Affairs Committee
HMIP	HM Chief Inspector of Prisons
ICE	IE Immigration Compliance and Enforcement
ICIBI	Independence Chief Inspector of Borders and Immigration
ICO	Information Commissioner's Office
IE	Immigration Enforcement
ILPA	Immigration Law Practitioners' Association

ILR	Indefinite leave to remain
IMA	Independent Monitoring Authority for the Citizens' Rights Agreements
IMBs	Independent monitoring boards
IND	Immigration and Nationality Directorate
IRC	Immigration removal centre
JCHR	Joint Committee on Human Rights
MAC	Migration Advisory Committee
MoJ	Ministry of Justice
NAO	National Audit Office
OVM	NHS Overseas Visitor Manager
PAC	House of Commons Public Accounts Committee
PHSO	Parliamentary Ombudsman and Health Service Ombudsman
PPO	Prisons and Probation Ombudsman
PSED	Public Sector Equality Duty
PSU	UKVI Professional Standards Unit
QA	Quality assurance
STHFs	Short-term holding facilities
TPC	Tribunal Procedure Committee
UKBA	UK Border Agency
UKIAT	UK Immigration Appeal Tribunal
UKVI	UK Visas and Immigration
UNHCR	United Nations High Commissioner for Refugees
UTIAC	Upper Tribunal (Immigration and Asylum Chamber)
VAC	Visa application centre

TABLE OF CASES

TABLE OF LEGISLATION

Council of Europe

International Law

1

Administration and Law

I. Immigration Administration

This book is a study of public administration and administrative law in operation and in context. The context is the administration of immigration policy in the UK and the specific administrative agency is the UK's immigration department. In formal terms, this is the government department called the Home Office or, more specifically, the three directorates within that department responsible for different aspects of immigration administration. These three directorates are: UK Visas and Immigration; Immigration Enforcement; and Border Force.[1] This book presents an administrative law analysis of what the immigration department does and how it does it. It critically examines how this department makes and implements policy, and how it is held to account and monitored. The book also examines how this area of administration and administrative law could be reformed and improved.

The immigration department is one the UK's major administrative agencies. It is the institutional embodiment of the ability of the UK state to control immigration, one of the defining characteristics of a modern state. The department's decisions and actions intimately affect the lives of millions of immigrants and their families both inside and outside the country. Its operations and performance are of acute interest to both politicians and the public. Furthermore, the immigration department performs various core administrative functions. It makes and implements immigration law and policy. The department has substantial law-making powers. It makes an extensive body of administrative rules and guidance. Each year, the department's caseworkers take millions of immigration casework decisions to decide the immigration status of people seeking to enter or remain in the country. The department is also responsible for ensuring compliance with and the enforcement of immigration law. By any measure, it is a very large, complex and important administrative agency.

The department is also one of the UK Government's most unstable and problematic administrative agencies. Few other government departments have been subject to as much persistent criticism and upheaval. Senior government ministers

---

[1] The phrase 'administrative agency/department/body' is used here as a generic synonym of 'government department', a more UK-specific phrase.

have described the department as not fit for purpose and as a troubled organisation with a closed, secretive and defensive culture. The department has long suffered from multiple difficulties and problems. It has been repeatedly criticised for the variable quality of its casework decisions on immigration and asylum applications, for delays in making decisions, and huge backlogs. The department has enforced immigration controls against people who have the legal right to remain in the country and who should not have been removed or subjected to enforcement action. Conversely, it has failed to enforce such controls against people who do not have the right to remain in the country. The department attracts a higher proportion of legal challenges than any other government agency. At times, the department has struggled to perform the most basic tasks. There are always operational difficulties somewhere within the immigration system and others looming on the horizon.

These problems arise in part because of the department's policy context and its operational environment. The task of managing and controlling immigration is inherently problematic. It presents all governments with one of the most organisationally challenging, politically contentious, and heavily legalised areas of administration. The department's problems go beyond the ordinary challenges that afflict other areas of administration and public management; they are deep-seated, endemic and systemic. Such problems generate considerable concern, but there is also the need to understand why such difficulties exist and what can be done about them.

The purpose of this book is, then, to provide a detailed analysis of the immigration department to understand and evaluate how it perform its functions and the challenges it faces, and to consider what can be done to improve its operations. But there is a wider purpose beyond examining the intrinsic importance of immigration administration. Studying the operations of government can enable us to arrive at a more informed understanding of how administrative law works in practice. This is significant because administrative law constitutes administration and concerns the organisation and activities of administrative institutions and how they are held to account. The administrative process itself often raises many novel and interesting problems. Indeed, administrative law is inextricable from the administrative agencies that make and administer such law and which in turn are also controlled by administrative law. However, despite the scale and complexity of administrative organisations and their importance, few scholars have grappled with the challenging issues and problems presented by the operations of such bodies, how they undertake their tasks, how they are organised, and how they make, apply, and enforce law and policy in practice.

To undertake this type of analysis, this book approaches and analyses administrative law from an institutional and functional perspective. It examines the administrative and legal issues that arise in light of the policy challenges facing government. From this perspective, the book then investigates the actions and behaviours of administration and its institutional competence and capacity to perform its tasks. The book's title, *Administrative Law in Action*, captures the nature of the dynamics involved. Administration exercises fundamental tasks and it is necessary to examine carefully how it performs them in practice, the problems encountered, and the different types of administrative law that are both made by government itself and imposed externally upon it. It is also necessary to consider how this area of government could be reformed and improved. To this end, the book provides an informed and realistic analysis of which reforms to administration are both required and possible.

II. Models of Administrative Law

Given the broad approach taken here toward administrative law, it is necessary to explain where this book sits within the wider body of administrative law scholarship. In much conventional legal thought, administrative law is principally conceptualised as the corpus of legal doctrines developed by the courts for the purpose of reviewing the legality of administration. This approach has a strong preference for viewing administrative law as comprising the legal principles of judicial review which apply across the broad range of government and public bodies. These legal principles are then subject to doctrinal and theoretical analysis in order to uncover their normative basis and how they are applied by the courts. Consequently, much of the conversation about administrative law concerns judicial review. This way of understanding administrative law will be readily familiar. It can be described as the 'legality' model of administrative law that is largely concerned with identifying the legal limits of administrative action. An important aspect of this model is the assumption that there actually is a clear dividing line between administration and law.

The principles and theories of judicial review are significant topics and deserve continued study. Nonetheless, there have long been concerns that a court-focused approach misses much of the action, not least the basic nuts and bolts of how administrative systems operate in practice and develop over time. Only a small number of administrative decisions are ever challenged by way of judicial review. The focus on courts and judicial reasoning tends to overlook other non-legal influences on administrative behaviour. The result is that more time is spent analysing how the courts review administration than investigating and analysing administrative action itself. Studying the legal limits of administrative action is important, but so is investigating the choices made within those limits. The result is that the legality model, with its court-centred focus, largely ignores huge areas of actual administration. This in turn constrains our understanding of key problems of administrative law and how they might be addressed.

Further, the notion that administrative law comprises a coherent and unified body of legal principles overlooks the highly diverse and variegated range of administrative contexts and functions. It also tends to neglect the fact that the growth of administrative governance has fundamentally transformed the nature of law itself. Modern law is principally concerned with making policy and its implementation by administrative institutions. Accordingly, a traditional focus on the coherence of legal doctrines as a self-contained set of principles now appears to be somewhat out of date and should be replaced by a focus upon the effectiveness of specific governmental institutions in making and implementing law and policy in practice.[2]

Highlighting the limits of a court-focused approach is nothing new and these points have long been rehearsed. It is important not to push them too far for the following reasons. First, some administrative lawyers have recognised the need to study administrative law in context, and there have been many studies. Second, the courts remain significant players in the workings and actions of administration despite, and indeed sometimes because of, the existence and operation of other forms of administrative law beyond the conventional legal principles. Nonetheless, in reality, much, though far from all, of administrative law in practice concerns the organisation and activities of administration and how policy is to be implemented. Administration itself is a major actor in this process and the functioning of administrative governance has raised many pressing and important issues that deserve analysis. Recent scholarship has highlighted that legal analysis of general legal principles often overlooks the fact that the grounds of judicial review are applied in the context of specific administrative-legal frameworks; more contextual analysis of judicial review is then required.[3] This is an important and valuable perspective. By extension, it can also be said that there is a need to study in context the various other forms of administrative law in action that exist outside the courts and the range of purposes they serve. In short, there is a need for a pluralistic approach that approaches the same subject matter – governmental operations – from a variety of different angles.[4]

An alternative way of studying and understanding administrative law might be termed a 'governance' model. From this perspective, administrative law is not solely or even principally concerned with the limits of administrative action. Instead, it should analyse the practical affairs of administrative governance, that is, 'what administrative agencies actually do, how they do it, and the internal ethics that both motivate and restrain their behaviour'.[5] This involves examining the basic organisation and operation of government agencies, how they are designed, how they make and implement policy, the mechanisms and instruments they use and their efficacy, and how these agencies are scrutinised and held to account. This approach recognises the degree of the transformation that has occurred as a

---

[2] EL Rubin, *Beyond Camelot: Rethinking Law and Politics for the Modern State* (Princeton, Princeton University Press, 2005); EL Rubin, 'From Coherence to Effectiveness: A Legal Methodology for the Modern World' in R van Gestel, HW Micklitz and EL Rubin (eds), *Rethinking Legal Scholarship: A Transatlantic Dialogue* (Cambridge, Cambridge University Press, 2017).

[3] J Bell, *The Anatomy of Administrative Law* (Oxford, Hart Publishing 2020).

[4] P Daly, 'Plural Public Law' (2020) 51 *Ottawa Law Review* 395.

[5] J Mashaw, 'Between Facts and Norms: Agency Statutory Interpretation as an Autonomous Enterprise' (2005) 55 *University of Toronto Law Journal* 497.

result of the growth of administrative governance and the need to investigate how administration works in practice.

Undertaking this type of analysis requires different ways of approaching and analysing law and administration when compared with a predominantly court-focused approach. The focus is not principally upon restraining administration, but on how to develop and promote effective and humane means of governing. It is therefore necessary to take seriously the institutional competence and capacity of administration, how administration is organised, the problems that arise, and the impact of political and organisational forces upon administration. Another feature is the recognition that the courts do not have any monopoly over administrative law. There are other forms of administrative law that exist both outside of administration and are also generated internally within administrative practices. It is therefore necessary to investigate and analyse how different types of administrative law operate and critically examine their effectiveness.

III. Concepts and Ideas to Investigate Administration and Law

This book examines how the immigration department makes and implements policy and how it is controlled by law. To this end, it focuses upon both the behavioural and the normative aspects of administration. That is, it examines how a particular administrative organisation – the immigration department – in fact operates, how it is organised, the effectiveness of its activities, and how it could potentially be improved. In doing so, it contributes to the long-standing endeavour of widening the focus of administrative law scholarship.[6] To understand, analyse and evaluate administration and administrative law in this way, it is necessary to examine in some detail the history of the department, its structure and how it performs its functions. To this end, conceptual tools are required.

One starting point is the concepts and tools provided by the legality model of administrative law. These include the various principles of judicial review and associated case law. However, there is an irremediable problem with the model of legality. It is focused almost exclusively upon identifying the legal limits of administrative action rather than starting with the functions and tasks that administration undertakes and how it performs them. Accordingly, this model fails to supply the appropriate conceptual tools with which to analyse and evaluate the organisation and activities of administrative governance. The model of legality remains of some use, particularly as regards the judicial control of the department, although even in this respect, such control itself involves a significant degree of judicial

---

[6] C Harlow and R Rawlings, *Law and Administration*, 5th edn (Cambridge, Cambridge University Press, 2021) ch 1.

management of administration. However, in order to evaluate administration and law, the conceptual tools to be used should themselves reflect the behavioural and normative orientation of administration. A more promising source of analytical tools and norms is not then the concept of legality, but the concept of administration.

Administration is the principal institutional means by which public policy is made and delivered. It is based on the principle of instrumental rationality, that is, the major purpose of administration is to implement policy as effectively as possible.[7] To this end, administrative organisations share common features: specialised jurisdiction; full-time officials; a hierarchical structure; formal rules, routines and procedures; and extensive reliance on case files. The concept of instrumental rationality is an ideal type and not a description of how administration works in practice. Nonetheless, the principal demand placed upon administration is that it implement policy effectively. While specific governments and ministers change regularly, administrative institutions comprise the permanent structure and basis of the governmental system and they have a purposive orientation. Higher-level policy decisions are taken by elected ministers who are responsible to Parliament, although ministers are almost entirely reliant upon officials who develop and work up policy proposals, provide advice, and make lower-level policy decisions and decide how higher-level policy goals are to be implemented. Senior officials play a significant role in both managing administrative organisations and in making policy. Front-line officials perform specific functions such as making individual decisions and enforcement action. This is the structure through which policy is administered.

The basic point is that instrumental rationality – implementing policy effectively – comprises the substantive standard of administrative action. Both politicians and the public expect and want administration to be functionally effective. This substantive standard comprises an internal norm that motivates administration. It is also the standard by which government departments and external agencies, such as independent inspectors and the National Audit Office, scrutinise and assess administrative action. It also informs the vast bulk of the administrative laws made by government agencies. The specific detail of what effective administration and administrative law looks like varies considerably from one context to another. Each government agency has its own unique function and the world of government is highly diverse. Further, government has been experiencing a number of transformational changes through trends such as outsourcing functions to private companies and the increased use of IT and automated decision processes. Nonetheless, instrumental rationality is the principal standard that informs and is used to evaluate administrative action.

A number of other analytical concepts and tools flow from the concept of instrumental rationality. By using such ideas, we can expand our vision in order

---

[7] M Weber (eds G Roth and C Wittich), *Economy and Society* (London, University of California Press, 1978) 217–23 and 956–1002.

to understand and evaluate how administration and administrative law work in practice and the possibilities for their improvement. For the purposes of this book, the following concepts and ideas will be used extensively to analyse the organisation and activities of the immigration department.

A. Organisational Competence

In order to make and implement policy, administration must have the formal legal powers and the ability to make its own rules. This is necessary, but far from sufficient. What is also required is effective administrative action. Turning policy aspirations into practical social reality involves an enormous range of actions, but above all it requires organisational competence. Administration must possess the necessary capacity and capabilities to perform its tasks effectively. It must be organised and managed effectively. Different administrative activities need to be coordinated so that policy goals can be implemented.

The need for competent government – getting the basics right – is familiar enough. The language of competence, capacity and capability regularly feature in discussions about both government in general and the immigration department in particular. Organisational competence reflects the expectations of politicians, the public in general and individuals who interact with administration. Politicians and the public expect government to be competent so that it can deliver policy outcomes. Individuals who interact with administration expect it to do its job properly when it comes to making correct decisions on their entitlements and legal rights. Organisational competence is also directly relevant to the reputation and legitimacy of both particular agencies and the wider governmental system in general. People are more likely to tolerate things that they disagree with if government agencies are competent. In short, organisational competence is an essential foundation of effective administrative action. It is also a means of understanding, and an integral component of, administrative law.[8]

Many of the issues concerning the competence of administration are specific to the particular administrative agency, its functions, structure, tasks and operating environment. However, there are aspects of organisational competence that are common across many administrative institutions. One concerns the capacity and ability of an administrative organisation to understand its internal operations

---

[8] PJ Weiser, 'Institutional Design, FCC Reform, and the Hidden Side of the Administrative State' (2009) 61 *Administrative Law Review* 675, 676 (administrative law scholars need to examine 'questions related to institutional competence and institutional structure that determine whether administrative regulation can be effective'); M Elliott and R Thomas, *Public Law*, 4th edn (Oxford, Oxford University Press, 2020) 403; E Fisher and S Shapiro, *Administrative Competence: Reimagining Administrative Law* (Cambridge, Cambridge University Press, 2020) (arguing that administrative competence is essential to understanding administrative law as the law of public administration and that much administration and administrative law depends upon administrative competence).

and the impact of its activities in terms of policy delivery. Another is the ability of senior officials to communicate the right messages and guidance downwards throughout the organisation to front-line staff. There also needs to be effective coordination between different parts of the same organisation. Such matters in turn depend upon management information, IT systems, and internal monitoring and supervision.

It is also important to recognise that the organisational competence of government agencies is always constrained by the real-world conditions in which they operate. Such agencies have the backing of the state's fiscal resources and its law-making powers. They can undertake complex tasks on an enormous scale. But they are not all powerful. Their capacities are constrained in all sorts of ways. Administrators have limited time and resources. Given the limits of bounded rationality, administrators satisfice rather than maximise; they look for good enough solutions rather than perfect ones.[9] Other constraints include: the skills, behaviours, and self-interests of officials; how effectively administrative systems are designed, resourced, organised, coordinated, managed and supervised; and the variable abilities of government agencies to learn. The consequences of such constraints become evident in various ways. Administration can fail by not getting the job done and/or by imposing significant harms on people who must, of necessity, interact with it. Organisational competence is always a matter of degree, and its assessment requires close examination of how any particular administrative institution operates and the cognitive and institutional constraints under which it operates.

A related point concerns the degree to which an administrative agency anticipates and recognises the limits of its organisational competence and takes appropriate steps to deal with them. For instance, a government agency that takes millions of individualised administrative decisions will be constrained by the limits of both its decision processes and the competence of individual decision-makers. The question then arises as to whether the agency has introduced appropriate mechanisms to counterbalance those limits and, if so, the effectiveness of those mechanisms. Another fundamental aspect of organisational competence concerns the capacity of administration to learn and respond to changes in its operating environment. The task environment of any particular administrative organisation is always in a state of constant flux. Administration must adapt to such changes or else risk becoming out of date and ineffective.

Turning to the immigration department, there are various aspects of the department's operations and its performance to examine. To anticipate subsequent discussion, the department may have reasonable organisational competence when it comes to processing a mass of individual casework decisions efficiently and quickly. However, quantitative capacity and volume is only one aspect

---

[9] HA Simon, *Administrative Behavior*, 4th edn (New York, Free Press, 1997) 118–20; HA Simon, *Reason in Human Affairs* (Stanford, Stanford University Press, 1983) 19–23.

of organisational competence. What of the quality of those decisions? Other administrative functions – making policy, legislation, and rules, and undertaking enforcement action – call for quite different skills, capacities and capabilities. Sitting above the various sub-systems of operational delivery, higher-level managerial competence is required to coordinate and oversee the overall system as a whole. We also need to investigate matters such as the IT systems by which management information on the organisation's activities are collected, and the alignment of policy with organisational structures, systems, staff and administrative cultures.

B. Internal Administrative Law

In order to implement policy, administrative organisations need to be managed and supervised. A significant means of doing this is through internal administrative law, the forms of administrative law generated internally within administration. Administrative legislation and judicial review are commonly recognised sources of administrative law. But large-scale organisations comprising thousands of officials work primarily on the basis of internal written instructions, policies, guidance, performance standards and monitoring systems to guide and manage their operations.[10] Internal administrative law refers to the internal systems and processes within administration by which higher-level officials oversee, supervise and monitor the work of front-line officials in order to motivate and manage them and to hold them accountable. It is not made by Parliament or the courts, but by senior officials and ministers as a means of structuring the activities of front-line officials and for supervising them. Internal administrative law therefore has a very different structure from, for instance, the legal principles of judicial review. When viewed from the administrator's perspective, administrative law is principally a means of getting things done by organising, and managing what are often large and complex administrative institutions.[11] The principal purposes of internal administrative law are to allocate responsibility for, limit, guide and motivate administrative action and to impose administrative accountability on front-line officials and thereby ensure that their actions and behaviours align with higher-level policy and organisational goals. The specific forms that internal administrative law assumes will be highly contingent upon the contexts, structures and functions of specific administrative organisations.

---

[10] R Rawlings, 'Soft Law Never Dies' in M Elliott and D Feldman (eds), *The Cambridge Companion to Public Law* (Cambridge, Cambridge University Press, 2015).

[11] At an abstract level, there are various ways in which senior officials can seek to control those working on the front line. These include: *duress*, the threat or use of sanctions and/or the withholding of rewards; *exchange*, the winning of cooperation by the mutual recognition of contribution and obligation for pecuniary rewards, status or symbols of esteem; and *identification*, the assuring of collaboration through shared values, purposes, and outlook. See A Dunsire, *Control in a Bureaucracy* (Oxford, Martin Robinson, 1978) 35.

The notion of internal administrative law has been predominately generated within US administrative law scholarship where it is understood as a form of administrative accountability by which higher-level officials control and direct subordinate officials and through which they call them to account for their work.[12] It has come to be recognised over recent decades, although this has been, in large part, a modern reinvigoration of its earlier recognition by previous scholars.[13] In the UK, internal administrative law has not received the same degree of attention and some caution is required when drawing comparisons with the US. Nonetheless, internal controls and systems clearly exist within UK government departments and agencies and can be incorporated within the analysis of administrative law. Furthermore, the importance of internal administrative law has long been recognised.

In the first text published on administrative law, FJ Port explained that:

> [T]he prime object of Administrative Law is motion or function; but in order that the law may be carried out, it is necessary to constitute not only central departments, but also subordinate bodies and local agents, so that the application of the law may be effective. It is right to have motion as the *ultimate* idea, but the immediate one may be constituent. This is necessarily so where the Government deals with an area which is larger than can be administered at first hand. The links of the chain must be forged in order that the will expressed at one end may operate at the other end, and the structure of the links is rightly studied in dealing with that operation of properly expressed will. There need therefore be no hesitation in bringing within the scope of Administrative Law the constitution of Bodies or the appointment of Agents whose primary function is the operation of the law and not its enactment or judicial interpretation. Dynamic Administrative Law must be based on static Administrative Law.[14]

Implicit within this description of the forging of the 'links of the chain' and their 'structure' are the internal forms of administrative law issued to front-line officials to guide, motivate and constrain their activities so that the 'properly expressed will' becomes effective. The notions here of function, constituent structure, administrative operations, and dynamic and static conceptions of administrative law highlight the close connections between instrumental rationality, organisational competence and internal administrative law. They are relevant throughout this book.

Other scholars have similarly recognised the role of internal administrative law. Griffith and Street noted that the control of administrative bodies and the

---

[12] JL Mashaw, *Bureaucratic Justice: Managing Social Security Disability Claims* (New Haven, Yale University Press, 1983); SA Shapiro, 'Why Administrative Law Misunderstands How Government Works: The Missing Institutional Analysis' (2013) 53 *Washburn Law Journal* 1; GE Metzger and KM Stack, 'Internal Administrative Law' (2017) 115 *Michigan Law Review* 1239; NR Parillo (ed), *Administrative Law from the Inside Out* (Cambridge, Cambridge University Press, 2018) 1–12.

[13] FJ Goodnow, *The Principles of the Administrative Law of the United States* (New York, Putnam's, 1905); B Wyman, *The Principles of the Administrative Law Governing the Relations of Public Officers* (St Paul, Keefe-Davidson, 1906).

[14] FJ Port, *Administrative Law* (London, Longmans, Green and Co, 1929) 12.

exercise of their powers were 'more a matter of administrative practice than of law.'[15] Consequently, the subject matter of administrative law extends beyond the borderline of law into administrative practices and organisation; ignoring these features would present an incomplete picture and fall into the fallacy that there is a clear dividing line between law and administration.[16] Other scholars have highlighted how the subject matter of administrative law extends beyond lawyer's law and includes both administrative guidance and the internal structures and organisation of government departments.[17]

When viewed from a conventional court-centred approach, the notion of administration-generated administrative law may seem unusual and perhaps even troubling, or it might seem trifling. After all, how can administrative guidance assume an importance equal, for instance, to a Supreme Court judgment articulating major norms of legal principle? But this is to overlook the fact that internal administrative law is the practical day-to-day reality within government agencies that engage in operational delivery of policies. Its role is to guide the behaviours and practices of front-line officials. Internal administrative law exerts continual influence upon administration whereas judicial intervention is typically more episodic. It is also the means by which court judgments, and other forms of external accountability, are incorporated into administrative routines and processes.

For these reasons, we need to examine how this type of administrative law works in practice. What are the various forms of internal administrative law that exist within the immigration department and how do they operate in practice? How effective are they? How do they interact with external administrative law? Do front-line operational staff have the capacity and resources to implement the internal law? What happens when different forms of internal law embody competing tensions? And what happens when internal administrative law and its forms are dysfunctional or are manipulated for politically self-interested ends?

C. Accountability and Institutional Design

A related set of issues concern the performance of administrative institutions and how they are held to account. This in turn depends on the range of values and interests imposed upon government by different accountability systems.

---

[15] JAG Griffith and H Street, *Principles of Administrative Law*, 4th edn (London, Pitman, 1973) 6.
[16] ibid.
[17] JF Garner, *Administrative Law* (London, Butterworths, 1970) 2, 22–23; J Willis, 'Canadian Administrative Law in Retrospect' (1974) 24 *University of Toronto Law Journal* 225, 237; T Daintith and A Page, *The Executive in the Constitution: Structure, Autonomy, and Internal Control* (Oxford, Oxford University Press, 1999).

Broadly speaking, the accountability framework of public administration spans the three distinct but related realms of politics, administration and law.[18] First, in a democracy, administration must be politically accountable to the people. Political accountability is achieved through elections and the appointment of ministers who head up government departments, and through parliamentary scrutiny of administration via ministers. A second form of accountability concerns the operation of administrative bodies and is focused upon their efficacy and effectiveness. Administration must seek to get things done by being competent, effectively implementing policy, and achieving value for money. This form of control is undertaken both internally within administration itself through internal administrative law, and externally by independent audit and inspection bodies. Third, there is legal accountability. Administration exercises power over people's lives. It must therefore be legally accountable for its decisions and actions that affect the rights and interests of affected people. There must be legal remedies by which such individuals can challenge the legality of administration and secure redress.

Viewed from this perspective, there is a range of demands placed on administrative bodies. They must be politically responsive, operationally effective, and act lawfully. All of these values are essential components of what legitimate administration looks like, but they often pull in different directions. As Mashaw has explained, 'the task of administrative law in structuring and controlling administrative institutions is the task of managing tensions among these competing demands'.[19] From one perspective or another, administration will fail or be seen to be failing. However, this approach brings into focus the tensions within a wider model of administrative law as the design and organisation of administrative institutions. This involves taking account of the full range of different interests and values in play and being pursued by different accountability systems. It also involves extending the inquiry into administrative law beyond judicial control by including other mechanisms of control. From this position, the task of administrative law is to generate institutional designs that appropriately balance the simultaneous demands of political responsiveness, efficient administration, and respect for legal rights.[20]

The interests served by accountability regimes – political responsiveness, administrative effectiveness and efficiency, and legality – can be pursued by different mechanisms of accountability. For instance, legal accountability is principally focused upon protecting legal rights and ensuring lawful administrative action. At the same time, courts and tribunals play a role in protecting

---

[18] P Day and R Klein, *Accountabilities: Five Public Services* (London, Tavistock, 1987) ch 1; R Mulgan, *Holding Power to Account: Accountability in Modern Democracies* (Basingstoke, Palgrave Macmillan, 2003).

[19] JL Mashaw, 'Structuring a "Dense Complexity": Accountability and the Project of Administrative Law' (2005) *Issues in Legal Scholarship*, Article 4, 14.

[20] ibid.

administration from undue political pressure and in ensuring competent administration. Administrative accountability is concerned with effective implementation of policy, but it can also protect individual rights through internal monitoring and review systems. Parliamentary select committees and independent reviews can articulate norms of legality. The Windrush scandal (considered in chapter three) was characterised by large-scale unlawful administrative decision-making. This occurred without any recourse to the courts or tribunals. Instead, the department's failures were identified and analysed in detail by committees, an independent review, and the Equality and Human Rights Commission.

This wider project of designing administrative institutions is by no means a simple endeavour, not least when undertaken in highly contentious areas such as immigration. The task of promoting effective governance is, to put it mildly, a highly problematic and inherently compromised endeavour. It raises difficult challenges when brute political forces impact upon large-scale and partly dysfunctional mass administrative systems, which then produce actions and decisions that might or might not be effective, legal or respectful of individual rights. The design of institutions is directly related to questions about their organisational competence and the corresponding possibilities for and limitations of administrative reform and improvement.

Another point is that the task of designing and organising administration can never be resolved once and for all; it is necessarily an ongoing project without any defined end point. The operational and political contexts in which administrative institutions exist never stand still. This has significant implications as regards their organisation, control and effectiveness. Nonetheless, the framework of accountability and viewing administrative law as part of the project of designing administrative institutions assists in defining and understanding the complex demands placed upon administration.

As regards the immigration department, it is necessary to examine how the different forms of accountability work in practice and which different institutional designs could be adopted. What is the balance between political control and accountability relative to administrative and legal forms of control and accountability? To what extent does the predominance of one type of control and accountability limit the effectiveness of other types? Where does the appropriate balance lie? And what are the implications for how a particular administrative system is to be designed?

D. The Organisational Foundations of Administrative Law

Another means of understanding administrative law is to identify the different organisational foundations or premises of administration.[21] The basic idea is that

---

[21] WH Simon, 'The Organizational Premises of Administrative Law' (2015) 78 *Law and Contemporary Problems* 61.

the various types of administrative law controls over administrative action come to reflect different understandings of public administration and how it is organised and functions. Such administrative law controls include both external judicial control and internal administrative and managerial supervision.

There are various understandings of administration adopted by administrative law, but for present purposes two such conceptions are particularly relevant. The first sees administration as a traditional bureaucracy, that is, an administrative machine that produces individual outputs from its processes. This includes, for instance, mass individualised administrative decision-making concerning people's entitlements and enforcement action. The archetypal notion of British administrative action has been the single individualised administrative decision that determines the status or entitlements of a person under the relevant rules and policies. The discrete and individualised nature of these decisions and action in turn generate a need for administrative law controls and remedies that are similarly focused on the individual decision or case. Such controls include, for example, the internal checking of individual decisions by higher officers and case-by-case adjudication by tribunal appeals and the courts by way of judicial review.

A second and more recent understanding of administration views it as a performance-based organisation that is focused not just on individual outputs, but also on achieving wider policy outcomes. This understanding emphasises the systemic and structural nature of administration and its ability to deliver policy. From this perspective, individualised decisions and actions are not just individualised decisions and actions; they are the product of overarching administrative systems and processes which in turn underlie and frame them. Accordingly, to be effective, the controls over such systems themselves come to assume a systemic and supervisory character that is often focused upon monitoring the overall performance of administration.

Looking ahead, we will consider how the organisational bases of administration and administrative law operate in practice in the context of the immigration department's core functions, such as casework and enforcement. Which different types of control and scrutiny – both internal/external and administrative/judicial – have adopted more systemic forms? What has been their success and effectiveness? To what extent should this trend be taken further? We will consider these questions in the context of both administrative and judicial supervision of the immigration department.

* * *

These concepts and ideas are part of the toolkit used in this book. Put together, they comprise an overall conceptual framework by which we can understand and evaluate the complex, messy, and sometimes contradictory realities of politics, administration and law. It might be argued that this framework lacks consistency with an overarching higher-level theory and that deeper theoretical underpinning is required. But that would miss the point. The value of these concepts and ideas is not their abstract theoretical coherence, but their practical utility when it comes to evaluating and improving administration and administrative law in practice. This pragmatic orientation is particularly appropriate given that actual government agencies that are themselves far from perfect, subject to multiple and competing pressures, and must get along as best they can in the circumstances.

Other ideas and analytical tools will be used when examining in detail how the department exercises its core functions and operations, such as policy-making, casework decisions and enforcement. As regards policy-making, an initial point is whether administrative law can be usefully recharacterised as policy-making and implementation. If so, then the issues are: what are the features of a good policy-making process; and to what extent do actual policy-making endeavours adhere to them? Related themes are the significance of management information to effective internal administrative supervision and control and the importance of administration systematically evaluating the effectiveness of its policy-making and enforcement activities.

Another core function – individual casework decision-making and redress mechanisms – also raises wider systemic issues concerning administrative performance. These include the role and effectiveness of quality assurance systems within high-volume casework processes and whether the inherent limits of external redress mechanisms can be ameliorated by internal systems of proactive error correction. We will consider the role of the courts in ensuring legal accountability by identifying the limits of administrative action and how this in turn involves the courts in managing administration. Further, to understand how individuals interact with the immigration department, we will examine the pervasive and deep-seated problem of bureaucratic oppression. By expanding the administrative law toolkit in these ways, it is possible to get a better understanding of the vast majority of administrative action that is often sidelined by a court-focused approach. It will also enable assessment, critique and prescriptive recommendations for improving administration.

IV. The Plan of the Book

So much for the purposes of the book and its conceptual framework. What is needed now is a road map of how this book will examine the work of the immigration department.

Chapter two introduces the work of the immigration department in detail. It provides a detailed contextual overview and analysis of the department's functions, its structure and history, and how it is constituted. The chapter also highlights and explores some of the behavioural features of both the immigration department and government in general. After this overview, subsequent chapters examine how the department performs its core functions in practice.

The first two functions concern how the department makes policy and how it makes rules and guidance. These then influence how the department performs its core operational functions of making immigration casework decisions and immigration enforcement. Chapter three examines immigration policy-making through a case study of the department's major policy initiative of the 2010s, commonly referred to as the 'hostile environment'. The chapter examines how officials worked up the hostile environment policy and its disastrous consequences for a large cohort of people – the Windrush generation – who, as Commonwealth citizens, were allowed to enter the UK before 1973. When the department came to devise the hostile environment measures in the early 2010s, it had entirely lost sight of this group of people, with the consequence that they were exposed to the adverse effects of the hostile environment measures. The chapter analyses the underlying causes of this flawed policy-making.

Another way in which administration makes policy is through administrative rule-making. Immigration administration is dominated by highly detailed, complex, technical and fast-moving sets of rules and guidance. Chapter four considers cross-cutting issues raised by the immigration rules and guidance. These include: the types of rules used to administer policy; the role of guidance and human rights law; the complexity of the rules; and the need to evaluate whether the rules achieve their policy objectives. This chapter finds that the complexity of the rules and guidance often work to the disadvantage of both those who interact with the immigration system and those who operate it.

Once rules have been made, they must be administered. This occurs through the department's two other core functions: casework decisions and enforcement action. Chapter five examines immigration casework and the fundamental challenge it poses: the need to process a huge volume of immigration applications and the consequent impact upon the quality of those decisions. The chapter considers the department's culture of applying the rules and the organisational problems involved in managing a large-scale casework process. In addition to front-line casework, there are also additional internal processes adopted by the department to improve and assure the quality of casework decisions. The effectiveness of these mechanisms are analysed.

As with most administrative decision systems, people who apply for an administrative decision concerning their individual circumstances (eg whether or not they qualify for immigration status) and are then refused can feel aggrieved and seek redress. This is the area often known as administrative justice. Chapter six examines how the various redress systems concerning initial casework decisions – administrative reviews, tribunal appeals and 'individual' judicial reviews mostly undertaken by the Upper Tribunal (Immigration and Asylum Chamber) – work in practice and their relative advantages and disadvantages. Each of these processes has its place and they could be enhanced. But they all share a common feature: they are reactive. Accordingly, the chapter argues that a model of internal administrative law based upon the proactive correction of errors could usefully address some of the shortcomings of the redress systems.

Chapter seven examines how the department seeks to enforce immigration controls and its performance in this respect – a neglected but important aspect of administrative law in action. The chapter considers the different enforcement and compliance mechanisms used by the department. This invites analysis of the department's internal organisation and which type of enforcement action is likely to be most effective in securing compliance with immigration law. Consideration is given to the internal means used within the department to manage its operations. The challenges the department faces in trying to enforce the rules have been the subject of detailed critiques, which are examined in detail.

In addition to the mass processing of thousands of fact-specific individual and tribunalised judicial reviews (examined in chapter six), the higher courts undertake more wide-ranging and in-depth judicial scrutiny of administrative policies and actions, which involves imposing legal norms on the department and evaluating its practices. Chapter eight examines how the courts undertake this wider scrutiny of the immigration department by subjecting the department to legal accountability through judicial review. It presents a model of judicial review as managing administration through which the courts, taking a pragmatic approach, assess administrative practices and impose legal norms on administration to bring its operations back into line. Key trends, such as the courts' developing systemic unfairness case law and other cases concerning substantive legality, are analysed. The cases show the courts responding to the department's organisational shortcomings and political interference with administrative and legal processes. This in turn involves considerable judicial supervision of the department's activities.

A significant number of people who interact with the immigration department come off much the worse because for it, but they are often without an effective remedy. Chapter nine investigates the phenomenon of bureaucratic oppression, that is, administrative behaviour and action that results in unnecessary harm to people. The chapter explores the causes of this phenomenon. It argues that bureaucratic oppression is a deep-seated and pervasive feature of immigration administration throughout its different settings, such as casework, outsourcing, immigration detention, and hostile environment measures. The chapter critically evaluates the effectiveness of current solutions and argues that the most effective solutions to countering oppressive administrative behaviour will include changes to internal administrative cultures and structural reforms within administration itself.

The final chapter, chapter 10, summarises the analysis and proposes a set of reforms for the immigration department. In doing so, the chapter addresses wider issues of institutional design and administrative legitimacy. The chapter argues that specific reforms to the department's operations need to be accompanied by a new institutional and constitutional framework for the department.

Overall, the operation of this administrative system is analysed as a dynamic process through which administrative law is generated in various ways, including: how officials make policy; the processes through casework decisions are taken; how the rules are enforced in practice; and the institutional systems and processes through which administrative operations are organised. The analysis supports the need for administrative lawyers to get to grips with the practical affairs of governance in order to understand and evaluate the effectiveness of administrative action and law.

2

The Immigration Department

A study of public administration and administrative law is necessarily concerned with administrative institutions. Inevitably imperfect and prone to both inertia and institutional pathologies, administrative organisations are purposive bodies. When government acts, it does so through administrative institutions that mobilise laws, money and officials to produce programme outputs and policy results.[1] This chapter provides a scene-setting overview of the immigration department, its organisation, functions, structure, operations, history, and the multiple contexts within which it operates. This is a prerequisite before proceeding to consider in detail the department's activities and its use of and control by administrative law.

But it is necessary to do more than just describe institutional form and administrative history. To analyse and evaluate the challenges and problems raised by administration and administrative law, it is also important to understand the substantive issues involved in the specific policy-administrative context and the political and organisational forces that impact upon administration. There are also the immigration department's specific operations and cultures – in addition to its malfunctions, self-interests, and the limits of its organisational competence. A behavioural understanding of how administration operates must also be placed against the normative values that prescribe how administration should operate. Administration should be competent, functionally effective and operate fairly and lawfully. We start by considering how the department is constituted and structured.

I. Constituting Administration

Administrative institutions exist because, at some stage, the politicians decided that the public interest required them to exist. Their role is to address a specific set of social, economic and policy problems. These problems are so insistent, large and complex that they can only be managed by permanent large-scale administrative systems. This process of constituting and designing administrative institutions

---

[1] R Rose, *Understanding Big Government* (London, Sage, 1984) 151.

is intrinsically related to their functions and structures. Administration exists to perform specific functions and pursue policy goals. It is then necessary to construct and devise an administrative structure that is attuned to such functions and goals. Statutory and other powers and duties, such as rule-making, decision-making and enforcement powers, are necessary. Administration also needs to be organised, resourced, operated, overseen, monitored and held to account. Furthermore, administrative institutions develop over time in response to changes in their social, economic, policy and operational environments. More powers and responsibilities will be conferred and structures may become more intricate and complex. In turn, administration is reconstituted and restructured.

A. Immigration Administration: Functions and Structures

What then of the UK's immigration department? This administrative institution takes the form of a large, heavily staffed operational department focused on individual casework. It has four core tasks. First, to make immigration policy through primary legislation to establish the overall legal framework for immigration operations. Second, to make immigration policy through detailed rules – the immigration rules – that lay down the criteria to determine who can and cannot enter and remain in the country. Third, to administer those policies and rules by making casework decisions on incoming applications to decide which applicants qualify under the immigration rules to enter or remain in the country. Fourth, to ensure compliance with and enforcement of the rules by preventing people without leave to enter from entering the country, and by removing those without leave to remain.

The scale of the enterprise is illustrated by some basic facts. In any particular year, the department receives and makes decisions on approximately four million immigration applications. The immigration rules are over 1,000 pages long and frequently revised. The department seeks to ensure compliance with and the enforcement of immigration law through a variety of different means, such as pre-entry checks, immigration detention, forced removals, deportations and other interventions and sanctions. This complex organisation, with 27,000 staff and a budget of over £2 billion, is organised into various directorates, sub-directorates, and then into various case-working and compliance and enforcement units and teams.

The department's structure naturally assumes a particular organisational model. It is not an independent expert agency that exercises its professional expertise in a small number of very large decisions. Instead, it is a traditional machine bureaucracy that has to cope with a large, repetitive and routine workload and therefore has standardised processes and a clearly defined hierarchy.[2] A large administrative

---

[2] H Mintzberg, *The Structuring of Organizations* (Englewood Cliffs, Prentice-Hall, 1979) 314–47.

entity such as the immigration department will have many organisational layers. At the top of the organisation will be ministers and senior civil servants to set the political direction and take major policy decisions. Beneath this is the senior managerial level, which in turn supervises the middle management, who in turn supervise and control front-line operational staff. Operational delivery is under- taken by casework staff and enforcement officers; they undertake the repetitive and routine tasks that generally do not require distinct professional skills. Rules programme the standard operating procedures amongst the operating core, which enables them to cope with the workflow. This level is also differentiated vertically between different front-line units and sub-units undertaking discrete functions. The middle management are complemented by the techno-structure, which scrutinises the organisation's processes and its capacity for change and improve- ment. A further defining characteristic is a ubiquitous control mentality over the operating core and an incessant search for more efficient means of processing the workload. The obsession with control is necessary because of the pressures placed on the operating core. A great deal of the time of the middle and senior managers is taken up with just trying to keep operations working in the face of incoming political and operational pressures.

Such organisations generate a deep-seated ambivalence.[3] From one perspec- tive, given its ability to mobilise power on an unprecedented scale, administration is technically superior to other forms of organisation. From another perspective, it generates a range of dysfunctional behaviours: the failure to implement policy goals; the mistreatment of people; and legalism, the displacement of ends in favour of means through the rigid and formulaic adherence to rules at the expense of individuals' circumstances and policy goals.[4] Nonetheless, an administrative system provides the only conceivable way of efficiently managing the huge work- flows required. Such organisations may appear to be stable and mature, but in practice they are often unstable and riddled with stress and their internal coor- dination is often variable. All these aspects feature heavily in the immigration department. There is a pervasive need for control – the basic task is immigration control – but there is also a need for internal control within the department and external political and legal control.

There are many other cross-cutting tensions. Consider the department's conflicting cultures. Some parts of the department, such as UK Visas and Immigration, which handles and processes immigration applicants, is tasked with providing a high-quality customer service toward the vast number of 'desirable' immigrants who qualify under the rules. On the other hand, other parts of the department adopt a quite different and more coercive approach toward those

---

[3] See, eg, M Crozier, *The Bureaucratic Phenomenon* (Chicago, University of Chicago Press, 1964).

[4] RK Merton, 'Bureaucratic Structure and Personality' in *Social Theory and Social Structure* (New York, Free Press, 1968) 249; PM Blau and MW Meyer, *Bureaucracy in Modern Society*, 3rd edn (New York, McGraw-Hill, 1987) 141–42; J Jowell, 'The Legal Control of Administrative Discretion' [1973] *PL* 178, 192–94.

'undesirable' people who do not qualify and thereby typically demonstrate quite the opposite of customer care. The Immigration Enforcement directorate is much more of a law enforcement agency that undertakes criminal investigations to disrupt organised criminal gangs and forcibly remove irregular migrants. Enforcement officers have coercive powers to enter premises, seize goods and property, and to place people into immigration detention without judicial authority. Other parts of the department function more as a welfare agency by providing support and accommodation to vulnerable asylum claimants. Each incoming government will also have its own particular policies and ideas about what to do about immigration, but the core tasks of making rules, casework and enforcement remain pretty much the same and are the means by which specific policies of particular governments are implemented.

Put in this way, the department's tasks seem quite simple. But the actual mechanics of getting things done are often quite complex and challenging in practice. The vast bulk of the department's work is not policy-making, but operational delivery, and this involves detailed work by multiple units which need to be coordinated. Indeed, the experience of the immigration department demonstrates how implementation matters just as much, if not more, than policy or ideology. It also illustrates how challenging operational delivery is. The accumulated features of grinding casework, complex rules, pressures on enforcement, the blizzard of political forces, and the mass of administrative detail produces a culture of almost constant crisis management. As a former immigration minister has noted, in terms of running things, 'the British government is quite poor; large organisations that do repetitive things, employ people at relatively low wages, who are not managed very effectively – that's certainly the problem with the immigration system, a huge transactional organisation'.[5]

In another sense, there is no coherent overall immigration system. Instead, it is more of a collection of largely uncoordinated functions. The department's casework and enforcement systems operate almost entirely separately from each other. They are staffed by separate teams and have their own processes. This, in turn, has led to poor internal communications and coordination. The department has also suffered from outdated IT systems and poor data quality. Consequently, the department has been unable to track individual cases from application to removal. Common features have included case files getting lost and delayed. The disjointed nature of the system informs many aspects of the department's organisation and activities. The department has also increasingly contracted out or outsourced many of its activities and tasks, such as managing immigration detention centres and providing accommodation for asylum claimants.

The ongoing task of constituting administration extends beyond organisational and structural issues, however. Administrative institutions are constituted

---

[5] Institute for Government, 'Ministers Reflect: Damian Green' (December 2015) 5. Damian Green MP was Minister of State for Immigration, 2010–12.

by law; there are different legal structures or models which embody different notions of how such institutions both do and should operate. Furthermore, in liberal democracies, public institutions operate within systems of public accountability. We therefore need to consider the competing legal structures that constitute the immigration department and the accountability contexts in which it operates.

B. Legal Models of Immigration Administration

At a general level, the constitutional and legal status of UK central government departments is obscure. It is usually explained by reference to the prerogative and the role of the Secretary of State.[6] However, this overlooks the fact that these entities are complex administrative organisations and their existence is a brute political reality. At the same time, their administrative processes are suffused with law. Legislation delegates extensive administrative powers to officials.[7] Administration itself makes the bulk of the detailed rules that prescribe application processes and the criteria for making front-line decisions and enforcement action. It also generates the large body of internal guidance that allocates tasks within the administrative structure and guides officials. But the law constituting the immigration department goes deeper than this. There are general, overarching legal models of administration. These models reflect competing modes of legal thought about how the immigration department both does and should operate in practice. These models are familiar within the structure of both policy and legal discussion and reflect different understandings of what the immigration department is for.

The principal model is based on state sovereignty. Controlling immigration is a core aspect of the sovereign state.[8] The critical tool here is that of authority, the power of administration to 'command and prohibit, commend and permit, through recognised procedures and identifying symbols'.[9] Under this model, the department has almost exclusive power to exercise its powers, with only very limited judicial control, in order to protect the state's borders. This top-down model looms large within departmental thinking, although it has been moderated over time by other models drawing upon quite different values. Since the

---

[6] See generally T Daintith and A Page, *The Executive in the Constitution: Structure, Autonomy, and Internal Control* (Oxford, Oxford University Press, 1999) ch 2.

[7] For instance, the power to give or refuse leave to enter is to be exercised by immigration officers whereas the power to give, refuse, or vary leave to remain is to be exercised by the Secretary of State, but by virtue of *Carltona*, is in practice exercised by case workers: Immigration Act 1971, s 4; *Carltona Ltd v Commissioners of Works* [1943] 2 All ER 560 (CA).

[8] *Musgrove v Chun Teeong Toy* [1892] AC 272 (JCPC); *Attorney-General for the Dominion of Canada v Cain* [1906] AC 542 (JCPC).

[9] CC Hood and HZ Margetts, *The Tools of Government in the Digital Age* (Basingstoke, Palgrave Macmillan, 2007) 50.

late 1960s, a competing model based upon procedural fairness and administrative justice has developed.[10] This model finds natural institutional reflection in judicial review and immigration tribunals. Its focus is upon judicial, independent and reasoned adjudication and the ability of migrants to participate in decisions that affect their lives. The next stage, from the 1990s onwards, was the increasing relevance of human rights law which grounded another model of immigration administration. Immigrants are not just entitled to the correct and fair application of the rules; they are also rights-bearing individuals. The main rights are: the right to seek asylum; the prohibition against torture and inhumane and degrading treatment (Article 3 ECHR); and the right to private and family life (Article 8 ECHR).[11] A human rights model simultaneously constrains administration and extends judicial power.

The potential for judicial-executive tensions with both the administrative justice and human rights models is obvious and extensive. As regards administrative justice, until 1993, the department had resisted appeal rights for asylum claimants on the basis that they would prevent the department from removing those with groundless claims.[12] More recently, the Immigration Act 2014 has significantly restricted appeal rights. Human rights have been similarly problematic. Extensive litigation over the right to private and family demonstrates both the difficult factual and legal problems involved and has resulted in clashes between ministers and courts and tribunals.

All these legal models of administration are familiar. The concepts of sovereignty, administrative justice and human rights are deeply embedded within legal practice and thought. However, administrative law is also generated internally within administration. The principal task of administration is implementing policy and it has numerous legal powers to this end. Accordingly, a model of administrative law grounded in effective performance and operational delivery emerges. This model is clearly reliant upon internal administrative law as the means by which administration is organised and held to account internally. These forms of law are found within the internal organisation of the department, through mechanisms such as guidance and instructions to front-line staff, customer performance standards, targets and internal coordination. A major area of inquiry, then, involves examining the effectiveness of such internal structures and the associated 'living' administrative law.[13]

---

[10] *In Re HK (An Infant)* [1967] 2 QB 617 (CA); Home Office, 'Report of the Committee on Immigration Appeals' (Cmnd 3387, 1967); Immigration Appeals Act 1969; *Bugdaycay v Secretary of State for the Home Department* [1987] AC 514 (HL); Asylum and Immigration Appeals Act 1993; R Thomas, 'The Impact of Judicial Review on Asylum' [2003] *PL* 479, 481–84.

[11] Refugee Convention, 1951; European Convention on Human Rights, 1950; Human Rights Act 1998.

[12] Home Office, 'A Report on the Work of the Immigration and Nationality Department' (1984) 25.

[13] cf Daintith and Page, *The Executive in the Constitution* (1999) 13–14.

C. Accountability Contexts

The preceding models of how law constitutes administration highlight the importance of legal control and legal accountability of administration. Of course, accountability regimes and systems overseeing administration extend further than this. In general terms, a government department is only part of a wider set of policy, social, legal and other systems with which it merges at the edges and all of which intersect with each other.[14] These wider systems include various actors whose existence are principally or partly parasitic upon the department's existence and operations. This institutional framework comprises a number of accountability or scrutiny bodies and other actors that in turn pursue a range of different values and interests.

Obviously, there is the wider public and electorate, as informed by the media and mediated by ministers, who are responsible to Parliament. Detailed scrutiny is provided by parliamentary select committees, principally the Home Affairs Committee (HAC). Scrutiny for value for money, efficiency and effectiveness is undertaken by both generalist bodies (the National Audit Office (NAO) and the Public Affairs Committee (PAC)) and the department's dedicated inspectorate, the Independent Chief Inspector of Borders and Immigration (ICIBI) ('the Chief Inspector'). Policy expertise is provided by the Migration Advisory Committee with contributions from the wider policy community. Individuals can seek redress from the courts and immigration tribunals to secure fairness, legality and protection of their human rights. Non-legal redress is provided through complaints via MPs' casework, the department's internal complaint-handling bodies, and complaints to ombuds for maladministration. Beyond this, there are various immigration campaigning and advocacy bodies which lobby on issues of policy and delivery.

Put together, these bodies and actors comprise the accountability framework in which the department operates. Yet, the department itself is several times larger and more powerful than these oversight bodies. A key issue is, then, the extent to which accountability pressures actually result in changes to administrative operations.

II. The Development of the Immigration Department

So far, we have painted with a broad brush. The preceding discussion illustrates the variety and complexity of the demands placed upon administration. To make further progress, we need a more contextual understanding of the

---

[14] RGS Brown and DR Steel, *The Administrative Process in Britain*, 2nd edn (London, Methuen, 1979) 209.

department's recent history. After all, government departments and their organisational systems and designs are highly path-dependent. The immigration department, in particular, has accumulated plenty of historical baggage and legacy issues. UK immigration controls date from 1905, but the focus of this book is on the department's current operations over the last three decades or so. We can then conveniently start with the 1990s.

For many years, the immigration department had been formally constituted as the Immigration and Nationality Directorate (IND), a Home Office directorate. Before the 1990s, IND had focused principally upon immigration casework, particularly family migration from the Indian sub-continent. This all changed in the 1990s with the huge surge in asylum claims. IND had been entirely unprepared for the scale of this challenge. Indeed, it had been run down. The number of experienced caseworkers had been reduced by over 1,000. Staff were shed in anticipation of – and in order to pay for – a new computerised system that would introduce a paperless casework process, but which never actually materialised.[15] This coincided with the IND, in effect, losing control of the burgeoning asylum intake. Having laid off experienced case-workers, it was then very difficult to recruit new ones while the number of incoming applications and the backlog of old cases were increasing. The decision to get rid of experienced caseworkers before a new IT system was in place verged on 'administrative negligence'.[16] In 2007, the asylum legacy programme had been introduced to try and clear the enormous backlog of some 460,000 undecided asylum claims. In 2009, an additional 40,000 immigration legacy cases of which the department had been unaware were added to the programme.[17]

The backlog of undecided asylum cases produced all sorts of challenges and problems. During this period, IND seemed almost permanently on the verge of collapse. At one stage a minister described attempts to improve IND's performance as being akin to 'trying to turn round a supertanker with a ship that was actually sinking'.[18] It took years for IND to even attempt to get out of the crisis. Problems were compounded by the adoption of dysfunctional retreatist tactics, such as 'defective non-compliance' asylum claims.[19] During the late 1990s and for much of the 2000s, the asylum intake and all of its attendant problems were the dominant and overriding issue for IND as reflected in high-level targets such as the asylum 'tipping point' target, which involved removing more failed asylum-seekers than

---

[15] NAO, 'The Immigration and Nationality Directorate Integrated Casework Programme' HC 277 (1998–99).

[16] Public Administration Select Committee, 'Ombudsman Issues' HC 448 (2002–03) [29].

[17] HAC, 'The Work of the UK Border Agency' HC 105 (2009–10).

[18] HAC, 'Oral Evidence: Asylum Applications', 8 May 2003, HC 218 (2003–04) Q 18 (Beverley Hughes MP, Minister of State, Home Office).

[19] IND would refuse to consider asylum claims on the ground that claimants had not returned their statement of evidence forms within the required 10-day deadline, but in many cases, the claimants had in fact met the deadline; the problem was that IND had failed to link up their statements with the file case, thereby generating extensive satellite judicial review litigation, leading to further unnecessary delays and additional costs.

the number of new unfounded applications, and making substantial reductions in asylum support costs. Nonetheless, the number of unsuccessful asylum claimants removed was very low.

The focus on asylum meant equally important matters were sidelined. In 2006, the foreign national prisoners crisis occurred: over 1,000 foreign national prisoners had been released from prison without being considered for deportation by IND, 'a classic example of departmental maladministration and endemic administrative incompetence'.[20] The toxic nature of the scandal – convicted serious offenders and immigration – prompted the resignation of the then Home Secretary, Charles Clarke. In a clear effort to deflect future ministerial responsibility and blame, the new Home Secretary, John Reid, described IND as 'not fit for purpose'.[21] This was the most devastating critique ever made publicly by a minister of his own department and a clear signal of the loss of confidence in civil servants. According to Reid, IND was inadequate in terms of its scope, information technology, leadership, management structure, systems and processes. In an era of increased global migration, the department had sought to cope with old and inadequate processes and systems that were incapable of responding effectively.[22] This was confirmed by a civil service capability review, which gave the Home Office the lowest score of all government departments. A fundamental overhaul was required.

In 2009, IND was abolished and reconstituted as an executive agency, the UK Border Agency (UKBA), operating at arm's length from ministers and run by a chief executive. Such agencies had been a feature of UK central government since the late 1980s as a means of introducing managerially separate units focusing on delivery rather than policy.[23] The establishment of the UKBA was a late addition to the list of the many other executive agencies. However, things quickly changed. With the coalition Government (2010–15) came austerity, budget cuts and a strong policy drive to reduce incoming immigration and to make life uncomfortable for people in the country without the right to remain – that is, the hostile environment. Operational crises continued. In 2011, the Home Secretary, Theresa May (2010–16), forced the head of Border

[20] C Painter, 'A Government Department in Meltdown: Crisis at the Home Office' (2008) 28 *Public Money and Management* 275.

[21] HAC, 'Oral Evidence: Immigration Control', 23 May 2006, HC 775 (2005–06) Q 866 (John Reid, Secretary of State for the Home Department). Other MPs have described the department as 'the United Kingdom's most opaque and unhelpful bureaucracy' (*Hansard*, HC Vol 473 col 1183 (20 March 2008) (Andrew Stunnell MP) and 'a fundamentally dysfunctional organisation' (HAC, 'Oral Evidence: The Work of the UK Border Agency', 26 March 2013, HC 792 (2012–13) Q 62 (Michael Ellis MP)).

[22] Cabinet Office, 'Capability Review of the Home Office' (2006).

[23] Executive agencies are delivery bodies of their parent government department and have no independent constitutional existence. They continue to act under the authority of the Secretary of State to whom they are responsible: *R v Secretary of State for Social Security, ex p Sherwin* (1996) 32 BMLR 1 (HC). See generally O James, *The Executive Agency Revolution in Whitehall: Public Interest versus Bureau-Shaping Perspectives* (London, Palgrave Macmillan, 2003); K Jenkins, *Politicians and Public Services: Implementing Change in a Clash of Cultures* (Cheltenham, Edward Elgar, 2008).

Force to resign after he had, without ministerial approval, relaxed border checks to deal with four-hour queues at airports and staff shortages.[24] This refuelled ministerial distrust of officials. At the same time, the department had been working on a transformation plan to address significant underlying weaknesses in its structures, procedures, culture and notoriously weak IT systems. Significant budgetary and staff reductions had clearly impacted upon operations compounding numerous administrative problems and delays.[25] The depth of concern was evidenced by regular and highly critical scrutiny from the HAC, highlighting routine administrative problems, lost files, huge backlogs, lengthy delays and poor-quality decisions. In 2012, the Committee criticised the UKBA for its 'bunker mentality' and for providing inconsistent information thereby undermining the Committee's scrutiny role.[26]

The endemic problems would not and could not go away. As one MP and former Home Office minister with long experience of immigration noted in 2012,

> the biggest problem is trying to get the Home Office administration to do what it says on the tin – to do what the rules say to make sure that the administration is efficient and effective. It is not, and it has not been for decades.[27]

Matters culminated in another highly critical report in 2013.[28] For some years, the UKBA had consistently told the HAC that legacy asylum claimants were no longer in the country; an extensive checking programme carried out over five years had not found any trace of them. In fact, contrary to these claims, the agency had simply not performed its full programme of checks. For six years, it had consistently given the Committee patently wrong information concerning the number of irregular migrants who had not been removed and it had continued to do so until an inspection report had brought the matter to light. Deeply unimpressed, the Committee noted that the agency's behaviour was 'hardly the mark of a transparent organisation which recognises its accountability to Parliament. Instead, UKBA appears to have tried to sweep its mistakes under the carpet in the hope that they would remain unnoticed.'[29] If the agency had not been attempting to mislead the Committee, then this had been 'a sign that senior officials had no idea as to what was actually going on in their organisation'.[30] Senior officials had either been duplicitous or incompetent.

---

[24] HAC, 'UK Border Controls' HC 1647 (2010–12).

[25] NAO, 'The UK Border Agency and Border Force: Progress in Cutting Costs and Improving Performance' HC 467 (2012–13).

[26] HAC, 'The Work of the UK Border Agency (August–December 2011)' HC 1722 (2010–12) [21].

[27] *Hansard*, HC Vol 547 col 957 (4 July 2012) (Fiona Mactaggart MP, Home Office minister 2003–06).

[28] HAC, 'The Work of the UK Border Agency (July– September 2012)' HC 792 (2012–13).

[29] ibid [15].

[30] ibid [16].

Theresa May responded by abolishing the UKBA. May's analysis was that the UKBA had created a 'closed, secretive, and defensive culture' and had been 'a troubled organisation'; its performance had not been good enough.[31] It had lacked the capacity to modernise its structures and systems and to get on top of its workload given the levels of mass immigration. The agency had struggled with the volume of its casework, which had led to historical backlogs running into the hundreds of thousands. Removals had not kept up with the number of irregular migrants. According to May, UKBA's problems stemmed from four main issues. First, its sheer size meant that it had conflicting cultures and all too often focused upon crisis management at the expense of other important work. Second, it lacked transparency and accountability. Third, the agency had been hindered by inadequate IT systems that involved manual, instead of automated, data entry and paper files instead of modern electronic case management. Fourth, the agency's policy and legal framework meant that it had often been 'caught up in a vicious cycle of complex law and poor enforcement of its own policies, which made it harder to remove people in the UK illegally'.[32]

The UKBA's responsibilities were then passed to three directorates within the Home Office: a case work agency focused on providing a high-quality, customer-focused service (UK Visas and Immigration); a law enforcement agency focused on deterrence, compliance and enforcement (Immigration Enforcement); and another providing controls and checks at the border (Border Force). The idea was that having three functional directorates rather than one large, all-purpose organisation would make the overall system more manageable, although there was considerable scepticism about what, if any, difference this would actually make.[33] The next major developments were the hostile environment policy and the Windrush scandal, which are examined later.[34]

These two key changes to the agency's institutional framework – the transition from IND to UKBA and the latter's abolition – illustrate much more than the different responses of two ministers to the same basic problem. Naturally enough, matters of administrative politics themselves become politicised and the underlying concern of politicians is often blame-avoidance. 'Agencification' was presented as a proven successful catalyst for change elsewhere in government. The IND needed to 'become a different kind of organisation: a more powerful agency with the operational freedoms it needs to deliver its services, but more clearly accountable to Parliament and the public'.[35] But Reid had clearly been motivated

---

[31] *Hansard*, HC Vol 560 col 1501 (26 March 2013) (Theresa May MP, Secretary of State for the Home Department).

[32] ibid.

[33] See, eg, HAC, 'Oral Evidence: The Work of the UK Border Agency', 26 March 2013, HC 792 (2012–13) Q 20.

[34] See ch 3.

[35] Home Office, 'Fair, Effective, Transparent and Trusted: Rebuilding Confidence in our Immigration System' (2006) [3.13].

by politically self-serving needs and had invoked a classic blame-shifting tactic: the defensive reorganisation of government agencies. As Hood has noted, 'when deflecting or diffusing blame is of the essence, the emphasis typically goes on designing organisations to achieve disconnection among different units and disconnection from past structures'.[36] With Clarke's recent resignation, abolishing the failure-laden and toxic IND brand and reconstituting it as an executive agency separate from the Home Office was the means of moving the target of blame for past failures while simultaneously shifting future blame from ministers to the new agency's chief executive.[37] It would take years for the agency to come to grips with its organisational challenges, and Reid's tactic was clearly designed to evade criticism of himself and future ministers for operational failures.

By contrast, Theresa May instinctively wanted much more directive top-down control: the new directorates would therefore report directly to ministers, not a chief executive, through a command-and-control structure. The depth of May's distrust of officials was evident. When a Home Secretary complains that her own agency had created a closed, secretive and defensive culture and has not been transparent and accountable, then the very last thing this suggests is a sudden ministerial Damascene conversion in favour of greater parliamentary and judicial scrutiny. May had clearly been intensely frustrated by the agency's organisational incompetence, defiance of her wishes, and officials acting behind her back and covering matters up because they feared the potentially punishing consequences. May desired greater accountability of the agency to her will and no one else's.

From a wider perspective, both episodes illustrate the endless reorganisational churn so characteristic of British governmental practice – the seductive, but ultimately illusory, aspiration that structural changes actually resolve endemic operational problems. In practice, such changes tend to be more symbolic, politically motivated interventions by ministers to be seen to be doing something. There was an evident risk that dividing UKBA into three directorates might only reinforce existing silos making joint working and a common focus on objectives more difficult.[38] Overall, organisational restructurings often tend to have only 'distractor effects': they consume resources and generate instability, but do little to address underlying operational problems.[39] Another response has been for the

---

[36] C Hood, *The Blame Game: Spin, Bureaucracy and Self-Preservation in Government* (Princeton, Princeton University Press, 2011) 69.

[37] Although formally designated as 'an executive agency of the Home Office', the UKBA had in fact remained an integral part of the department.

[38] I Macgee, 'Institute of Government Statement on the Decision to Scrap the UKBA' (3 April 2013) available at www.instituteforgovernment.org.uk/news/latest/institute-statements-decision-scrap-ukba

[39] A White and P Dunleavy, *Making and Breaking Whitehall Departments: A Guide to Machinery of Government Changes* (London, IfG, 2010).

department to legislate extensively and repeatedly, although this alone is hardly a solution to its endemic problems; 'legislation without administrative control and direction will not work'.[40] More recent trends reinforce the importance of national administration and law. Post-Brexit and the ending of freedom of movement, policy over EU migration has been restored to the department along with casework decision-making.

III. Getting under the Surface

The preceding sketch suggests a need to delve much deeper and in the process uncover other contextual and behavioural characteristics of both the immigration department and British government in general. The department operates within a variety of different contexts. Obviously, there are the immediate political, administrative and constitutional environments, but there is also the wider globalised nature of immigration to consider. As regards administrative operations, it is also necessary to go beyond formal structures by highlighting the behavioural dimensions of administration and how it operates in practice.

A. Political, Policy and Constitutional Contexts

One place to start is with the policy and politics of immigration. Immigration has long been a highly politically sensitive area with competing and ultimately irresolvable arguments for and against allowing people to enter the country. Politicians have, for many years, sought and struggled to manage these tensions. The basic truth is that a modern open economy needs immigration. But there are many other reasons for immigration apart from economic immigration. There are immigration routes for family, visit, study and protection purposes. But precisely how much immigration should be allowed, by whom, and under what conditions? The security dimension to immigration has also come much more to the forefront in the light of international terrorism, but it also includes the handling of foreign national prisoners. There is inevitably much policy debate about the scope and limits of immigration as informed by public attitudes, which vary enormously. There are deep-seated concerns about the security of borders and the need to manage immigration effectively by taking account of such concerns while not pandering to prejudice. At the level of high politics, there has been far greater continuity between different governments, Labour and Conservative, than there have been differences. To a large extent, the differences between the parties have often been synthetic, artificially manufactured for the purposes of blame and

[40] *Hansard*, HC Vol 496 col 255 (14 July 2009) (Keith Vaz MP). Immigration Acts were enacted in 1993, 1996, 1999, 2002, 2004, 2006, 2008, 2009, 2014 and 2016.

political point-scoring. Another significant continuity has been the difficulties of managing the system and its operations.

The underlying causes of the policy challenge are not to be found in domestic politics, but in the fraught, complex, dynamic and globalised nature of international migratory pressures set against domestic public opinion. National governments retain the formal powers to control immigration, but how much real substantive power do they possess in the context of wider global migratory forces? It has been argued that governmental efforts to control immigration have often failed because of more powerful structural factors – the needs of employment markets, wealth inequalities and political conflicts in countries of origin – matters over which national governments have little or no influence.[41] Despite the empirical challenges in determining the effectiveness of immigration policies, it has been concluded that national immigration policies 'have a less prominent role affecting the overall scale of migration when compared to other migration determinants, such as economic drivers, social networks, cultural and geographical proximity'.[42] If so, then the administrative endeavour of controlling and managing immigration may carry less force than many governments would be prepared to accept.

Of course, few politicians, let alone a minister, could ever publicly acknowledge this, although some might well privately consign immigration to the 'too difficult' box.[43] Either way, the point highlights the potential for a distinct clash between what the public and ministers want and the capacity of the organisation to respond effectively. This tension is particularly acute in the immigration department, which necessarily operates within a highly – often toxically – charged context of blunt short-term political forces, in particular, the need to restore and maintain public confidence in the system. Policy is not altogether immaterial, but the unpredictability of 'events' often matter more. The political pressures vary, but at times can be intense, and this in turn drives both political and administrative behaviour.

Ministers must then respond to public concerns about immigration. After all, they are elected, in the media glare, and are accountable to Parliament. Naturally, ministers want results quickly. It is common for Home Secretaries, on the parliamentary or media stage, to make knee-jerk reactions to newspaper headlines, to announce crack-downs on immigration because of abuse of the system. It is equally common for such ministerial behaviours to be criticised, but, in the real

---

[41] For an overview of the debate, see M Czaika and H de Haas, 'The Effectiveness of Immigration Policies' (2013) 39 *Population and Development Review* 487.

[42] European Commission Joint Research Centre, 'International Migration Drivers: A Quantitative Assessment of the Structural Factors Shaping Migration' (Luxembourg, Publications Office of the European Union, 2018) 8.

[43] See generally C Clarke (ed), *The Too Difficult Box: The Big Issues Politicians Can't Crack* (London, Biteback, 2014).

world of politics, it is inevitably difficult for politicians not to do otherwise. From one perspective, it could be viewed as political responsiveness to public concerns; from another, it is pandering to prejudice. Either way, it is an inherent fact of political life. No area of administration, not least such a politically contentious areas such as immigration, could ever be entirely separated from politics, but how far should ministerial influence extend? Ministers can potentially intervene in day-to-day operations irrespective of the consequences. In the tax context, individual decisions have been entirely removed from direct ministerial control because of concerns over potential political interference.[44] By contrast, while immigration decisions are taken by junior officials, they remain within ministerial control and potentially subject to ministerial influence.

In constitutional terms, immigration policy is then exclusively a matter for the department and, in particular, the Home Secretary, subject to such scrutiny as Parliament is able to muster. There are no legislatively mandated policy goals other than the bland statutory requirement that the Secretary of State lay immigration rules before Parliament to regulate immigration.[45] These rules are statements of executive – not legislative – policy and how the Home Secretary will exercise her discretion to grant or refuse leave to enter or remain.[46] Matters of executive organisation are wholly within the province of central government. The major reorganisations of the immigration department were announced to Parliament as *faits accomplis* with no scope for any parliamentary scrutiny at all.[47] The traditional power-hoarding nature of the UK central state is thereby confirmed.

B. Political and Administrative Control of Administration and Organisational Challenges

Yet, none of this means that ministers actually get much, let alone all, of what they want. A minister is just a politician – the political head of a department, but not necessarily an expert in either administrative operations or the specific policy domain. In politically divisive and administratively problematic areas of government, such as immigration, ministers will often be tempted to take short-cuts to blame the opposition and seek favourable media coverage.

---

[44] Commissioners for Revenue and Customs Act 2005.

[45] Immigration Act 1971, s 3(2).

[46] *Odelola v Secretary of State for the Home Department* [2009] UKHL 25, [2009] 1 WLR 1230.

[47] As Reid noted: 'it was not and has never been the normal practice of Administrations to make oral statements on the machinery of government': *Hansard*, HC Vol 458 col 1641 (29 March 2007) (John Reid, Secretary of State for the Home Department). There is an important difference between the statutory nature and detail of the law governing the organisation of non-ministerial bodies departments (eg Ofcom and the Food Standards Agency) and the almost lack of hard law as regards the organisation of ministerial departments.

Within their department, ministers can only exercise fragmentary oversight of what is and is not happening within it. There will be huge parts of the organisation that ministers will never be able to penetrate. Even should a minister want to know more, they are entirely reliant upon officials for such information and there is no guarantee that officials will necessarily disclose all relevant information. Another option is for the minister to go fully native, to allow themselves to become captured by the department, and thereby act as its spokesperson, both inside and outside the government machine, by advancing the department's interests rather than those of the elected government. This trait is sometimes noticeable through the institutional defensiveness of some ministers when being scrutinised in Parliament.

There are added twists in the Home Office, a government department with unique challenges.[48] Being Home Secretary is, after all, the most demanding and hazardous of all ministerial offices.[49] Most Home Secretaries come to see the world in Hobbesian terms, a clash of forces threatening social order requiring the imposition of authority. But in practice, the individual office-holder's measure of success is likely to be their personal day-to-day survival without being toppled by some unforeseen crisis. Further, the tensions inherent in the ambiguous nature of the minister-official relationship are more acute within the Home Office than in other government departments.[50] Ministers have, at times, been openly distrustful of officials. Indeed, the minister-official relationship has often been particularly problematic in the Home Office, sometimes toxically so because of the clash between political pressures and the slow operation and variable performance of the administrative machinery.[51] Ministers may see officials as obstacles because of their conservative risk-averse nature. Officials may, on occasion, be obstructive and sometimes for good reason, not least to ensure that the department complies with court rulings.

However, the wider problem is that operational delivery systems, by their very nature, rarely respond to short-term ministerial desires or frustrations. In general terms, the political and administrative practices of government often

---

[48] T Rutter, 'No place like the Home Office: former top officials on the department's unique challenges' *Civil Service World* (10 May 2018).

[49] As a former Home Secretary has noted, 'The Home Office confronts each incomer with a tangle of problems emerging from the entrails of our society. To put it mildly, it is not a department of fun and laughter': D Hurd, *Robert Peel: A Biography* (London, Phoenix, 2007) 64. There is also a junior minister for immigration. A former junior immigration minister once informed the author that the position had the reputation for being the worst ministerial job in government, with a lot of very unglamorous, tedious and routine work. According to Damian Green MP (Minister of State for Immigration, 2010–12), 'a lot of the life of an immigration minister is trying to devise the laws, statutory instruments and so on, to stop the will of the Government being frustrated by judges, trying to make legislation watertight so it can't be over-interpreted by judges': Institute for Government, 'Ministers Reflect' (n 5) 8–9.

[50] RAW Rhodes, *Everyday Life in British Government* (Oxford, Oxford University Press, 2011); R Bacon and C Hope, *Conundrum: Why Every Government Gets Things Wrong and What We Can Do About It* (London, Biteback, 2013) chs 14 and 15.

[51] P Wintour, 'Why do so many Home Secretaries fall out with their officials?' *Guardian* (20 November 2020).

embody a fundamental tension between short-term ministerial timescales and the inherent constraints of managing large-scale administrative systems that rarely respond quickly to political pressures. The principal administrative challenges are how to deliver policy and how to ensure that the delivery chain between policy-makers and front-line officials operates effectively. We need to explicate these organisational challenges in a bit more detail.

As the principal substantive standard of administration and administrative law, instrumental rationality is rooted in the overriding need for government agencies to achieve desired outcomes. This involves assumptions about the cause-and-effect relationships between policy ends and the means used to achieve them. Delivering policy in practice within large-scale administrative systems is inherently complex and problematic. The major organisational challenge is to align policy objectives throughout multiple streams of institutionalised action, such as organisational structures, rules, processes, technical systems and front-line operations. There are also issues of staffing and administrative cultures to deal with.

In this implementation process, higher-level officials devise the means for achieving desired policy goals, which in turn become an end in themselves for operational staff. But there is often a lack of effective and thorough integration throughout this means-ends hierarchy.[52] There will often be gaps in the delivery chain between policy goals and front-line processes, or inherent mismatches between them. There will be varying degrees of operational disconnect between policy and implementation, the traditional division between those officials who craft policy and those engaged in operational delivery.[53] This will often be accompanied by a limited understanding as to how policy goals are being implemented on the ground and a lack of adequate management information and evaluation to link up operational delivery with policy. In large systems, there will also often be a lack of coordination between different operational units responsible for delivering the same policy goal. This sub-optimal vertical and horizontal integration will inevitably result in varying types of policy implementation gaps and/or harm to affected people who of necessity interact with the department and whose lives depend upon it. Another issue is that the selection of means to achieve policy ends will seldom be value-free or non-political. Ministers may prefer one particular way of achieving a desired goal in order to stake out a political position and to send out a political message. However, this can in turn close off consideration of alternative ways of delivering policy and the means preferred by ministers may turn out to be unworkable, harmful or dysfunctional.[54]

The adaption problem also comes into play; that is, the capacity of the organisation to identify and respond effectively to changes in its wider environment and then implement new policies and processes effectively. Consider the hierarchical

---

[52] HA Simon, *Administrative Behavior*, 4th edn (New York, Free Press, 1997) 73–75.

[53] A King and I Crewe, *The Blunders of our Governments* (London, Oneworld, 2013) ch 19.

[54] The trend is similarly pronounced in the benefits context. See M Adler, *Cruel, Inhuman or Degrading Treatment? Benefit Sanctions in the UK* (London, Palgrave Macmillan, 2018).

structure of administrative institutions and the degree to which it is open or closed to external variables from its wider operational or task environment.[55] Such organisations have three interdependent layers: leadership positions at the top (ministers and senior officials); policy staff and middle management; and the front-line operational delivery. They need to cope with significant uncertainty arising from their operating environment and therefore have to be flexible and open, but they also need to reduce uncertainty so that work can get work done. This tension and the consequent need for both flexibility and certainty is distributed differently across the three organisational layers. Those at the top have to be open to multiple variables (political pressures, media, the public, policy, large-scale and immediate changes in the task environment and technological change). By contrast, front-line operational staff – caseworkers processing individual decisions and enforcement staff preparing cases for returns – need to be protected from such wider and quick-changing forces. There is a real need to eliminate uncertainty from the operating core so that front-line staff have the stability to undertake the mass of the detailed work involved. They need to work within closed systems which are characterised by planned and controlled action and certainty within institutional structures, rules, systems and processes.

To reframe this, the administrative enterprise embodies a paradox. It involves hitting a moving target, itself comprised of several moving components, and therefore flexibility is required. Yet, the officials engaged in front-line delivery on the ground need certainty and stability in the systems and processes they use – otherwise nothing would get done. There are, of course, gradations in the ability of operational systems to absorb and adapt to different types of change. For instance, incremental and piecemeal adjustments, such as new rules, can be absorbed fairly easily. Even more significant changes such as whole new work streams and processes (such as the post-Brexit EU Settlement Scheme) can be established with sufficient planning and resources. However, larger-scale system reform is far more challenging given the multiple, complex and shifting variables involved and the need to keep the machine working in the meantime. The perennial risk is that the operational environment imposes intense demands for change and adaptation that delivery systems cannot keep up with and that the casework and enforcement machinery become out of date. Yet, constantly changing front-line technologies and operational systems risks getting it badly wrong. It is neither easy nor simple to resolve this fundamental paradox of administration. In fact, it can only be managed, and even then with difficulty. Highlighting this fundamental challenge does, though, illustrate the sheer complexities involved in administering policy at scale.

Within the immigration department itself, there are all the usual shortcomings of bureaucratic institutions: an excessive focus on process over outcomes; an

---

[55] See specifically JD Thompson, *Organizations in Action: Social Science Bases of Administrative Theory* (New Brunswick, NJ, Transaction Publishers, 2006) and in general B Burnes, *Managing Change*, 7th edn (Harlow, Pearson, 2017).

inward-looking focus; fragmented operational structures; a concentration upon organisational hierarchies and complexity; poor internal communications; poor organisational learning; internal turf wars; and the inability to self-examine critically its performance, instead preferring to be defensive and cover up difficult problems.[56] Other points to note concern staffing and culture. Externally, a government department may appear to have an inner solidity, but within the workforce this is often transient, with officials coming and going and being moved around internally thereby diminishing institutional memory. In terms of administrative culture, the Home Office is Whitehall's chief tough nut and has a quite different outlook and character from other government departments.[57] At the same time, the scale of operations, the administrative malaise, and its political context will produce resignation at the likely inability of the system to resolve matters thereby in turn creating an endemic blame culture and a desire to cover up problems. The department's internal culture has been characterised by low morale and low staff engagement, with a fear of communicating bad news being commonplace.[58] As a result, problematic issues have not been dealt with quickly and have on occasion only reached the attention of senior managers after they have irrevocably transformed into intractable problems.

In this context, there is a real need for effective internal administrative control.[59] Yet, it cannot be assumed that senior officials and managers are really any more in control of administrative operations than ministers. The business of modern government is fundamentally about managing large-scale systems of operational delivery. This requires division or unit-level and higher-level managerial skills and competencies, something historically lacking in the immigration department. Achieving desired real-world outcomes at scale involves the ability to run and supervise large and complex organisations and the effective coordination of operations, structures, cultures, resources, planning, people and information. By any measure, this is challenging.

Yet, managerial skills have rarely been valued as a key competency within the Whitehall elite.[60] The focus of senior mandarins is principally upon advising ministers, helping them out of tricky situations, and crafting policy. This elite includes people of very high intellectual calibre. Nonetheless, the courtier role prevails despite the undoubted need for and importance of managerial competence and

---

[56] J Bourn, *Public Sector Auditing: Is It Value For Money?* (Chichester, Wiley, 2006) ch 2.

[57] cf W Davies, 'Home Office Rules' *London Review of Books* Vol 38 No 21 (3 November 2016): 'the Home Office has long been identified as the voice of the working class inside Whitehall, and feels looked down on by the Oxbridge elite in Downing Street and the Treasury. … the ethos of the Home Office [is akin] to that of Millwall fans: "No one likes us, we don't care". See also D Trilling, 'Cruel, paranoid, failing: inside the Home Office' *Guardian* (13 May 2021).

[58] NAO, 'Reforming the UK Border and Immigration System' HC 445 (2013–14) [3.15].

[59] As the then HAC chair noted in 2009: 'What we actually need is administrative control of the Border Agency': *Hansard*, HC Vol 496 col 252 (14 July 2009) (Keith Vaz MP).

[60] Bacon and Hope, above n 50, 281–304; Rhodes, above n 50; Jenkins, above n 23.

skills. Part of the explanation is the inherently political nature of governmental activity, the reliance of ministers upon senior officials to guide them through the political minefields, and the instinctive and assumed role of senior officials to provide assistance. Effective management and delivery of programmes is rarely adequately rewarded.

C. Administrative Brass Tacks: Management Information, Internal Accountability, Organisational Competence and Resources

There are other related shortcomings. One concerns inadequate internal knowledge about administrative operations. Perhaps the most important of all core governmental functions is to know what is going on. Yet, the basic fact is that the UK central state possesses very little good-quality management information on what it does, its effectiveness and whether it provides value for money.[61] This is an especially acute problem in the immigration department. Senior officials have openly admitted that they lack a detailed understanding of what is and is not going on within their department, and the policy and wider impacts and consequences of its actions. As a former permanent secretary noted in 2018: 'there are defects in our data and there are defects in the systems we have to manage that data, which are quite old'.[62]

Management information is either incomplete or there is too much of it, but it is not the right sort of information.[63] All too often such information concerns activities undertaken as opposed to impacts, outcomes and results produced. Furthermore, it is not just an issue of having the right type of management information, but also of devising appropriate means for driving and measuring

---

[61] See Bacon and Hope, *Conundrum* (2013) 290–91 ('the difficulties in finding good information have been among the hardiest of perennials in the debate about failure in Whitehall … Too often, Whitehall doesn't have the right information'); Bourn, *Public Sector Auditing* (2006) 32 ('There are problems with much of the enormous amounts of data collected by government'); NAO, 'Challenges in Using Data Across Government' HC 2220 (2017–19).

[62] PAC, 'Oral Evidence: Windrush Generation and the Home Office', 17 December 2018, HC 1518 (2017–19) Q 125 (Sir Philip Rutnam, Permanent Secretary, Home Office). See also: HAC, 'Oral Evidence: Immigration Control', 6 June 2006, HC 775 (2005–06) Q 947 (Lin Homer, Director General, IND): 'our data collection systems are not good … the importance of good quality accurate information being collected, being used, and being shared is clearly not driven through the organisation yet'; PAC, 'Oral Evidence: Windrush Generation and the Home Office', 17 December 2018, HC 1518 (2017–19) Q 139 (Shona Dunn, Second Permanent Secretary, Home Office): 'I could not say right now that we could be sure of having absolute line of sight down into all the parts of the organisation'; PAC, 'Oral Evidence: Immigration Enforcement', 13 July 2020, HC 407 (2019–21) Q 49 (Shona Dunn, Second Permanent Secretary, Home Office) recognising that 'the dearth of information in some aspects of the activities that the immigration force undertake … is something that we need to continue to work on, and that is regrettable.'

[63] PAC, 'Immigration Enforcement' HC 407 (2019–21) [9]–[10].

administrative effectiveness. Inappropriate tools, such as some performance targets, can have all sorts of unintended distorting effects with adverse consequences, a matter evident in the Windrush scandal. The problems are heightened by the department often lacking a detailed and informed understanding of its policy context and of how its policies upon impact affected people. And all of this has important practical consequences, not just for operational delivery, but also government accountability and administrative law.

The role of management information may seem some distance from mainstream administrative law, but it is central to how administrative organisations work and their effectiveness and performance. The essence of instrumental rationality is whether administration action in fact produces desired policy outcomes. When administrative law is viewed as an instrument for getting things done, then good quality management information really is crucial. It is necessary to understand how statutory and other legal powers are being used by administration to implement policy goals. Without such information it is difficult, if not impossible, to understand and measure administrative performance, how policy is being effectively delivered on the ground, and the impacts of administrative action, both intended and otherwise. It is equally difficult for those bodies that scrutinise the department to hold it to account for its performance and to make informed judgements and recommendations.

A related issue is the department's internal culture of accountability. In 2006, IND's director had raised before the HAC both the importance of and difficulties in creating an internal culture of accountability. Such a culture involves officials seeing themselves as collectively responsible for overall organisational performance.[64] Yet, the reality was an overall picture of junior staff struggling to deliver with inadequate resources and leadership whilst neither their own immediate management nor more senior management felt able to insist on better performance.[65] As the Committee recognised, the biggest single management challenge for the department was to create lines of responsibility and accountability and to foster a culture at each organisational level in which staff felt responsible for overall performance rather than just their own individual tasks.[66] Without such a profound change of culture, individual targets or performance measures were unlikely to lead to the desired improved performance. Simply issuing written instructions top-down and expecting them to be implemented by front-line officials is unlikely to be effective without the right structures and cultures in place.[67] The wider point is that the efficacy of internal administrative law depends

---

[64] HAC, 'Immigration Control' HC 775 (2005–06) [539]–[540].
[65] ibid.
[66] ibid [543].
[67] D Ramsbottom, 'The Ministry of Chaos' *Guardian* (26 May 2006).

significantly upon having appropriate and robust internal organisational norms and cultures.[68]

Much of the time these features are hidden away, but they become most visible during the department's various crises. A notable feature of modern government is the potential for unexpected problems to arise given the complexity of unstable, overloaded, under-resourced, and uncoordinated administrative systems (and sub-systems). Large, fragmented, silo-based operational processes, such as the casework and enforcement systems within the immigration department, are particularly prone to this. As one former Home Secretary (Kenneth Baker, 1990–92) once candidly advised another (Jack Straw, 1997–2001):

> [J]ust remember as Home Secretary, there will be 50 sets of officials working on schemes to undermine your government and destroy your political career, and the worst is not only will you not know who they are, but neither will they.[69]

This is not mere hyperbole. Precisely this happened during the foreign national prisoners crisis of 2006. The underlying operational problems had included: a lack of coordination between the department and the prison service; increased caseload outstripping administrative capacity; and wholly inadequate internal supervision and oversight of the department's Criminal Casework team.[70] The patchy and inadequate nature of the IND's management information and its consequences was also evident: officials did not know how many foreign national prisoners had been sent to prison or how many had been later released without being considered for deportation.[71] There had been an entire lack of managerial competence and oversight. Senior officials later recognised the need to raise junior management competence from its low base. A culture of administrative blame-avoidance had also played an important role. Given the department's 'good news' culture, junior officials aware of the problems had delayed escalating matters upwards until it was too late. The crisis illustrates many continuities to the present day: poor data collection systems and management information; limited and variable administrative competence; and the department's inability to reform and change itself.

During the HAC's extensive post-mortem, it was apparent that the immigration system had been managed on the basis of available, rather than relevant, information, which had often been inadequate. IND's director, Lin Homer, told the Committee that developing proper management information and targets were

---

[68] E Fisher and S Shapiro, *Administrative Competence: Reimagining Administrative Law* (Cambridge, Cambridge University Press, 2020) 85–93.

[69] Quoted in M Cockerell, 'Home Secretary: Do you have what it takes to do Britain's most demanding job?' *The Independent* (24 May 2006).

[70] HAC, 'Immigration Control' (n 64) [516]–[535]; Committee of Public Accounts, 'Home Office Resource Accounts 2004–05 and Follow-up on Returning Failed Asylum Applicants' HC 1079 (2005–06); S Hyde, 'A Review of the Failure of the Immigration and Nationality Directorate to Consider Some Foreign National Prisoners for Deportation' (2007).

[71] NAO, 'Returning Failed Asylum Applicants' HC 76 (2005–06) [3.10].

central to her strategy of turning the department around.[72] Homer accepted that it would several years for better performance management to become reality, but she had clearly wanted every key part of the department's activities to be tracked effectively, which the HAC strongly supported.

Anyone might then assume that, given the importance of such matters, the department would have, over the next decade and a half, devised, introduced and operated an extensive range of systems for collecting and analysing performance and management information. Quite the contrary. In 2020, following another ruinous failure – Windrush – the department was still effectively in the same position. The department's lack of organisational competence and its dysfunctionality had resulted in significant harm to people. It still lacked adequate management information and knowledge with which to understand the impact and consequences of its activities.[73] It was again criticised for lacking basic competence, and the latest reform plan was met with scepticism as to what it would actually amount to, thereby reinforcing the perception that this is a largely unreformed and perhaps unreformable system.

These problems are, if anything, accentuated by the department outsourcing key aspects of operational delivery to private contractors and others.[74] Outsourced tasks have included: the processing of visa applications; the provision of asylum accommodation; the management of immigration detention centres; escort services for removal purposes; and immigration checks that are part of hostile environment measures. Outsourcing gives the department a means of trying to manage its limited capacity, although in some instances, it has enabled the department to shift the blame when things go wrong.[75] Complaints about the substandard services provided by profit-taking contractors are common. Outsourcing also raises further challenges concerning the department's oversight of contractors. Further separating operations from policy risks further breaks in the delivery chain and this requires capacity from the department to ensure effective monitoring of contractors. In practice, the reality is that the department may 'outsource and forget' and then problems arise.

It is important not to paint too black a picture or to overstate the general point. Administrative reality is nuanced, especially within such a large fragmented administrative system. The department has recognised the need to improve. It has introduced new IT data collection and management systems. Internal cultures of accountability are not monolithic. They change over time and vary from one unit or sub-unit to another. Many officials seek to do their job as effectively as possible and recognise the need to be held accountable. There is a real challenge for officials

---

[72] HAC (n 64) [562] (Lin Homer, Director General, IND).

[73] NAO, 'Immigration Enforcement' HC 110 (2019–21).

[74] See generally R Thomas, 'Does Outsourcing Improve or Weaken Administrative Justice? A Review of the Evidence' [2021] *PL* 542.

[75] 'Home Office outsourcing immigration operations "on the cheap" due to funding shortages and lack of ministerial interest, says chief inspector' *The Independent* (14 July 2019); A Bowman et al, *What a Waste: Outsourcing and How it Goes Wrong* (Manchester, Manchester University Press, 2015) ch 2.

in keeping on top of the caseload in a changing operational and political environment, especially if they lack the tools necessary and have to work with outdated
and overloaded systems. Further, an extreme negativity bias applies: officials
receive little, if any, credit for their successes, but copious amounts of criticism and
blame when things go wrong.[76] Nonetheless, deep-seated problems are inherent
within this system.

What then of resources? They are a key determinant of organisational
competence and capacity. The Chief Inspector of Borders and Immigration has
identified the

> by now familiar picture of a system (or more accurately a set of related but not always
> connected or coherent functions) that does not have the capacity, and in some instances
> the capabilities, to do everything required of it all of the time, with the result that some
> things are not done well or not at all.[77]

The basic reality is that the department is not properly resourced to deal with the
volumes it has to handle and the scale of its legal duties and the political goals
placed upon it; its business exceeds its capacity to manage. The system is stretched
to such an extent that the department's response to the latest priority or crisis is
typically at the expense of performance elsewhere.[78] The Inspector has recognised
the perceived harshness of continuing to criticise the department for its failures
– poor record-keeping, poor quality management, and poor internal and external
communications – but has also emphasised that unless these issues are addressed,
the department would continue to find it hard to use its already over-stretched
resources both effectively and efficiently.[79]

If current resources are inadequate, then, given the political saliency of immigration, perhaps extra resources could be allocated to resolve or at least ameliorate
matters? The need for additional resource is, of course, a cross-government issue,
but, by its very nature, the immigration department has an additional hurdle to
surmount in this regard. In 2018, the then immigration minister had explained
that the department 'needs more resources. It needs more people. It needs more

---

[76] Hood, *The Blame Game* (2011) 9–14.

[77] ICIBI, 'Annual Report 2018–19' (2019) 10.

[78] See HAC, 'Oral Evidence: Home Office Delivery of Brexit: Immigration', 10 October 2017, HC 421
(2017–19) Q 31 (David Wood, former Director General of Immigration Enforcement): 'The history
… has been of a poorly resourced system. The whole system was sort of managed, but you felt being
in charge of it at times that you were playing … nine-year-old football. You were all chasing the ball.
You suddenly had a problem because you had to move resources to try to deal with the problem knowing that, if we have to keep them there too long, we are going to have problems with where they came
from'; *Hansard*, HC Vol 640 col 391 (2 May 2018) (Meg Hiller MP, Home Office Minister 2007–2010):
'Dealing with the administration of immigration with never enough resources has been a challenge for
the Home Office for years'.

[79] See 'Home Office outsourcing immigration operations "on the cheap" due to funding shortages and lack of ministerial interest, says chief inspector' *The Independent* (14 July 2019): (the Chief
Inspector likened the department's predicament to trying to 'change a tyre as you're driving down the
motorway').

experienced caseworkers who are in a position to be able to process claims accurately and effectively.[80] However, as the minister later explained:

> The basic resource for the management of the immigration system is wholly inadequate and always has been. And the fundamental reason for that is if you're the Minister and you go to the Chief Secretary [of HM Treasury] and you say, 'I want more money for the immigration service', they say 'you must be joking – you think the British public would support that?'.[81]

D. The Customers

So far, we have considered matters from an administration-centred perspective, but we also need to consider the position of those who are subject to the process. This prompts a shift of focus to more familiar administrative law concerns: ensuring fair treatment; lawful decisions; and redress for often powerless people. Immigrants are a highly diverse group of people seeking entry either lawfully or otherwise. Applying for immigration status is often a life-changing event. From the perspective of applicants, the system will appear to be overwhelmingly monolithic and monopolistic. Migrants have no option but to interact with the system or suffer the consequences of becoming an irregular migrant with an insecure immigration status, or no such status at all.

The department can process most of the incoming caseload with relatively few problems, but a sizeable proportion of people experience a range of well-rehearsed problems, such as backlogs, delays and poor-quality decisions.[82] The immigration rules are highly complex and dense. Anyone would experience difficulties in navigating the complexity of not just the rules, but the whole system, without specialist advice. Some people may inadvertently apply for an inappropriate immigration status. It is virtually impossible for an applicant to contact their caseworker even when difficulties arise. It has also been consistently argued that the poor quality of case-work decisions arises from a culture of disbelief in which caseworkers are predisposed to rejecting applications and view applicants as inherently suspect.

All of this generates a real need for administrative justice processes and legal control via appeal tribunals and judicial review. From the perspective of an immigrant, the judicial process – independent and fair procedures – offers

---

[80] HAC, 'Oral Evidence: Immigration Detention', 8 May 2018, HC 913 (2017–19) Q 355 (Caroline Nokes MP, Minister for Immigration).

[81] 'Windrush Lessons Learned Review: Independent Review by Wendy Williams' HC 93 (2019–20) 68.

[82] As one MP asked in 2012, 'How on earth did we get into this position, where so many of my constituents come to me with heart-wrenching stories of how their lives have been eviscerated by this country's utter incompetence, over a long period in sorting out its immigration?' (*Hansard*, HC Vol 547, col 953 (4 July 2012) (Richard Fuller MP)).

the best means of participating in the administrative process. Like other 'problematic people' subject to administrative control systems (eg prisoners and people detained under mental health legislation), immigrants cannot vote. Such authority-based administrative systems explicitly reject the need for the consent of the governed, an otherwise essential legitimising value of administration. It is no surprise then that the immigration department is the typical respondent in administrative law litigation. It receives a greater proportion of legal challenges than any other part of government. It also has a particularly bad reputation for not just stretching the limits of administrative legality, but also, on occasion, for defying binding judicial rulings, whether because of contumacious intent or muddled incompetence.

This concern is always in the back of the minds of lawyers and judges. In 2008, a judge described the unlawful detention of an immigrant for nearly 22 months as

> shocking even to those who still live in the shadow of the damning admission by a former Secretary of State that a great Department of State is 'unfit for purpose'. They are scandalous for what they expose as the seeming inability of that Department to comply not merely with the law but with the very rule of law itself.[83]

Evidently, there is an acute need for legal control. Yet, to foreshadow later discussion, ministers have, over recent years, significantly restricted the system of legal remedies against immigration decisions through legal aid restrictions and the withdrawal of various appeal rights and their replacement with administrative review, despite the high proportion of successful appeals.

There are then those who experience the sharper end of the system: people caught working illegally and those detained, removed, or deported will experience the department's more coercive side. The department also plays a role in protecting those at risk of harm from others, such as victims of human trafficking. Like all administrative systems, the immigration process exists to perform crucial social functions and its work often raises challenging and sensitive issues. Yet, the administrative system itself becomes part of the problem when it oppresses people – and this occurs not just in dark, hidden corners, but also through mundane administrative routines, complex, contradictory and rigid rules, and the behaviours of individual officers. The immigration system seems more prone to such oppression than other systems. Just as any administrative process exists to serve the public good, there is also the need to ensure fair process, just and legal outcomes, and that people subject to the process are treated with dignity.

By contrast, the department will adopt a different perspective. It has no control over the selection of its clientele. It has to deal with all types of individuals, and some migrants will opportunistically seek to evade attempts by the department to enforce the rules against them. And some will do so by making extensive use of legal challenges. Yet, the risk is that the department adopts a wider tough and

---

[83] *R (SK) v Secretary of State for the Home Department* [2008] EWHC 98 (Admin) [2] (Munby J).

enforcement-minded approach to all cases rather than just in relation to those cases in which it is really needed. The potential for injustice for affected individuals is enormous.

Given the consequences of wrong decisions and the department's overall attitude toward judicial legality, there is a real need for effective redress for individuals and legal control of administration. Despite legal aid restrictions, there is a vibrant sector of immigrant campaigning and support groups. Those arguing in favour of the rights and interests of migrants lobby sympathetic MPs and naturally they also look to unelected parts of the constitution, the House of Lords and the courts. In legal terms, they place considerable reliance upon international human rights conventions, in particular the European Convention on Human Rights and the Refugee Convention. At its root, their argument is not to abolish the immigration department (the assertion of rights against government often requires positive administrative action), but for a more humane and fairer vision of administration focused upon protecting rights. The potential for clashes here with ministers is obvious and there have at times been acute tensions between various Home Secretaries and the judiciary.[84]

IV. Conclusion

Where then does all of this leave matters? We can reassess by going back to first principles. Administration, and the law governing it, is or should be guided by and operate in the public interest. This includes the ability of elected and politically accountable ministers to set policy goals and the need for competent, effective, lawful, and fair administration to implement them. It seems clear that both the public and immigrants want competent administration that can do the job properly. Yet, the department operates in a highly fraught political environment and its administrative operations are often dysfunctional. These factors are deeply embedded in practice and have significant distorting effects on the quest for more effective forms of administration. Indeed, the department can be seen as embodying an acute and ongoing legitimation crisis as evidenced by foreign national prisoners, Windrush and a constant stream of lower-level imbroglios.

At some stage in any discussion, the point will be made that, standing back and looking at matters as a whole, it is a problem of neither administration nor law; it is all just raw politics in a different guise: ministers decide and the department responds. And it is precisely this type of claim that seems simultaneously persuasive and contestable. Politics clearly motivates ministerial and administrative behaviour and there are significant elements of ministerial and official game-playing and blame-shifting. Yet, there are core features of the administrative process

---

[84] See, eg, 'Theresa May criticises judges for "ignoring" deportation law' *BBC News* (17 February 2013); 'Britain's top judge attacks Theresa May's criticism of judiciary' *Daily Telegraph* (4 March 2013).

and the law governing it that cannot be simply dismissed as just politics. These principally comprise the normative requirements imposed upon administration. This point applies far beyond immigration. Administration should be competent and functionally effective. It must also follow fair process in its interactions with affected people and act lawfully. These normative values reflect society's acceptance of and indeed desire for an overall system of administrative governance as the only viable means of managing complex social problems. The values of effectiveness, competence, legality and fairness prescribe society's normative vision as to what a legitimate system of government looks like and how it should operate in practice. At the same time, designing and operating an administrative system that satisfies these values in real-world conditions is a very problematic endeavour.

There have long been strong arguments for reforming the immigration department and for enhancing its effectiveness, fairness and compliance with the law. There is no viable alternative agenda. The department is an 'immortal' government agency. However it is labelled and categorised, the department is basically indestructible. It will only cease to exist if all immigration law and policy were to be altogether renounced – a political impossibility.

At the same time, dissatisfaction with the department is near universal. Indeed, this entire chapter may well have conveyed a profound sense of disillusionment with the immigration system, its drab and dreary workings and routines, its multiple failures and crises, and the limited possibilities for systemic improvement. The causes differ somewhat, but the same feelings extend to virtually all actors within the wider system – not just applicants, but also ministers, officials, representatives, judges, complaint-handling bodies, and so on. Further, while the particular nature of such disenchantment is specific to the immigration context, matters do not seem so very different in other large operational systems, such as the benefits system. Both systems have experienced similar trends in terms of tough austerity-induced policies, variable delivery of policies and organisational performance, deep-seated concerns about the quality of individualised decisions, and limitations to redress mechanisms.

Yet, this cannot be the end of the matter. There is no reason why immigration administration should remain always as it always has been. The past may shape the future, but does not necessarily determine it. The nature of administration itself – comprising over-arching systems and processes in need of monitoring and supervision – need not necessarily be accepted as inadequate. The normative force of the values of administrative competence, effectiveness, fairness, and legality not only remains, but has become more insistent. There is a strong argument that administrative law can improve and enhance public administration. In a sense, the immigration department is suspended between different visions of what it currently is and what it could potentially become. The alternative to disillusionment and dispiriting pessimism is optimism, but this is near impossible to maintain. The next best option is then a realistic optimism. Even this will be particularly challenging and will at times be tested almost to destruction in the chapters that follow. The degree to which it remains unscathed or even at all will depend upon the perspective adopted.

As the following discussion and analysis will demonstrate, there have and will continue to be fundamental administrative errors and failures. Examining and analysing the department's operations can provide a clearer understanding of the current system's operations, what goes wrong, why, and whether it can in future be avoided. But, in addition to this, there are important current trends in immigration administration that strongly indicate the desired course of direction. As the next chapter highlights, the department's most recent egregious failure – the Windrush scandal – also generated a future design of how it could operate and be reformed. Further, there are various types of administration-generated legal processes that rarely get the attention or analysis that they deserve, which could be developed to enhance the department's performance. Also, the courts have increasingly come to undertake judicial review on the basis of systemic unlawfulness and unfairness, with a view to improving not just the department's performance, but also enhancing its internal supervision and systemic compliance with legal and procedural norms. There is also a real need for reform when it comes to the endemic problem of bureaucratic oppression. The argument advanced here is that such trends need to be developed further and formalised through legislation where appropriate. In short, the task of trying to improve administration and administrative law in the immigration context is inherently problematic and success is not guaranteed, but it is essential.

3

Administrative Policy-making: The Hostile Environment Policy and Windrush

In an administrative state, most laws take the form of legislation enacted by Parliament and regulations made by government departments and agencies to implement their policy goals. These laws are 'first and foremost the legal expression of a policy developed within a particular government department'.[1] They are an integral part of the wider process by which government agencies make and implement policy. This is not a new development.[2] By contrast, conventional court-focused administrative law scholarship has focused largely on legal doctrine rather than substantive policy. Yet, substantive policies are the principal products and determinants of administrative behaviour. Accordingly, the substantive policies of government departments need to be fully incorporated into the analysis of administrative law.[3]

A more radical argument is that the growth of administrative policy-making, through the development of administrative organisations, has not merely supplied more materials for investigating administrative law; it has also led to a fundamental structural change in the nature of *law* itself. The concept of law of a coherent body of legal principles with its own inherent order or logic and which is accessible to reason or as a set of rules governing human conduct is deeply embedded within legal scholarship. It rests upon the somewhat dubious assumption that law and politics can actually be formally separated. Another basic problem is that this conceptual approach no longer adequately accounts for the vast majority of administrative laws that govern society. These laws – legislation and regulations – are made by Parliament and government to embody and

---

[1] P Goldsmith, 'Parliament for Lawyers: An Overview of the Legislative Process' (2002) 4 *European Journal of Law Reform* 511, 513.

[2] CP Ilbert, *Legislative Methods and Forms* (Oxford, Oxford University Press, 1901) 210–13 and 219 noted that the bulk of the statute book consisted of administrative legislation rather than lawyer's law and that, as long ago as 1837, the Home Office had been the principal source of administrative legislation.

[3] E Gellhorn and GO Robinson, 'Perspectives on Administrative Law' (1975) 75 *Columbia Law Review* 771; RL Rabin, 'Administrative Law in Transition: A Discipline in Search of an Organizing Principle' (1977) 72 *North Western University Law Review* 120.

deliver policy. Further, these laws put into action changes – such as creating and organising government agencies, conferring powers upon them, and allocating resources – that extend far beyond the idea that law concerns subjecting human conduct to the governance of rules.[4] Such laws are also intimately concerned with the behaviours and actions of administrative departments.

Administrative law is then better understood if it is recharacterised as policy and implementation.[5] Legislation and regulations are explicitly adopted to achieve policy goals; their implementation by government agencies accounts for the largest part of the work of those institutions. When compared with a conceptual approach of law, with its attendant court-centred focus, this understanding of administrative law has real advantages. It can connect legal scholarship with other disciplines, such as political science and public administration. It better reflects the nature and character of administrative government and its instrumental role in addressing social problems. It also encompasses the full range of activities undertaken by government in carrying out its tasks. This approach can also be used to undertake detailed analyses of how government operates in practice. It might then provide a potentially profitable perspective on how administrative law operates and functions in practice. When viewed from this perspective, some of the central issues of administrative law concern the policy-making process within government and the quality and effectiveness of its outputs and outcomes.

It is from this perspective that this chapter examines a major instance of immigration policy-making known as the hostile environment policy. This general policy comprised various measures introduced principally through the Immigration Acts 2014 and 2016 to make life uncomfortable for irregular migrants. The chapter examines the policy-making process and the subsequent adverse consequences of the hostile environment policy, as demonstrated by the Windrush scandal. Overall, the policy was deeply flawed because of acute failures in the department's policy-making process. Consequently, if reform of administrative law is desired, the principal and most beneficial reforms should focus upon improving and enhancing the processes by which government departments make and implement policy.

I. Policy-making

To begin, we can briefly consider policy-making itself, the process by which government agencies identify policy goals and select the appropriate means of

---

[4] EL Rubin, 'Law and Legislation in the Administrative State' (1989) 89 *Columbia Law Review* 369; B Tamanaha, *A Realistic Theory of Law* (Cambridge, Cambridge University Press, 2017) ch 5 and 126: 'No existing theory of law adequately accounts for government entities that utilize legal mechanisms in myriad ways in their activities'.

[5] EL Rubin, *Beyond Camelot: Rethinking Politics and Law for the Modern State* (Princeton, Princeton University Press, 2005) 203–14.

achieving them. This is a huge issue and has generated a correspondingly large literature.[6] It is generally recognised that a good-quality policy-making process possesses certain characteristics. Policy-makers should first identify the problem that they want to resolve and identify their goals. They should generate a range of alternative solutions for addressing that problem and achieving their goals. They should then evaluate the likely effectiveness of those solutions by drawing upon the available evidence and identify the trade-offs involved. Evaluation and learning should be built into the implementation process. Policy-makers should adopt both forward- and outward-looking perspectives.[7] They should take a long-term view, based on statistical trends and informed predictions, of the likely impact of policy. An innovative and creative approach should be preferred by questioning established assumptions and established ways of doing things. The process should be informed by the best available evidence and stakeholders should be involved throughout. Policy-makers should take account of the impact of policy upon those affected. Systemic evaluation should be built into the policy-making process. Policy should be kept under review. Policy-makers should draw lessons about what works and what does not.

These characteristics of policy-making are certainly desirable, although they suggest an ideal model of policy-making which is often at odds with the real-world conditions of political and administrative life. Policy-making and implementation is rarely a rational, linear process; the distinction between policy goals and the means of accomplishing them is often blurred in practice. The whole enterprise is an intrinsically difficult and problematic process influenced by various complex and intersecting political, organisational and behavioural variables. It is also informed by the nature of relationships between officials and ministers. The former might be unwilling to challenge their minister's policy proposals; speaking truth to power may be seen by ministers as obstruction with negative consequences for civil servants' careers. In practice, policy officials undertake their work through 'invited authority' and 'improvised expertise'.[8] The design and implementation of policy is also constrained by a wide number of complex organisational and administrative variables and factors.[9]

The policy process also needs to be set against the wider backdrop of well-documented systemic and human behavioural malfunctions within British

[6] M Moran, M Rein and RE Goodin (eds), *The Oxford Handbook of Public Policy* (Oxford, Oxford University Press, 2008); P John, *Analyzing Public Policy* (London, Routledge, 2012); M Howlett, *Designing Public Policies: Principles and Instruments*, 2nd edn (London, Routledge, 2019).

[7] Institute for Government, 'Policy Making in the Real World: Evidence and Analysis' (London, IfG, 2011) 23.

[8] EC Page and B Jenkins, *Policy Bureaucracy: Government with a Cast of Thousands* (Oxford, Oxford University Press, 2005).

[9] JL Pressman and A Wildavsky, *Implementation*, 3rd ed (Oakland, University of California Press, 1984).

central government.[10] These include: the political pressures upon ministers and their limited experience in terms of making policy; the culture of the senior civil service; the gaps between those who make policy and those who implement it; the over-concentration of power within central government departments; their relative lack of accountability and of internal deliberation; the issue of civil service skills; and the often peripheral and reactive role of Parliamentary scrutiny, amongst many others. Then there are recent trends within the specific context of the Home Office: reduced department budgets following years of austerity; the high-pressure political context; and a department feeling embattled following repeated criticism for being not fit for purpose. It is in this context that we consider the hostile environment policy.

II. The Hostile Environment

A. The Immigration Problem

For many years, immigration has presented successive governments with a major problem. This problem is complex, multi-factorial, and multi-dimensional, but it can, for present purposes, be stripped down to one basic aspect. Given the growing number of people present in the country without immigration status and who are not known to the immigration department, increased concern from the public about immigration, and the need for ministers and the department respectively to win re-election and to maintain public confidence, how is it possible for government to secure greater compliance with and enforcement of immigration law in light of the department's reduced budgets and increased political demands placed upon it?

The department's traditional response has been to enforce immigration controls forcibly through removal and deportation procedures. This costly and complex process may remove some of the most difficult immigration 'offenders', but these people comprise only a small proportion of all of those without immigration status. The principal alternative has been to encourage irregular migrants to leave voluntarily – a less costly process, but, by its nature, a voluntary one. Some people may return voluntarily to their home country, but again, they form a small proportion of those without immigration status. This leaves a considerable number of other people who cannot be forcibly removed easily and many who are highly unlikely to return voluntarily. In light of public concern and the need to be

---

[10] For the government failure literature, see: P Dunleavey, 'Policy Disasters: Explaining the UK's Record' (1995) 10 *Public Policy and Administration* 52; A King and I Crewe, *The Blunders of Our Governments* (London, Oneworld, 2013); R Bacon and C Hope, *Conundrum: Why Every Government Gets Things Wrong and What We Can Do About It* (London, Biteback, 2013); W Jennings, M Lodge and M Ryan, 'Comparing Blunders in Government' (2018) 57 *European Journal of Political Research* 238.

seen to be doing something, the department has been compelled to address this problem by identifying further policy instruments by which it could seek to secure greater compliance with immigration law. It has had to do this in a highly pressurised political environment and also within an overall framework of government accountability that emphasises not just political responsiveness, but also administrative effectiveness and acting lawfully and fairly.

B. A Hostile Solution

The policy solution has been to restrict and prevent irregular migrants from undertaking activities and accessing essential services that almost everyone needs to live an ordinary life. These include: working; benefits and healthcare; housing; banking; and driving. These measures collectively comprised the 'hostile environment' policy. The overall purpose was to make life uncomfortable for irregular migrants by denying them access to services and thereby encouraging them to either regularise their status or leave voluntarily.

The 'hostile environment' is sometimes used to describe the department's overall approach toward immigration, including restrictive immigration rules, but it is more appropriately used to describe the specific measures designed to restrict access to services and thereby encourage irregular immigrants to leave the country voluntarily. In 2012, the political signalling from Theresa May, Home Secretary, was that irregular migrants could expect to receive a 'really hostile reception' in the UK.[11] The basic idea has deep roots in immigration law. The Immigration Act 1971 had imposed sanctions upon those who facilitate illegal immigrants residing in the UK – a forerunner of the Right to Rent scheme considered below.[12] Restrictions on employing irregular immigrants were introduced in 1996.[13] Under carriers' liability schemes, introduced in 1987 and extended in 1999, penalties are imposed on air carriers, haulage operators and ferry operators responsible for transporting clandestine entrants to the country.[14] The department's 2007 enforcement strategy stated that individuals 'not prioritised for removal … should be denied the benefits and privileges of life in the UK and experience an increasingly uncomfortable environment so that they elect to leave.'[15]

Nonetheless, the policy momentum for a hostile environment escalated considerably during the 2010s. The Home Office's view was that the measures were built upon a framework of compliance, deterrence and industrial-scale

---

[11] 'Theresa May interview: "We're going to give illegal migrants a really hostile reception"' *Daily Telegraph* (25 May 2012).

[12] Immigration Act 1971, s 25. See also M Griffiths and C Yeo, 'The UK's Hostile Environment: Deputising Immigration Control' (2021) *Critical Social Policy* (forthcoming).

[13] Asylum and Immigration Act 1996, s 8.

[14] Immigration (Carriers' Liability) Act 1987; Immigration and Asylum Act 1999, Pt 2.

[15] Home Office, 'Enforcing the Rules: A Strategy to Ensure and Enforce Compliance With Our Immigration Laws' (2007) 17.

data-sharing with other government departments and private sector actors. Individual policies would, both individually and cumulatively, make life difficult for irregular migrants thereby encouraging them to either regularise their status or leave. This would, in turn, secure more effective enforcement but at lower costs than traditional enforcement methods. While there are a number of such measures, the Home Office stressed the importance of their cumulative impact on individuals.

The individual measures had some common features. First, while the department was responsible for devising and controlling this overall policy, it would enlist and compel other actors – other government departments and public bodies as well as private actors – to implement it in practice. The Home Office could rely upon other government departments to implement the policy through the principle of collective responsibility. As regards private actors, such as landlords and employers, the Home Office could impose sanctions and penalties on them if, for instance, they let property to or employed irregular migrants. The department had previously been criticised for introducing legislation that had been ineffective because it had not been matched by administrative action.[16] But the intention was that the hostile measures would obviate this criticism by compelling private actors to administer them.

A second feature was that the overall effect of the policy would 'internalise' immigration controls or 'the border' within the country. Previously, immigration controls had been physically located at the border and ports of entry. The UK had previously exported its border to many other countries by requiring that nationals from that country apply for and be granted entry clearance or a visa before travelling to the country.[17] The effect of the hostile environment was to internalise the border by requiring everyone – UK nationals and immigrants alike – to demonstrate and evidence their immigration status when, for instance, applying for employment or renting a property through the production of passports and other relevant documents. The assumption was that such documentary evidence would be conclusive of a person's immigration status; the converse assumption was that its absence would denote that the person concerned did not have immigration status and was therefore a 'disqualified' person who could not, for example, work legally or rent a property.[18]

Viewed in abstract terms as a means of securing compliance with immigration law, the idea of making life uncomfortable for irregular migrants to encourage them to leave had considerable attractions for the department. There were none of the costs associated with detention and enforced removals. Instead, government would create the conditions in which people without immigration

---

[16] See, eg, *Hansard*, HC Deb Vol 496 col 255 (14 July 2009) (Keith Vaz MP).

[17] There are also 'juxtaposed controls' under which the UK operates border controls in France and Belgium.

[18] For instance, Immigration Act 2014, s 21 is entitled 'Persons disqualified by immigration status or with limited right to rent'.

status would be encouraged to leave voluntarily. After all, government uses indirect methods to secure compliance with the rules by its own citizens. Given the public concern about immigration, why not then devise and apply similar methods against people who are not its citizens? Nudge techniques have become increasingly common within government through the utilisation of behavioural insights.[19] The hostile environment policy could, arguably, be viewed as a range of 'very hard-nudge' techniques. Government could portray the response of irregular migrants to the various measures as an individual, conscious choice: people could remain and tolerate the lack of access to services or leave voluntarily. Yet, the overall policy was intensely controversial. It was met with particular criticism during the scrutiny of legislation through Parliament. Such criticism intensified following the Windrush scandal. These matters are considered below, but it is first appropriate to provide a brief overview of the individual hostile environment measures.

C. Hostile Measures

i. Illegal Working

A long-standing policy assumption is that illegal working acts as a pull factor for irregular migrants and results in the exploitation of workers, unfair competition and revenue evasion. In 1996, it was made a criminal offence for employers to employ irregular migrants.[20] Since 2006, there has been a civil penalty regime.[21] Civil penalties are now the principal means of dealing with cases of non-compliance by negligent businesses employing irregular workers. To respond to concerns that some employers deliberately do not check whether their employees have the right to work (and could only be liable for a civil penalty rather than criminal prosecution), the 2016 Act made it easier to bring criminal prosecutions in such cases. The Act also created a new offence of illegal working with the aim of ensuring that the act of illegal working is always an offence, unless the individual does not know or has reasonable cause to believe that their immigration status disqualifies them from working.[22] The earnings of illegal workers can be seized under the Proceeds of Crime Act 2002. Employers can check online whether employees have the right to work.[23]

---

[19] R Thaler and C Sunstein, *Nudge* (London, Penguin, 2008); D Halpern, *Inside the Nudge Unit: How Small Changes Can Make a Big Difference* (London, Allen, 2015).
[20] Asylum and Immigration Act 1996, s 8.
[21] Immigration, Asylum and Nationality Act 2006, s 15.
[22] Immigration Act 2016, s 34.
[23] 'Right to work checks go fully digital' *Public Technology* (17 December 2018).

ii. Social Security

The 1999 and 2002 Immigration Acts restricted welfare benefits for individuals without leave to remain in the country. Individuals applying for benefits from the Department for Work and Pensions (DWP) must confirm their immigration status; those in receipt of benefits can have them cancelled.

iii. The Right to Rent Scheme

This scheme prevents irregular migrants from renting private accommodation. Landlords must confirm the lawful immigration status of potential tenants by carrying out 'reasonable enquiries' to establish that prospective tenants have the 'right to rent' before agreeing to lease them premises 'for residential use'.[24] This is enforced by way of a civil penalty regime and criminal offences for those landlords and agents who deliberately and repeatedly fail to comply with the Right to Rent scheme or fail to evict individuals who they know or have reasonable cause to believe are disqualified from renting as a result of their immigration status.[25] It is also a criminal offence knowingly to lease a property to a disqualified person. The 2016 Act also enables landlords to terminate tenancies where the tenant is a disqualified individual.[26]

iv. Illegal Driving

Since 2010, the Driver and Vehicle Licensing Agency (DVLA) has been obliged to refuse driving licences to anyone unable to demonstrate that they are lawfully resident.[27] Existing licences of irregular migrants can be revoked.[28] The police and immigration officers can also search for and seize UK driving licences belonging to an irregular migrant and impound vehicles.[29] It is a criminal offence for an irregular migrant to drive.[30]

v. Banking

Under the 2014 Act, irregular migrants cannot access banking services.[31] Banks and building societies must refuse an application for a UK current account from

---

[24] Immigration Act 2014, ss 20–37.
[25] Immigration Act 2016, s 39.
[26] Immigration Act 2016, s 40. In *R (Joint Council for the Welfare of Immigrants) v Secretary of State for the Home Department* [2020] EWCA Civ 542, [2021] 1 WLR 1151 the Court of Appeal dismissed a wide-ranging human rights challenge against the scheme.
[27] *Hansard*, HC Vol 508, col 70ws (25 March 2010).
[28] Immigration Act 2014, s 47.
[29] Immigration Act 2016, s 43.
[30] Immigration Act 2016, s 44.
[31] Immigration Act 2014, ss 40–43.

an individual listed as a 'disqualified person'. They must also undertake periodic checks and to notify the Home Office when a person disqualified with a bank account is identified.[32] The department may then apply to freeze the individual's accounts, although there is an exception to ensure people's essential living needs are met.

vi. NHS Healthcare

Since 1977, the NHS has been able to charge people not ordinarily resident in the UK.[33] Regulations from 1982 imposed a charging regime in respect of hospital treatment for overseas visitors. In 2015, regulations (as amended) imposed charges on secondary (hospital) care and community care services, although some services, such as A&E, are specifically excluded. GP services, and primary dental and ophthalmic services, remain outside the scope of the overseas charging regulations.[34]

vii. Concerns

Pre-Windrush, a number of deep-seated concerns were raised with these measures. The general concern was essentially that the measures had inhumane consequences for irregular migrants. A related concern was that those affected would include not just irregular immigrants, but also people present entirely lawfully, but who could not evidence their immigration status. There can be a very blurred line between the two. Linked to this were concerns that the department had not considered the equality and diversity issues and that it was relying heavily upon the use of private actors, such as employers and landlords, which could well distort the implementation of the policy because they would be motivated by financial considerations. Take the Right to Rent scheme, perhaps the most high-profile and contentious hostile environment measure. Landlords complained about the burdens of undertaking checks. There were also concerns that landlords, wishing to avoid financial penalties, could well in practice err on the side of caution by refusing tenancies to ethnic minorities and thereby resulting in racial discrimination.

The reliance upon the sharing of data was also problematic given the department's poor reputation as regards the quality and accuracy of its data. And this turned out to be the case. The restriction of banking and driving licences has been weakened by incomplete or incorrect immigration records for individuals

---

[32] Immigration Act 2016, Sch 7.

[33] National Health Service Act 1977, s 121.

[34] National Health Service (Charges to Overseas Visitors) Regulations, SI 2015/238 and SI 2017/756; Department of Health and Social Care, 'Guidance on Implementing the Overseas Visitor Charging Regulations' (2020).

(for instance, data placed in the wrong fields) and by delays in updating records.[35] A final concern was the lack of detailed evidence as to the effectiveness of the measures. In 2018, the Chief Inspector concluded that the Right to Rent scheme still had to demonstrate its worth as a tool to encourage immigration compliance.[36] The Inspector's wider uneasiness illustrated how the hostile environment measures had been based more on conviction than upon evidence and the very limited evaluation of how the measures worked in practice.

The department's consistent response has been that the measures were right in principle, enjoyed public support, and necessary to enforce immigration control. From the perspective of political accountability, ministers could plausibly argue that the measures had been introduced in response to public opinion favouring more effective action against illegal immigration. But they could not plausibly claim that there was direct democratic support for the measures. There had been no mention at all of the hostile environment policy in the Conservative Party's 2010 party manifesto.[37] There had been a manifesto commitment to reduce immigration from the hundreds of thousands to tens of thousands a year, although this concerned immigrants entering the country as opposed to those already present. In any event, while political support for a general policy is clearly necessary and desirable, the hostile environment policy raised other questions as to whether it would also be administered effectively, lawfully and fairly in practice.

III. Windrush

In 2017, a journalist began reporting that many people who had been lawfully settled and permanently resident in the UK for decades had been wrongly refused access to services, placed in immigration detention, removed, and refused permission to re-enter because they had been unable to prove that they had the right to remain and live in the UK.[38] Such people belonged to the Windrush generation – an estimated 500,000 people who had come predominantly from Commonwealth Caribbean nations to the UK between 1948 and 1973 and who were largely of Caribbean ethnic and national origin.[39] Under the Immigration Act 1971, these

---

[35] ICIBI, 'An Inspection of the 'Hostile Environment' Measures Relating to Driving Licences and Bank Accounts' (2016) [2.21].

[36] ICIBI, 'An Inspection of the 'Right to Rent' Scheme' (2018).

[37] Conservative Party, 'Invitation to Join the Government of Britain: The Conservative Manifesto 2010' (2010). A related point is that the Conservative Party did not achieve a majority in the 2010 general election and entered into a coalition with the Liberal Democrats.

[38] A Gentleman, *The Windrush Betrayal: Exposing the Hostile Environment* (London, Guardian Faber, 2019).

[39] For a social history of the Windrush generation, see M Phillips and T Phillips, *Windrush: The Irresistible Rise of Multi-racial Britain* (London, Harper Collins, 1998).

people had a statutory right of abode in the UK because they had arrived before 1 January 1973 (when the 1971 Act came into force) and had been specifically and explicitly conferred a distinct immigration status – the right of abode – by that Act.[40] They were exempt from deportation and immigration detention.[41] When Windrush people entered the UK, the department did not, at that time, give them any formal official document to demonstrate their status. The department did not itself keep any records and later destroyed landing cards. Thousands of members of the Windrush generation were children at the time and had travelled on their parents' passports and did not therefore possess their own documents. Over the following decades, the Home Office's institutional memory of the particular position of the Windrush generation faded. The department lost sight of this cohort of people in light of many subsequent developments in immigration, not least the increase in asylum claimants during the 1990s and 2000s. In turn, the department's focus became increasingly dominated by the perceived need to tighten and enforce immigration controls and, during the 2010s, developing and applying hostile environment measures.

The subsequent problem was that many Windrush people – lifetime residents in the UK – were not formally identified as having the right to live in the country by the department. Many of them had been caught by the hostile environment measures. People with a legal right to remain had lost their jobs, benefits and tenancies, and been refused healthcare. In some cases, people had been detained, removed from the country, prevented from re-entering, and separated from their family. Overall, members of the Windrush generation had been treated as if they had been in the UK illegally whereas, in fact, they had been lawfully resident for many years. In short, they had been subject to not just unlawful administrative decisions and actions, but also significant forms of unjustifiable and unnecessary harm. It is no exaggeration to say that many people had their lives destroyed by the Home Office because they had caught up in hostile environment measures. That policy was intended to make life uncomfortable for people without immigration status, but it had directly affected people who had a legal right to be in the country.

In this context, Windrush people could seek to regularise their immigration status on the basis of settlement due to long residence, as returning residents, or request a 'No Time Limit' endorsement, a process which is not an application for indefinite leave to remain, but for formal confirmation that the individual already has that status.[42] Many applied to the department for a decision, but were refused,

---

[40] Immigration Act 1971, s 1(2). See further RM White, 'The Nationality and Immigration Status of the "Windrush Generation" and the Perils of Lawful Presence in a "Hostile Environment"' (2020) 33 *Journal of Immigration, Asylum, and Nationality Law* 218.

[41] Immigration Act 1971, s 7(1).

[42] This concerns an application by a person who is already a permanent UK resident to have an endorsement in their passport or Biometric Residence Permit which demonstrates that there is 'No Time Limit' concerning their stay in the UK or an application to transfer an indefinite leave to remain status onto a biometric residency permit.

despite having supplied often considerable volumes of documents about their personal history in the UK. Caseworkers assessed such applications by considering whether applicants had demonstrated their case to the criminal standard of proof ('beyond reasonable doubt'). The department's decision systems and caseworkers equated a lack of formal documentation with a lack of immigration status; this wrong-footed Windrush people and illustrated the superficiality of the department's casework decisions.[43] Many people were – wholly incorrectly – deemed to be irregular migrants and were therefore denied access to public services and subjected to immigration detention and removal. Some had visited their country of origin for a short visit, but then been unable to return to the UK, even though they had lived there for decades.[44]

There was considerable fall-out from Windrush as it became increasingly clear that the department had been directly responsible for imposing harm on many innocent people. Windrush generated feelings of betrayal and distrust, and concerns that the department was, under a thin veneer, acting in an institutionally racist way. From the perspective of Commonwealth Caribbean countries, the scandal was part of an established pattern of persistent cruelty imposed on them by the UK.[45]

There were also immediate political consequences. During the crisis, the Home Affairs Committee (HAC) undertook detailed scrutiny. Amber Rudd MP, then Home Secretary (2017–18), had incorrectly informed the Committee that there had not been any performance targets concerning the number of people without immigration status that were to be removed – either forcibly or voluntarily – from the country by Immigration Enforcement.[46] In point of fact, not only did such targets exist, but there had been a specific target to increase enforced returns by 10 per cent over the course of the year.[47] What is more, the removal targets had directly influenced administrative behaviour. Enforcement officers had focused on going after the easiest cases for removal purposes – the 'low-hanging fruit' – to meet their targets. Such cases included vulnerable people, and also members of the Windrush generation, people who were present legally and posed no threat of harm by remaining in the country.[48]

---

[43] See further ch 5 at 117–118.

[44] For subsequent legal challenges, see: *R (Howard) v Secretary of State for the Home Department* [2021] EWHC 1023 (Admin) (applying good character guidance to refuse applications for naturalisation as British citizen made by members of Windrush generation was irrational given their long-residence and integration); *Mahabir and others v Secretary of State for the Home Department* [2021] EWHC 1177 (Admin) (Windrush person separated for more than 40 years from her UK family returned to secure her status in the UK, but to do so, was separated from her Trinidad close family; the Home Office then refused to waive unaffordable application fees for her close family to join her in the UK, which amounted to colossal interference with her family life and was discriminatory and unlawful).

[45] G Hewitt, 'The Windrush Scandal: An Insider's Reflection' (2020) 66 *Caribbean Quarterly* 108.

[46] HAC, 'Oral Evidence: Windrush Children', 25 April 2018, HC 990 (2017–19) Q 85 (Amber Rudd MP, Secretary of State for the Home Department).

[47] 'Amber Rudd was sent targets for migrant removal, leak reveals' *Guardian* (28 April 2018).

[48] The Windrush Review – 'Windrush Lessons Learned Review: Independent Review by Wendy Williams' HC 93 (2019–20) 10 – quoted a former senior official: "'There'd be a whole range of targets

This particular way of gaming governmental targets – 'output distortion' – involves the deliberate manipulation of the reporting on administrative action by 'hitting the target, but missing the point'.[49] Enforcement action had served the defensive self-interests of enforcement officials who had been placed under considerable pressure to meet their performance targets as set by ministers. By contrast, only limited enforcement action had been taken against the most difficult immigration cases, which included those whose illegal presence in the country posed a much higher potential risk of harm. Rudd immediately removed the targets which she had denied existed and later resigned for having inadvertently misled the Committee.[50]

Having a parliamentary committee expose a lack of knowledge by the Home Secretary on a fairly basic aspect of the department's operations was clearly embarrassing for both the minister concerned and (some) senior officials.[51] The last point is necessarily qualified because sources within the department had leaked to the media that Rudd had been informed about removal targets by officials before giving evidence to the Committee – contrary to her claim that she had been unaware of them.[52] A subsequent review concluded that the Home Secretary had not been properly supported by officials before the committee.[53]

Ministerial resignations, tensions between officials and ministers within a government department, and leaks to the media are the stuff of day-to-day politics. But, in the grand scheme of things, they are fairly peripheral events. Resignations

including number of removals, voluntary departures, foreign national offenders that would be removed. So there'd be a … range of targets across the organisation." The official noted that (in their view, with or without targets) staff would, "pick the low hanging fruit … because you go into … operations, the poor illegal immigrant has got his passport in his pocket, he's arrested and on a plane within 24 hours probably … because there's no obstacle to get the person out the country …'".

[49] C Hood, 'Gaming in Targetworld: The Targets Approach to Managing British Public Services' (2006) 66 *Public Administration Review* 515, 516. The problems are compounded if, as Hood argues, central managers do not check performance data, take performance gains at face value, or lack a coherent anti-gaming strategy. The Home Office had none of these mechanisms.

[50] Exemplifying both contemporary patterns of seemingly futile ministerial behaviour and how ministers can be just as much victims – as well as masters – of the political-governmental system, Amber Rudd had responded to speculation within the Westminster bubble about her political future through a series of defiant late-night tweets. Having been Home Secretary for less than a year, Rudd had not been personally responsible for the Windrush scandal, although she had unintentionally misled the HAC.

[51] It was not the only incorrect statement made to the Committee. During the hearing, the senior official appearing alongside the Home Secretary, Glyn Williams (Director General for Borders, Immigration and Citizenship) had to correct Rudd after she had inaccurately told the Committee that there were 'opportunities for people to appeal the decision'. In fact, the right of appeal had been withdrawn under the Immigration Act 2014, s 15. See: HAC, 'Oral Evidence: Windrush Children', 25 April 2018, HC 990 (2017–19) Qs 154–55.

[52] The Home Office source told *The Guardian*: 'We were gobsmacked by what she said, and that she stuck to her guns. It is inconceivable that Amber Rudd did not know about the targets'. See 'Amber Rudd was sent targets for migrant removal, leak reveals' *Guardian* (28 April 2018); 'Amber Rudd resigns hours after Guardian publishes deportation targets letter' *Guardian* (30 April 2018); and then, inevitably, M Foster, 'Amber Rudd allies accused of "turning fire" on Home Office staff over her exit' *Civil Service World* (1 May 2018).

[53] Home Office, 'Sir Alex Allan Review: Executive Summary' (2 November 2018).

change the personnel at the top and briefly dominate the news agenda, but do nothing whatsoever to address the underlying structural and systemic administrative problems. Ministers come and go, whereas government departments are inherent and permanent features of the machinery of government. What is much more important is how these departments make and implement policy. Indeed, the principal causes of the Windrush scandal were directly traceable to significant shortcomings in the department's policy-making processes when it had developed the hostile environment measures. It is this to which we now turn.

IV. Policy-making Failures

Windrush prompted various reports from three parliamentary select committees and the NAO, and an independent Windrush Lessons Learned Review (the 'Windrush Review') was undertaken by Wendy Williams who had been commissioned by the Home Office to uncover why the scandal arose and to make recommendations.[54] These reports generally arrived at similar conclusions, although the Windrush Review was the most authoritative report; Williams and her team had direct access to official documents and also interviewed former ministers and officials. Furthermore, all of these reports were highly critical of the Home Office. The Windrush Review was extremely critical – damning – about both the department's policy-making process for developing the hostile environment measures and its conduct when making decisions about whether members of the Windrush generation were entitled to remain in the country. In light of the sensitivities involved, the report concluded that the department had demonstrated 'institutional ignorance and thoughtlessness towards the issue of race and the history of the Windrush generation'.[55]

Collectively, these reports concluded that Windrush people had been caught up by a series of different policy, legal, cultural and organisational changes in the Home Office. These included: the removal of caseworker discretion; the use of targets to influence the throughput of casework decisions; restrictions on independent checks and appeals; stronger controls at the border; and the substance of hostile environment measures targeted at irregular migrants, but affecting people with the right to remain, who could not evidence their immigration status because the Home Office had never physically issued documentation to them. A key factor was the department's lack of institutional memory: it had lost sight of the Windrush cohort and the rights they had as Commonwealth citizens under the Immigration Act 1971.

---

[54] HAC, 'The Windrush Generation' HC 990 (2017–19); JCHR, 'Windrush Generation Detention' HC 1034 HL 160 (2017–19); PAC, 'Windrush Generation and the Home Office HC 1518' (2017–19); NAO, 'Handling of the Windrush Situation' HC 1622 (2017–19); Windrush Review (n 48).
[55] ibid 7.

These reports highlighted the deeply flawed policy-making process that produced the hostile environment. Those measures had been based on the erroneous assumption that people unable to evidence their right to be in the country with specific documents were necessarily irregular migrants with no right to remain and were therefore to be denied access to services. The Windrush Review concluded that policy officials had been under intense political pressure to introduce tough immigration policies, and to do so quickly. It highlighted how the political pressure to get tough on immigration had adversely impacted on the overall culture within the department and led to ways of working that treated some people very harshly and meant that the department had not properly thought through its policies. The review did not explicitly reference 'groupthink', although it is quite clear that the whole of the policy momentum had been toward devising clear ways of taking a zero-tolerance approach toward illegal immigration and few, if any, officials voiced concerns. The Windrush Review concluded that there had been a deep cultural resistance within the Home Office to considering contrary views; instead, there had been a 'defensiveness, lack of awareness, and an unwillingness to listen and learn from mistakes'.[56]

The failures within the department's policy-making process were reflected in many other respects. The impact assessments accompanying the hostile measures had been inadequate. These assessments are intended to present a cost-benefit appraisal of a proposed policy and associated legislation by analysing its objectives and the intended effects, costs, benefits and risks of a range of different policy options.[57] But the assessments for the 2014 and 2016 Immigration Acts did not properly identify or address the possible risks of the proposed hostile environment policies. They did not contain sufficient understanding of the policy context and affected populations. Nor did they identify the Windrush generation as a cohort of people likely to be adversely affected. Impact assessments are meant to be at the centre of the policy-making process, but those prepared were more akin to a tick-box exercise produced towards the end of it. They had been framed in terms of 'do this or nothing' – a blunt, simplistic and binary choice confirming a lack of nuance and subtlety. Consequently, the department did not adequately assess the risk of unintended or unfair consequences of its policies when implemented in practice.

Another failure was that the department did not possess a detailed understanding of immigration law, its historical development, and the implications as regards people caught up in hostile environment. Over time, the Immigration Act 1971 had been overlaid by many statutes aimed at restricting immigration. This resulted in a highly detailed and complex statutory framework concerning immigration and nationality law. Even the department's experts struggled

---

[56] ibid 90.
[57] HM Treasury, *The Green Book: Central Government Guidance on Appraisal and Evaluation* (2018) [3.19]–[3.21].

to understand how each new change in legislation affected and interacted with previous legislation. The significant turnover of officials also diminished institutional memory within the department. The long-term result was that the department was unable to comprehend and understand properly its own legislation and the consequences as regards specific cohorts of people, such as the Windrush generation. When the Windrush scandal broke, senior officials had to educate themselves about the legal implications of the right of abode in the Immigration Act 1971 because they did not know about it. In short, the department lacked an historic understanding of its own legislation, and the implications of this legislation were not considered when the hostile environment policy was devised.

The department had also adopted a narrow and insular approach when devising the hostile environment measures. It had not collected relevant information to ensure it had a good understanding of the issues. It had also ignored clear warnings about the likely negative consequences. A 2014 report entitled 'Chasing Status' published by the Legal Action Group raised concerns relating to the impact of the hostile environment on certain groups, including Jamaican migrants who arrived in the UK before 1973, and how people who had been lawfully resident for many years were being treated as if they were illegally resident.[58] During the Commons Public Bill stage of the Immigration Act 2016, the Joint Council for the Welfare of Immigrations had told MPs that

> the entire target of the Bill, as of the 2014 Act, is to create a hostile environment, purportedly for unlawful migrants, but, actually, what we are really concerned about and what we have already seen happening is that it targets all migrants: lawful migrants here and, indeed, citizens of this country.[59]

In 2016, a diplomatic telegram was sent by the Foreign Office to the Home Office that referred to warnings made to the UK Government by Caribbean Commonwealth ministers about Windrush cases. In an act of gross negligence, the department ignored these warnings. Instead, the order of the day was departmental defensiveness and its 'resolute conviction that the implementation of the relevant policies was effective, should be vigorously pursued, and would achieve the policy intent.'[60]

More broadly, there were few effective constitutional restraints upon the Home Office. Within the structure of the UK central state, government departments, such as the Home Office, are highly autonomous institutions subject to only weak constitutional constraints. A classic critique of the constitutional relationship between the executive and legislature in the UK has focused upon the relative

---

[58] F Bawdon, 'Chasing Status: The 'Surprised Brits' Who Find They Are Living With Irregular Immigration Status' (London, Legal Action Group, 2014).

[59] Public Bill Committee, 'Immigration Bill', Fourth Sitting, 22 October 2015, PBC (Bill 074) 2015–16, col 138 (Saira Grant, Joint Council for the Welfare of Immigrants).

[60] Windrush Review (n 48) 137.

weakness of the latter.[61] The legislative process is largely dominated by government, which sets the policy agenda and makes the vast bulk of legislation. By contrast, Parliament is not a policy-making body; it debates, scrutinises, amends and enacts the Government's proposed legislation rather than making its own.[62] Recent scholarship indicates a more nuanced approach in which Parliament exerts more influence than previously assumed.[63] Nonetheless, the passage of the 2014 and 2016 Acts suggests that governmental dominance of the legislative process, or at least a remnant of it, remains. During the Parliamentary passage of the legislation, some MPs raised concerns about the possible adverse consequences of both the 2014 and 2016 Bills, but these concerns were not properly considered by ministers. Instead, ministers repeated their mantra that tough measures were needed. The basic problem with having a strong governmental power in the constitution is that it becomes just as easy to make bad policies as it is to make good ones – because of either insufficient parliamentary scrutiny and deliberation or because of government's dismissal of concerns legitimately and properly raised.[64]

More generally, the department's policy-making had been highly conditioned by its culture and view of the world. As the UK Government's law, order and security department, the internal culture of the Home Office has long emphasised the need to be 'tough' on immigration and to reach instinctively for punitive enforcement instruments. These assumptions had been illustrated by the department's use of aggressive and confrontational language: 'cracking down on illegal immigrants and foreign prisoners' who 'play and abuse the system', and 'activist lawyers'.[65] From this insular perspective, ministers and officials had, without much conscious self-scrutiny, adopted a particular social construction of the type of immigration 'offender' they wanted to deter.[66] As a senior official later explained:

> We designed the [hostile environment] for the worst kind of offender if you like ... we had in our minds the determined people who were knowingly, overtly ... frustrating

---

[61] M Flinders, 'MPs and Icebergs: Parliament and Delegated Governance' (2004) 57 *Parliamentary Affairs* 767; M Flinders and A Kelso, 'Mind the Gap: Political Analysis, Public Expectations, and the Parliamentary Decline Thesis' (2011) 13 *British Journal of Politics and International Relations* 249.

[62] P Norton, 'Parliament and Legislative Scrutiny: An Overview of Issues in the Legislative Process' in A Brazier (ed), *Parliament, Politics and Law Making: Issues and Developments in the Legislative Process* (London, Hansard Society, 2004) 5.

[63] M Russell and D Glover, *Legislation at Westminster: Parliamentary Actors and Influence in the Making of British Law* (Oxford, Oxford University Press, 2017).

[64] King and Crewe, *Blunders* (2013) chs 25 and 27.

[65] According to a highly respected former senior Home Office civil servant, D Faulkner, *Servant of the Crown: A Civil Servant's Story of Criminal Justice and Public Service Reform* (Reading, Waterside Press, 2014) 183: 'Governments should avoid using the images and terminology of exclusion, confrontation and especially warfare, with their implication that some people are of less value, or do not "belong", because of who they are or the situation in which they are placed. Language should not be "loaded" to score political points'.

[66] See generally P Berger and T Luckmann, *The Social Construction of Reality* (London, Penguin, 1967); H Ingram, AL Schneider and P Deleon, 'Social Construction and Policy Design' in P Sabatier (ed), *Theories of the Policy Process* (New York, Routledge, 2007).

and abusing the system in a way that was very calculated. We did not have in our minds at all people who were caught up in a web of complexity that was really not of their making at all because of historical circumstances.[67]

There was demonstrably a distinct mismatch between how the department had socially constructed the nature of the immigration problem and the more messy and complex social reality. The department's culture and outlook coloured its definition of both the problem and its policy response. In other words, the hostile environment was more reflective of the department's internal values, norms and modes of thought than it was of the range of complex situations facing immigrants and those who fell under the 'Windrush' umbrella. While some immigrants seek to evade the system, many do not. Furthermore, the department had imposed its presuppositions upon a much wider group of people – those who could not evidence their immigration status, which included members of the Windrush generation. Having done so, the possibility that the hostile environment policy could have been administered without causing harm to people was so remote as to be altogether negligible.

There had also been a failure by the Home Office to consider equality and diversity issues, an important aspect of the policy-making process. This was somewhat surprising in at least two respects. First, there is a complex interplay between immigration policy and issues of race and ethnicity. Second, under the Equality Act 2010, all public authorities are subject to the public sector equality duty (PSED) which requires them, when carrying out their functions, to have due regard to the need to eliminate discrimination, advance equality of opportunity and foster good relations.[68] Both of these considerations strongly suggest a pressing for the department to have considered the equality and diversity aspects of the hostile environment policy, but it failed to do so. Indeed, the Windrush Review noted that, when asked about the perception that race might have played in the scandal, some of the officials interviewed had been 'unimpressively unreflective, focusing on direct discrimination in the form of discriminatory motivation and showing little awareness of the possibility of indirect discrimination or the way in which race, immigration, and nationality intersect'.[69]

This was reinforced by the Equality and Human Rights Commission (EHRC), which found that the department had failed to comply with the PSED by not understanding the impact on the Windrush generation and their descendants when developing, implementing and monitoring the hostile environment.[70] More specifically, the EHRC found as follows. The department had repeatedly ignored, dismissed and disregarded the severity of the negative impacts of the hostile measures that had been identified. Its engagement with stakeholders representing

[67] Windrush Review (n 48) 87.
[68] Equality Act 2010, s 149.
[69] Windrush Review (n 48) 13.
[70] EHRC, 'Public Sector Equality Duty Assessment of Hostile Environment Policies' (2020).

Windrush people and their descendants had been limited even when the severe effects of the hostile environment measures had emerged. The analysis of equality evidence had been completed too late in the policy-making process to be effective. The exceptions to the PSED for immigration functions had been interpreted too broadly, incorrectly and/or inconsistently. There had also been a lack of an organisation-wide commitment, including by the department's senior leadership, to the importance of equality and the PSED. Its responses to negative equality impacts had been perfunctory and insufficient.

Senior officials did not consider the position of Windrush people – nor did the department properly understand how people and communities were likely to be affected by its policies. The department failed to consider the complex relationships between immigration and nationality policy with issues of race. This made the process of assessing and evaluating policy even more critical to ensure officials could identify, understand and mitigate potential effects. Indeed, the lack of diversity amongst senior officials meant that the department lacked the input of different perspectives; most of the policy-makers were white and most of the people adversely affected were black.

Furthermore, contrary to the norm that evaluation be built into the policy-making process, the department had made little real attempt to monitor or evaluate how hostile environment measures were operating in practice and their cumulative impact. Such evaluations could have given the department important information about how the hostile measures were operating, but they did not happen. The department's failure to monitor the policy's impact on vulnerable people amounted to a 'dereliction of duty'.[71] This conclusion was bolstered by the fact that significant aspects of the policy's delivery had been outsourced to landlords and employers. By 2020, the department admitted it had no specific evidence base to support the effectiveness of the measures and was unable to measure whether hostile policies encouraged people to leave voluntarily.[72]

Failures in policy-making were compounded by flawed casework decisions.[73] Of the various mechanisms of external administrative law by which people can challenge immigration decisions, neither judicial review nor the making of complaints to the ombudsman were used by Windrush people to challenge decisions. Tribunal appeals had been withdrawn by the 2014 Act.

None of the methods of internal administrative law – internal guidance instructions to caseworkers and internal quality assurance checks over their decisions – prevented the scandal from occurring while the setting of removal targets for immigration enforcement officers positively contributed to it. In 2006, the department had issued guidance in response to what was then seen as an emerging problem. A 'General Group Instruction' had been issued to caseworkers; this

---

[71] PAC, 'Windrush Generation and the Home Office' HC 1518 (2017–19) [3].
[72] NAO, 'Immigration Enforcement' HC 110 (2019–21) [2.9].
[73] See further ch 5 at 117–118.

noted that the department had been receiving a 'steady trickle of applications from people' who were in the UK on or before 1 January 1973 (the cut-off date in the Immigration Act 1971 for those Commonwealth citizens present in the UK qualifying for a right of abode in the UK). The guidance noted that 'such applications should be treated sensitively, as there is a significant risk of adverse publicity if they are handled inappropriately or wrongly refused'. It noted that such people

> may have difficulty in providing documentary evidence of their status on or before 1 January 1973 or continuous residence since then. Please be sensitive in dealing with this aspect. If there is no conclusive documentary evidence of settlement on 1 January 1973, they may be deemed to have been settled on that date if other evidence is reasonably persuasive ... Under no circumstances should such applicants be regarded as overstayers ... without the authorisation of a Chief Caseworker.[74]

Unlike a fair amount Home Office immigration guidance, this particular guidance instruction was not made publicly available on the department's website and nor was it released to immigration practitioner groups, the common means by which such guidance becomes known. Furthermore, the instruction was not followed by caseworkers deciding Windrush applications, but instead was overlooked or forgotten about within the departmental bureaucracy.

All in all, there had been considerable ministerial and political pressures on officials, administrative errors, omissions, incompetence and many failures in the policy-making process. The Home Office has developed the hostile environment policy at speed under considerable pressure from ministers, but with very little consideration of its possible impacts, especially on people from minority and ethnic backgrounds. The department had failed to assess fully the effect of the measures on people who were present in the UK entirely legitimately and lawfully. The position of the Windrush generation had been overlooked completely. When stakeholders raised concerns, they had been ignored. The social and political pressures on the department exacerbated pre-existing problems. These included the department's separation between policy design and implementation, and its neglect of the social impact of its policies. The lack of diverse perspectives at senior levels made it less likely that the assumptions underpinning the hostile measures and their implementation would be challenged. Staff did not feel confident to raise any doubts of their own. This was compounded by a complex legal framework and a casework culture that did not recognise the problems caused for affected people and which generated flawed operational decisions. All of this led to appalling consequences that disproportionately affected members of the Windrush generation. 'Ultimately, the department failed to look, engage, listen and learn, across all stages of making and implementing' the hostile environment policy.[75] This was the result of the

---

[74] Home Office, General Group Instruction 'Applications from people who were settled in the UK on 1 January 1973' (16 January 2006) cited in Windrush Review (n 48) 10.
[75] ibid 119.

external social and political pressures placed upon the department, its rules-based operational environment, its introspective culture, and its seeming indifference toward, and lack of curiosity in, the impact of its policies on affected people.

V. After and Beyond Windrush

It is difficult to see how the department's failures could have been any worse. The Windrush generation had a lawful right to be in the UK, but had become caught up in the hostile environment, and suffered foreseeable and avoidable harm and distress as a result. It is difficult to overestimate the intense and unnecessary injustice caused to people who had lived their lives in the UK for many decades when they received formal letters from the Home Office notifying them that they were immigration offenders who needed to take immediate action to return to countries they had not visited for decades. Such distress would have only been exacerbated by then being arrested, placed in immigration detention and, in some cases, being removed from the UK or unable to return to it.[76]

The degree of failure was so profound that the Government could not seek to avoid it. Windrush had taken the department by surprise, but to others it had been both 'foreseeable and avoidable'.[77] When presented with problems, all governments can usually select from a range of different tactics by which they can seek to avoid or deflect blame.[78] On this occasion, that was not possible. The Home Secretary accepted the Windrush Review and its recommendations in full and made a full apology.[79] Immigration policy is politically controversial and different people take very different views as to the correctness of such policy. However, there was near total unanimity across the political spectrum that the effect of the hostile environment policy as regards members of the Windrush generation had been a calamitous failure.

Despite the failures, Windrush has also provided the opportunity for both learning for the future and for reform. Indeed, the Windrush Review reads as not just a detailed and devastating critique, but also as a blueprint for a more effective and humane vision of what the immigration department could become. In an

---

[76] See 'Windrush campaigner Paulette Wilson dies aged 64' *Guardian* (23 July 2020); PHSO, 'An Investigation into UK Visas and Immigration's Handling of Windrush Man's Status' (2021) (the department acted with maladministration by wrongly telling a Windrush man, in the last years of his life, that he had no immigration status and then missing opportunities to put things right, which made him depressed and anxious and caused severe distress to his family).

[77] Windrush Review (n 48) 7.

[78] C Hood, *The Blame Game: Spin, Bureaucracy and Self-Preservation in Government* (Princeton, Princeton University Press, 2011); M Hinterleitner, *Policy Controversies and Political Blame Games* (Cambridge, Cambridge University Press, 2020); SL Resodihardjo, *Crises, Inquiries, and the Politics of Blame* (London, Palgrave Macmillan, 2020).

[79] *Hansard*, HC Vol 673 col 1154 (19 March 2020) (Priti Patel MP, Secretary of State for the Home Department).

important sentence, the review recommended that ministers and senior officials provide their staff with 'a clear understanding of what effective public administration looks like by establishing an organisational culture and professional development framework that values the department's staff and the communities it serves'.[80] The Windrush Review project can then be viewed as part of a wider project of institutional design to improve the accountability, effectiveness, fairness and legitimacy of the immigration system. It is this model of administrative law as institutional design that informs the analysis throughout this book.

As we will see, there are inherent difficulties in improving and reforming the immigration agency. The immigration system embodies an inherent tension between, on the one hand, welcoming legitimate migrants and, on the other hand, enforcing immigration controls against those without immigration status. Striking the right balance is difficult because of the organisational complexity and because immigration is intensely politicised and highly contentious. Further, it is not an area where there is 'always a common view of what "good" looks like'.[81] Nonetheless, the Windrush Review noted that the department 'should aspire to lead the way as an exemplar of effective public administration'.[82] To this end, it made 30 detailed recommendations covering a broad range of wider themes, which the Home Office accepted.[83] These recommendations and the themes underlying them are considered throughout this book. For present purposes, given the present focus on administrative policy-making, the hostile environment and the Windrush scandal, the following recommendations are particularly pertinent.

First, the review made specific recommendations focused on righting the wrongs suffered by members of the Windrush generation, for instance, by continuing with the Windrush compensation scheme. In practice, concerns have arisen relating to significant delays for applicants, compensation awards and the operation of the scheme.[84] Second, some of the other recommendations reminded the Home Office, a longstanding government department, of the most basic and rudimentary requirements of good government. The department needed a clear statement of its purpose, mission and values. It had to improve its historical understanding of immigration law and to ensure staff were trained on equalities and human rights law. Clearer guidance for caseworkers was required. The rudimentary and basic level of the recommendations indicates the depth of the malaise.

---

[80] Windrush Review (n 48) 14.

[81] ibid 135.

[82] ibid.

[83] Home Office, 'The Response to the Windrush Lessons Learned Review: A Comprehensive Improvement Plan' (CP 293, 2020).

[84] HAC, 'Oral Evidence: The Windrush Compensation Scheme' 9 December 2020 HC 1013 (2019–21); NAO, 'Investigation into the Windrush Compensation Scheme' HC 65 (2021–22).

Third, other recommendations concerned improvements to the department's policy-making and to ensure that it was in future both robust and inclusive. The department had to undertake a full evaluation of the hostile environment policy and its component measures, both individually and cumulatively. Other recommendations concerned the need for improved future policy-making. All policies and proposals for legislation had to be subject to rigorous impact assessments that did not merely present the binary option of 'do this or nothing'. There was a need to invest in training for senior officials who advise ministers. The department's data quality, management information and performance measures had to improve. Policy submissions for ministers and permanent secretaries had to consider the risks to vulnerable individuals and groups and equalities. Better record-keeping, such as a central archive of record departmental submissions and minutes, was required to provide a clear audit trail. The department needed to improve its understanding of the groups and communities affected by its policies through improved engagement. Officials would have to seek out a diverse range of voices and prioritise community-focused policy through such engagement. As regards promoting an inclusive workforce, it was recommended that the department establish a strategic race board, revise its diversity and inclusion strategy, review its diversity, inclusion and unconscious bias training, and review successful employment tribunal claims brought by members of staff relating to race discrimination, harassment or victimisation. The department later agreed a legally binding agreement with the EHRC committing it for two years to demonstrating that it was properly considering evidence from stakeholders representing affected groups and taking active progress to understand the equality impacts of its policies and practices.[85]

VI. Conclusion

This chapter commenced with the point that most administrative laws take the form of legislation and regulations. Consequently, administrative law is better understood if it is recharacterised as policy and implementation. After all, policy is principally made and implemented by administrative institutions. The principal test for evaluating such administrative law is not its internal legal coherence or consistency with precedent, but its practical effectiveness. These points are demonstrated by the episode of the hostile environment policy. The legislation embodying this policy reflected a political will to deal with the problem of immigration as defined by ministers and officials. The detail of the legislation had been designed by policy officials and comprised a range of six administrative programmes, which

---

[85] 'Home Office signs legal agreement to ensure Windrush failures are not repeated' *Guardian* (1 April 2021).

involved collaboration between the Home Office, other public bodies and private actors. The legislation conferred additional powers upon the department. It also specified in detail how the hostile environment policy was to be organised and delivered.

Yet, all of these efforts to make and implement policy turned out to be deeply, profoundly flawed. As a case study of government policy-making, the hostile environment policy raises wider questions about the department's policy-making competence and the relationship between ministers and civil servants. In general terms, administration must be politically responsive to ministers. There are risks in deviant officials not doing what ministers want, but there are also risks in officials being entirely subservient to ministers especially if it leads to people's legal rights being so severely undermined. The political pressure on the immigration department to develop the hostile environment measures demonstrably overrode virtually all of the accepted principles and norms of good administrative policy-making. Almost every policy-making mistake and omission that could be made was made. Many of the errors and failures were deep-rooted in the development of immigration law, the Home Office's policy and organisational failures, and the wider structural administrative-political-constitutional context in which it operated. The normal checks over the quality of policy-making were either superficial or absent.

Such failures would normally matter principally in terms of policy not achieving its goals and/or not providing good value for money. But the essential problem of the failures in the making of the hostile environment policy, combined with the Home Office's operational culture, was that it had appalling consequences for the Windrush demographic. This represented not just a fundamental failure by administration to apply the law. It went far beyond an 'ordinary' episode of maladministration or administrative injustice. Windrush was one of the biggest mass blunders ever to have been afflicted on people by the immigration department – and this really is something, given the department's record. It was a clear instance of a government department undermining the statutory rights by acting unlawfully and thereby positively causing harm to innocent people through its organisational incompetence and carelessness.

The underlying causes were political, institutional, cultural and behavioural, but, above all, they stemmed from failures in the department's policy-making and implementation processes. These underlying causes were too profound and deep-seated to be resolved by, for instance, 'surface-level' reforms such as improved legislative drafting or the use of legislative standards to check the quality of legislation.[86] That the Windrush Review made various detailed recommendations on such basic and rudimentary aspects of the core task of any government

---

[86] See, eg, D Oliver, 'Improving the Scrutiny of Bills: The Case for Standards and Checklists' [2006] *PL* 219; Political and Constitutional Reform Committee, 'Ensuring Standards in the Quality of Legislation' HC 85 (2013–14).

department – making and implementing public policy effectively, lawfully and fairly – was a clear indictment of the department's multiple failures. Having experienced the failures of Windrush, the real challenge for the department will be in the content and implementation of its future policy endeavours.

Looking to the future, three key issues arise. The first concerns the hostile environment policy itself. The Home Office had committed itself to evaluating the operation of this policy. It is possible that modification and amendment will be the result, rather than the policy as a whole being withdrawn. Nonetheless, political and policy debate over the hostile environment will continue. The second longer-term issue concerns future Home Office policy-making. The quality of future policy-making will be scrutinised against the recommendations of the Windrush Review. It remains to be seen how robustly the Home Office implements these recommendations over the years and indeed decades to come. The third issue is similarly profound, but it may be corrosive for the department. The failures of the hostile environment and of the Windrush scandal significantly eroded the administrative legitimacy of the department. It was a ministerial and political failure. But it was also an administrative failure in the sense that the department is a permanent institution of government that needs to try to secure legitimacy for its actions. The degree to which the Windrush recommendations improve matters remains to be seen, but criticism of the compensation scheme cautions against any undue optimism.

We will return to the wider issues of compliance and enforcement in a later chapter. In the meantime, the department uses other instruments to make and implement policy apart from primary legislation, such as the secondary-level administrative rules and tertiary level guidance. These mechanisms are used to provide the fine-print and detail of policies, and they in turn require detailed scrutiny.

4

Administrative Rules and Guidance

In addition to legislation, government departments also make and implement policy through administrative rules. Such rules are made entirely by government subject to ministerial approval with little, if any, parliamentary scrutiny and certainly no opportunity for amendment. Compared with the more episodic character of primary legislation, administrative rule-making is much more of a continuous process in which new rules are introduced and then amended over time. The resulting rules are often highly detailed and voluminous. But rules are not the end of the matter. There is also administrative soft law, the informal tertiary-level guidance that comprises the various policies and internal instructions issued within the department to front-line officers. In practice, it is these guidance documents that officials rely on rather than the actual rules. At the same time, above the level of the rules, human rights law has come to play an increasingly important role in immigration.

This chapter considers immigration rules and guidance. It does not focus upon their ever-changing content and detail. Instead, the chapter examines the principal cross-cutting issues raised by the rules and associated guidance. These include: the department's choice of rule-type (discretion-laden rules or hard-edged objective rules?); the development of and interrelationship between the rules and policy guidance; their complexity and the scope for simplification; and the need to evaluate how the rules work in practice. These issues in turn raise wider questions How does the type of rules adopted affect how the department organises its activities? Does the department possess the necessary organisational competence to make effective rules? How are such rules and guidance used as a means of internal administrative law to control and guide front-line officials?

I. Immigration Rules

Before proceeding further, some general points are needed. First, administrative rules are an essential tool in areas of mass administration that involve determining people's entitlements. The immigration rules guide caseworkers about the criteria to be applied when deciding immigration applications. They also inform applicants and their advisors as to the requirements they need to meet to qualify, and which documentary and other evidence is required. The rules provide a central focus for tribunals and courts when adjudicating upon challenges against initial refusal decisions. Beyond this, rules comprise a principal form of internal administrative law. Not only are they used to translate policy into law, they also provide a means to control and coordinate the activity of thousands of caseworkers and enforcement officers. Administrative rules are also a key starting place from which to try to improve the quality and effectiveness of decision-making. The converse is also true: complex rules are more likely to hinder effective decision-making and result in injustice for individuals.

Second, there is the unique legal status of the immigration rules.[1] They are not ordinary secondary legislation but statements of executive policy as to the practice to be followed in the administration of the Immigration Act 1971.[2] Statements of changes to the Immigration Rules must be laid before Parliament and can be disapproved within 40 days through a resolution passed by either House, although there is no minimum length of time that Statements must be laid before Parliament before taking effect. Beyond this, the department has occasionally consulted on major changes to the rules. In 2006, the department consulted about a major change consultation concerning the introduction of the points-based scheme.[3] There was another consultation of changes to the family migration rules in 2012.[4] But this is very much the exception. Almost all statements of changes to the immigration rules are made without prior consultation and many have been introduced at short notice thereby significantly weakening the ability of Parliament to scrutinise them before their entry into force. The courts have refused to impose a common law duty on the department to consult when making immigration rules.[5]

A third point concerns the complexity of the rules. The 1994 statement of changes to the rules was 80 pages long. Since then, the rules have been amended on numerous occasions.[6] The current set of immigration rules is well over 1,000 pages long.[7] There are also 3,000 pieces of policy guidance available to staff on the Home Office intranet which range from single-page documents to some that are over 100 pages long, depending on the particular immigration route and its complexity. Such guidance may or may not be published.[8] Anyone surveying this highly intricate, detailed and shifting set of rules and guidance

---

[1] *Odelola v Secretary of State for the Home Department* [2009] UKHL 25, [2009] 1 WLR 1230 [6] (Lord Hoffmann); *Pankina v Secretary of State for the Home Department* [2010] EWCA Civ 719, [2010] 3 WLR 1526 [12]–[13] (Sedley LJ).

[2] Immigration Act 1971, s 3(2); *Odelola v Secretary of State for the Home Department* [2009] UKHL 25; [2009] 1 WLR 1230 [35] (Lord Brown); *Hesham Ali (Iraq) v Secretary of State for the Home Department* [2016] UKSC 60; [2016] 1 WLR 479 [16]–[18] (Lord Reed).

[3] Home Office, 'A Points-Based System: Making Migration Work for Britain' (Cm 6741, 2006).

[4] Home Office, 'Family Migration: A Consultation' (2011).

[5] *R (Bapio Action Ltd) v Secretary of State for the Home Department* [2007] EWCA Civ 1139 [18]–[47] (Sedley LJ).

[6] 'Revealed: immigration rules in UK more than double in length' *Guardian* (27 August 2018).

[7] Home Office, 'Immigration Rules', available at www.gov.uk/guidance/immigration-rules.

[8] Home Office, 'Visas and immigration operational guidance: detailed information', available at www.gov.uk/topic/immigration-operational-guidance.

could only conclude that it is a dense and impenetrable mass that defies easy comprehension. The problem of complexity features in the tax and benefit systems, but in the immigration context, this pathology has been taken to the extreme. As Irwin LJ has noted, 'the Immigration Rules are, in truth, something of a disgrace'.[9] There have been numerous substantive changes in the nature of the rules that have made them increasingly complex. This complexity creates all sorts of problems and difficulties. Having made poorly thought-through rules, the department has then had to make new rules to address problems that have arisen in their practical operation, and then more new rules, and so on. The result has been a mess of rules. As Beatson LJ has noted, 'the architecture of the Rules is not the grand design of Lutyens' Delhi or Haussmann's Paris, but more that of the organic growth responding to the needs of the moment that is a feature of some shanty towns'.[10] The question then arises as to whether the rules can be made less complex, but first it is necessary to consider in more detail how such complexity arises in the first place.

II. Choice of Rule-type

When government agencies make rules, they are often confronted with various design questions. Which type of rules provide the best means of administering policy? To what extent should the rules give discretion to decision-makers? Alternatively, are prescriptive and detailed rules desirable? When are discretion and detailed prescription productive or counter-productive? What is the best way of organising a system of mass casework decision-making?

A. Discretion v Bright-Lines

In general terms, a government agency that makes decisions concerning people's entitlements can select from two broad types of rules. It can make general standards or guidelines that require officials to exercise judgement (discretion-laden or flexible rules). Or it can make prescriptive and highly detailed rules that specify precise decisional criteria (bright-line or rigid rules). There is a generally recognised distinction between 'guidance' that is open-textured, discretionary and advisory, and hard-edged 'rules' that are prescriptive, mandatory and compel a particular outcome.[11] Clearly, these labels relate to substance and not the formal

---

[9] S Irwin, 'Complexity and Obscurity in the Law and How We Might Mitigate Them' (Peter Taylor Memorial Lecture, Professional Negligence Bar Association, 17 April 2018).

[10] *Secretary of State for the Home Department v Khan* [2016] EWCA Civ 137, [2016] 4 WLR 56 [40] (Beatson LJ).

[11] *R (Alvi) v Secretary of State for the Home Department* [2012] UKSC 33, [2012] 1 WLR 2208 [114] (Lord Walker) and [120] (Lord Clarke).

description of secondary rules and tertiary policy guidance. 'Guidance' requires decision-makers to exercise judgement and evaluation when making decisions. This involves exercising common sense when applying the rules and making pragmatic, reasoned decisions. By contrast, prescriptive 'rules' are detailed and specify hard-edged requirements. Decision-makers do not need to exercise judgment, but merely tick the relevant boxes. There are also various intermediate positions on this continuum which blend together different rule-types. The rule-type chosen will also be affected by and have significant repercussions for an agency's organisational structure and decision processes. A critical issue for those who design administrative institutions is then to determine which types of rules to use.

Taking a broad sweep, the substance of the immigration rules has, over the years, shifted from largely discretionary rules toward hard-edged rules and detailed prescription, although substantial pockets of discretion remain. Originally, the rules conferred extensive discretion on decision-makers (immigration officers, entry clearance officers, and Home Office caseworkers). The key issues were typically the credibility of the applicant, for instance, whether they were a *genuine* student, and the *adequacy* of their ability to maintain and accommodate themselves without recourse to public funds. This discretionary focus for decision-makers went hand in hand with an application process based upon the completion of application forms, the presentation of documentary evidence, and in-person interviews (whether at the border, the overseas entry clearance or visa office, or at the Home Office). Further, because such discretion could be exercised incorrectly, there had to be a system of appeals against initial decisions in which the applicant, or their UK-based sponsor, could participate in the judicial and independent tribunal process.

Then, in the mid-2000s, the department took a conscious decision to introduce bright-line or hard-edged rules through the points-based scheme for work and study routes.[12] This was introduced in part to replace discretion entirely with objective evidence and prescriptive eligibility criteria. For instance, previously when assessing whether an applicant had adequate maintenance funds, the caseworker would assess whatever documentary evidence was presented. By contrast, under the points-based rules, there is a highly prescriptive set of evidential requirements. For instance, an applicant for a Tier 4 (General) student visa wishing to study at a university outside London must score 10 points for funds. The applicant will only be awarded these points if she has sufficient funds to pay the full course fees for an academic year plus £1,015 for each month of the course up to a maximum of nine months. Furthermore, the applicant must provide particular documents in the specified format to show that the funds are available to them. Applicants who do not meet the precise requirements will be refused. By specifying a simple and readily intelligible requirement, the rule is

---

[12] Home Office, 'A Points-Based System' (n 3).

predictable and transparent. Applicants can self-assess their eligibility, thereby reducing speculative and erroneous applications. In theory, the rule is easy and efficient to administer and should produce uniform outcomes.

B. Rule-type Trade-offs

Both approaches have the potential for humane and efficient administration and for institutional pathologies. Rules embedded with discretion can be applied flexibly to take account of the particular circumstances of individual applications. But this also diminishes predictability and risks arbitrary, wrong and inconsistent decisions. The appeals process provides a means of challenging such decisions, but adds cost, time and complexity. By contrast, bright-line rules provide certainty and predictability about how decisions will be reached and can be applied quickly and efficiently. But there are the downsides of a rigid rule-bound administration that blindly applies a dense body of highly detailed rules that can lead to 'near misses'.

Both approaches envisage different roles for decision-makers. With judgemental rules, decision-makers operate as street-level bureaucrats who make policy at the ground-level.[13] Yet, such policy is largely unsystematic and ad hoc as it is made by thousands of caseworkers in response to individual applications. By contrast, prescriptive rules change the nature of decision-making to a 'tick-box' exercise undertaken by relatively junior caseworkers to process applications quickly and efficiently. In turn, responsibility for policy is moved upwards within the department making the overall system easier to coordinate and more manageable.

This shift to bright-line rules occurred for various reasons. The department wanted a more efficient process and to take paper out of the system. Interviewing applicants takes time and was largely done away with by the move to objective criteria. The move to bright-line rules also avoided the increasing criticism that decisions reflected the prejudices of caseworkers. Entry clearance officers located overseas were frequently criticised for carrying out subjective assessments in which their own biases came into play. There were also criticisms that different officials would interview applicants differently and that different overseas visa posts adopted different approaches, resulting in different success rates for claimants. Some posts (eg Islamabad and Lagos) adopted a defensive approach whereas other were more customer-focused. In presentational terms, the move to objective and prescriptive eligibility criteria for work and study routes was in the interests and certainty, predictability and administrative efficiency, but it also served as a defensive blame-avoidance tactic.

---

[13] M Lipsky, *Street-level Bureaucracy: Dilemmas of the Individual in Public Services* (New York, Russell Sage, 1980).

There were also strong political forces at work. Hard-edged rules are often hard-line rules that can be used by ministers when taking a tough stance to eliminate abuse and restore public confidence.[14] To give some illustrations, following the foreign national prisoner crisis, more restrictive rules were introduced for criminal deportation cases. The previous rules – under which, in considering whether to deport, the public interest had to be balanced against any compassionate circumstances – went beyond the requirements of the Human Rights Act 1998.[15] New rules created a strong presumption in favour of deportation, only to be outweighed in exceptional cases[16] and were followed by legislation which established a scheme of automatic deportation.[17] A similar trend can be seen in relation to the general grounds for refusal.[18] Previous rules had enabled caseworkers to exercise discretion when issuing sanctions, such as re-entry bans, against those who had breached immigration law (eg by overstaying or working illegally). Subsequent rules set out a clear period during which a previous immigration offender would have any future applications refused; for instance, an applicant who has used deception to enter will be automatically banned for 10 years.[19] The ministerial rationale was that blanket rules send out a clear message that breaches of immigration law will not be tolerated.[20]

C. Excessive Formalism

However, far from entering the heaven of efficiency, clarity and predictability, critics and representatives have persistently argued that immigration decision-making merely entered an alternative form of complex, rigid, rule-bound hell. The arbitrariness of discretion and its costs and delays have been replaced with the arbitrariness of blanket rules applied in tick-box fashion without regard to the circumstances of individual applications or the underlying purposes of the rules. When individual circumstances arise that are not catered for by a bright-line rule, then decision-makers cannot exercise discretion.[21] Applicants who do not present the required documents must be refused. There is no scope for any concept of a 'near miss'; the applicant either meets the requirements or not.

---

[14] G Manning and J Collinson, 'Complexity in the Immigration Rules: Politics or the Outcome of Judicial Review?' (2019) 24 *Judicial Review* 85.

[15] Immigration Rules HC 337 (1994) r 364; *Hansard*, HC Vol 446 cols 77–81ws (23 May 2006); *CM v Secretary of State for the Home Department* [2005] UKIAT00103 [36].

[16] Immigration Rules HC 1337 (2006) r 364.

[17] UK Borders Act 2007, ss 32–39.

[18] Immigration Rules, r 320; now Pt 9 of the Rules.

[19] Immigration Rules HC 321 (2008) r 320(7B).

[20] *Hansard*, HC Vol 475 col 1351 (13 May 2008) (Liam Byrne MP, Minister for Borders and Immigration).

[21] For instance, applicants who fall short of the required amount of funds even by a trivial amount, such as £1, for a short period of time, such as one day, will not qualify irrespective of any extenuating circumstances. See *NA & Others v Secretary of State for the Home Department (Tier 1 Post-Study Work-funds)* [2009] UKAIT00025 [47] and [103].

Highly prescriptive rules can often undermine their underlying purposes in practice. For instance, the points-based scheme specifies in great detail the evidence required by the claimant to satisfy the maintenance requirement. Bank statements must include the applicant's name, account number, date of each statement, the bank's name and logo, and be printed on the bank's letter head; or electronic statements must be accompanied by a supporting letter confirming that the statement is authentic. However, some banks are unwilling to provide documents that meet these requirements, with the result that an application will be refused as it does not fulfil the formal prescribed requirements, even though it in substance qualifies.

Likewise, the rules governing evidential requirements for the maintenance of family members have been highly prescriptive. The policy is to ensure that family members will not be a burden on the state. To implement this, the rules prescribed which evidence would be accepted to satisfy caseworkers that applicants could meet the minimum income requirement of £18,600 per year. But the rules did not cover all situations for people earning money, such as people who were paid in cash. In such instances, the rules did not appear to be functioning as intended: individuals with genuine sources of income and who in substance qualified, did not qualify in formal terms because they had not satisfied the prescribed financial requirements. There were many appeals before tribunals in which all concerned accepted that the applicant was earning over the required amount, but such appeals had to be dismissed because the rules did not provide for people paid wages cash-in-hand. Such rules impose burdens on people for no real purpose – other than the ostensible need to follow the rules for their own sake; they also undermined the purpose of the relevant rule. This in turn led to more piecemeal changes and amendments to the rules.

The move to hard-edged rules was accompanied by the progressive weakening of appeal rights. A key component of the points-based scheme has been the substitution of tribunal appeals with administrative review.[22] This started by preventing appellants from relying upon new evidence on appeal.[23] Since 2015, appeals against points-based scheme applications have been entirely removed (apart from appeals on human rights grounds).[24] From one perspective, abolishing appeals and using rigid rules can enable the department to get it right first time: the scope for error is eliminated because the rules themselves provide the mechanism of control.[25] But this hollow perspective simply conflates technical errors with the substantive error costs induced by the over- and under-inclusiveness of rigid rules.

What then of judicial intervention? The courts have emphasised that procedural fairness must be understood in light of the overall purposes of the

---

[22] Nationality, Immigration and Asylum Act 2002, s 88A.
[23] Nationality, Immigration and Asylum Act 2002, s 85A.
[24] Immigration Act 2014, s 15.
[25] Home Office, 'Report on Removal of Full Appeal Rights Against Refusal of Entry Clearance Decisions Under the Points-Based System' (2011).

points-based scheme to simplify the application procedure and to enable high volumes of applications to be processed in a fair and efficient manner by specifying precisely the evidence applicants must submit.[26] Occasional harsh outcomes are the price to be paid for certainty and efficiency. For instance, if an applicant has not submitted all specified documents, the department is not obliged to conduct a preliminary check of all applications to see whether they are accompanied by the specified documents, or to contact applicants where this is not the case and to give them an opportunity to supply the missing documents.[27] Likewise, the fact that the department knew that the Confirmation of Acceptance for Studies letter on which a student applicant relied for leave to remain had been mistakenly withdrawn by the college did not then require the department to notify the applicant of the problem and provide an opportunity to rectify the situation.[28] Any requirement to make such inquiries would have resource implications, extend the length of the decision-making process, and undermine the intended straightforward and relatively automatic operation of decision-making. Overall, the judicial approach has been that the focus on certainty and efficiency in the points-based scheme informs how the general public law duty of fairness operates; its application should not jeopardise the working of a scheme that uses objective criteria in order to be clear and predictable.

The department has made some concessions such as its evidential flexibility policy. Given the highly prescriptive nature of the points-based scheme, both in terms of eligibility criteria and its evidential requirements about specified documents, applicants can easily make mistakes and present incomplete or incorrect documents. To mitigate the potential harshness of refusals in such cases, under the evidential flexibility policy, caseworkers can exercise a degree of flexibility. If an applicant either has not submitted a specified document or has submitted documents, some of which are missing, in the wrong format, or incomplete, then the caseworker may contact the applicant to request the document or the correct version. The courts have stressed that the policy was not designed to give an applicant the opportunity to remedy any defect or inadequacy in the application or supporting documentation so as to save the application from refusal after substantive consideration.[29] Furthermore, requests for further information will not be made where addressing the error or omission would not lead to a grant because the application would be refused for other reasons.[30] The evidential flexibility

---

[26] *EK (Ivory Coast) v Secretary of State for the Home Department* [2014] EWCA Civ 1517, [2015] Imm AR 367 [28]–[31] (Sales LJ); *Nyasulu v Secretary of State for the Home Department* [2016] EWCA Civ 1145 [17] (Sales LJ); *Talpada v Secretary of State for the Home Department* [2018] EWC Civ 841 [36]; *R (Taj) v Secretary of State for the Home Department* [2021] EWCA Civ 19.

[27] *Alam v Secretary of State for the Home Department* [2012] EWCA Civ 960.

[28] *EK (Ivory Coast)* (n 26). See also *Secretary of State for the Home Department v Rodriguez* [2014] EWCA Civ 2.

[29] ibid.

[30] Immigration Rules, r 245AA; Appendix FM-SE, para D. See also *Mandalia v Secretary of State for the Home Department* [2015] UKSC 59; *Mudiyanselage v Secretary of State for the Home Department* [2018] EWCA Civ 65, [2018] 4 All ER 35.

policy was introduced in 2009 through guidance and subsequently inserted into rule 245AA in 2012. By 2018, eight versions of the guidance had been issued and rule 245AA had itself been variously amended.

More generally, the frequency of changes to the rules and guidance has made it increasingly difficult for all concerned to know what the rules actually are and what the rules were when the applicant (now litigant) made their original immigration application. For instance, during the first four years of the points-based scheme, there were over 180 changes to the Tier 4 (student) rules and guidance.[31] All concerned – applicants, sponsors, advisors, caseworkers and legal teams – had to familiarise themselves with new sets of rules and guidance thereby generating enormous uncertainty as to which set of rules applied. Caseworkers have, at times, been working with three different versions of the guidance, depending on the date applications were made (decisions are made on the basis of the rules and guidance in place at the time of application). As the Upper Tribunal noted in 2012, the rules 'change so frequently that it is always difficult to know what rules were in force at a given time in the past'.[32] The negative consequences for legal certainty are evident.

III. Guidance and Policies

At this point, it is appropriate to consider tertiary level or soft-law guidance and policies. Like all administrative organisations, the department makes extensive use of staff instructions, policies and administrative guidance to explain and interpret legislation and the rules. From a lawyer's perspective, such guidance seems rather low down in the legal hierarchy, but it is typically the first and perhaps often the only port of call for caseworkers.

Such guidance has various functions. It can fill in the gaps in the rules. For instance, when the rules have required caseworkers to exercise discretion, guidance has often informed caseworkers as to which factors to consider. There have also been instances in which an applicant has not qualified under the rules, but could rely on an extra-statutory concessionary policy.[33] Some policies often incorporated a discretion that might be exercised in favour of a person who did not meet the requirements of the immigration rules and also specified which

---

[31] ICIBI, 'An Inspection of Tier 4 of the Points Based System (Students)' (2012) [6.1]–[6.6].

[32] *Rajbhandari v Secretary of State for the Home Department (PBS: funds – available) Nepal* [2012] UKUT 364 (IAC) [8].

[33] For many years, it was assumed that 'extra-statutory' concessionary policies made outside of the rules were issued under the prerogative; see *R v Secretary of State for the Home Department, ex p Rajinder Kaur* [1987] Imm AR 278, 291 (HC). However, in *R (Munir) v Secretary of State for the Home Department* [2012] UKSC 32, the Supreme Court held that such policies had a statutory basis under the Immigration Act 1971.

factors were relevant in decision-making. For instance, under the seven-year concession policy, there was a general presumption that enforcement action would not normally proceed in a case involving a child who had either been born and had lived continuously in the UK to the age of seven, or had seven years or more of continuous residence.[34] Some concessionary policies, such as the long residence policy, have been incorporated into the rules; and some policies, such as the R refugee family reunion policy, were partially incorporated into the rules. Guidance then is primarily issued within the department as a form of internal administrative law as instructions to front-line operational staff, especially caseworkers. It is also of particular interest to those advising and representing applicants. In terms of administrative law, a related purpose of guidance is to ensure consistent decision-making by guiding front-line staff as to how the rules are to be applied. This is permissible provided that guidance is clear and does not conflict the rules, that discretionary powers are exercised for proper purposes, and that decision-makers do not shut their ears to claims that fall outside such guidance and policies.

A. Problems with Guidance

In practice, the use of guidance has created various problems. It is necessary at the outset to distinguish between formal published policies, such as White Papers, formal internal policies, and informal internal administrative practices.[35] As regards internal guidance, consider the largely ad hoc and excessively informal manner in which it has been issued. Guidance has often come to light through ministerial letters to MPs and representatives, or instructions and guidance published on the department's website or has not been published, but instead surfaced through leakage. It has often been necessary for practitioners to piece together the content of such policies from various statements and practices, not all of which have been widely known.[36] Guidance has often been generated by different casework teams within the department without any overall oversight or coherent approach to what guidance has been issued, whether it is consistent with the rules, or if it has been well drafted. There have also been cycles of juridification in which informal policies come to be relied upon by applicants, are then subject to judicial interpretation, and become 'legally hardened' and are then placed into the formal rules or legislation. For instance, the courts interpreted the seven-year concession as introducing not just a presumption against removal

---

[34] DP 5/96 (The 7 Year Child Concession); *Hansard*, HC Vol 326, cols 309–10 (24 February 1999) (Mike O'Brien, Minister of State for Immigration).

[35] cf *R (WL (Congo)) v Secretary of State for the Home Department* [2010] EWCA Civ 111, [2010] 4 All ER 489 [53]–[58] (Stanley Burton LJ).

[36] R McKee, 'Home Office Policies' (2006) 20 *Journal of Immigration, Asylum and Nationality Law* 289.

where the parent's child had seven years' residence, but a presumption that the Home Office would grant leave in such cases.[37] The policy was withdrawn in 2008 because it had been 'overtaken' by the Human Rights Act 1998, but this was probably more motivated by the political need to prevent overstayers and others from accruing rights to remain.[38] However, the essence of the seven-year concession for children was later put into statute.[39] The department has also, on occasion, (unlawfully) adopted secret policies and guidance in especially sensitive matters (eg following the foreign national prisoners crisis of 2006) to give effect to ministerial wishes.[40]

Another persistent practical problem with guidance has been the frequent failure of caseworkers to apply or to even be aware of relevant policy guidance, even when it is directly relevant to casework decisions. There is no apparent mechanism by which Home Office presenting officers, who represent the department before tribunals, are kept informed of relevant changes in guidance and can identify what guidance was in place at any particular time.[41] The cause is poor internal dissemination and communication of such guidance to front-line staff: another facet of organisational incompetence. In such instances, a refused applicant whose case had been decided without reference to relevant guidance could argue that there had been a failure to act in accordance with established principles of administrative or common law; not taking account of or giving effect to policy or guidance. Consequently, the casework decision had not been taken 'in accordance with the law'.[42] Tribunals could only apply the immigration rules, not policy guidance, but could allow an appeal if relevant guidance had not been applied and then send the matter back to the department to be re-decided by applying the facts as found by the tribunal.[43] Following the restriction on appeal rights under the 2014 Act, it is no longer possible to appeal on the ground that an immigration decision was not in accordance with the law. The only remedy lies by way of judicial review, although policy guidance could play some role in Article 8 ECHR right to family life appeals.[44]

---

[37] *N (Ghana) v Secretary of State for the Home Department* [2008] EWCA Civ 906; *R (A) v Secretary of State for the Home Department* [2008] EWHC 2844 (Admin).

[38] *Hansard*, HC Vol 485, col 49WS (9 December 2008) (Phil Woolas MP, Minister for Borders and Immigration).

[39] Nationality, Immigration and Asylum Act 2002, s 117D(1) (as inserted by the Immigration Act 2014, s 19).

[40] See *Lumba v Secretary of State for the Home Department* [2011] UKSC 12, [2012] AC 245 examined in ch 8.

[41] Upper Tribunal (Immigration and Asylum Chamber), 'Response to Law Commission Consultation on Simplifying the Immigration Rules' (2019) 9.

[42] Immigration Act 1971, s 19(1)(a)(i); Nationality, Immigration and Asylum Act 2002, s 86(3); *DS Abdi v Secretary of State for the Home Department* [1995] EWCA Civ 27, [1996] Imm AR 148 (CA).

[43] *SS v Secretary of State for the Home Department (Jurisdiction – Rule 62(7); Refugee's family; Policy) Somalia* [2005] UKAIT 00167; *AG and others v Secretary of State for the Home Department (Policies; executive discretions; Tribunal's powers) Kosovo* [2007] UKAIT 00082.

[44] See *Mandalia* (n 30), considered in ch 8.

Other problems have included the ambiguous and poor drafting of guidance and inconsistencies with the rules. The precise scope and content of the seven-year concession policy has caused confusion, as demonstrated by successive legal challenges.[45] There have also been inconsistencies between the rules and guidance. At one point, the guidance concerning the evidential flexibility policy created a much wider obligation than the rules.[46] Underhill LJ suspected this was the unintentional 'result of incompetence ... It would hardly be the first time that such mistakes have occurred in the Home Office: the web of Rules and Guidance has become so tangled that even the spider has difficulty controlling it'.[47] The department has, on occasion, adopted different sets of localised guidance when applying the same immigration rules. In-country and overseas casework teams have applied different versions of the evidential flexibility guidance thereby leading to inconsistent outcomes between applicants of different nationalities.[48] This prompted the Chief Inspector to highlight the importance of ensuring that clear processes and guidance are in place to ensure that nationals of particular countries are not disadvantaged due to different approaches taken in different posts. Having different casework teams applying the same guidance differently or applying different guidance are particularly odd outcomes given that one purpose of guidance is to promote consistency in how the rules are applied in practice.

The most egregious failures have concerned the accretion of additional requirements through administrative practice without them having any basis in the rules or guidance. Caseworkers considering applications made by Windrush people seeking a 'No Time Limit' endorsement required them to demonstrate their case to the criminal standard of proof – beyond reasonable doubt, a wholly inappropriate and unlawful practice. In administrative law fact-finding exercises, the standard of proof is always the balance of probabilities.[49] No one in the department either knew or was willing to identify why the criminal standard had been adopted, which had the effect of reducing successful applications.[50]

---

[45] *R (Dabrowski) v Secretary of State for the Home* Department [2003] EWCA Civ 580; *Baig v Secretary of State for the Home Department* [2005] EWCA Civ 1246; *R (Sadowska) v Secretary of State for the Home Department* [2006] EWHC 797 (Admin); *R (Tozlukaya) v Secretary of State for the Home Department* [2006] EWCA Civ 379; and *N (Ghana) v Secretary of State for the Home Department* [2008] EWCA Civ 906.

[46] *SH (Pakistan) v Secretary of State for the Home Department* [2016] EWCA Civ 426.

[47] *Mudiyanselage* (n 30) [54] (Underhill LJ). See also *Mahad (Ethiopia) v Entry Clearance Officer* [2009] UKSC 16, [2010] 1 WLR 48 [11] (Lord Brown): 'It is evident that IDIs [the Immigration Directorate's Instructions] have on occasion been issued inconsistently with the Rules as interpreted by the courts ... [owing] ... to a regrettable lack of coordination'.

[48] ICIBI, 'A Thematic Inspection of the Points-Based System: Tier 2 (Skilled Workers)' (2010) [5.77]–[5.103]; ICIBI, 'An Inspection of Tier 4 of the Points Based System (Students)' (2012) [4.61]–[4.66].

[49] The exception is asylum cases where the standard of proof is a reasonable degree of likelihood, which is lower than the normal civil standard of the balance of probabilities.

[50] 'Windrush Lessons Learned Review: Independent Review by Wendy Williams' HC 93 (2019–20) 98.

As a member of the Windrush generation noted, 'the onus is not on them to tell us, it's on us to find out, but we don't know'.[51] It is difficult to understand precisely how the standard of proof had been raised through administrative practice to an unlawfully and unreasonably high standard other than by highlighting politically driven hostile environment policies. It is precisely episodes such as this that raise concerns about the need to insulate caseworkers from being put under, or second-guessing, political pressures from much higher up within the departmental structure. Consider also DNA tests. In 2018, the Home Secretary told Parliament that DNA tests from immigration applicants were voluntary, not compulsory.[52] It then came to light that caseworkers had in fact been requiring certain applicants to undertake DNA testing. Legally, there was no power to mandate such tests.[53] Again, an additional and unlawful requirement had been inserted through administrative practice.

From an organisational perspective, what is striking is the multiple sources of guidance and its uncoordinated and unsystematic dissemination within the department's fragmented internal structure, and how this in turn prompts judicial correction. The department has, over many years, sought to simplify, streamline and clarify its guidance by promulgating formal guidance with a central 'owner' within the department and reviewing guidance.[54] However, the scale and complexity of the department's siloed operations have in practice often worked against this laudable goal. For instance, operational staff have taken the view that policy guidance produced for them by policy officials has not been written in a way that could help them in their day-to-day work.[55] This has, in turn, led to locally produced guidance being issued to interpret policy in an operational context, which will itself fail if it is inconsistent with the immigration rules or adds a gloss to them. Guidance produced within different teams has been successively updated, with the consequence that there is considerable scope for inconsistency and uncertainty about which guidance is applicable and whether it is correct and up to date. Moreover, the amount of new and amended guidance is so vast that it

[51] ibid.

[52] *Hansard*, HC Vol 648 col 467 (25 October 2018) (Sajid Javid MP, Secretary of State for the Home Department).

[53] R Alcock, 'Internal Review of the Government's Policy on Requirements to Provide DNA in Visa and Asylum Cases' (2018); D Singh, 'Independent Review of the Home Office Response to the Mandating of DNA Evidence for Immigration Purposes' (2019); Home Office, 'Darra Singh's Review of Home Office Response to Mandating of DNA Evidence: Home Office Response' (2019).

[54] This push for better and more centralised guidance was part of the wider move in 2009 to simplify the rules, which itself never materialised: Home Office, 'Simplifying Immigration Law: A New Framework for Immigration Rules' (2009) 9–10. The intention was to reduce the amount of guidance and ensure that guidance was of a better quality. A fair amount of new-style 'unified' guidance was issued, but did not prevent ad hoc guidance from being generated. Also in 2009, the department wanted to reform the complex primary legislation and published a single draft immigration bill, but following the 2010 election, attention clearly moved to other matters, such as introducing the Coalition government's migration cap. See Home Office, 'Simplifying Immigration Law: The Draft Bill' (Cm 7666 and Cm 7730, 2009).

[55] Singh (n 53) [9.6].

is difficult for operational staff to keep on top of it when they are subject to targets concerning the decisions to be taken daily. All of this is reinforced by siloed working and differences in cultures and dynamics within different units and sub-units of the organisation.

To ensure a more coherent approach, the department's simplification and streamlining programme aims to provide a single and authoritative source for guidance, policy and rules, and to ensure that information is consistent and accessible for both caseworkers and the public. Part of this is to ensure that all centrally published internal guidance for staff is accurate and up to date, and any out-of-date or inaccurate material is removed.[56] Nonetheless, a considerable amount of work is then required to improve the drafting, consistency and dissemination of policy guidance.

B. Judicial Interventions

Unsurprisingly, the problems with guidance have resulted in extensive litigation. In general terms the courts have rarely invalidated specific immigration rules.[57] But in *Pankina* and *Alvi*, the courts made a major intervention as regards the relationship between the points-based scheme rules and policy guidance by limiting the department's ability to introduce hard-edged 'rules' through guidance.[58] Having introduced the framework of the points-based scheme in 2008 through the immigration rules, the department then placed many of the scheme's detailed substantive eligibility requirements in policy guidance published on its website rather than through immigration rules. In doing so, the department had introduced hard-edged 'rules', such as the requirement that an applicant demonstrate that she had a balance of £800 in a bank account for a three-month period. However, the department had clearly not anticipated the judicial reaction and the different substantive legal consequences attendant upon embodying policy within the different legal forms of guidance or immigration rules. The courts held that the immigration rules now had the status of being law. Accordingly, only the rules could be used to introduce hard-edged binary requirements. By contrast,

---

[56] Home Office, 'Response to Mandating of DNA Evidence' (n 53).

[57] For a classic example of the courts finding an immigration rule to be ultra vires, see *R v Secretary of State for the Home Department ex parte Manshoora Begum* [1986] Imm AR 385 (HC). More recently, the courts have intervened specifically concerning the imposition of the 'No Recourse to Public Funds' condition as regards Art 3 ECHR treatment and the welfare of children: *R (W, A Child By His Litigation Friend J) v Secretary of State for the Home Department* [2020] EWHC 1299 (Admin) (the No Recourse to Public Funds condition could not be imposed where the applicant was suffering inhuman or degrading treatment (contrary to Art 3 ECHR) by reason of lack of resources); *ST v Secretary of State for the Home Department* [2021] EWHC 1085 (Admin) (the No Recourse to Public Funds condition, under para GEN1.11A of Appendix FM to the Immigration Rules, did not comply with the department's duty to safeguard and promote the welfare of children who are in the UK (Borders, Citizenship and Immigration Act 2009, s 55)).

[58] *Pankina* (n 1); *Alvi* (n 11).

guidance was not law but policy, and therefore had to be applied flexibly and adapted fairly in the light of the circumstances of the particular circumstances; administrative discretion cannot be fettered. Accordingly, the hard-edged binary nature of the points-based scheme could only be introduced through immigration rules and not policy guidance. The department responded by transferring a considerable amount of detail from guidance into the rules.[59] Further, as highly prescriptive rules need to be frequently changed and updated, this in turn made the rules more detailed and complex.

Another judicial technique has been to preserve areas of judgemental discretion within the immigration rules and guidance by preventing the department from replacing discretion with standardised tick-box rules that are easier to apply, but which disadvantage claimants with more complex situations than such standardisation recognises. In *Ishtiaq*, the Court of Appeal held that guidance prescribing the types of evidence to be accepted in domestic violence cases did not remove the fact-finding task conferred by the rules on caseworkers to consider other types of relevant evidence that could be used to make a valid finding of domestic violence.[60] The department's approach had been to adopt a prescriptive approach to the evidence required, but this defeated those domestic violence victims who could not present such evidence, an approach which undermined the purpose of the relevant rule and was unlawful.

Similarly, *Mahad* concerned the blanket refusal by entry clearance officers of applications made by relatives overseas seeking to join family members in the UK on the basis that they were relying upon third-party support in order to fulfil the requirement of being adequately maintained without recourse to public funds.[61] The Supreme Court held that the rules did not support such a blanket approach. The purpose of the rules was to ensure entrants could be maintained without recourse to public funds rather than to prohibit third-party support. Instead, it was for the applicant in each case to satisfy the entry clearance officer that the third-party support being relied upon was assured and adequate. Again, we can see the disconnections between formal rules on the one hand and the reality of administrative policies and practices on the other. The instinctive bureaucratic impulse toward standardisation prompted judicial intervention to protect against a more restrictive blanket approach. This type of judicial intervention has performed a valuable role by preventing discretion from being undermined by an administrative processing mentality. Another variant has been to employ human rights law. In *Quila* the flat rule that increased the qualifying age for a marriage visa from 18 to 21 years of age in order to safeguard potential victims of forced marriage

---

[59] The statement of changes introduced immediately after the Supreme Court's ruling in *Alvi* was almost 300 pages in length. See Home Office, 'Statement of Changes in Immigration Rules' (Cm 8423, July 2012).
[60] *Ishtiaq v Secretary of State for the Home Department* [2007] EWCA Civ 386, [2007] Imm AR 712.
[61] *Mahad* (n 47).

inevitably included those not being forced into marriage and was contrary to the right to family life under Article 8 ECHR.[62]

IV. Human Rights and Rules

In contrast to guidance that operates below the level of the rules, human rights law operates over and above the rules. Of all the Convention rights, the right to respect for private and family life (Article 8 ECHR) has produced the most litigation and been a frequent source of controversy. Under Article 8, migrants without leave to remain can claim that their removal would be unlawful because it would infringe their private and/or family life that they have developed in the country. As Article 8 is a qualified right, its application includes a balancing exercise between the right to private and family life and the public interest in maintaining immigration control. This balancing exercise is to be undertaken on the basis of the specific facts and circumstances of the individual case.

Article 8 embodies a moral demand from migrants that, as rights-bearing individuals, their right to family life can outweigh the public interest in controlling immigration. In *Huang* the House of Lords recognised that people are social beings; they live in families and depend upon them for their well-being; there comes a point at which an individual's separation from their family becomes so serious that it breaches their fundamental right to family life. On the other hand, there are countervailing considerations that weigh in favour of immigration control: the general administrative desirability of applying known rules to ensure the system of immigration control is workable, predictable, consistent and fair as between one applicant and another; the damage to good administration and effective control if this system is perceived by applicants internationally to be unduly porous, unpredictable, or perfunctory; the need to discourage non-nationals admitted to the country temporarily from believing that they can commit serious crimes and be allowed to remain; and the need to discourage fraud, deception and deliberate breaches of the law.[63]

The result is that Article 8 adjudication is fact-specific and inherently judgemental. Cases are decided initially by the department and on appeal by tribunals. Further, the courts have intervened to prevent the department from constructing hard and fast rules concerning the application of Article 8. For instance, in *Chikwamba*, the department's blanket requirement that a failed asylum-seeker, wishing to remain in the UK on the basis of her family life, return to her home country to apply for immigration status in the UK was unlawful because of the disruption to her family life.[64] 'Policies that involve people cannot be, and should

---

[62] *R (Quila) v Secretary of State for the Home Department* [2011] UKSC 45, [2012] 1 AC 621.
[63] *Huang v Secretary of State for the Home Department* [2007] UKHL 11, [2007] 2 AC 167, [16].
[64] *Chikwamba v Secretary of State for the Home Department* [2008] UKHL 40, [2008] 1 WLR 1420.

not be allowed to become, rigid inflexible rules. The bureaucracy of which Kafka wrote cannot be allowed to take root in this country and the courts must see that it does not.[65] Furthermore, the department's own unreasonable delays in processing asylum applications could reduce the importance it placed on of maintaining immigration control if those delays resulted from 'a dysfunctional system which yields unpredictable, inconsistent, and unfair outcomes'.[66]

The problematic issues have concerned exactly who is to undertake the Article 8 balancing exercise and how. For obvious policy reasons, the department has seen Article 8 as a threat to the integrity of the immigration rules; unsuccessful asylum claimants and others present in the country without immigration status can seek to spin their cases out for as long as possible and develop a family life in order to prevent their removal. A related risk is that Article 8 comes to be used by tribunals as a general dispensing power to allow migrants to remain even though they did not qualify under the strict requirements of the rules. The role of the European Court of Human Rights interpreting the ECHR has also proven controversial. The most sensitive issue has been the degree to which foreign national prisoners can seek to use Article 8 as a basis for remaining in the UK when the immigration department wants to remove them in the interests of public safety and protection.

Concerned at its loss of control and overly generous judicial applications of Article 8, the department, initially through immigration rules in 2012,[67] and then through the Immigration Act 2014, has specified the weight to be accorded to the public interest in Article 8 cases.[68] Under the 2014 Act, maintaining effective immigration controls is in the public interest. It is also in the public interest that applicants speak English and be financially dependent. Little weight is to be given a private life, or relationship with a qualifying partner established by a person in the country unlawfully or whose immigration status is precarious. But, the public interest does not require a person's removal where there is a genuine and subsisting parental relationship with a qualifying child and it would be unreasonable to expect the child to leave the UK. There are additional considerations concerning foreign criminals. Deporting such people is in the public interest; the more serious the offence committed by a foreign criminal, the greater the public interest.[69] There is detailed provision about various exceptions depending upon the length of imprisonment.

---

[65] ibid [4] (Lord Scott).

[66] *EB (Kosovo) v Secretary of State for the Home Department* [2008] UKHL 41, [2009] 1 AC 1159 [16] (Lord Bingham).

[67] Immigration Rules HC 194 (2012). See also Home Office, 'Statement of Intent: Family Migration' (2012); Home Office, 'Grounds of Compatibility with Article 8 of the European Convention on Human Rights' (2012); *MF (Nigeria) v Secretary of State for the Home Department* [2013] EWCA Civ 1192.

[68] Nationality, Immigration, and Asylum Act 2002, s 117B (as inserted by the Immigration Act 2014, s 19).

[69] Nationality, Immigration, and Asylum Act 2002, s 117C (as inserted by the Immigration Act 2014, s 19).

This form of 'governmentally prescribed interpretation of Article 8 through both rules and statute' was clearly aimed to reduce judicial discretion. The Supreme Court has held that, while the rules are a relevant consideration, the ultimate question is one of proportionality.[70] The Court has also criticised the obscure drafting of the provisions as regards the deportation of foreign criminals. Those provisions were intended to provide clarity, but, because of their obscure drafting, have instead generated uncertainty.[71] Overall, tribunals and courts must take account of numerous detailed and sometimes overlapping rules and then apply an overarching test to determine whether removal would be proportionate under Article 8.

V. Complex Rules and Simplification

Making rules involves inherent trade-offs. Increased consistency and predictability come at a cost in terms of a lack of flexibility in hard cases and vice-versa. Nonetheless, the overall effect of the department's efforts to simplify the rules has often been to make them more complex. Paradoxically, more and more prescriptive rules which are then constantly amended and changed increases the uncertainty that such rules were, in part, intended to reduce. The causes of such complexity are various and go beyond the prescriptive and detailed character of the points-based scheme and other sets of rules. The courts have noted that 'rebarbative' drafting has produced unclear and inconsistent rules that are far from simple and accessible.[72] Indeed, the rules have become so detailed and have been amended so many times that there are probably only one or two officials that truly understand them.

Virtually all concerned recognise that the immigration rules are not only complex, but often unnecessarily, chronically and excruciatingly detailed and complex. The courts have repeatedly raised concerns about the complexity of the rules and the urgent need for simplification.[73] In 2013, Jackson LJ noted that the rules 'have now achieved a degree of complexity which even the Byzantine

---

[70] *R (Agyarko) v Secretary of State for the Home Department* [2017] UKSC 11, [2017] Imm AR 764.

[71] See, eg, *KO (Nigeria) v Secretary of State for the Home Department* [2018] UKSC 53, [2018] 1 WLR 5273 [14] and [57] (Lord Carnwath): 'It is profoundly unsatisfactory that a set of provisions which was intended to provide clear guidelines to limit the scope for judicial evaluation should have led to such disagreement among some of the most experienced Upper Tribunal and Court of Appeal judges. ... It has taken almost four years for these cases to reach the Supreme Court. In the meantime there have been significant differences of approach and conflicting decisions at each level. The view of the Department itself, at least of the effect of section 117B(6), seems to have changed over time. I have noted the continuing debate before the Upper Tribunal and the Court of Appeal. Unfortunately these differences are far from surprising given the unhappy drafting of the statutory provisions.'

[72] *Singh v Secretary of State for the Home Department* [2015] EWCA Civ 74 [59] (Underhill LJ).

[73] *Sapkota v Secretary of State for the Home Department* [2011] EWCA Civ 1320, [2012] Imm AR 254 [127] (Jackson LJ).

Emperors would have envied'.[74] Such statements are nothing new.[75] The issue of simplification has long been mooted. In the late 2000s, the department sought to simplify immigration law, but nothing came of it.[76] In 2020, Underhill LJ explained:

> This Court has very frequently in recent years had to deal with appeals arising out of difficulties in understanding the Immigration Rules. This is partly a result of their labyrinthine structure and idiosyncratic drafting conventions but sometimes it is a simple matter of the confused language and/or structure of particular provisions. This case is a particularly egregious example. The difficulty of deciding what the effect of paragraph 276B (v) is intended to be is illustrated by the facts not only that this Court itself is not unanimous but that all three members have taken a different view from that reached by a different constitution in *Masum Ahmed*. Likewise, the Secretary of State initially sought to uphold *Masum Ahmed* contrary, it would seem to her own Guidance – but, as we have seen, shortly before the hearing executed a *volte face*. (This illustrates a different vice, also far from unique, that the Home Office seems to have no reliable mechanism for reaching a considered and consistent position on what its own Rules mean.) Of course, mistakes will occasionally occur in any complex piece of legislation, or quasi-legislation; but I have to say that problems of this kind occur far too often. The result of poor drafting is confusion and uncertainty both for those who are subject to the Rules and those who have to apply them, and consequently also a proliferation of appeals.[77]

Another judge said that the solution was simply to discard the current set of rules entirely and start again.[78]

The negative effects of this sprawling mass of complex rules are clear. Ordinary people often find the rules impenetrable and incomprehensible. It is easy for anyone to get so lost in the detail that it becomes increasingly difficult to understand what the requirements of the rules actually are. Beatson LJ has noted that the detail, the number of documents to be consulted, the number of changes in both the rules and guidance, and the difficulty in ascertaining which version of them apply present 'real obstacles to achieving predictable consistency and restoring public trust in the system, particularly in an area of law that lay people and people whose first language is not English need to understand'.[79] The risk of

[74] *Pokhriyal v Secretary of State for the Home Department* [2013] EWCA Civ 1568 [4] (Jackson LJ). See also *R (Robinson) v Secretary of State for the Home Department* [2019] UKSC 11 [66] (Lord Lloyd-Jones): 'the structure of both primary and secondary legislation in this field has reached such a degree of complexity that there is an urgent need to make the law and procedure clear and comprehensible'.
[75] In *Zenovics v Secretary of State for the Home Department* [2002] EWCA Civ 273, [2002] INLR 219 [33] Schiemann LJ had noted that 'the law is riddled with obscurities and regularly amended by primary and secondary legislation and by rules'. For parliamentary criticism, see HAC, 'Home Office Delivery of Brexit: Immigration' HC 421 (2017–19) [54] and [73].
[76] Home Office, 'Simplifying Immigration Law: A New Framework for Immigration Rules' (2009).
[77] *Hoque and others v Secretary of State for the Home Department* [2020] EWCA Civ 1357 [59] (Underhill LJ).
[78] ibid [96] (McCombe LJ).
[79] *Hossain v Secretary of State for the Home Department* [2015] EWCA Civ 207 [30] (Beatson LJ).

poor-quality decisions is also increased and legal certainty eroded. Underhill LJ has noted that officials 'have at least some of the same difficulties in keeping up with the consequences of the kaleidoscopic changes in their own rules as the rest of us do'.[80] Complex rules make it more likely that errors in decision-making will arise, therefore increasing the need for reviews and appeals, thereby adding more delay and uncertainty.

Complexity presents the department with a paradox: it simultaneously works both for and against its self-interests. In light of their inward-looking disposition, government agencies often require people to think and act like officials; in turn, the rules end up serving the needs of officials more than those of individuals. Complexity can also alienate people from the system.[81] Given the restrictive nature of immigration policy, this has often suited the department's needs. Complex rules are all of a piece with the difficulties applicants experience in attempting to navigate a complex system and being unable to interact with caseworkers, and the very limited efforts taken by the department to guide applicants and help them understand the process. As a senior official has noted, 'my biggest reflection really, from the outside in, is what a difficult organisation we've been to seek help from'.[82] Yet, at the same time, the department itself also becomes entangled by the complexity of its own rules – as evidenced by the many appeals that proceed to tribunals and the higher courts on highly formalist points of interpretation. Badly drafted rules generate avoidable litigation. This in turn weakens the department's ability to perform its own functions because of the frequent uncertainty as to the precise meaning of the rules in specific cases; the department's complicated legal framework often works against it.[83]

More simple rules are then required, but how and to what extent is this to be achieved? Complex rules reflect the complex nature of immigration policy which changes frequently. There will always be short-term pressures to change the rules to meet specific needs and pressures. There is some indeterminacy in distinguishing between, on the one hand, the legitimate need to change the rules and guidance quickly in response to policy changes and to close down unforeseen gaps, ambiguities and contradictions and, on the other hand, unnecessarily complex rules that can and should be simplified. More generally, other parts of government – tax and benefits – have struggled to reduce legal complexity. The tax simplification project illustrates how simplifying the law is anything but simple.[84] What then can be done to simplify the rules and guidance?

---

[80] *Singh* (n 72) [57].

[81] J Bourn, *Public Sector Auditing: Is It Value For Money?* (Chichester, Wiley, 2006) 28–32.

[82] *Windrush Review* (n 50) 98.

[83] *Hansard*, HC Vol 560 col 1501 (26 March 2013) (Theresa May MP, Secretary of State for the Home Department).

[84] S James, 'The Complexity of Tax Simplification: The UK Experience' in S James, A Sawyer, and T Budak (eds), *The Complexity of Tax Simplification: Experiences From Around the World* (London, Palgrave Macmillan, 2016). On the complexity of benefits law, see N Harris, *Law in a Complex State: Complexity in the Law and Structure of Welfare* (Oxford, Hart, 2013).

The Law Commission's report on simplifying the immigration rules presented a detailed analysis of the causes and consequences of complexity and specific recommendations to simplify the rules.[85] It recommended that the rules should be underpinned by the following principles: suitability for the non-expert user; comprehensiveness; accuracy; clarity and accessibility; consistency; durability (a resilient structure that accommodates amendments); and capacity for presentation in a digital form. The rules needed to be overhauled entirely, better structured, organised and drafted. The Law Commission made other detailed recommendations, including the creation of a simplification review committee to look at the drafting and structure of the Rules. The department accepted the Law Commission's analysis and the bulk of the recommendations and committed itself to overhauling the rules.[86]

As regards substantive matters, the principal choice has been between reverting from a prescriptive approach to a wholesale return to a more discretionary approach or by seeking to ameliorate some of the difficulties of a prescriptive approach. The dilemma here is that previous discretionary rules had the safety net of appeals against poor initial decisions. Reintroducing wide-scale discretion without better quality decisions and the safety net of appeals would increase arbitrary casework.[87] The Upper Tribunal noted that a less prescriptive system would require additional qualities and competences from caseworkers, such as being appropriately trained and aware of principles of public law (eg procedural fairness), and to have specialist knowledge of the category of the rules and the underlying policy, and sufficient time to make reasonable assessments and, where necessary, to liaise with applicants.[88] The big question is whether the department has the organisational competence to make such changes. Many representatives would doubt it.

The Law Commission therefore recommended that the department use a less prescriptive approach to evidential requirements, in the form of non-exhaustive lists of the types of evidence that will be accepted. Instead of highly prescriptive evidential requirements, the rules could provide lists of evidential requirements specifying which evidence would be accepted, together with a category or categories of less specifically defined evidence which the decision-maker could consider with a view to deciding whether an applicant met the underlying requirement of the rules. This recommendation would apply principally in relation to points-based scheme applications concerning, for instance, financial requirements. It would allow a more flexible and purposive approach to

---

[85] Law Commission, 'Simplification of the Immigration Rules: Report' HC 14 Law Com No 388 (2019–21).

[86] Home Office, 'Simplifying the Immigration Rules: A Response to the Law Commission's Report and Recommendations on Simplification of the Immigration Rules' (2020).

[87] Law Commission (n 85) [5.117].

[88] Upper Tribunal (Immigration and Asylum Chamber), 'Response to Law Commission Consultation on Simplifying the Immigration Rules' (n 41) 16.

be adopted in hard cases by allowing caseworkers to reach a more common-sense outcome when an applicant who in substance qualifies is defeated by not fulfilling every technical requirement of the formalistic rules. As regards policy guidance, the Law Commission recommended that such guidance should be simplified, rationalised and subject to coordinated oversight.

In response to the Law Commission's report, the department established a Simplification of the Rules Review Committee and committed itself to reducing unnecessarily prescriptive rules, especially as regards evidential requirements.[89] Simplifying the rules is necessarily a long-term project. Few other large, complex administrative systems (eg tax and social security) have been able to simplify rules without encountering significant challenges. The success of any such attempt in the immigration context would need to be assessed over a period of some years to ascertain whether more simple rules have been introduced and maintained despite the changes inevitably made to them. It is not currently possible to undertake this type of assessment, although the outlook seems somewhat negative. Consider the department's first major and 507-page-long statement of changes to the rules following its acceptance of the Law Commission's recommendations.[90] The length and complexity of these rules were criticised for making 'effective parliamentary scrutiny virtually impossible' and ignoring 'a key criterion of the Government's definition of "good law", in that it makes the law less accessible to the citizen'.[91]

VI. Evaluating Rules

A final matter concerns the need to evaluate how the rules work in practice. Given that the rules embody policy, the issue then arises as to the degree to which the rules successfully implement their policy goals. As instrumental rationality is the principal norm of administration, it is then necessary to evaluate how sets of rules work in practice. Such evaluations will also inform future policy developments. In general terms, government has only rarely evaluated and monitored the implementation of law and policy. During the 2000s, there was a significant move toward post-legislative scrutiny.[92] However, the momentum behind this largely seems to have dissipated.[93] Overall, there are strong behavioural forces within government

---

[89] Home Office (n 86) 10.

[90] Home Office, 'Statement of Changes to Immigration Rules' 22 October 2020, HC 813 (2019–21).

[91] Secondary Legislation Scrutiny Committee, '33rd Report of Session 2019–21: Statement of Changes in Immigration Rules' HL 161 (2019–21) 1.

[92] House of Lords Constitution Committee, 'Parliament and the Legislative Process' HL 173 (2003–04) [165]–[193]; Law Commission, 'Post-Legislative Scrutiny' (Cm 6945, 2006); Office of the Leader of the House of Commons, 'Post-Legislative Scrutiny: The Government's Approach' (Cm 7320, 2008).

[93] A Burrows, *Thinking About Statutes: Interpretation, Interaction, Improvement* (Cambridge, Cambridge University Press, 2018) 128 ('the official line on post-legislative scrutiny is not being adhered to in practice').

that limit the potential for evaluating past policies and rules. More often than not, government focuses on current problems and developing new policies.

What then of the evaluations of the immigration rules? Senior officials have recognised that 'the Department should be evaluating its policies ... not just in relation to activity, but also impact'.[94] Over recent years, changes to the rules have included a commitment to monitor and review by laying a report to Parliament within five years, although no such reports have yet been published. There has been some evaluation of immigration rules and routes. In 2011, the NAO concluded that part of the points-based scheme – Tier 1 for highly skilled migrants – had met, in part, its objective of attracting highly skilled applicants into the UK with an estimated 60 per cent of Tier 1 migrants working in skilled or highly skilled professions, although the evidence was not robust.[95] It was also found that the department's lack of robust and useful management information had limited its ability to detect systematic abuse and to target its resources effectively.

But this has been very much the exception. As the episode of the hostile environment illustrates, the department has, overall, not evaluated its policies. In 2020, the Migration Advisory Committee (MAC) highlighted the importance of evaluating immigration rules and policy.[96] Good-quality and accessible data and evaluation were vital to ensure effective monitoring of the operation of immigration routes introduced by the rules and to be able to make necessary adjustments in a timely fashion. Indeed, with the new points-based system introduced post-Brexit, the MAC stated that there needed to be more active monitoring and evaluation of how it works in practice as there would inevitably be uncertainty about impacts. Without such monitoring, there was 'a danger that the UK, unable to learn from the past, continues to lurch between an overly open and overly closed work migration policy without ever being able to steer a steady path'.[97] However, the Committee highlighted the paucity of data and the 'difficulty of access' which made evaluation problematic.[98] In naturally anodyne language, the MAC recommended that the department improve its retention of historical data in a suitable format, make progress in linking relevant datasets, and share this data so that outcomes, such as migrant employment, could be tracked and evaluated.

The implications of this are not difficult to decipher. When a government advisory committee complains about the difficulties of accessing data from its own sponsoring department, then the problem is not merely an overlooked email. The more likely explanation is a deep reluctance amongst senior officials to share such data because of a fear as to what any evaluation might uncover, the inevitable

[94] PAC, 'Oral Evidence: Windrush Generation and the Home Office', HC 1518 (2017–19) Q 95 (17 December 2018) (Sir Philip Rutnam, Permanent Secretary, Home Office).
[95] NAO, 'Immigration: The Points Based System – Work Routes' HC 819 (2010–11) 6.
[96] Migration Advisory Committee, 'A Points-Based System and Salary Thresholds for Immigration' (2020) 3 and 11.
[97] ibid 3.
[98] ibid 11.

uncertainties as to how things might play out politically, and the risk of ministers being embarrassed. Suppose that a major policy heralded by ministers as 'the solution' turned out in practice to be counter-productive and ineffective? The reality is that ministers, driven by their short-term political agendas, do not want evidence-based policy: they want policy-based evidence.[99]

Evaluations have been published and made use of – when they have suited ministerial needs. For instance, the purpose of Tier 1 (General) Migrants of the points-based scheme, which was open 2008 to 2015, was to widen the pool of highly skilled individuals and maintain labour market flexibility by allowing those without a job offer to work in the UK. The scheme was introduced under the Labour Government. A 2010 assessment found that 29 per cent of Tier 1 (General) visa holders were in skilled roles, 21 per cent were in unskilled roles (stacking shelves, driving taxis or working as security guards) and half had an unclear employment status.[100] This assessment was used to introduce restrictions on the immigration route by Theresa May early in her tenure as Home Secretary.[101] The department may then have undertaken other evaluations, but it is unlikely that those with negative implications will be published. This seems unacceptable; a mature system of government would recognise the need for empirical and published evaluations to inform policy and public debate.

VII. Conclusion

As a form of modern administrative or regulatory law, the immigration rules and guidance illustrate the department's variable organisational competence. The rules and guidance fail in multiple ways; they are, in significant respects, unnecessarily complex. Any set of rules governing a complex area of policy are likely to be complex and dense, but the immigration rules far exceed what is necessary. This in turn makes the rules inaccessible and leads to errors in their application. All parties concerned struggle to understand the confusing and complex rules. As a mass casework organisation, both the department and applicants benefit from bright-line rules, but this trend has been taken to the extreme and, in the process, form has been exalted over substance and purpose, thereby reducing legal certainty. There are inconsistencies between the rules and guidance. The problems in the formulation and dissemination of guidance within the department indicates not just a lack of effective internal communication, but also the degree of operational disconnect between those who make policy and those who administer it.

---

[99] D Taylor and S Balloch (eds), *The Politics of Evaluation: Participation and Policy Implementation* (Bristol, Policy Press 2005) 3–5.

[100] Home Office, 'International Group Points Based System Tier 1: An Operational Assessment' (2010).

[101] Immigration: Home Secretary's Speech (5 November 2010), available at www.gov.uk/government/speeches/immigration-home-secretarys-speech-of-5-november-2010.

Implementing the Law Commission's simplification recommendations is clearly required, but simplification needs to be much more than a one-off event; it needs to be embedded within the administrative rule-making process. The use of guidance should be formalised. Guidance should be consistently produced and published online. It should be explained clearly for the benefit of both officials and claimants and be consistent with the rules. Guidance should also be effectively disseminated and communicated within the department so that caseworkers can apply it. There also needs to more effective parliamentary scrutiny of the rules and more understanding and evaluation of how they work in practice. The department should publish evaluations of how the rules work in practice. Improvements along these lines are necessary and would be beneficial in terms of transparency, accessibility and scrutiny. However, the discussion so far is incomplete. We also need to consider how the rules are applied and enforced in practice, and it is this to which we now turn.

5

Caseworking

Casework – individual decision-making – involves analysing evidence, finding facts, applying rules, making decisions and giving reasons. It may not be a glamorous task, but casework is an essential part of the wider administrative law task of applying the rules to implement policy. Given the scale of administration, casework must be undertaken in bulk. This in turn raises perennial tensions between throughput and quality. As a caseworking organisation, the immigration department is almost entirely focused on processing large volumes of applications within agreed service standards. This can only be achieved through standardisation of processes. The fundamental challenge is then to produce good-quality decisions in the context of organisational and political pressures to take an enormous volume of applications as efficiently and quickly as possible. Accordingly, issues of administrative capacity and organisational competence are very much at the forefront.

This chapter examines how the department handles this challenge. It considers how caseworking is organised, the quality of decisions, the operational contexts in which caseworkers work and the pressures that influence their work; the style of administrative decision-making adopted; and internal administrative mechanisms to assure and improve casework decisions. From a wider perspective, the performance and organisation of casework also raises questions about the effectiveness of internal administrative law and organisational competence: how are caseworkers motivated and supervised? To what extent does the department possess the capacity and capability to resource, operate and manage an effective and complex mass casework system? How effective are internal methods to assure and improve the quality of decisions?

I. Caseworking in General

Immigrants seeking to enter or remain in the UK must apply for a decision as to whether they qualify under the Immigration Rules. There are many different routes under which applicants can apply to enter or remain for purposes. Most casework is undertaken in response to applications made either out of country or in-country under a particular immigration route, such as work, study, family, visit, asylum, European casework and settlement, and long residence. There are also other casework decisions that are not made in response to applications, such as Immigration

Enforcement's Returns Preparation (which relate to public safety and security concerns) and its Criminal Casework team, which handles criminal deportations. Above front-line casework are quality assurance systems and other casework units dealing with challenges against refusal decisions by way of administrative reviews, tribunal appeals and judicial review litigation. New decision-making categories have, of necessity, been added piecemeal in response to events, such as the EU Settlement Scheme (following Brexit) and the Windrush compensation scheme.

Broadly speaking, two general types of casework apply to the various immigration categories. First, there is 'binary work stream processing': trans-actional, rule-based decisions that require minimal problem-solving skills or judgement and only an objective assessment whether valid specified evidence has been provided. These applications are considered by junior officials on the basis of the papers only. The second type of casework involves judgemental decisions in areas such as asylum, domestic violence, statelessness and human rights applica-tions. In such contexts, caseworkers must assess the credibility of applicants and make subjective assessments following interviews.

Casework varies in terms of its legal and factual complexity. Visit visas and student visas are amongst the most routine. By contrast, asylum, decisions to remove status, and criminal deportations are more complex. The different immi-gration routes in turn produce a complex and shifting organisational structure and a plethora of caseworking units and changing organisational structures.[1] Figure 5.1 shows UKVI's organisational structure.

Figure 5.1 UKVI organisational structure (2021)

Visas and citizenship	Strategy Transformation and Performance	Immigration and Protection	Resettlement Asylum Support and Integration
Customer and Commercial Services	Strategy and Planning	Appeals Litigation and Administrative Review	Asylum Support and Specialist Casework
Visits and Family	Strategy Transformation and Performance – Central Operations	Asylum Operations	Better Regulation, Cross-Cutting, Devolution and Wales Unit
European Casework and Settlement		Family and Human Rights Unit and Shared Service Centre Network	
Work, Study, Citizenship and Windrush Taskforce	Transformation Design and Delivery	Immigration, Information, Improvement and Support	Integration and Vulnerability
Windrush Compensation Scheme Operations		Immigration and Protection Hub	Resettlement Transfer and Operations
		Refused Case Management	

Source: UKVI

In formal constitutional terms, casework decisions are made in the name of the Secretary of State. Some sensitive decisions (eg exclusion from entry and depri-vation of citizenship on grounds of the public good) must personally be made

---

[1] For instance, the Status Review Unit (SRU) is one casework unit within Refused Case Management (RCM), which is a unit within Immigration & Protection, which is a unit within UKVI, itself a directo-rate of the Home Office.

by the Home Secretary, but the vast majority of decisions are taken by casework-ers. The mundane reality is that executive power is exercised on a day-to-day basis by armies of junior civil servants working in office blocks in Croydon and Sheffield that must take 20,000 decisions per day. Caseworking is not a properly recognised profession within government. In practice, it is a low-level, low-pay and low-status position undertaken by relatively junior officials.[2] There is, then, a dissonance between the important consequences of decisions taken by casework-ers and their relatively low status and position. Caseworkers are not subject to the same training and regulatory requirements as immigration advisers to ensure they are competent.[3] Asylum caseworkers receive a five-week training course and then six months of mentoring.

Another feature of casework is the high turnover of staff. The department has often been criticised for its workforce planning; the loss of experienced staff; lengthy staffing gaps; high levels of inexperienced new recruits; and concerns that casework units struggle due to under-resourcing.[4] The high staff turnover rate has produced great demand for training. The impact of this is particularly acute given the complexity of the system and the fact that it can take up to six months to train and assure the standards of case officers.[5] 'Agency staff' have often been used as a flexible resource to deal with casework backlogs.[6] The overall perception is a continual inflow and outflow of staff, prompting repeated concerns over the loss of experienced staff and staff shortages.[7]

The overriding pressure on the department is to process the incoming caseload quickly, yet because of staff and resource shortages, the building up of undecided backlogs of applications is a perennial problem.[8] Overall, the department makes something like four million immigration decisions per year. In numerical terms, visitor applicants account for the bulk of the caseload; there were 1.4 million entry clearance visit applications in 2019–20, around three-quarters of all entry clearance applications. But all of this is subject to quick changes and seasonal

---

[2] Binary work stream casework is mostly undertaken by administrative officer decision-makers; other casework is undertaken by higher-level officials at the grade of executive officer. Casework managers are at the grade of higher executive officer.

[3] In 2006, the HAC, 'Immigration Control' HC 775 (2005–06) [217] recommended that caseworkers should be subject to the same requirements as immigration advisers. Only by 2019 had the department partnered with the Chartered Institute of Legal Executives to offer accredited quali-fications as part of a new immigration specialist academy for caseworking staff. See Immigration Enforcement, 'Our IE – Delivering Our Organisational Priorities' (2019) 11.

[4] HAC, 'The Windrush Generation' HC 990 (2017–19) [109].

[5] R Alcock, 'Internal Review of the Government's Policy on Requirements to Provide DNA in Visa and Asylum Cases' (2018) [54]–[55].

[6] 'Gap-Year Students Deciding Asylum Claims' *Guardian* (25 February 2016).

[7] HAC, 'The Windrush Generation' (n 4) [104].

[8] HAC, 'Oral Evidence: Home Office Delivery of Brexit: Immigration', 10 October 2017, HC 421 (2017–19) Q 31 (John Vine, then ICIBI): 'throughout the nearly seven years I was the Independent Chief Inspector, I found myself in a position of telling three Home Secretaries about backlogs that they did not seem to know about … You need to get through the volume but … in a way that ensures that the right decisions are made, quality of decision-making is made. It is difficult to see how you can do that without the correct level of resources to do the job properly.'

variations resulting in pinch-points. For instance, student applications typically reach a peak in the run-up to the start of the academic year; visitor applications are highest in the second quarter of the year as visitors plan to visit in the summer. The asylum intake will be affected by a wide range of other factors, such as: a deterioration of conditions in countries that generate asylum claimants; the ability of agents to bring people into the country; and the scope for abuse. From its successive inquiries, the Home Affairs Committee (HAC) concluded that the pressures facing caseworkers have increased over recent years; the time available to take decisions may have remained the same, but the number of decisions to be taken within that time has increased.[9]

Given that the department overall lacks sufficient resources to do its work, the volume of applications, the pressure to meet processing targets, and the fluctuations in demand create an unstable operational environment and a relentless managerial challenge. The bane of the department's life, and an inherent and intractable feature of its operations, has been the building-up of backlogs of undecided claims needing to be cleared. Even a single day not taking decisions would significantly jeopardise its performance. A redesign of the process, such as onshoring entry clearance applications, or new immigration rules, can also result in difficulties, delays and hold-ups. Asylum backlogs in particular have been a major feature, leading to intense scrutiny from the HAC and litigation, but backlogs exist in other areas also. The managerial challenge is then to eliminate all possible uncertainty so that the machine can operate as smoothly as possible, but given the impossibility of fully achieving this, organisational structures inevitably become ridden with tension.

II. Processing Targets and Decision Quality

Processing targets are the means by which managers drive and assess the performance of caseworkers. Daily productivity targets are seen as essential to stay on top of the high volumes of applications. Without processing targets, there would be no means of monitoring performance and no standard against which to measure such performance. Yet, this inevitably adversely impacts upon the ability of caseworkers to make good-quality decisions and reasons for refusal. Casework, then, can descend into quick processing to meet targets with consequent low-quality decisions.

A. Targets

As regards immigration caseworking, there are at least two types of targets: those relating to the number of decisions to be taken per day by a

---

[9] ibid [102].

caseworker; and those that relate to the timeliness of processing. The targets vary between the type and complexity of decision made within different casework units, and over time depending on the pressures. Targets have ranged from 10 EU settlement decisions per day to four family and human rights cases per day. Student curtailment caseworkers have had a target of completing 25 case considerations per day.[10] In 2013, entry clearance officers had to process 45 visitor applications per day – 10 minutes per application; unsurprisingly, quality was poor.[11] Settlement caseworkers are expected to complete a certain number of cases per week adjusted for the type of case and its complexity. Settlement decision targets have been reviewed regularly by management, in consultation with staff, and have been challenging but achievable.[12] In the context of binary work streams, the key issue for managers will be managing workflow and monitoring productivity; caseworkers work to benchmarks concerning the number of decisions they should complete within a single shift. These productivity targets for caseworkers – daily 'stats' – are seen as essential to stay on top of the high volumes of applications.

Processing targets are complemented by timeliness service standards, which vary between each immigration route and the type of service requested by the application. For instance, in 2019, the 'standard' target for processing and deciding most applications for Leave to Remain and Indefinite Leave to Remain was six months across many immigration routes (eg ECAA, long residence, no time limit, domestic violence, points-based scheme (Tiers 2 and 5), protection (asylum)). For some routes, the standard was eight weeks (eg points-based scheme (Tier 1 General, Tiers 2, 4, and 5), Spouse/Partner). Applicants can, for an additional fee, apply for priority (five working days) or super-priority (next day) customer service standard. In 2020, the standard processing time was reduced from six months to eight weeks across most, though not all, routes. As regards entry clearance (applications made out of country and previously decided out of country, but now largely decided in-country), the service standards have been as follows: settlement (60 working days); and points-based scheme (Tier 1 General, Tiers 2, 4, and 5) and visitors (15 working days). There is another cross-cutting dimension. Applications are classified as either straightforward and therefore subject to service standards or non-straightforward, that is, complex and not subject to service standards. Processing targets also provide applicants with a guide to the timescale in which they can expect an outcome on their applications,[13] and transparency for the public.[14] Organisational performance is assessed by the percentage of applications, for each route, caseworkers process within service standards.

[10] ICIBI, 'A Short Notice Inspection of the Tier 4 Curtailment Process' (2016) [6.4].

[11] ICIBI, 'A Short-Notice Inspection of Decision-making Quality in the Warsaw Visa Section' (2013).

[12] ICIBI, 'An Inspection of Settlement Casework' (2015) [4.3].

[13] The UKVI has published service standards.

[14] See Home Office, Migration Transparency Data, available at www.gov.uk/government/collections/migration-transparency-data.

Most straightforward applications are processed with service standards.[15] However, this hides a submerged number of applications categorised as 'non-straightforward' which can take much longer. For instance, the longest time an applicant had to wait for indefinite leave to remain between 2014 and 2017 was 719 days and the longest an application was on hold for during the same period was 1,001 days.[16] It also needs to be borne in mind that application fees often far exceed the unit cost of processing applications.[17] For instance, the fee for an in-country application for indefinite leave to remain is £2,389 compared with a unit processing cost of £243.[18] Work that does not contribute to processing targets, such as calling social services because of concern about an unaccompanied asylum-seeking child, is not valued and therefore disincentivised.[19]

B. Decisional Quality

The consequences of all this are obvious. Processing targets provide benchmarks for organisational performance and individual workloads, but they become dysfunctional when meeting them becomes an end in itself and clearing the caseload takes priority over making good-quality decisions. To cope with the pressure, applications can be deemed non-straightforward. The sheer volume of decisions required, the department's serious resource issues, the high turnover of staff, unrealistic workloads, staff being poorly supported and overworked and the pressure from targets often lead to errors and mistakes with life-changing consequences.[20] The resulting casework decisions are often of poor or variable quality. The Public and Commercial Services Union has raised its concerns that staff shortages have meant there 'was not enough time to prepare cases. Unrealistic targets and lack of

---

[15] For most routes, the percentage of straightforward applications processed within service standards is over 95%, though in some instances it is nearer 80%. See UKVI, 'Transparency Data: Visas and Citizenship Data: February 2021 Q4 2020', table VC_02, available at www.gov.uk/government/publications/visas-and-citizenship-data-february-2021.

[16] 'Home Office Visa Delays "Inhumane"' *BBC News* (3 October 2017).

[17] UKVI has a cost recovery target of 203%; additional fee income subsidises other parts of the system. In 2019–20, UKVI's expenditure was £1.7 billion whereas its income was £2.3 billion: Home Office, 'Annual Report and Accounts 2019/20' HC 334 (2019–20) 147. In *R (Project for the Registration of Children as British Citizens) v Secretary of State for the Home Department* [2021] EWCA Civ 193, the Court of Appeal held that the fee charged to children applying to be registered as British citizens was unlawful.

[18] Home Office, 'Visa Fees Transparency Data', available at www.gov.uk/government/publications/visa-fees-transparency-data There are also hidden costs depending on the type of application. For indefinite leave to remain, other costs would include document translations, English language test, Life in the UK test and lawyer fees.

[19] Anonymous, 'I Worry Asylum Caseworkers are Failing People in their Darkest Hour' *Guardian* (8 April 2017): 'If you wanted to do the right thing, you would have to take the productivity hit and risk performance management procedures, ultimately with the threat of dismissal.'

[20] HAC, 'Home Office Delivery of Brexit' (n 8) [69]–[71].

training and mentoring are having an impact on the quality of decision making'.[21] In 2020, a senior official explained:

> I think with the case working culture, what … I used to rail against was they never met a migrant and somehow lived in a kind of bubble where the most important thing was how many files you got through.[22]

A persistent and widespread concern from immigration representatives is that caseworkers often fail to give proper and adequate reasons when refusing applications. Practice varies. Some immigration refusal notices are brief; asylum reason for refusal letters can be 20 pages long with long quotations from case law and country information, but with short conclusory reasons. There are real problems with the quality of decisions.[23] Reasons may not be tailored to individual circumstances, but instead cut and paste from a standard template or contain basic factual and legal errors. The Supreme Court has noted that the common use of standardised reasons through IT, decision templates, and drop-down menus to process large numbers of decisions efficiently is not in itself legally objectionable, provided the reasons explain adequately why the decision has been taken.[24] Nonetheless, the pervasive concern is that the quality of reasons in decision letters and refusal notices is often highly variable.

Yet, there are pockets of specialist and high-quality casework. Some specialist casework teams are 'highly knowledgeable about the complex legislation, rules and policies' they apply.[25] The vast majority of settlement decisions have been found to have been made efficiently and effectively, in line with the rules, guidance, service standards and internal quality targets, although in a small number of cases, both grants and refusals, the rules or guidance had not been correctly applied.[26]

Another powerful influence on casework is the immediate policy context of deciding who can and cannot enter or remain in the country. Each immigration decision is potentially fraught with difficulty: is the applicant genuine or an irregular migrant who is abusing the process? The question is constantly present and often determined by influential proxy measures such as credibility or a poor immigration history. From a critical perspective, it has consistently been argued that casework is informed by a culture of disbelief. At the same time, recognising

---

[21] Public and Commercial Services Union, written submission to the HAC, 'Home Office Delivery of Brexit: Immigration' HC 421 (2017–19).

[22] Quoted in 'Windrush Lessons Learned Review' HC 93 (2019–20) 104 ('Windrush Review').

[23] Freedom From Torture, *Lessons Not Learned: The Failures of Asylum Decision-making in the UK* (London, Freedom From Torture, 2019); L Schuster, 'Fatal Flaws in the UK Asylum Decision-making System: An Analysis of Home Office Refusal Letters' (2020) 46 *Journal of Ethnic and Migration Studies* 1371; ICIBI, 'Short Notice Inspection of the Tier 4 Curtailment Process' (n 10) [6.14]: 'Curtailment letters were not tailored to individual circumstances and were generated using a standard template'.

[24] *R (Agyarko) v Secretary of State for the Home Department* [2017] UKSC 11, [2017] 1 WLR 823 [71] (Lord Reed).

[25] ICIBI, 'An Inspection of the Review and Removal of Immigration, Refugee and Citizenship "Status"' (2018) [7.11] and [9.17].

[26] ICIBI, 'Settlement Casework' (n 12).

the highly different political perspectives on immigration, the issue is often a paradoxical one. To some extent, a culture of disbelief does exist and varies over time in line with ministerial influence. Yet, most immigration applications are issued.

These tensions are most acute in the asylum context. Concerned at the length of time taken to decide asylum claims, the HAC in 2013 recommended a six-month target.[27] The department then introduced a service standard that 98 per cent of straightforward asylum claims would receive an initial decision within six months, although the Committee later warned that the target would not be met without additional resources and funding.[28] By 2017, the 'relentless' focus on meeting the six month target had pushed some officials to the limit.[29] When combined with difficulties concerning the recruitment and retention of staff, caseworkers had been placed under extreme pressure to deliver the target. This led to the informal quality benchmark for decisions being reduced from 'good' to 'good enough' with threats of disciplinary action for staff who missed the target. Managers acknowledged quality issues with substantive interviews and asylum decisions. Internal quality assurance process found that 25 per cent of decisions were unsatisfactory. Caseworkers responded by significantly increasing the number of claims categorised as 'non-straightforward' (which were not included within the target).

Another concern was that the six-month target did not allow the department to prioritise applications from the most vulnerable people in the system if their claim is 'non-straightforward'. As regards the quality of decisions, managers accepted the need for improvements and that they had moved away from the idea of 'gold plated' decisions to a more realistic aim of 'good' decisions. The Chief Inspector concluded that improvements needed to focus not just on the technical skills of caseworkers, but also on vision, aims and objectives, and the performance standards expected of caseworkers; the 'starkly different perspectives' of caseworkers and managers about the effects of the six-month target suggested that communication between managers and caseworkers needed to be greatly improved. In 2019, the target was abandoned.[30] Instead, the department would reprioritise cases according to need (eg by focusing on late asylum claims made in detention, those frustrating removal, and acute vulnerability cases, such as unaccompanied asylum-seeking children) while also increasing capacity and making process improvements to produce better decisions.

[27] HAC, 'The Work of the Immigration Directorates (October – December 2013)' HC 237 (2013–14) [47]; HAC, 'Asylum' HC 71 (2013–14) [7].

[28] Home Office, 'Government Response to the Seventh Report from the HAC, Session 2013–14 HC 71': *Asylum* (Cm 8769, 2013) 3; HAC, 'The Work of the Immigration Directorates (Q3 2015)' HC 772 (2015–16) [15].

[29] ICIBI, 'An Inspection of Asylum Intake and Casework' (2017).

[30] Letter from Caroline Nokes (Minister of State for Immigration) to Yvette Cooper MP (Chair of the Commons HAC) (19 March 2019); 'Home Office abandons six-month target for asylum claim decisions' *Guardian* (7 May 2019).

The lesson here is that imposing simplistic targets upon an under-resourced process is likely to have dysfunctional consequences. Instead, realistic and appropriate targets agreed upon between managers and staff in which good-quality decisions can be made, and sufficient resources are required. Nonetheless, there will always be competing pressures between quality and processing the incoming caseload. Post-Windrush, the department was reviewing its performance standards and key performance indicators, and thereby generating principles to enable it to understand performance across the immigration system and to its reporting framework.[31]

C. Casework Capacity

The traditional response of stakeholders and representatives has been to criticise the poor quality of initial decision-making and attribute it to a culture of disbelief. But what has not received equal attention is what would be required in both organisational and resource terms to improve the quality of decisions. If better decisions are required, then this presupposes increased better resourcing of caseworking and a move toward professionalising caseworking within government. Cost is a major consideration, and it is difficult to improve immigration casework without additional substantial investment.

In the absence of this and an increasing volume of applications, the department has resorted to digital methods to clear the volume quickly. In 2015, an algorithmic 'streaming tool' was introduced in the highest volume immigration route – visit visas. Applicants were assigned a risk category based on nationality and refusals, which was then used to inform decision-making, but which operated more as a de facto decision-making tool.[32] The streamlining tool was challenged on the basis that it contributed to refusal decisions for certain nationalities; applicants rated as red were more likely to be refused, thereby leading to more refusals. The department preferred to withdraw the tool rather than defend its legality in court.[33] Such criticism is understandable, although it is equally understandable for an under-resourced department to seek out alternative and more efficient ways of processing an enormous caseload quickly so that people wishing to visit get a decision within sufficient time to travel. It is highly likely that the department will wish to develop more digital tools in particular immigration routes, especially in high-volume binary work stream routes.

In areas of judgemental decision-making, there is certainly a strong case for more resources in specific areas. Perhaps the one area most in need of

---

[31] Home Office, 'The Response to the Windrush Lessons Learned Review: A Comprehensive Improvement Plan' (CP 293, 2020) [103].

[32] ICIBI, 'An Inspection of the Home Office's Network Consolidation Programme and the "Onshoring" of Visa Processing and Decision Making to the UK' (2020) [3.15].

[33] R Jennings, 'Government Scraps Immigration "Streaming Tool" before Judicial Review' *Human Rights Law Blog* (6 August 2020).

improvement, professionalisation and resourcing is asylum caseworking.[34] As noted above, basic errors feature in asylum decisions; this is before one gets to more complex issues of asylum law and country conditions. The process has been described as a lottery.[35] Tribunals regularly allow over 40 per cent of appeals, suggesting clear weaknesses in initial casework decisions. Moreover, the sensitive task of making asylum decisions – the careful fact-finding exercise concerning both an applicant's credibility and country of origin information and applying the particular standard of proof, the reasonable degree of likelihood – is likely to exceed the competencies of many caseworkers. Complaints have included the use of aggressive interviewing techniques which applicants, some of whom will be victims of torture, find to be dehumanising and traumatic.[36]

The need for more expert, professional and better qualified caseworkers is obvious and compelling, but the department simply lacks the capacity, capabilities and resources to professionalise asylum decision-making. It is almost inconceivable that the department could, for instance, employ staff at the same level of tribunal judges. A quick look at the wider trends of asylum caseworking indicates why.

Between 2014 and 2020, the number of asylum applications made fluctuated between around 6,000 to 10,000 per quarter. However, the proportion of asylum claims decided within six months declined from 87 per cent in 2014 to 20 per cent in 2020 (Figure 5.2). The asylum backlog – the number of asylum claimants awaiting an initial decision – increased from 4,851 in 2011 to 20,300 in 2016, and then doubled to 42,745 in 2020 (Figure 5.3). An increasing number of asylum applicants had to wait over a year for an initial decision (Figure 5.4). The total asylum work in progress also increased significantly.[37] Asylum backlogs increase asylum support and accommodation costs. The unit cost of processing an asylum claim actually fell from £15,415 in 2010–11 to £9,279 in 2019–20. But, over the same time period, total asylum operations costs increased from £567 million to £956 million. The number of asylum caseworkers has fluctuated significantly from below 300 in 2015–16 to nearly 600 in 2019–20, thereby illustrating the degree of turnover and the limited opportunity for staff to develop expertise.[38] In 2020, amidst the backlog and COVID-19 challenges, the department was exploring the possibility of using a third-party supplier to conduct substantive asylum interviews to increase interview throughput, speed up decisions, and

---

[34] Another area in need of significant improvement is the statelessness determination procedure. See UNHCR, 'Statelessness Determination in the UK' (2020).

[35] 'Asylum offices "in a constant state of crisis", say whistleblowers' *Guardian* (25 December 2017); K Brewer, 'Asylum decision-maker: "It's a lottery"' *BBC News* (8 May 2018).

[36] Freedom from Torture, 'Beyond Belief: How the Home Office Fails Survivors of Torture at the Asylum Interview' (2020).

[37] Total asylum work in progress is the number of cases not concluded at the given point in time, which includes undecided cases, those cases awaiting an appeal outcome and those cases awaiting removal.

[38] 'Caseworking staff' is defined as all staff responsible for delivering the following stages of the asylum operations system: interviewing and deciding asylum operations claims.

reduce outstanding cases.[39] This prompted predictable and legitimate concerns.[40] Overall, without a major injection of resources, the department's inability to operate a trusted asylum decision process is unlikely to change.

Figure 5.2 Asylum applications received and completed within six months

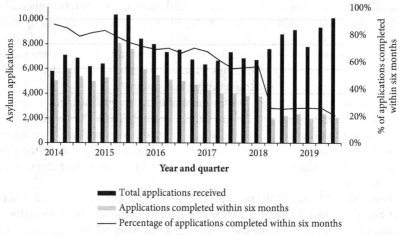

Source: UKVI, 'Transparency data Immigration and protection data' (2020)

Figure 5.3 Asylum work in progress, 2011–20

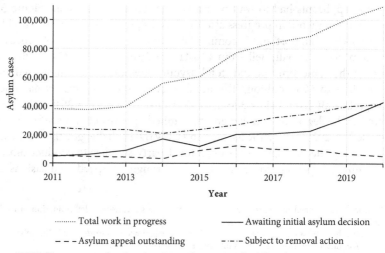

Source: UKVI, 'Transparency data Immigration and protection data' (2020)

[39] Letter from UKVI Asylum Operations, 'Third Party Interviewing External Communication' (22 September 2020).
[40] 'People Seeking Refuge in UK Face "Serious Risk" of Injustice as Home Office Plans More Asylum Outsourcing Despite Warnings' *The Independent* (23 September 2020).

Figure 5.4 Length of time to take initial asylum decisions

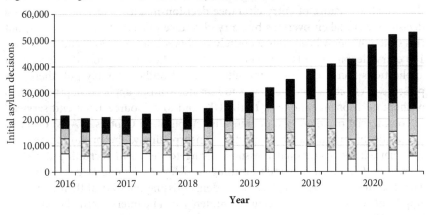

□ Less than 3 months   ▨ 3–6 months   ▨ 6–12 months   ■ 12 months+

Source: UKVI, 'Transparency data Immigration and protection data' (2020)

III. Organising Caseworking

Casework is not just about individual decisions. It also concerns how the whole casework process is managed and organised. Organising casework effectively has some key components.[41] Caseworkers and managers must share a clear purpose. Staff should be properly trained and supported. Realistic performance targets should be applied fairly. Quality assurance must identify and correct wrong decisions and provide timely and constructive feedback to improve future performance. There should be relevant performance measures and data-capture concerning matters such as case progression and outcomes so that managers can evaluate effectiveness. Managers should take a responsive and effective approach when problems or delays arise. Middle-level managers must themselves be supported higher up within the hierarchy and receive sufficient resources. A senior responsible owner should oversee related casework units. Higher-level policy staff need to understand the challenges caseworkers face.

There also needs to be effective coordination and communication between different caseworking units and other parts of the wider system. For instance, decisions to grant asylum should be followed by the conferral of refugee status and leave to remain. Likewise, in-country refusal decisions should be progressed to enforcement units to identify cases suitable for removal action. Set against this framework, successive reports from the Chief Inspector have consistently reiterated the need for the department to improve its effectiveness in managing casework.

---

[41] ICIBI, 'Review and Removal of Immigration, Refugee and Citizenship 'Status' (n 25) [3.8].

There are also cross-cutting organisational issues and changes. One concerns the globalised nature of entry clearance decision-making. For many years, visa decisions were taken overseas by entry clearance officers at overseas posts, but this system has now been almost entirely 'onshored'. Between 2008 and 2018, over 100 entry clearance posts were closed.[42] During the same period, the number of applications increased from 1.95 million to 3.4 million. Simply put, there was pressure to cut costs. The result was to introduce online application processes, to onshore decision-making back to the UK, and to outsource 'front end services' to commercial partners who operate Visa Application Centres (VACs) overseas to handle biometrics and passports.[43] Unsurprisingly, the onshoring process was marked by operational pressures owing to delays in recruiting decision-makers and seasonal demands resulting in delays in issuing large numbers of Tier 4 student applicants with some students missing the start of their courses.[44] Applicants overseas, such as 'genuine students', can be interviewed via video link by the UK caseworker.[45]

A. Modelling Casework Systems

Another issue concerns the best model for organising work within casework teams. Much binary work stream is high-volume 'once and done' casework. By contrast, more specialist and complex casework (such as whether to remove status from people who have lived in the UK for many years) can involve multiple sequential stages.[46] How then is more complex casework best organised? One model is termed 'end-to-end': the same caseworker is responsible for a case from inception to completion and performs all actions throughout. This can enable clear and continuous 'ownership' of cases throughout the process and consistency of approach and prevents any double handling. Alternatively, in a 'stage-by-stage' model, rather than having a single case owner responsible for a case throughout, one caseworker completes one action or stage before passing the case to another caseworker for the next action. This can be more efficient as work is differentiated so that some of it can be done at a lower grade and hence lower cost.

[42] ICIBI, 'Home Office's Network Consolidation Programme' (n 32).
[43] This is a global trend. The global technology and outsourcing company, VFS Global, processes visa applications for over 60 countries including the UK.
[44] ICIBI (n 32) [5.22]–[5.32].
[45] Applicants from 'low risk' countries are less likely to be interviewed.
[46] In particular, casework concerning criminal deportations, the removal of indefinite leave to remain and citizenship, and 'status reviews' of migrants previously granted indefinite leave to remain and refugee status. Legislation and the immigration rules contain a number of mechanisms for removing a person's immigration status, depending on the grounds for doing so. The removal of immigration status is variously described as 'revocation', 'curtailment', 'cancellation', 'cessation' and 'deprivation', but the effect is the same; the person becomes liable to removal from the UK or will be refused entry if outside the UK.

However, there are subtle pros and cons to both models. To illustrate, the Status Review Unit (which reviews the immigration status of refugees, those with indefinite leave to remain, and British nationality) used an end-to-end model, which had been inefficient, with cases taking too long to conclude. By contrast, Criminal Casework (a unit of some 800 officers, which handles criminal deportations) had found that end-to-end led to caseworkers being responsible for too many live cases at the same time, resulting in cases not being monitored effectively and lower throughput. Criminal Casework then switched to a stage-by-stage model. This enabled significantly more effective progressing of cases, although, in some respects, Criminal Casework had failed to establish clear and continuous 'ownership' of deportation cases. Further, it was unclear whether the stage-by-stage model resulted in more prompt removals of foreign national prisoners.[47] Over the years, asylum casework has shifted from a staged model to end-to-end and then back to a staged model. Overall, an end-to-end model is probably most effective for more complex high-consequence decisions, such as asylum. The wider point is that casework units need effective management in light of a changing task environment, with variables such as caseload demand, performance standards, resources, whether a team is dealing with a known population, etc.

The organisation of specific teams must also be accompanied by effective coordination and communication between the teams that handle related casework issues. Given the dominant structure of fragmented silo-based casework, this is a challenge. For instance, despite their commonalities, the three casework units responsible for removing immigration status had for years worked entirely separately from each other without any collaboration, which led to inconsistent approaches. For over two years, two separate casework units (the Status Review Unit and Criminal Casework's Cancellation, Cessation and Revocation unit) adopted very different approaches toward the cessation of refugee status for particular nationals, in particular Somali nationals, and on whether it was safe to return people who previously had been granted refugee status.[48] There had been no 'recognition of this, let alone any analysis of how it was possible given that Home Office decision makers are supposed to draw on the same internally-produced Country Policy and Information Notes'.[49] The lack of communication between two units performing essentially the same task undermined consistent application of the same evidential materials and legal rules. Coordination mechanisms were subsequently introduced.[50] There are other examples of the same set

---

[47] ICIBI (n 25) [3.5]–[3.12]; NAO, 'Managing and Removing Foreign National Offenders' HC 441 (2014–15); ICIBI, 'An Inspection of the Home Office's Management of Non-Detained Foreign National Offenders' (2017).

[48] ICIBI (n 25) [3.4]. Cessations of refugee status concerning Somali nationals by Criminal Casework were significantly higher than those of the Status Review Unit.

[49] ibid.

[50] Home Office, 'The Home Office Response to the Independent Chief Inspector of Border and Immigration, An Inspection of the Review and Removal of Immigration, Refugee and Citizenship 'Status'' (2018) 3.

of rules being applied differently between overseas posts and in-country teams, and the importance of administrative mindset in this respect.[51] Within a largely fragmented siloed system of casework units, there is a constant need to ensure coordination between different parts of the overall system.

Such organisational problems abound, but two overarching issues in particular need highlighting. Should the department adopt a functional or reactive model of casework compared with a proactive model? And what are and should be the links between policy and casework staff?

B. Reactive or Proactive Casework Systems

In general terms, a casework department can adopt either a reactive or a proactive approach. It can organise its casework units under functional lines and consider whether applicants qualify under the rules that apply to the particular type of application. Alternatively, it can organise casework around the position of applicants and consider which application route or status best suits an individual's circumstances. Which approach is adopted has significant implications for how applicants are treated, how caseworkers interact with them, and how user-friendly the process is.

The department's longstanding approach has been a reactive and compartmentalised one: it receives and processes applications under the specific rules that apply to that type of application. Fragmented casework units are grouped around particular immigration categories and rules; caseworkers do not consider someone's whole status or entitlement to enter or remain under the rules. This is reinforced by the department's systems and IT systems which focus on the case number rather than the individual applicant's overall situation. If the applicant is refused, then it is for the refused applicant to decide what to do next. Applicants cannot contact caseworkers to raise queries, and caseworkers are not empowered to give applicants advice and support.

Needless to say, this approach is far from customer-focused. Caseworkers do not guide applicants to help them understand the application process and decide which immigration category or status would be most appropriate for them.[52] Consequently, many applicants (who pay high application fees) are bewildered

---

[51] ICIBI, 'An Inspection of Family Reunion Applications' (2020) [3.11] and [9.16] (overseas family reunion decision-making characterised by taking insufficient account of applicants' circumstances the applicants, readiness to refuse, unreasonable expectations as to supporting evidence, and limited quality assurance. By comparison, in-country decisions showed more awareness of the nature of these applications and greater sensitivity as reflected in grant rates, the quality of decisions, reason-giving, and extent of stakeholder engagement; in-country decisions were better considered and better explained and refusals were harder to challenge and overturn than overseas refusal decisions).

[52] At best, caseworkers will refer applicants to the department's published guidance, which staff themselves struggle to understand or navigate: Windrush Review (n 22) 51. As regards human rights/asylum claims, the Upper Tribunal has emphasised that when a human rights claim is made, but the

by the complexity of the system and find it very difficult to navigate. Unaware of which immigration route is suited to their circumstances, people can make inappropriate applications, which are refused, and then seek to challenge it. This leads to unnecessary work, inefficiencies and confusion for applicants.[53]

The alternative would be to adopt a proactive and person-focused approach. Under this model, caseworkers would help applicants navigate their way through the system and complex rules. When refusing applications, caseworkers could adopt a proactive approach by which they could assist applicants to find their way through the system or be considered under a different, more appropriate category, or give advice as to what type of information and evidence could help strengthen a reapplication.[54] This would involve a considerable shift both organisationally and culturally. To some extent, this has been pursued with regard to the EU Settlement Scheme through the use of automation to collect applicants' official records. But this is only a relatively small in-road. Reorganising caseworking from a functional approach to a more proactive approach would involve considerable reform of the department's processes. Post-Windrush, the department announced the Future Casework initiative, which would more effectively identify appropriate immigration routes based on an applicant's characteristics and have more customer interaction throughout the application process.[55]

C. Casework and Policy

The relationship between policy and casework officials is another organisational relationship that goes to the centre of the link between policy and implementation. Whether policy is actually delivered will depend in large part on the degree

---

claim could also provide the basis for asylum, then the department should draw this to the claimant's attention: *JA v Secretary of State for the Home Department* (human rights claim, serious harm) Nigeria [2021] UKUT 97 (IAC).

[53] For an illustrative exchange of views, see PAC, 'Windrush Generation and the Home Office: Oral Evidence' 17 December 2018 HC 1518 (2017–19): Q 142 Caroline Flint MP: '[W]hat practical steps you are taking to ensure that you test out policies, forms and online services with the very people you are asking to use them, to ensure they are easily understood, and maybe also test them out with your staff so that they feel confident about deploying the policies that are brought down from on high. What are you doing practically to test them and ensure they are fit for purpose?' Sir Philip Rutnam (Permanent Secretary, Home Office): '[W]e recognise it as an issue and we are starting to try to put it at the heart of the way in which we work on policy, and turning it into operations –'. Q 143 Caroline Flint MP: 'Some people would be really shocked at that answer, because to be honest, Sir Philip, why for the last 20 years has that not been the policy of the Home Office?' Sir Philip Rutnam: 'The policy of the Home Office under successive Governments has been to receive applications and process them under the rules that apply to that application. We have not, in truth, had a proactive approach to trying to help people to find their way through the system. That would be my observation.'

[54] D Singh, 'Independent Review of the Home Office Response to the Mandating of DNA Evidence for Immigration Purposes' (2019) [9.4]: 'Decision makers need to be empowered and equipped to make decisions on the person they are considering, not just the application form in front of them.'

[55] Home Office, 'The Response to the Windrush Lessons Learned Review: A Comprehensive Improvement Plan' (CP 293, 2020) [103].

to which policy staff are conscious of what is happening at the level of operational delivery. If policy officials are cocooned away at a higher level and lack an awareness of operational matters, believing they can merely tell operations what to do and assume that it will actually get done, then problems are inevitable. Caseworkers can be presented with situations that policy officials did not foresee or are issued with guidance that is unworkable in practice. Alternatively, if caseworkers have to make complex decisions, but are not given enough time because of processing targets, then this results in dysfunctional behaviours such as siphoning off excess applications into non-straightforward routes to ease the pressure.

In general terms, large operational bodies typically have a sharp formal separation between those who make policy and those who deliver it. In the context of the immigration department, the deep structural and geographical separation between policy and operations has negative effects.[56] There is little cooperation and support between policy and operations, and little assessment of how policy is delivered in practice. Reviews have identified mixed views on the working relationships between policy and operations.[57] Some operational staff have highlighted a disconnect with policy staff and guidance not being suited to the needs of caseworking units, which then leads to local guidance being issued to interpret the policy intent in an operational context. The high degree of turnover amongst both policy and casework staff will also hinder effective communication and cross-working.

There is a clear need for policy officials to have a better understanding of operational practices and to own the end-to-end development and implementation of policies and associated guidance. Likewise, busy operational teams have a role to play in informing policy development and guidance.[58] Further, the experience and needs of applicants should be more prominent. Some measures have improved connections between policy and casework teams. During the introduction of the EU Settlement Scheme, policy staff operational teams sat together to process applications and test the policy intent against operational reality. For instance, the EU policy lead provided advice and support on initial decisions and administrative reviews on a case-by-case basis.[59] There are instances of good working relationships between policy and operational staff, working through issues collaboratively, but the wider separation of policy and operations has negative effects, as evidenced by poor coordination and problematic delivery. There is a need for more joint working to bridge the gap between policy and operations and to facilitate communication and feedback.[60]

---

[56] Institute for Government, 'Managing Migration after Brexit' (2019) 35–37.
[57] Singh, 'Independent Review' (n 54) [9.6]–[9.7].
[58] Alcock, 'Internal Review' (n 5) [51]–[52].
[59] ICIBI, 'An Inspection of the EU Settlement Scheme' (2019) [6.93].
[60] Institute for Government (n 56) 39.

IV. Styles of Immigration Rule-Application and Administrative Culture

We now consider how internal culture and the structuring of the administrative decision system influence how decisions are taken and rules are applied. One way into this dynamic is to examine the familiar problem, present in all rule-based decision systems, of how to decide hard cases. In such cases, applying the rules literally would produce outcomes that undermine the underlying policy and/or result in unfairness for individuals. This poses a choice for the department as to its preferences: should it apply the rules literally even though this means unfairness for the individuals concerned and/or not attaining its policy goals? Or should it use discretion or adopt a legally creative approach by interpreting and applying the rule in a manner that is consonant with its both policy goal and a fair and just outcome?

A. Approaches to Applying Rules

The internal cultures of rule-application adopted by government agencies will reflect different ways of accommodating the tension between formal adherence to the rules and prioritising fairness and policy goals.[61] Kagan has identified four styles of applying rules. A 'legalistic' approach involves rigidly adhering to the rules over meeting policy goals, even though decisions may not make sense or result in unjust outcomes in particular cases. A second approach is 'discretionary judgement', that is, ad hoc departures from the rules to fulfil policy goals or to be responsive to the variety of individual situations that arise. A third approach – 'legal creativity' – involves caseworkers prioritising both adherence to the rules and fulfilling policy goals by creatively interpreting the rules or introducing new sub-rules in response to particular cases. A fourth approach, 'retreatism', is adopted when a government agency values neither adherence to the rules nor meeting policy goals. When adopting this approach, 'officials deal with difficult choices by temporising and accumulating backlogs of undecided cases, or by making endless demands for more information, or by processing cases in a pro forma, ritualistic fashion, with little attention to legal accuracy or consequences.'[62]

The approach adopted will be influenced by various organisational, political and other factors.[63] Organisational factors, such as, resource constraints, a high volume of applications to be decided, and the pressures on caseworkers to process decisions in a timely way, will often induce caseworkers to adopt

---

[61] RA Kagan, 'Varieties of Bureaucratic Justice: Building on Mashaw's Typology' in N Parillo (ed), *Administrative Law From the Inside Out* (Cambridge, Cambridge University Press, 2017) 260–63.

[62] ibid 263.

[63] ibid 263–70.

legalistic or retreatist approaches. The degree of interaction between caseworkers and applicants is also significant. If caseworkers meet applicants face-to-face, they are more likely to become better informed about the nature of the applicant's problems and circumstances. Conversely, making decisions solely on the papers will likely generate a legalistic or retreatist decision-making culture.[64] A third factor is the status of caseworkers, their professionalism, and their work culture. If caseworkers are professionals with the authority to exercise their own judgement, this may enable them to adopt a legally creative approach. There are also political factors. Political messaging from ministers will set the tone in which caseworkers operate. A stringent political approach is likely to incline caseworkers adopting a legalistic approach whereas a legally creative approach may well be perceived as a dangerous aberration that is likely to be punished if uncovered. By contrast, a strict application of the rules will provide caseworkers with a defence if criticised.

B. Immigration Casework

Where does immigration decision-making fit within this analytical framework? Overall, the department's default approach is legalism: the rigid application of the rules has become a policy goal in itself. In general terms, the system adopts an acute degree of legal formalism in which any failure by an applicant to meet all of the strict requirements of the immigration rules will mean refusal irrespective of whether this defeats the purpose of the rules or results in an unjust decision. While the internal culture of immigration decision-making has long been slanted toward legalism, this has been accentuated over recent years. The resource constraints, high caseloads, pressures to meet targets and service standards, the number of decisions caseworkers are expected to make each day, the low status of caseworkers and their lack of professional autonomy, and the checklist nature of decision-making have all contributed to an increasingly rigid rule-based decision-making culture in which a minor error by an applicant is likely to lead to refusal. The pressure to decide a huge volume of applications according to targets severely restricts the ability of staff to exercise judgement and discretion in hard cases. Exercising judgment and being legally creative involves time, energy and initiative.

Caseworkers have an important responsibility in terms of making decisions about people's lives, but they are junior officials closely monitored by managers and under pressure to deliver more decisions in less time. The notion that a caseworker could challenge decisions where rules have produced what she considered to be the wrong outcome has been entirely discouraged.[65] A 'legal creativity' approach is beyond the capabilities and competence of caseworkers and at odds with the department's culture. Indeed, such an approach is not exactly encouraged

---

[64] ibid 265.
[65] Windrush Review (n 22) 106.

at the level of the First-tier Tribunal, but can be undertaken by the Upper Tribunal and the higher courts.[66]

C. Windrush Decision-Making

While a legalistic approach is the default mode, the particular pathologies of immigration have increased the scope for retreatism. Consider Windrush case-work decisions. Members of the Windrush generation applied for 'No Time Limit' endorsements to confirm they had indefinite leave to remain. Caseworkers decided these applications by applying a checklist which undermined the stat-utory right of abode. This resulted in intense unfairness for the individuals concerned. People had their applications refused because they could not provide prescribed documents. Caseworkers required applicants to present multiple addi-tional documents to prove their presence in the UK for each year of residence far beyond what could reasonably be expected. Evidence was assessed against the criminal standard of proof. The inadequate training of caseworkers and organisational pressures on them to meet processing targets meant there was no opportunity for them to exercise judgement.[67] Caseworkers lacked not just the professional ability to exercise judgement, but also an historical understanding of the complex legal position concerning the Windrush generation. They did not know that when Windrush people entered the country over the years 1948–73 the department did not at that time issue official documents or keep consistent records.[68] Caseworkers who might have wanted to raise ethical concerns about decisions were unable to do so.[69]

These features were exacerbated by the lack of personal interaction between caseworkers and applicants and by deciding applications solely on the papers. This is not necessarily a problem when the rules are clear and decisions are

---

[66] 'Discretionary judgement' is present, albeit to a limited degree, when the immigration minister exercises her residual discretion to grant immigration status to a migrant who does not qualify under the rules. Such instances occasionally arise follow media and/or parliamentary pressure or personal lobbying to the immigration minister. This route enables individual cases to receive consideration, but also introduces the influence of political considerations and favours into decision-making. The obvious concern is that ministerial discretion to depart from the rules risks undermining the whole system of rules and their administration and opening up the system to political favours.

[67] In at least one instance, these dysfunctional pressure led one caseworker, fearful of being challenged for not meeting processing targets, to hide the casefile because they wanted to consider more evidence; it would have been quicker and easier for them to refuse the application. Another caseworker said that 'meeting service standards is like a religion'. See Windrush Review (n 22) 104.

[68] Of course, why should caseworkers have known this? As noted above, front-line staff need to work within a structure that provides certainty and prevents staff being overloaded with detail so they can do their job. Yet, senior officials should have been aware of the need for greater knowledge and expertise and acted accordingly to ensure caseworkers were properly equipped.

[69] According to Lucy Moreton, General Secretary of the Immigration Services Union (ISU), 'it was ... all but impossible for the staff compelled to enact these policies to raise those concerns internally': HAC (n 6) [100].

straightforward, as in decisions governed by objective criteria. But it is much more problematic when people have complex immigration histories or where the evidence submitted is inherently fragmentary and an assessment of the applicant's credibility is required.

Windrush illustrates these difficulties. Handling applications on the papers went hand-in-hand with a tick-box approach to making decisions, as opposed to a full and informed evaluation. Consequently, caseworkers did not become aware of the problems facing Windrush applicants because they were not forced to really listen to understand their situations. Nor were caseworkers compelled to consider the impact of their decisions upon applicants or the unfairness of their decisions. Windrush case files showed evidence of poor record-keeping, decision-making by inappropriate checklists, minimal use of discretion, and lengthy and confusing decision letters to applicants that rarely recorded the reasons for decisions.[70] A related complication was that the highly fragmented and silo-based nature of the department's organisational structure was unable to cope with Windrush cases. When an administrative structure is divided into multiple different parts – different casework units, different parts of the enforcement system – then individual officials will only consider the aspect of a person's case that they are concerned with. No single official could consider a person's overall circumstances. The potential for poor decisions was enormous.

Windrush also illustrates how the notion of a policy goal can itself be problematic when caseworkers are motivated by a desire to implement the latest government policy which is inconsistent with long-standing legislation. Windrush casework had been heavily influenced by the hostile environment to reduce migration. However, what had been completely overlooked was that members of the Windrush generation had a statutory right of abode. The result was that the policy goal being pursued by caseworkers was not to give effect to the statutory rights of the Windrush generation, but the more recent ministerial policy of reducing immigration. The result was systemic administrative failure and mass unlawful decision-making.

D. Post-Windrush: Casework Reforms

The department subsequently changed its handling of Windrush decisions. It sought to shift its casework culture from one of heavy compliance to a more customer-focused approach.[71] Caseworkers allowed more time for applicants to submit documents or, when refusing applications, signposted other routes or approved immigration advisers and showed sensitivity and care to ensure

---

[70] Windrush Review (n 22) 106 and 146.
[71] ICIBI, 'A Reinspection into Failed Right of Abode Applications and Referral for Consideration for Enforcement Action' (2019) [3.10] and [6.66]–[6.70].

applicants' circumstances were fully considered. Caseworkers also exercised discretion and focused on getting decisions right first time. The department undertook to improve contact with applicants by, for instance, introducing opportunities for people suspected to be in breach of the rules to have more face-to-face encounters and interactions with caseworkers, and has introduced a mechanism by which caseworkers can raise ethical concerns.[72]

More broadly, the department announced that it wanted to change the culture of decision-making and develop an ethical decision-making model, built on the Civil Service Code and the principles of fairness, rigour and humanity, and a right-first-time approach.[73] This is to be complemented by professionalisation of casework and a 'licence to operate' for caseworkers to raise their skills and capability. These could well be positive developments. There are obvious tensions here between the additional time required for ethical consideration and escalation routes, on the one hand, and meeting administrative processing targets and policy imperatives, on the other. Much will depend on what actually happens in practice.

V. Internal Mechanisms to Enhance Decision Quality

To summarise the discussion so far: casework systems are structured and routinised because they must cope with a high volume; those systems are under-resourced and lack capacity; consequently, the quality of the decisions produced is often variable. One answer is to give applicants legal remedies. We will consider remedies in chapter six, but jumping straight to external legal remedies is to overlook another, equally valid way of ensuring good decisions. Immigration casework is an administrative system. What then can be done within the administrative process itself to assure and improve the quality of casework decisions?

This section considers three mechanisms of internal administrative law that have been introduced over recent years and are likely to develop further: 'minded to refuse' notices; quality assurance of casework operations; and the Chief Caseworker Unit. In each instance, there is at least the potential within the administrative process to ensure better quality casework, although their practical effectiveness at present may well be limited.

A. Minded to Refuse

Casework operates on the basis that applicants bear the burden of advancing their case and relevant evidence. If the evidence presented is insufficient, then

[72] PAC, 'Immigration Enforcement: Oral Evidence', 13 June 2020, HC 407 (2019–21) Q 68 (Tyson Hepple, Director General, Immigration Enforcement, Home Office).
[73] Home Office, 'Response to the Windrush Lessons Learned Review' (n 55) [91]–[95].

the application will be refused and it will be for the refused applicant to decide whether to bring a challenge. Unsurprisingly, there is a high volume of legal challenges. Could inserting a 'minded to refuse' stage prevent disputes from escalating in the first place?

'Minded to refuse' is a familiar enough concept; it encapsulates the well-known *Doody* principles that a person likely to receive a negative decision should first be informed of the gist of the case against them and be allowed to make representations.[74] It promotes both fairness and efficiency. Making better decisions first time can prevent the additional costs and delays of onward challenges.

'Minded to refuse' has also increasingly featured in both political and legal discussion about immigration casework. When the Windrush scandal first broke in 2018, Amber Rudd, then Home Secretary, raised the prospect of introducing a 'minded to refuse' stage for decisions attracting a right of appeal for two reasons. First, to have 'more of a human face for individuals who would otherwise have to go to appeals' and because tribunals often allow appeals when new information is presented for the first time.[75] This was supported by the HAC as an addition to, but not an alternative to, existing appeal rights.[76] In response, the department accepted that 'minded to refuse' would not replace existing appeal rights and commenced a 'minded to refuse' pilot scheme in asylum cases to learn lessons and then possibly scale it up to other immigration decisions if it improved the quality of decision-making whilst enabling timely decisions.[77]

The department has, though, rejected introducing 'minded to refuse' across all immigration routes.[78] The concerns are obvious. Such a change could, in effect, double the amount of administrative resources and time involved in those applications that are currently refused. These costs would arise from segmenting the current single stage of a decision into two stages. In the first stage, caseworkers would consider applications, decide whether they were minded to refuse, and then set out those concerns to the applicant. The second stage would then involve considering the applicant's response and making a final decision with reasons. It is possible that the same caseworker could undertake both stages, but this would seem unlikely given long-established departmental behaviour. Given the already intense pressure from the volume of applications, the inevitable risks are a build-up of backlogs and delays. Alternatively, caseworkers might well be inclined just to refuse without a 'minded to refuse' stage simply to keep on top of the volume and not to give themselves additional work. Either way, this tension again illustrates how administrative pressures and processing continually threaten the department's already limited capacity to deliver high-quality casework.

---

[74] *Doody v Secretary of State for the Home Department* [1994] 1 AC 531 (HL).

[75] HAC, 'Windrush Children: Oral Evidence' 28 April 2018 HC 990 (2017–19) Q 185 (Amber Rudd, Secretary of State for the Home Department).

[76] HAC (n 4) [100].

[77] HAC, 'The Windrush Generation: Government Response to the Committee's Sixth Report of Session 2017–19' HC 1545 (2017–19) 6.

[78] JUSTICE, 'Immigration and Asylum Appeals – A Fresh Look' (2017) 80.

At this point, the courts come into the picture. Given the department's general disinclination toward introducing a 'minded to refuse' stage, the courts have, on occasion, insisted upon it irrespective of onward rights of challenge. A consistent theme is that the courts may hold that procedural fairness requires a 'minded to refuse' stage when judgemental decisions are involved and carry serious consequences for applicants.[79] There is a clear distinction with the largely non-interventionist approach taken by the courts as regards points-based scheme applications.[80] While judicial intervention has been grounded in procedural fairness, there is also a close connection between this and the obligation on decision-makers to take into account all material information considerations when taking decisions.

The leading recent case is *Balajigari*, which concerned refusals under rule 322(5) in 'earnings discrepancy' cases.[81] The Court of Appeal held that where the department was going to refuse indefinite leave to remain because of the applicant's alleged dishonesty, a 'minded to refuse' stage was required.[82] Given that the refusal of leave to remain was functionally equivalent to a removal decision and the seriousness of being labelled as dishonest, 'minded to refuse' was necessary to ensure fair process. A post-decision administrative review was insufficient; reviewers can only consider the evidence before the original decision-maker and not consider new evidence adduced to rebut a finding of dishonesty. Nor were post-refusal representations adequate given the natural tendency of caseworkers to confirm decisions already taken. The minded to refuse process could be undertaken by way of an interview, but in most cases, a written response would be sufficient. The key elements include informing applicants of the concerns about their case and giving them the opportunity to show cause why they should not be refused.

'Minded to refuse' was duly incorporated into operational guidance.[83] The Upper Tribunal then held that where the applicant has a right of appeal, for instance on human rights grounds, the Home Office is not obliged to operate a 'minded to refuse' stage.[84] The tribunal process would fill the gap because, in such

---

[79] The courts have required a 'minded to refuse' stage in relation to: asylum decisions (before a right of appeal was introduced); nationality applications; and deciding the genuineness of marriages of convenience: *R v Secretary of State for the Home Department ex parte Thirukumar and Others* [1989] Imm AR 402 (CA); *R v Secretary of State for the Home Department, ex parte Fayed* [1998] 1 WLR 763 (CA); *Miah v Secretary of State for the Home Department* (interviewer's comments: disclosure: fairness) [2014] UKUT 515 (IAC).

[80] See ch 4 at 79–80.

[81] These cases involved migrants being refused indefinite leave to remain owing to minor tax discrepancies and clerical errors, which the department and HMRC often viewed as falsely inflated earnings in order to meet the minimum financial requirement for ILR.

[82] *Balajigari v Secretary of State for the Home Department* [2019] EWCA Civ 673, [2019] 1 WLR 4647.

[83] Home Office, 'False Representation: Guidance for Caseworkers' (2019) 8–10. 'Minded to refuse' has also been subsequently incorporated into decisions concerning student language cases: Home Office, 'Educational Testing Service (ETS): Casework Instructions' (2020).

[84] *Ashfaq v Secretary of State for the Home Department* (Balajigari: appeals) [2020] UKUT 226 (IAC); *R (Mansoor) v Secretary of State for the Home Department* (Balajigari – effect of judge's decision) [2020] UKUT 126 (IAC).

cases, the applicant has the opportunity to advance her case on appeal. At the same time, over a year later and despite *Balajigari*, many highly skilled migrants subject to rule 322(5) refusals reported not actually having received a 'minded to refuse' letter.[85]

Overall, 'minded to refuse' should in principle improve the quality of casework decisions, although this needs to be subject to empirical evaluation to assess its costs and benefits. It is also highly dependent upon administrative capacity and willingness to operate it effectively.

B. Quality Assurance

Another internal mechanism to improve casework is quality assurance (QA). In general terms, the QA of casework decisions involves three aspects: devising standards to assess the quality of decisions; using those standards to generate data about the quality of decisions; and then taking action to remedy the concerns identified.[86] The department has, at various times, used ad hoc QA methods such as: entry clearance manager (ECM) reviews of refusal decisions;[87] second pair of eyes (the review of a decision by a senior officer before being dispatched to the applicant); and the quality initiative project with the United Nations High Commissioner for Refugees (UNHCR) as regards asylum decision-making.[88] Overall, the quality of such processes, in particular the ECM reviews, have been variable and unsystematic.[89] QA also overlaps with and can merge with other mechanisms, such as: pre-appeal reviews (reviews of new evidence in appealed decisions before the appeal is heard);[90] administrative review; and formal legal remedies, such as tribunal appeals and judicial review.

The department's QA processes have developed over time, following various promptings from the NAO. Initially, QA was focused on asylum decisions, although in practice the department did not do enough to follow-up on QA

[85] Migrant Rights Network, 'Highly Skilled Migrant Indefinite Leave to Remain Refusals & Covid-19 Realities' (2020).

[86] JL Mashaw, *Bureaucratic Justice: Managing Social Security Disability Claims* (New Haven, Yale University Press, 1983) 149–52.

[87] NAO, 'Visa Entry to the United Kingdom: The Entry Clearance Operation' HC 367 (2003–04) [2.24].

[88] Between 2004 and 2008, the Home Office and the UNHCR worked together to improve the quality of initial asylum decisions through the Quality Initiative project. See UNHCR, 'Quality Initiative Project: Key Observations and Recommendations' (2008).

[89] ICIBI, 'Entry Clearance Decision-Making: A Global Review December 2010 – June 2011' (2011) and 'A Re-inspection of the Family Reunion Process, Focusing on Applications Received at the Amman Entry Clearance Decision Making Centre' (2018) [3.5], [4.41] and [4.70].

[90] Pre-appeal reviews were introduced to deal with appeals that had been waiting for hearings for long periods of time. See Letter from Home Office to the Immigration Law Practitioners' Association (30 November 2018).

findings to address the causes of variable-quality decisions.[91] QA was later extended to immigration decisions. QA standards have also developed and been refined over time. The current operational QA strategy is based upon a 'three lines of defence' model which is common throughout both public and private sectors.[92] First line assurance is undertaken by line managers within casework teams. Senior caseworkers review a random sample of two per cent of decisions that are representative of the range of decisions taken. Decisions are assessed against the Decision Quality Framework. Second line assurance is undertaken centrally by the UKVI Central Operations Assurance Team (COAT).[93] This team is separate from specific casework teams. It undertakes routine sampling of cases to 'check the checker' and thematic targeted assurance reviews. Overall, it focuses upon assessments of first-line assurance, targeted assurance reviews on decision quality by local casework units, and assurance statements for each work area. COAT also encourages a culture of continuous improvement. At each level, there are upwards reporting requirements to local assurance boards to monitor results and then to higher level Joint Executive Board and the Risk and Assurance Committee. Third line assurance is undertaken by external agencies: the Government Internal Audit Agency; the Chief Inspector; and the NAO.

In 2017, UKVI implemented a new decision quality framework (DQF) to improve decision quality through its QA programme (Table 5.1).[94] The aim is to ensure initial immigration decisions and administrative reviews are taken to specified standards in line with guidance, legislation and court judgments, to identify and address areas of concern and poor practice, and to highlight and share good practice.[95] The DQF informs first- and second-line assurance, and structures the QA process to ensure consistency. It also provides clear expectations for

[91] NAO, 'Improving the Speed and Quality of Asylum Decisions' HC 535 (2003–04) [4.12]–[4.24] and 'Management of Asylum Applications by the UK Border Agency' HC 124 (2008–09) [2.11]–[2.13].

[92] Under this widely used general model, first-line assurance is undertaken within business operational areas. Second-line assurance is associated with oversight of management activity; it is separate from those responsible for delivery, but not independent of the organisation's management chain. Third-line assurance is independent, often external, and undertakes more objective assurance focused on the role of internal audit. See generally HM Treasury, 'Assurance Frameworks' (2012); NAO, 'Recent Developments in Government Internal Audit and Assurance' (2013).

[93] COAT is located within UKVI's Strategy, Transformation and Performance directorate. See Figure 5.1.

[94] Until 2013, QA of asylum decisions used a percentage-based auditing framework which assessed whether decisions complied with relevant policies, procedures and case law. In 2013, a more comprehensive QA method required assessors to assess the impact of any errors. Each sampled decision was rated as 'satisfactory', 'weak' or 'fail'. Where decisions only contained minor errors which had little or no impact on the decision, these decisions were considered to be satisfactory, though that did not mean that all cases judged weak or fail contained an incorrect decision – many will have contained the correct decision, but the supporting reasoning was not robust. In 2015, further changes were made: satisfactory decisions containing less than 20% of minor errors were scored as high/DQ1 while those satisfactory decisions containing more than 20% of minor errors were scored as moderate/DQ2.

[95] UKVI, 'Operational Assurance Strategy' (2017).

caseworkers, and a formal process for delivering feedback for identifying training and/or development needs and to identify whether quality is measurably improving. Senior caseworkers review a random sample of two per cent of decisions prior to the decision letter being served. Within each casework unit, there is an assurance lead responsible for ensuring first-line assurance results are monitored

Table 5.1 UKVI Central Operations Assurance Team, Decision Quality Framework[96]

Decision Quality Framework: Error Markings	Decision Quality Framework: Final Assurance Ratings
Correct: The consideration is fully justified and adheres to legislation, policy and guidance – there are no risks to the customer, Home Office or the UK	**DQ1** • Decision to grant or refuse is correct, with sufficient evidence available, provided, gathered; and • Decision made in accordance with current rules, legislation, case law, policy and guidance/standards; and • Decision contains fewer than 20% minor errors and no significant or fail errors; and • No apparent risks to the customer, Home Office or the UK.
Minor: An error which does not detract from the consideration and would not affect the outcome of the decision and should be quickly rectified – there are no apparent risks/negative impact on the customer, Home Office or the UK	**DQ2** • Decision to grant or refuse is correct, with sufficient evidence available, provided, and gathered; and • No apparent risks to the customer, Home Office or the UK; and • Decision contains 20% or more minor errors which require correction and no significant or fail errors.
Significant: An error which detracts from the quality of the decision or casts doubt on the outcome of the decision and requires attention to address serious weaknesses or omissions – there are potential risks to the customer, Home office or the UK	**DQ3** • Decision to grant or refuse is reasonable (based on the evidence presented); but • There is one or more significant error(s) which without corrections or re-work might present risks to the customer, Home Office or the UK.

(continued)

[96] Supplied by the UKVI Central Operations Assurance Team.

Table 5.1 *(Continued)*

Decision Quality Framework: Error Markings	Decision Quality Framework: Final Assurance Ratings
Fail: An error which not only detracts from the consideration but also affects the decision such that the outcome cannot necessarily be relied upon and immediate attention is required to address the critical failure(s) – there are significant risks/negative impacts to the customer, Home Office or the UK as a result of this error.	**DQ4** • Decision to grant or refuse is reasonable (based on the evidence presented); but • There are one or more fail errors which means that little confidence can be placed in the validity of the consideration; and/or • There are potential or evident risks to the customer, the Home Office or the UK. **DQ5** • Decision to grant or refuse is wrong; and • There are one or more fail errors which means that little confidence can be placed in the validity of the consideration; and/or • There are potential or evident risks to the customer, the Home Office or the UK.

and analysed to understand strengths and weaknesses and to ensure findings drive improvements, for convening quarterly boards, for monitoring and reporting actions against identified issues and recommendations, and for liaising with and facilitating second line assurance. Following QA assessments, caseworkers receive feedback on their decisions and issues or errors are fed back to the team and included in training material. Second-line assurance by COAT is separate from casework units and seeks to add value by understanding end-to-end work streams and cross-cutting impacts, sharing best practice and consistency of approach, and conducting deep dives into high-risk areas.

Figure 5.5 shows the proportion of initial asylum decisions assessed through QA as satisfactory and unsatisfactory between 2013 and 2019. The sample size ranged between two and five per cent. Given changes in QA assessment methods, it is not possible to compare directly all the data. Nonetheless, the data presents QA assessments under the method used at the time. First-line assurance was complemented by second-line assurance in 2017. The proportion of asylum decisions assessed as satisfactory has varied; it was 55 per cent in 2014–15 and only exceeded 80 per cent in 2016–17, before declining.

How then does the QA system measure up? The process is important in terms of monitoring and potentially raising the quality of decisions, but it has significant limitations. The effectiveness of first-line assurance by a manager and not an independent officer is likely to be influenced by the nature of the

Figure 5.5 Asylum decision quality assurance outcomes, 2013–19[97]

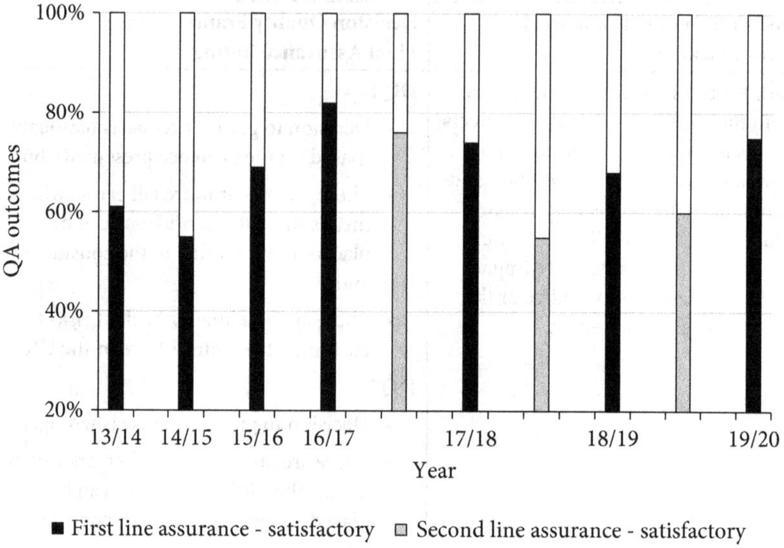

First line assurance - satisfactory   □ Second line assurance - satisfactory

continuing relationship between caseworker and manager. Much also depends upon how rigorously the DQF is applied in practice and the available capacity to undertake effective QA. The two per cent sample size is unlikely to provide a sufficient level of assurance or to identify problematic issues. The two per cent sample was introduced in 2014 as the default, but can be varied depending on resources and priorities. Nonetheless, it has been applied irrespective of the complexity of decisions or the risks involved. QA is the only mechanism that regularly considers the quality of initial positive decisions; external administrative law remedies, such as tribunal appeals and individual judicial, are wholly centred upon refusal decisions. However, the two per cent sample clearly skews the focus of QA. If 95 per cent settlement decisions are granted, then a two per cent QA sample will focus largely upon assessing positive decisions. Accordingly, QA focuses on the most common outcomes, rather than those where the risk of an incorrect decision is higher, or the potential impact greater.[98]

Another indicator of the limited effectiveness of the implementation of the QA strategy is the number of inspection reports that have flagged up concerns with

[97] Source: Home Office, 'Immigration and Protection UKVI Transparency Data Q2 2020' (27 August 2020) table ADQ_01A: The Decision Quality percentage of Decisions Sampled. In this figure, the data for 2015–16 aggregates the High/DQ1 and Moderate/DQ2 scores to indicate those decisions assessed as satisfactory. The changes in assessment methods mean that it is not possible directly to compare all the data since 2010.

[98] NAO, 'Handling of the Windrush Situation' HC 1622 (2017–19) [3.09]–[3.10].

casework when such concerns should have been identified through first or second line QA checks. In 2017, the Chief Inspector told the HAC:

> Getting decisions right, particularly visa decisions, and having the right sort of assurance processes in place to make sure that those decisions have been made correctly is challenging because of the volumes, often because there are staffing gaps or there are staff in post who have not had the training they require or have not had the assurance processes behind them to give the support and feedback that they might need ... the point I have stressed in a number of reports, and certainly stressed to the Department, is the issue of first-line supervision, the first-line manager whose role is to provide assurance, some level of checking, but also to coach and provide feedback to individual staff in order to improve overall decision-making. I think there has been a lot of pressure on those first-line managers to get through the volumes and so there is less capacity to provide that support, challenge, assurance function that is needed. That is an area where I have repeatedly said that more needs to be done.[99]

A glance back at Figure 5.5 confirms the point. Second-line assurance of the first-line assurance (checking the checker) shows that the quality of the latter is itself variable. For the years 2017–18 and 2018–19, second line assurance found that only 55 per cent and 60 per cent respectively of first-line assurance checks were satisfactory. In other words, 45 per cent and 40 per cent of first-line assurance checks were unsatisfactory. Having poor-quality initial decisions being subject to poor-quality first-line assurance is inefficient and illustrates the scale of the challenge. Failing to get the first-line QA right not only means wrong decisions not being identified and corrected; it also means that caseworkers' understanding and performance does not improve because of the lack of timely and constructive feedback.[100]

Other limitations are evident. First-line QA has often sampled below the required two per cent of decisions.[101] On some occasions, first-line QA has been suspended or downgraded to 'light touch reviews' because of acute staffing shortages.[102] Overseas assurance has often been ineffective.[103] Even if the two per cent

---

[99] HAC, 'Oral Evidence: Home Office Delivery of Brexit: Immigration', 29 November 2017, HC 421 (2017–19) Q 247 and Q 264 (David Bolt, ICIBI). In 2018, a senior official sought to reassure the PAC, 'Windrush Generation and the Home Office: Oral Evidence', 17 December 2018, HC 1518 (2017–19) Q 138 (Shona Dunn, Second Permanent Secretary, Home Office) that the 2017 assurance strategy was 'making a difference in terms of first and second line of defence assurance of decision making. It is focusing on the outcome of the decisions, not just the process steps. It is looking specifically at questions such as feedback loops, governance and skills – whether different casework teams have the sorts of skills necessary to deliver the sorts of decisions they are being asked to deliver, to the quality that they are being asked to deliver them.' Given the above evidence, this comment came across more as a senior official trying to put the best gloss on a process that has its weaknesses.

[100] ICIBI, 'Entry Clearance Processing Operations in Croydon and Istanbul' (2017) [3.20].

[101] ICIBI (n 12) [2.9] and [6.3]. See also Singh (n 54) [9.3]: 'We also found some units were selecting the two per cent for first line assurance by nationality. We did not see any specific strategy or related equality impact assessment concerning this practice.'

[102] ICIBI, 'Entry Clearance Processing Operations in Croydon and Istanbul' (n 100) [6.14]–[6.16]; ICIBI, 'An Inspection of Administrative Reviews' (2020) [3.27] and [7.135].

[103] ICIBI, 'An Inspection of Family Reunion Applications' (2016) [6.61].

sample is used, another issue concerns the 'span of control', that is, the ratio between a manager and the number of caseworkers; a higher ratio means more work for the manager. Similarly, a high intake of new staff (which are checked on 100 per cent of all decisions) will reduce capacity to undertake the two per cent assurance of other caseworkers.[104]

The department itself has described its QA processes as being 'to a fair extent effective' while recognising that 'more could be done to improve and strengthen the approach'.[105] First, there needed to be a greater focus on organisational performance. QA (especially at the first line) had been heavily focused on the performance of individual caseworkers rather than identifying areas of potential concern or weakness at the unit or organisational level. Second, there needed to be more focus on outcomes. QA had been focused too much on the process of assessing cases and not enough on taking effective action to address concerns identified or on wider assurance/performance-management practices that could improve casework. A persistent theme has been limited action taken to address QA findings about weak decisions.[106] That this concern, first expressed by the NAO in 2004, was still being made by the department in 2017 highlights the scale of the change required and how making real improvements to casework extends far into organisational, resource and cultural matters.[107] Third, there needed to be improved governance and partnership. The link between first- and second-line assurance and also policy, training and improvement teams had been inconsistent. Fourth, more clarity between first- and second-line assurance was required. Second-line assurance frequently duplicated first-line assurance and the lines of responsibility for managing risk and quality have sometimes been blurred. More effective use of second-line assurance was required to add value and increase capacity for targeted assurance work. The 2017 strategy sought to correct this through basing QA on agreed principles. QA would be: proportionate and risk-based avoiding both under- and over-assurance; integrated and holistic; timely; understood by caseworkers; robust; transparent; and consistent. It also introduced formal reporting requirements. Nonetheless, it is not apparent that the weaknesses identified in 2017 have been adequately resolved.

The effectiveness of QA also varies in light of the decision type. Binary work stream decisions are more suited to QA assessment; the hard-edged decision criteria make it easier for reviewers to identify shortcomings. By contrast, the Chief Inspector has recommended that credibility-based decisions (eg asylum

---

[104] Newly recruited and trained caseworkers are mentored during which time, 100% of their decisions are checked. Once a decision-maker consistently meets the required standard, then the number of checks falls to the two per cent random sampling.

[105] UKVI, 'Operational Assurance Strategy' (n 95) 3.

[106] See, eg, ICIBI, *A Re-inspection of the Tier 4 Curtailment Process* (2017) [2.24] (failure to refer to most appropriate immigration rule in significant proportion of sampled decision letters suggested QA checks were not yet rigorous enough).

[107] NAO, above n 91.

and domestic violence victims) receive enhanced QA beyond the two per cent sample size or more in-depth qualitative reviews.[108] But this has been rejected for the usual reasons (disproportionate use of resources; delay).[109] Another feature is that QA operates in the context of the department's functional fragmented structure; this is likely to hinder the identification of common issues across different casework teams and is expected to reinforce the problems. The different approaches taken toward the cessation of refugee status by the Status Review Unit and Criminal Casework is illustrative: the adoption of a different approach was only identified by the Chief Inspector and not first- or second-line assurance. Another point is that QA outcomes are spreadsheet-based scores on individual caseworkers to conduct trend analysis. Such information will have both the pros and cons of quantitative information; it may provide a wider spread of data, but at a thinner qualitative depth.

Windrush highlighted other gaps and shortcomings. QA had not identified flawed Windrush decision processes and outcomes. It had not been at all geared towards identifying or counteracting such situations, but instead had been narrowly focused on formal quality and process checks on decisions, as opposed to decision outcomes and impacts.[110] Nor did QA take full account of the complexity of decisions or the impact of different decisions or routinely analyse recurring issues. More generally, the whole episode had highlighted the department's default mode of adopting inward-looking, procedural and reactive measures that focused on tackling operational decisions at the end of the system and dealing with symptoms, not underlying causes.

The department's 2021 post-Windrush assurance strategy introduced important changes.[111] The blanket two per cent sampling which operated regardless of the complexity and risk levels in any casework stream was replaced by a more risk-based approach dependent upon the level of variability involved in decision-making. In essence, this means smaller sample sizes for areas of straightforward casework based on simple and easy-to-follow rules and in which previous QA checks have established that decision outcomes are correct and of high quality. The rationale was that the two per cent sampling had, in some circumstances, placed an unnecessary burden on high-volume/low-risk areas at the expense of sampling more high-risk decision areas. Future sampling would then vary in light of: the complexity of decision-making; the accuracy and robustness of first line assurance; previous quality scores; and appeal/administrative review win rates. Varying the sample size in accordance with these factors make sense if it enables more efficient, focused and meaningful assurance where it is needed. Another change was that first- and second-line assurance would check whether caseworkers sought support

---

[108] ICIBI, *An Inspection of Administrative Reviews* (2020) [4.1].

[109] Home Office, *The Home Office Response to the Independent Chief Inspector of Borders and Immigration's report: An Inspection of Administrative Reviews* (2020) [1.17].

[110] NAO, *Handling of the Windrush Situation* HC 1622 (2017–2019) [3.9].

[111] UKVI, *Assurance Strategy 2021* (2021).

in complex cases and use discretion based on the new ethical decision-making framework. A related aspect is the role of COAT in providing assurance statements on casework teams to ensure that first-line assurance is rigorous and consistent, that results are analysed and monitored, have clear governance arrangements, and that leaders promote continuous improvement. The 2021 assurance strategy also beefed up second-line targeted assurance reviews. These are commissioned internally by COAT and involve in-depth case-sampling. Significant weaknesses will then be reported upwards and accompanied by recommendations to alleviate or eradicate the underlying causes and embed a learning culture.

Overall, QA remains work in progress; it is likely to have improved casework, but there is significant scope for improvement. A more effective QA process would be better resourced, more able to identify wider thematic issues and respond quickly to them, and do more to improve overall organisational performance. The 2021 assurance strategy suggests that this is the course of direction and it highlights the importance of embedding a culture of continuous improvement, although it is too soon to say how it is working in practice. One gets a sense of the best of intentions, but likely implementation challenges driven by short-term pressures. We return to these issues in chapter six.

C. Chief Caseworker Unit

The third internal means of improving caseworking is by having senior dedicated casework leadership. Another post-Windrush initiative, the Chief Caseworker Unit (CCU) was established to improve caseworking expertise and ensure that caseworkers could raise concerns or request specialist guidance.[112] The unit is comprised of a cadre of experienced senior caseworkers. The focus is to enhance decision-making capability and to provide caseworkers with a clear escalation route to address concerns or to provide specialist guidance. The CCU also promotes the better exercise of discretion, explores systemic issues across UKVI, advises on particularly complex cases, and focuses upon building bridges between policy and operations so that the latter can play a greater role in the design and development of policy. The wider purpose is to establish a casework profession with a more customer-focused approach. The CCU is central to the department's efforts to professionalise casework and introduce externally validated accreditation and continuous development.[113] The CCU has also undertaken independent reviews of Windrush refusals, identifying gaps in published guidance and patterns or issues emerging from casework. Other planned work includes improving decisions in asylum, refused case management and family and human

[112] HAC, *The Windrush Generation: Government Response to the Committee's Sixth Report of Session 2017–19*, HC 1545 (2017–19) 6; *Hansard*, HC Deb, cW (21 December 2018) (Caroline Nokes MP, Minister of State for Immigration); ICIBI, *Administrative Reviews* above n 108 [3.28].
[113] HAC, *Government Response* above n 112, 6.

rights applications, and developing a communication campaign to help staff understand the effect their decisions have on people's lives.[114]

In its response to the Windrush Review, the department announced other changes to the CCU as part of the wider move to change the culture of decision-making.[115] The CCU structure would be established across UKVI by having a group of chief caseworkers to improve the consistency, quality and sustainability of decision-making. The CCU has also introduced an internal 'Face Behind the Case' campaign and training to encourage caseworkers to see applicants as people. Another initiative is a 'policy superuser network' to identify policies that do not reflect operational reality and could have unintended consequences for applicants, and to provide better support for casework teams when receiving and implementing policy and guidance changes. It will work to ensure that policies reflect operational reality, support effective decision-making and, crucially, are developed with the customer at the centre. The CCU will also undertake early warning reviews in response to systemic issues relating to long-standing or cross-cutting matters concerning policy, systems, or processes.[116] A UKVI Professionalisation Hub has also been introduced to professionalise caseworkers by ensuring they have the skills and capability to do the job.

The CCU is potentially a positive development in terms of improving casework quality, although concerns have been raised that it is just a short-term fix rather than a permanent fixture.[117] Ideally, it would become established as an independent statutory office thereby giving it a degree of permanence. The CCU should also exercise a leadership role in raising the profile and professionalisation of caseworking within the department as well as monitoring its quality. Much will depend upon resourcing and the personal standing and ability of chief caseworkers to exert influence internally.

In this respect, the experience of the chief adjudication officer (CAO) in the social security context is relevant. The CAO was established in the 1980s as a statutory body to monitor and review benefits adjudication. Social security adjudication officers were the first tier of the independent statutory authorities that adjudicated claims. There was an internal separation of powers between individual decision-making and policy-making. Importantly, there was a culture of *adjudication*, in the sense of deliberating upon claims, rather than straightforward processing. The CAO had advisory and monitoring roles, reported publicly on adjudication standards, and publicly evaluated the standards and quality of decisions.[118]

---

[114] *Windrush Review*, above n 22, 129.

[115] Home Office, *Response to the Windrush Lessons Learned Review*, above n 55 [107]–[110].

[116] UKVI, *Assurance Strategy 2021*, above n 111, 13.

[117] *Windrush Review*, above n 22, 129.

[118] AW Bradley, 'Recent Reform of Social Security Adjudication in Great Britain' (1985) 26 *Les Cahiers de Droit* 403; R Sainsbury, 'The Social Security Chief Adjudication Officer: the First Four Years' [1989] *PL* 323; J Baldwin, N Wikeley, and R Young, *Judging Social Security: The Adjudication of Claims for Benefit in Britain* (Oxford, Clarendon Press, 1992) 36–37; N Warren, 'The Adjudication Gap – A Discussion Document' (2006) 13 *Journal of Social Security Law* 110.

Over time, the post was downgraded and then abolished as the culture of benefit decision-making shifted away from adjudication to administrative processing and responsibility for benefit decisions was transferred to the Secretary of State.[119] The monitoring function was only partially reintroduced in the 2000s through the DWP's Decision-Making and Appeals Standards Committee and an annual report by the President of Social Security Tribunals.[120] However, neither of these formal reporting mechanisms had much, if any, real influence in raising the quality of benefit decisions. There were difficulties in using the monitoring reports effectively as a basis for instrumental reforms and improvements. Eventually, both mechanisms fell away. Concerns over the variable quality of benefit decisions are now as extensive as those concerning immigration casework.[121]

The story is simultaneously discouraging and instructive. The most effective internal means of raising the quality of casework is likely to be through dedicated proactive leadership and expertise within the department. Having senior experienced caseworkers on hand, working closely with casework teams and providing practical advice and assistance is likely to be significantly more effective than the production of another formal external report which diagnoses the same problems, but has limited practical impact. If the CCU receives support internally and comes to gain an important internal reputation within and across casework teams, it is likely to play an increasing role in raising the quality of casework decision-making, its culture and *esprit de corps*, and transform casework into more of a professional role within the department. As with QA, there is much work to be done. What will also be required is an evaluation of the effectiveness of both QA and the CCU in raising the quality of casework.

VI. Conclusion

As a core administrative function, casework is of considerable importance in terms of administering policy and making correct decisions on people's immigration status. The department has reasonable competence in terms of setting up and operating systems to process casework efficiently, but there are acute limits to its organisational competence in terms of quality. Binary work streams enable efficient processing, but the department has failed properly to resource more complex

---

[119] Social Security Act 1998, s 1; N Wikeley, 'Burying Bell: Managing the Judicialisation of Social Security Tribunals' (2000) 63 *MLR* 475, 479–480.

[120] See, eg, DWP, *Decision Making Standards Committee Annual Report 2009–2010* (2010); President's Report, *Report by the President of the Social Entitlement Chamber of the First-tier Tribunal on the Standards of Decision-making by the Secretary of State and Child Maintenance and Enforcement Commissioner 2009–10* (2010).

[121] R Thomas and J Tomlinson, 'A Different Tale of Judicial Power: Administrative Review as a Problematic Response to the Judicialisation of Tribunals' [2019] *PL* 537, 545–555.

casework – as evidenced by asylum and Windrush casework. A significant proportion of casework is substandard and results in poorly reasoned decisions and additional costs and delays through onward challenges. This has resulted in persistent and justified criticism of the quality of casework decisions and dysfunctional administrative behaviour. Limited organisational capacity and competence is reflected in poorly reasoned casework decisions, which in turn weakens administrative legitimacy.[122]

Processing targets have been deemed necessary to keep on top of the incoming volumes of applications, but they have clear adverse effects in terms of quality, which, as the next chapter suggests, shifts significant costs elsewhere in the wider system. On the other hand, other internal mechanisms, such as 'minded to refuse', the QA system and the CCU are potentially positive developments. These mechanisms reflect the department's implicit acceptance of the need to address the limits of its casework capacity. Yet, their basic weakness is that they are almost entirely reliant upon the same underlying casework processes which they are designed to improve. Beyond this, there is enormous amount of work to be undertaken to professionalise casework, improve training and mentoring, address the causes of high staff turnover, have more emphasis upon good quality and ethical decisions, improve QA processes and feedback loops, and learn from poor decisions.

Ultimately, the weaknesses of immigration casework can only be resolved by significant reforms designed to strengthen the quality and capacity of this administrative process, and this requires investment. We will return to these issues, but first we need to consider how refused applicants can challenge casework decisions.

---

[122] See generally JL Mashaw, 'Public Reason and Administrative Legitimacy' in J Bell, M Elliott, JNE Varuhas, and P Murray (eds), *Public Law Adjudication in Common Law Systems: Process and Substance: Process and Substance* (Oxford, Hart Publishing, 2016).

6

Redress and Legal Challenges

Once initial casework decisions have been taken, the question arises as to how affected individuals can challenge refusal decisions. In chronological terms, much – though not all – of the business of challenging decisions comes between initial casework and enforcement. Indeed, given the volumes, challenging decisions operates as an extension of the casework process. In light of the resources devoted to challenges – deciding administrative reviews and defending and responding to appeals and judicial reviews – it also qualifies as a core area of government activity by itself. Onward challenges are one point at which internal and external approaches to administrative law meet.

In a deeply embedded sense, administrative law is conventionally understood by lawyers as fundamentally about providing claimants with external legal remedies against administration. How could it be otherwise? The department often makes wrong decisions with huge adverse consequences for those concerned. Given the wider context of administrative governance, the whole pattern of people's everyday lives is so interwoven with administrative decision-making that one error or problem will often have significant repercussions for many other aspects of a person's life, especially when the decision concerns a person's immigration status. Administrative processing is seen as inherently inferior to judicial adjudication with its emphasis on participation, fair process and independent judges. This applies even more so as regards the immigration department, which some claimants and lawyers see as dysfunctional given its reputation of routine errors and mistakes, a culture of disbelief and its underlying policy agenda.

In other systems such as tax and benefits, the general departmental attitude is to accept legal challenges as a legitimate way of correcting initial decisions. By contrast, the Home Office has often viewed judicial remedies as open to abuse and an impediment to controlling immigration. In this context, lawyers will naturally incline towards the view that only judicial remedies before independent judges protected from executive interference will suffice. This is reinforced by two of the legal models constituting immigration administration: the administrative justice and human rights models. The institutional focus of both is upon external judicial remedies, whether the focus is upon ensuring fair process and correct decisions about immigration status or, over and above this, protecting migrants as rights-bearing individuals against the state.

The question then arises as to how the system of onward challenges is organised and its effectiveness. This chapter considers the principal means of redress: administrative reviews; tribunal appeals; and 'individual' judicial reviews. Other grievance routes, such as complaints and MP casework, are considered later on.[1] For convenience, the discussion here is organised along institutional lines, although the messy reality is that a single case can go through various systems both concurrently or consecutively and on multiple occasions. As the discussion unfolds, it becomes apparent that considering the effectiveness of these remedies involves identifying the underlying model of administrative law upon which they are predicated and its strengths and weaknesses. This in turn raises the question as to whether there is an alternative model of administrative law grounded upon a complementary and proactive means of detecting, preventing and correcting errors. As Birch Bayh once put it, 'you shouldn't have to sue somebody to get justice. It ought to come through administrative process'. If an alternative model of administrative law is to exist, what would be its conceptual structure? And how could it work in practice? But this is to get ahead of ourselves. It is first necessary to consider briefly the development of redress mechanisms and then evaluate their operation and effectiveness.

I. The Development of Immigration Administrative Law Remedies

The overall system of external administrative law remedies for immigration decisions has been subject to many changes. The principal remedy has been appeals to the dedicated immigration tribunal. Appeals were first introduced in 1971 on the basis that it was fundamentally wrong and inconsistent with the rule of law that decisions affecting a person's whole future should be vested solely in administrative officers without any appeal.[2] The existence of appeals are largely justified in terms of judicial control, participation, fairness and legality. The creation of tribunal appeals is also a recognition of the department's limited competence for making good-quality casework decisions and the need consequent need for important decisions to be retaken on appeal. Reduced casework capacity leads to more appeals. There is also scope for frivolous and vexatious appeals, as well as legitimate challenges.

As pressures on the system grew, it proved to be difficult to contain cases at the tribunal level. Challenges increasingly proceeded to the higher courts by way of both appeal from the tribunal and judicial review of both tribunal decisions and initial decisions.[3] In response to increased volumes, successive governments have

---

[1] See ch 9.

[2] Home Office, 'Report of the Committee on Immigration Appeals' (Cmnd 3387, 1967); Immigration Act 1971.

[3] cf *R v Immigration Appeal Tribunal, ex p Shah* [1998] 4 All ER 30, 48 (CA) (Staughton LJ): 'The tension between humanitarian concern on the one hand and self-interest on the other has produced in this country the whole apparatus of immigration control, with immigration officers, adjudicators,

sought to limit onward appeal rights and judicial review. The Labour Government in 2004 failed in its blunt attempt to abolish immigration judicial reviews.[4] In 2010, the tribunal was transferred into the First-tier and Upper Tribunal structure.[5] But ministerial frustration remained. In 2013, Conservative Home Secretary Theresa May described the appeals process as 'a never-ending game of snakes and ladders' open to exploitation by foreign criminals, immigrants and their lawyers to delay the enforcement of immigration law.[6] Appeal rights were significantly restricted by the Immigration Act 2014. Previously appealable decisions could now be challenged by way of administrative review and judicial review.[7] In broad sweep, the tribunal system process has changed from a system in which many refusal decisions attracted a right of appeal on general grounds of both law and fact to one in which appeals can only be brought on human rights and asylum grounds. In turn, administrative review has largely replaced appeals as a quicker and cheaper method of checking decisions. Judicial review remains a frequently used remedy.

So much for history; what of the effectiveness of such remedies? Tribunal appeals and judicial review are the established judicial remedies, but administrative review is now the first step on the redress ladder. We therefore start with administrative review and then consider appeals and judicial review.

II. Administrative Review of Administrative Decisions

Administrative review is a hybrid of internal quality assurance and a redress mechanism. Refused applicants can request a review of initial refusal decisions on the basis that it contained a caseworking error. Performed correctly, administrative review can enable higher-level oversight of the quality of decision-making and the protection of individual legal rights. It can also provide a more efficient and user-friendly mechanism than that provided by more legalistic remedies. A legal model that situates claimants and administration as adversaries is appropriate in many cases, but not all. A swift internal review has considerable advantages in terms of ease, efficiency, and providing a better way to resolve matters informally without the cost and delay of formal legal hearings.[8] For instance, a student visa

---

appeal tribunals, judicial review and a greater burden on the Civil Division of the Court of Appeal than any other single topic.'

[4] Asylum and Immigration (Treatment of Claimants etc) Act 2004.

[5] Tribunals, Courts and Enforcement Act 2007.

[6] Theresa May, Home Secretary, speech at the Conservative Party conference, Manchester, available at www.ukpol.co.uk/theresa-may-2013-speech-to-conservative-party-conference.

[7] There have always been some immigration decisions that do not attract a right of appeal. Some types of decisions, such as the curtailment of leave to remain, cannot be challenged through administrative review.

[8] In the social security context, see R Sainsbury, 'Internal Reviews and the Weakening of Social Security Claimants' Rights of Appeal' in G Richardson and H Genn (eds), *Administrative Law & Government Action* (Oxford, Oxford University Press, 1994); R Thomas and J Tomlinson, 'A Different Tale of Judicial Power: Administrative Review as a Problematic Response to the Judicialisation of Tribunals' [2019] *PL* 537, 545–52.

appeal may take months to be heard – and conclude long after the start of the academic year – whereas an administrative review can take 15 days. By filtering out clearly wrong decisions, administrative review can reduce unnecessary appeals and the associated costs and delays.

Unsurprisingly, lawyers, even if not deeply sceptical of the department, are culturally predisposed toward viewing administrative review as inadequate. It has none of the legitimising symbols, rituals, independence or substance of the judicial process. There are no hearings with oral evidence and submissions, no overriding objective to ensure cases are handled justly and fairly,[9] and no onward right of appeal. Reasons are given, although their quality varies. The handling by reviews by a separate unit within the department does not provide the same degree of institutional separation and safeguards provided by judicial independence. Seeking justice from administration, especially the immigration department, just does not measure up to a lawyer's conception of justice as an intrinsically judicial phenomenon.[10] Moreover, the risk with inserting a review process into a large organisational system is that it comes to exhibit the same type of pathologies that afflict initial caseworking. The lack of transparency and openness of administrative review compares poorly with the judicial process. Indeed, it has been suggested that the real attraction of administrative review is that it enables government to conceal the full inadequacies of initial decisions from public scrutiny.[11] However, any assessment should not necessarily compare administrative review with tribunal appeals, but instead involve a pragmatic evaluation based on how well reviews operate in practice.

Various review processes have operated in the immigration context and have been widely criticised. Reviews have been characterised by boilerplate reasons, inconsistencies and carelessness, and were often ineffective in identifying errors.[12] In 2004, only one per cent of entry clearance reviews succeeded compared with 40 per cent of appeals.[13] The department needed to improve quality.[14] Despite such concerns, reviews operated largely against the safety net of appeals. With the introduction of the points-based system, appeals were no longer seen as necessary and were replaced by administrative reviews.[15]

---

[9] Tribunal Procedure (First-tier Tribunal) (Immigration and Asylum Chamber) Rules, SI 2014/2604, r 2.

[10] See, eg, Council on Tribunals, 'Annual Report 1989/90' (1990) [1.9].

[11] TG Ison, '"Administrative Justice": Is It Such a Good Idea?' in M Harris and M Partington (eds), *Administrative Justice in the 21st Century* (Oxford, Hart Publishing, 1999) 39.

[12] Constitutional Affairs Committee, 'Asylum and Immigration Appeals' HC 211 (2003–04) [107]; ICIBI, 'An Inspection of Family Reunion Applications' (2016) [6.61].

[13] NAO, 'Visa Entry to the UK: The Entry Clearance Operation' HC 367 (2003–04) [2.24].

[14] Independent Monitor for Entry Clearance Refusals, 'Report for 2005' (2006).

[15] Immigration, Asylum and Nationality Act 2006, s 4(1); Home Office, 'Report on Removal of Full Appeal Rights Against Refusal of Entry Clearance Decisions Under the Points-Based System' (2011).

A. Replacing Tribunal Appeals with Administrative Reviews

Prior to the Immigration Act 2014, appeal rights were attached to specified immigration decisions.[16] The 2014 Act changed this approach by attaching appeals not to specific decisions, but to grounds. Appeals could only be brought on refugee and human rights grounds. All other pre-existing appeal rights were replaced with administrative review.[17] This controversial restriction was highly criticised. Concerns were expressed that administrative review was not being introduced to secure fairness and justice for individuals, but to reduce the number of immigrants who would have succeeded had they been able to put their case to a tribunal.[18] The department admitted that the high appeal success rate was largely attributable to its own errors: approximately 60 per cent of appeals were allowed due to case-work errors.[19] As one MP noted, 'the Government's response to this high margin of error is not to seek to improve the quality of their decision making, but rather to reduce the opportunities for challenge'.[20] By contrast, ministers argued that the delays and costs of appeals were 'not fair to applicants'.[21] Replacing appeals with reviews was estimated to save £261 million over 10 years.[22] In response, the JCHR quoted Baroness Hale: 'In this day and age a right of access to a tribunal or other adjudicative mechanism established by the state is just as important and fundamental as a right of access to the ordinary courts'.[23] Accordingly, withdrawing appeal rights undermined the common law right of access to justice.[24] But ministers were implacable: only fundamental rights cases justified the expense and delay of an appeal. Immigration decisions did not fall within the right to a fair trial (Article 6 ECHR).[25] The result is that only a small proportion of the four million immigration decisions per year now attract a right of appeal. Further changes increased the scope for human rights appeals taking place out of the country.[26]

To meet concerns, Parliament required the Chief Inspector to report on the effectiveness of administrative review in identifying and correcting case working

[16] Nationality, Immigration and Asylum Act 2002, s 82(2). Such decisions included the refusal of leave to enter, entry clearance, of a certificate of entitlement, to vary a person's leave to enter or remain, and so on.

[17] Immigration Act 2014, s 15; Immigration Rules, Appendix AR.

[18] *Hansard*, HL Vol 752 col 1353 (5 March 2014) (Lord Avebury).

[19] Home Office, 'Impact Assessment of Reforming Immigration Appeal Rights' (2013) 7.

[20] *Hansard*, HC Vol 569 col 199 (22 October 2013) (Barry Gardiner MP). See also *Hansard*, HC Vol 569 col 189 (22 October 2013) (Fiona MacTaggart MP).

[21] Home Office, 'Immigration Bill Factsheet: Appeals' (2013) 1.

[22] Home Office, 'Impact Assessment of Reforming Immigration Appeal Rights' (2013) 2.

[23] *R v Secretary of State for the Home Department, ex parte Saleem* [2001] 1 WLR 443, 458 (CA).

[24] JCHR, 'Legislative Scrutiny: Immigration Bill', HL 102 HC 935 (2013–14) [39]. See also House of Lords Constitution Committee, 'Immigration Bill' HL 148 (2013–14) [3]–[5].

[25] Home Office, 'Government Response to the JCHR, Eighth Report of Session 2013–14' (2014) 2; Home Office, 'Immigration Bill: ECHR Memorandum' (2013) 14–16.

[26] Immigration Act 2016, s 63. See P Jorro, 'The Enhanced Non-suspensive Appeals Regime in Immigration Cases' (2016) 30 *Journal of Immigration, Asylum and Nationality Law* 111.

errors and the independence of reviewers.[27] Ministers also gave assurances.[28] Administrative reviews would be undertaken by fully trained and experienced staff who would be independent of the original decision-maker and located in a separate operational unit. Feedback mechanisms would be established. The Home Office would also monitor the overturn rate on administrative review and investigate any discrepancy with the appeal success rate.[29]

In practice, none of these assurances were initially fulfilled, although the system has improved as tracked through successive inspection reports. The first report in 2016 found that reviews were being undertaken by low-level, untrained and temporary staff with limited or no experience of immigration law, a notoriously complex area.[30] The majority of staff in the in-country administrative review team had no previous experience of points-based scheme casework and limited experience of immigration casework. Quality assurance was minimal and ineffectual. Valid applications had been incorrectly rejected and this had not been picked up. To ensure a degree of independence, in-country reviewers had been organised into a functionally separate unit from initial decision-makers, but the unit had been staffed with junior and inexperienced officials. Complex cases were not referred upwards to more senior caseworkers. By contrast, overseas reviewers worked alongside primary decision-makers; although there was no evidence of bias, it was more difficult to demonstrate that reviewers were truly independent. As regards the quality of review decisions, reasons must be proper, adequate, intelligible and deal with the substantial points raised.[31] Some review decisions were characterised by 'an over-reliance on the initial refusal decision letter' with review 'decision notices reiterating the previous grounds for refusal without addressing the applicant's points' of challenge.[32] Perfunctory decision notices do not comprise an effective review.[33]

Success rates were far lower than those of appeals. Some 49 per cent of appeals were allowed under the former regime. The department had concluded that 60 per cent of allowed appeals succeeded due to caseworking errors. By contrast, in 2015–16, the success rate for administrative reviews was eight per cent for in-country reviews and 22 per cent for at the border reviews.[34] In 2016–17, the success rate was 3.4 per cent for in-country reviews and 6.8 per cent for border reviews.[35] This was far lower than the proportion of allowed appeals.

---

[27] Immigration Act 2014, s 16.

[28] *Hansard*, HL Vol 752 cols 1357–58 (5 March 2014) (Lord Wallace of Tankerness, Advocate General for Scotland).

[29] Home Office, 'Statement of Intent: Administrative Review' (2013) 4.

[30] ICIBI, 'An Inspection of the Administrative Review Processes Introduced Following the Immigration Act 2014' (2016).

[31] *In Re Poyser and Mills' Arbitration* [1964] 2 QB 467, 478 (CA); *MK v Secretary of State for the Home Department (duty to give reasons) Pakistan* [2013] UKUT 00641 (IAC).

[32] ICIBI, 'Administrative Review' (n 30) [2.10].

[33] *R (Akturk) v Secretary of State for the Home Department* [2017] EWHC Admin 297 [47] (Holman J).

[34] ICIBI (n 30) [2.29].

[35] ICIBI, 'A Re-inspection of the Administrative Review Process' (2017) [2.6].

Process significantly influences substantive outcomes. Legal rights and substantive entitlements are likely to become less effective when procedural rights are weakened.[36] Assurances that such discrepancies would be investigated were unfulfilled – as were promises of feedback loops to improve initial decision-making. The only assurance met was that reviews would be processed within 28 days. The Chief Inspector concluded that there was 'there was significant room for improvement in respect of the effectiveness of administrative review in identifying and correcting case working errors, and in communicating decisions to applicants'.[37] Even the normally robust Home Office recognised that 'quality has not consistently been of the standard to which we aspire'.[38] A subsequent inspection in 2017 found improvements as regards in-country administrative reviews, but slow progress for overseas and at the border reviews.[39] Remaining weaknesses included: the quality of reason-giving; the lack of a dedicated team for overseas reviews; and the variable level of quality assurance for overseas and border reviews. Overall, the department had failed to demonstrate that it had delivered an efficient, effective and cost-saving replacement for the previous appeals mechanisms.[40]

A third inspection in 2020 found further improvements.[41] It concluded that administrative reviews were generally effective at identifying and correcting 'objective' factual or process errors, albeit too slow to put things right in some cases. As regards the internal separation of the review function, since 2019, reviews concerning in-country and entry clearance casework decisions have been handled by the UKVI's Administrative Review Unit (ARU). The ARU comprises a separate dedicated team so that reviewers are separate from original decision-makers.[42] An internal review process will always struggle to demonstrate that it is wholly independent. Nonetheless, so far as is possible within an administrative structure, reviewers are separate. An internal separation of functions can in practice provide a high degree of operational independence and enable different administrative cultures to develop. But this somewhat loose arrangement can prompt questions as to the unit's longevity and whether detailed statutory regulation would be preferable. Further, an internal separation of functions is, to some extent,

---

[36] M Adler, 'Understanding and Analysing Administrative Justice' in M Adler (ed), *Administrative Justice in Context* (Oxford, Hart Publishing, 2010) 132–36; *R (Parmak) v Secretary of State for the Home Department* [2006] EWHC 244 (Admin) [27] (Sullivan J).

[37] ICIBI (n 30) 2.

[38] Home Office, 'Response to the Independent Chief Inspector's Report: An Inspection of the Administrative Review Processes Introduced Following the 2014 Immigration Act' (2016) 1.

[39] ICIBI, 'Administrative Review Process' (n 35).

[40] ibid 2.

[41] ICIBI, 'An Inspection of Administrative Reviews' (2020).

[42] Immigration Act 2014, s 16(1)(c). The Administrative Review Unit is part of UKVI's Appeals, Litigation and Administrative Review (ALAR), a senior civil service command within UKVI's Immigration & Protection (I&P) Directorate; original decision-making teams for all in-country and overseas eligible decisions, including EU Settlement Scheme decisions, are located in UKVI's Visas & Citizenship Directorate. See ch 5, Figure 5.1, 'UKVI Organisational Structure'.

weakened when reviewers revert cases to the original casework unit for substantive reconsideration once an error has been identified. Reviews concerning decisions made at the border decisions are handled separately within Border Force. There is no dedicated review team and reviewers are located within casework units and therefore have less independence and separation than a single dedicated team would have. Following prompting by the Chief Inspector, Border Force is to establish a dedicated review unit to deal with at the border administrative reviews, which is to be independent of operational managers involved in the initial decisions.[43]

B. The Limits of Administrative Reviews

Administrative reviews are constrained in various ways. Their scope is limited to identifying caseworking errors and reviewers are generally limited to considering only the same evidence presented to the original decision-maker.[44] There are limited exceptions where new information is submitted to demonstrate a caseworking error has been made or where new evidence is relied upon to demonstrate that a previously submitted document is genuine (to counter a decision based on false representation or failing to disclose a material fact in relation to a claimed previous application). The position is different as regards EU Settlement Scheme administrative reviews (the reviewer can consider new information not before the original decision-makers and, where appropriate, request further new information evidence).[45] Nonetheless, the general position is that administrative review is concerned with identifying whether the original caseworker made an error on the basis of the information then available. Consequently, the review process is more geared towards demonstrating that the Home Office has not made an error rather than ensuring the best outcome for the applicant.[46] This is at odds with the department's stated aim of providing excellent customer service and of specific concern with regard to vulnerable applicants. Allowing applicants to submit new information would enhance the effectiveness of the process from the applicant's position.[47] Administrative review is limited to 'eligible decisions'.[48] This excludes human rights decisions, which can be appealed to the tribunal.[49]

---

[43] Home Office, 'Response to the ICIBI's report: An Inspection of Administrative Reviews' (2020) [3.2].

[44] Immigration Rules, Appendix AR 2.4.

[45] Immigration Rules, Appendix AR(EU) 2.3 and AR(EU) 2.4. See also Home Office, 'Administrative Review: EU Settlement Scheme' (2020).

[46] ICIBI, 'Administrative Reviews' (n 41) [3.24].

[47] This happens in other administrative review processes, such as homelessness reviews and social security mandatory reconsiderations.

[48] Immigration Rules, Appendix AR 3.2, 4.2, 5.2.

[49] A human rights claim is not an eligible decision; reviewers are instructed not to engage with any human rights claims found in a review application.

One particular anomaly is that administrative review is not available to those refused visit visas, the largest immigration category with one of the highest refusal rates. Given the nature of established migrant and family networks, family members wishing to visit relatives in the UK for important family events will often wish to challenge refusals. The refusal of a visit visa will often prevent someone from securing one to visit other countries. Family visitor refusals used to be appealable on general grounds, but are now only appealable on (limited) Article 8 ECHR grounds.[50] In such cases, the delay and limitations of such appeals significantly weaken their effectiveness. An administrative review would be quicker and more efficient, but this is unavailable. The remaining option of judicial review also has its limits, but it may occasionally prompt a reconsideration.

Another limitation of administrative reviews concerns the type of evidence being reviewed. Reviews have been judged to be generally effective for identifying and correcting 'objective' errors: misapplying the immigration rules; overlooking relevant evidence; and granting of the wrong length or conditions of leave. Administrative review is the obvious remedy for refusals taken under the points-based scheme where hard-edged rules are applied objectively. However, reviews are of little or no value when initial refusals are based on credibility assessments.[51] Such decisions include domestic violence and genuine student applications. The obvious reason is that a paper-based review of evidence concerning, for instance, the credibility of a victim of domestic violence without any personal interaction between caseworker/reviewer and applicant is highly unlikely to go beyond a surface-level or to engage properly with the matter, given the significance of such decisions. Indeed, the inspector found some review decisions 'showed a readiness to side with the original decision-maker's opinions about the weight of the evidence provided that raised questions about institutional thinking. This was particularly evident in the application of the Genuine Student Rule.[52]

Accordingly, it was recommended that all review decisions relying on credibility be quality assured by a manager before being dispatched.[53] But, the department rejected this on the basis that it would be disproportionate and could impact negatively on current service standards, although it would consider

---

[50] Family visitor appeals were abolished by the Crime and Courts Act 2013, s 52. On post-2014 Act visit visa appeals, see *Kaur v Entry Clearance Officer, New Delhi (visit appeals; Article 8)* [2015] UKUT 487 (IAC) (tribunal only has jurisdiction under the Human Rights Act 1998 to decide whether the decision is unlawful, but the starting point is evidence about the appellant's ability to meet the requirements for visitors under the immigration rules); *Abbasi v Entry Clearance Officer, Karachi (visits – bereavement – Article 8)* [2015] UKUT 463 (IAC) (refusal of a visa to foreign nationals seeking to enter for a finite period to mourn with family members the recent death of a close relative was capable of interfering with Art 8 ECHR.).

[51] ICIBI (n 41) [3.23].

[52] ibid [3.25].

[53] ibid [4.1].

increasing 'second pair of eyes' (SPOE) checks using a risk-based approach.[54] On occasion the courts have highlighted poor refusal decisions.[55] Representatives report that the quality of reviews is very hit and miss. In general terms, the only onward route of challenge against an administrative review is by way of judicial review. The weakness is, as the tribunal itself has noted, the inability of the judicial review court to engage in fact-finding or to substitute decisions.[56] The lack of a tribunal appeal in sensitive and high-impact decisions that require careful evaluation of subjective evidence, such as domestic violence cases, is a source of injustice. Reviews have an important role in high-volume rule-based decisions, but they do not work effectively or provide an adequate safeguard in credibility-based decisions.

The administrative review process is focused on identifying any caseworking errors and is often regarded as completed at this stage. The process may also include the substantive reconsideration and substituting a new decision in, for example, points-based scheme applications. But in other instances, once the reviewer has identified a caseworking error, the case is then returned to the relevant casework unit for a fresh decision, thereby making the whole process more of an 'administrative judicial review' than a thorough 'reconsideration'. There are practical reasons for separating the review and reconsideration stages: a change of circumstances might mean the whole application requires reconsideration; it is not possible to interview applicants (to assess credibility) as part of the review process; and obtaining new evidence may require liaison with other agencies.[57] Different casework units use different ways of handling reconsiderations. In some units, the original decision-maker will conduct the reconsideration; it is seen as a learning opportunity for them. In smaller casework teams, reconsideration may be undertaken by a colleague of the original decision-maker. In other high-volume areas, there is a dedicated post-decision team to ensure objectivity. Indefinite 'leave to remain' reconsiderations are reviewed by a senior caseworker to add additional

---

[54] Home Office, 'Response to the ICIBI's report' (n 43) [1.17].

[55] See, eg, *R (AT) v Secretary of State for the Home Department* [2017] EWHC 2589 (Admin): the Administrative Court found a 'fairness deficit' from the Home Office for not giving an applicant for leave to remain as a victim of domestic violence the opportunity to comment on 'damning accusations' made by the alleged perpetrator/husband and a failure to evaluate impartially the competing accounts at both the initial decision and through administrative review. The initial decision letter contained 'disturbing' reasoning: the applicant's account was rejected *because* it conflicted with that of the husband; 'one is left with the uncomfortable feeling that the man's evidence counted for more than the woman's. A double standard was applied' (Kerr J). See also 'Abuse victims increasingly denied right to stay in UK' *Guardian* (16 August 2018) (comparing previous high success of domestic violence cases before the tribunal compared with much lower subsequent success rates through administrative review).

[56] *SM and Qadir v Secretary of State for the Home Department (ETS – Evidence – Burden of Proof)* [2016] UKUT 00229 (IAC) [102]; *R (Gazi) v Secretary of State for the Home Department (ETS – judicial review) IJR* [2015] UKUT 00327 (IAC) [36]–[40].

[57] Home Office, 'Administrative Review' (2019) 47.

assurance. There is a dedicated reconsideration casework team for student reviews. Rationalisation is required across casework teams to ensure that all reconsiderations are undertaken by senior caseworkers.

As regards timeliness, most reviews are considered within the service standard of 28 days. There is the usual balance between timeliness, staff capacity and resources, and quality. As a senior manager put it, '[We] can't slip on service delivery and can't slip on quality; both are equally as important'; it would be counter-productive to send out poor-quality review decisions just to meet the 28-day service standard.[58] But there is no timescale concerning the post-review reconsideration stage and no oversight or tracking of such cases. An applicant might be notified within 28 days that the original decision contained an error, but then wait months for a reconsidered decision. This 'effectively frustrates' the purpose of administrative review, which is not just to identify caseworking errors, but also to correct them.[59] Another shortcoming has been the lack of reliable and comprehensive data; data on overseas administrative reviews has been 'plagued by gaps and inconsistencies'.[60] What data is available has been collected to manage workflows. The data has not been up to scratch when it comes to seeking to understand why review application numbers fluctuate and trends in and the reasons behind outcomes with a view to improving both reviews and original decision-making. The department has committed itself to publish better data.[61]

C. Overall

A central purpose of introducing administrative reviews was to improve decision quality.[62] Overall, compared with appeals, reviews represent a weakening of redress. As regards substantive outcomes, review success rates vary; granular data is unavailable. Representatives report that reviews are very hit or miss. Increased success rates (Table 6.1) suggest reviews are not a rubber stamp, but do provide something approaching, but not quite achieving, a more effective remedy. Significant scope for improvement remains. In a sense, this is unsurprising. After all, administrative review is a relatively new process whereas appeals and judicial review have operated for decades; they have been refined over time. In their early decades, appeals were of uneven quality and have substantially developed since.

[58] ICIBI (n 41) [7.126].
[59] ibid [3.11].
[60] ibid [6.48].
[61] Home Office (n 43) [1.2].
[62] House of Commons Public Bill Committee, 'Immigration Bill 2013: Sixth Sitting' (PBC (Bill 110) 2013–14) col 199 (5 November 2013) (Mark Harper MP, Minister for Immigration).

Table 6.1 In-country Decisions and administrative reviews, 2015–19[63]

Year	Eligible decisions	Total administrative reviews	Reviews upheld	Reviews overturned	Other[64]
2015–16	199,315	6,313	5,289 (84%)	1,024 (16%)	741
2016–17	238,032	5,579	4,737 (85%)	842 (15%)	438
2017–18	227,669	5,350	4,295 (80%)	1,055 (20%)	364
2018–19	263,837	4,544	3,154 (69%)	1,390 (31%)	278

Improvements could include allowing applicants to submit new evidence and constituting an independent external quality assurance panel to examine samples of review decisions and then provide feedback.[65] Surveying applicants for their feedback would provide another source of information. Paper-based reviews should be focused on paper-based 'binary work streams' and objective rule-based decisions. There is an unassailable argument for having appeals against judgmental/credibility decisions with high consequences (eg domestic violence, statelessness). Visit visa refusals should attract an administrative review.[66] Post-review reconsiderations also need to be managed properly to prevent the bizarre situation in which some applicants are disadvantaged because they have successfully challenged a flawed initial decision. An overarching question is whether replacing many appeal rights with administrative review has brought the cost savings and benefits claimed for it. The Chief Inspector has chided the department's delay in producing the evaluation.[67] The evidence suggests that there is still some way to go before reviews become more effective.

III. Tribunal Appeals

Tribunal appeals provide refused applicants with an independent judicial remedy; a tribunal judge will consider the evidence, hear oral evidence and submissions,

[63] ICIBI (n 41) [6.38] and [6.41].
[64] This includes applications rejected as invalid and withdrawn applications.
[65] This was once raised by the Home Office, but never acted upon: Home Office, 'Response to the Independent Chief Inspector's Report' (n 38) 2 and [11.6].
[66] Visit visa decisions often involve assessing credibility. Family visitor appeals were prone to delays. An administrative review by an independently minded senior officer could provide a quick and effective remedy.
[67] Source: ICIBI (n 41) [4.4]. The 2014 Act appeal changes were brought into force in 2015; by mid-2021, the department was apparently nearing the completion of the scoping stage of the evaluation, but it was still to be published.

and then write up a detailed determination. This replaces the department's decision on matters of both law and fact, and binds the parties. Judicial review may be seen as superior remedy in terms of legal matters, but it is generally unable to resolve matters of fact. By contrast, handling evidence and making factual findings are the daily work of tribunals. In terms of fact-sensitive immigration cases, this often places tribunal appeals far above judicial review as an effective remedy.

The immigration tribunal was initially an informal process and not one that would pass muster under contemporary attitudes of administrative law; until 1987, immigration adjudicators were appointed by the Home Office. But, through the 1990s and 2000s, the appeal system became progressively judicialised and was then incorporated into the First-tier and Upper Tribunal structure. Given the sensitive nature of this jurisdiction and the potential for executive pressure, great importance has long been attached to judicial safeguards: a full rehearing of the evidence by an independent and judicial decision-maker; handling cases fairly and justly; adversarial hearings; detailed and reasoned tribunal determinations; and onward rights of appeal. The whole ethos of tribunals is one of a fair and swift individualised adjudication in which appellants can participate directly via oral hearings or now online. Tribunals apply the same rules as caseworkers, but decisions are taken by an independent judges before whom the appellant can appear in person, a feature that is likely to more instill confidence than the distanced, faceless, box-ticking culture prevalent in departmental casework routines. Located above the First-tier Tribunal (Immigration and Asylum Chamber) (Ft-TIAC), the Upper Tribunal (Immigration and Asylum Chamber) (UTIAC) considers onward error of law appeals and issues important legal guidance. A superior court of record, the UTIAC is recognised by the higher courts as an expert, specialist judicial body; it issues country guidance in asylum cases, and since 2013 undertakes the majority of immigration judicial review work.[68]

A. Appeals in Practice

For much of the time, tribunals work reasonably well and provide appellants with an effective and accessible remedy. Nonetheless, there are constraining factors. The tribunal is structurally independent; the Home Office cannot seek improperly to interfere with the determination of appeals. But it is not jurisdictionally independent; the ultimate power to add and withdraw appeal rights rests with the department, subject to the Government's parliamentary majority. While many representatives are highly committed and provide an excellent service, others are incompetent or unscrupulously exploitative, which

---

[68] Tribunals, Courts and Enforcement Act 2007, s 3(5); *R (Cart) v Upper Tribunal* [2011] UKSC 28, [2012] 1 AC 663, [40]; *AH (Sudan) v Secretary of State for the Home Department* [2007] UKHL 49, [2008] 1 AC 678; R Carnwath, 'Tribunal Justice – A New Start' [2009] *PL* 48.

disadvantages both appellants and the efficiency of the tribunal. There is also significant unmet need for legal advice and legal aid restrictions.[69] Given the procedural and substantive legal complexities, unrepresented appellants often lack the resources to present their cases effectively.[70] There are also communicative and cultural barriers. The department's behaviour in appeals has at times been heavily criticised.[71] The time taken for appeals to be heard varies, but significant delays do occur. This in turn has prompted the department to introduce 'appeal reconsiderations': the department will reconsider in-country appeals lodged and additional evidence (and it has actively encouraged representatives to submit new evidence) to try to conclude cases before they reach a formal tribunal hearing, thereby improving timeliness and reducing unnecessary burdens on the tribunal.[72]

The independence of tribunals is demonstrated by the high proportion of allowed appeals, but there are long-standing concerns that decision-making varies considerably between different judges.[73] A large part of the problem is that there is

[69] Legal Aid, Sentencing, and Punishment of Offenders Act 2012; F Meyler and S Woodhouse, 'Changing the Immigration Rules and Withdrawing the "Currency" of Legal Aid: The Impact of LASPO 2012 on Migrants and their Families' (2013) 35 *Journal of Social Welfare and Family Law* 55; S York, 'The End of Legal Aid in Immigration: a Barrier to Access to Justice for Migrants and a Decline in the Rule of Law' (2013) 27 *Journal of Immigration, Asylum and Nationality Law* 106; R Thomas, 'Immigration and Access to Justice: A Critical Analysis of Recent Restrictions' in E Palmer, T Cornford, A Guinchard, and Y Marique (eds), *Access to Justice: Beyond the Policies and Politics of Austerity* (Oxford, Hart Publishing, 2016); H O'Nions, '"Fat Cat" Lawyers and 'Illegal' Migrants: the Impact of Intersecting Hostilities and Toxic Narratives on Access to Justice" (2020) 42 *Journal of Social Welfare and Family Law* 319.

[70] In *AA (Nigeria) v Secretary of State for the Home Department* [2010] EWCA Civ 773 [88] Longmore LJ was 'perplexed and concerned how any individual whom the Immigration Rules affect can discover what the policy of the Secretary of State actually is at any particular time if it necessitates a trawl through Hansard or formal Home Office correspondence as well as through the comparatively complex Rules themselves. It seems that it is only with expensive legal assistance, funded by the taxpayer, that justice can be done'.

[71] Quality varies, but low points have included: 'files are not provided, documents are not available, they do not put it evidence that they ought to put in, they fail totally to produce any skeleton arguments, the list goes on and on and the Tribunal is simply getting fed up with it' – concluded that the Home Office does 'not seem capable of dealing with the appeals in the manner in which they ought to be dealt with. The result is that the Tribunal is left in an impossible position' (*Secretary of State for the Home Department v Tatar* [2000] 00TH01914 [3]–[4] (UKIAT)); 'it is hard to imagine any other department of state in this country where such incompetence would be tolerated ... it goes beyond mere institutional incompetence, into the realm of an institutional culture of disregard for adjudicators, who are the primary judicial authority in this country for making sure that immigration powers are efficiently, as well as fairly exercised' (*Secretary of State for the Home Department v Razi* [2001] 01TH01836 [16]–[17] (UKIAT)).

[72] Letter from UKVI to ILPA, 'Home Office Review of Older Cases' (30 November 2018). Initially, the department sent out such reviews to external lawyers and later set up a dedicated internal team. See Home Office, 'Reconsiderations' (2018).

[73] See R Thomas, 'Refugee Roulette: A UK Perspective' in J Ramji-Nogales, AI Schoenholtz and PG Schrag (eds), *Refugee Roulette: Disparities in Asylum Adjudication and Proposals for Reform* (New York, New York University Press, 2009); N Gill, R Rotter, A Burridge, M Griffiths and J Allsopp, 'Inconsistency in Asylum Appeal Adjudication' (2015) 50 *Forced Migration Review* 52; C Nye and L Sands, 'Asylum seekers face appeals "lottery"' *BBC News* (29 November 2017).

no objective standard of correct decision-making.[74] Some degree of inconsistency is to be expected, but it is not known how much there actually is. Beyond this, the general quality of First-tier Tribunal decisions is often good-to-high, although not consistently high.[75] Judges are under pressure to manage the throughput of cases, write up detailed determinations and apply complex rules.[76] There is also the long-standing phenomenon by which some appeals go round and round the system often over the course of years. For instance, a first-tier appeal is decided, found by the Upper Tribunal to contain factual or legal errors amounting to a material error of law, remitted back to the first-tier, reheard, and then appealed and so on, often prompting the latest judge of several to have considered the same case to note dryly that 'this case has an unfortunate procedural history'. Given that tribunals focus on case-by-case adjudication, there is no systematic feedback to the department on the quality of initial decisions. Inaction by the department in implementing allowed appeals has arisen due to administrative delays and politically motivated considerations prompting judicial review action.[77] The department has, at times, challenged a significant proportion of appeals allowed by the First-tier Tribunal. Nevertheless, despite the difficulties, tribunals provide appellants with an effective remedy.

B. Appeals Post-2014

Previous appeal arrangements were relatively straightforward: refused applicants could appeal specified immigration decisions, such as the refusal of leave to remain, and then the tribunal would hear the evidence and determine the appeal accordingly. Under the 2014 Act, an appellant can no longer appeal on the simple

---

[74] R Thomas, *Administrative Justice and Asylum Appeals: A Study of Tribunal Adjudication* (Oxford, Hart Publishing, 2011).

[75] See, eg, *MM v Secretary of State for the Home Department* [2017] (AA/06906/2014, 30 August 2017) (UTIAC) (serious errors in various decisions by the same Ft-T judge); *Secretary of State for the Home Department v Waheed* (IA/18828/2015, 22 August 2016) (UTIAC) (the Ft-T judge's 'tediously incompetent' determination had failed to engage with the Home Office's case and to analyse 'glaring weaknesses' in the appellant's case); *Secretary of State for the Home Department v EP* (HU/18412/2019, 10 September 2020) (UTIAC) ('the decision of the First-tier Tribunal in this particular case is so deeply flawed by legal error that it cannot stand').

[76] Compared with other tribunals that give brief decision notices, immigration tribunals differ in that the tribunal judge has to write up a detailed determination setting out the evidence, the findings of fact made, and the law. For every hour spent hearing an appeal, judges will, on average, spend two or three hours writing up the determination.

[77] See, eg, *AW v Entry Clearance Officer, Islamabad (Duties of Immigration Judge) Pakistan* [2008] UKAIT 00072 [4]: 'It is indeed within the knowledge of every member of this Tribunal that Entry Clearance Officers typically treat judicial directions, and regulations made by Parliament, with utter disdain.'

basis that the refusal decision was not in accordance with the immigration rules, but only on human rights and asylum grounds. One consequence of this has been to concentrate the tribunal's workload on more complex asylum and human rights-related cases by reducing the amount of high-volume and simpler appeal categories, such as such as family visitor appeals.

Another consequence is simply that the ability of migrants to seek 'ordinary' administrative justice in non-human rights cases has been substantially reduced. The 2014 Act therefore illustrates how the administrative justice model of constituting immigration administration has been significantly weakened, although the courts have, to some extent, intervened to protect appeals.[78] The legal complexity and formalism of appeal routes have increased.[79] For instance, the refusal of indefinite leave to remain is no longer an appealable decision; an applicant therefore needs to make a human rights application. This has to be made through the specified procedure (including the form to be used and the fee to be paid) to promote consistency and administrative efficacy.[80] An in-country applicant who has made a human rights claim that has been refused by the department has an in-country appeal on Article 8 ECHR grounds prior to removal.[81] However, if the department certifies an asylum or human rights claim as clearly unfounded, the applicant can appeal, but only from outside the UK; they can only return if the appeal is allowed.[82] There have been successful legal challenges to the fairness and effectiveness of such out-of-country appeals and the certification of a claim as clearly unfounded can be challenged by way of judicial review.[83]

Tribunals are the principal means of raising human rights issues, although there is considerable complexity and incoherence in which decisions can and cannot be appealed. Some domestic violence claims are also human rights claims (in which case, they are appealable), but not all domestic violence claims are human rights

---

[78] See: *Lord Chancellor v Detention Action* [2015] EWCA Civ 840, [2015] 1 WLR 5341 (fast-track detained process for asylum appeals was systemically unfair and unjust); *R (Mohibullah) v Secretary of State for the Home Department (TOEIC – ETS – judicial review principles)* [2016] UKUT 00561 (IAC) (the Home Office had abused its power by not using a decision-making mechanism that attracted a right of appeal); *R (Kiarie and Byndloss) v Secretary of State for the Home Department* [2017] UKSC 42 (out-of-country criminal deportation appeal process unfair); *Khan v Secretary of State for the Home Department* [2017] EWCA Civ 1755, [2018] 1 WLR 1256 (overturning the UTIAC, the Court of Appeal held that European Economic Area extended family members did have a right of appeal).

[79] For examples of the excruciatingly complex legalistic provisions concerning human rights claims, see *R (Shrestha) v Secretary of State for the Home Department* [2018] EWCA Civ 2810; *Balajigari v Secretary of State for the Home Department* [2019] EWCA Civ 673 [95]–[103]; *MY v Secretary of State for the Home Department (refusal of human rights claim: Pakistan)* [2020] UKUT 89 (IAC).

[80] Immigration, Asylum and Nationality Act 2006, s 50(1).

[81] Nationality, Immigration and Asylum Act 2002, s 92(3); Provisions of the Immigration Act 2016, brought into effect on 1 December 2016, mean that the Secretary of State can certify human rights cases not involving international protection but based on rights to private and family life, so that a person must leave the UK while their appeal is pending and pursue that appeal from abroad, returning only if they succeed.

[82] Nationality, Immigration and Asylum Act 2002, s 94B.

[83] *Kiarie and Byndloss* (n 78).

claims (in which case, they are not appealable, but challengeable through administrative review and then judicial review).[84] In other decisions, such as curtailment of an individual's leave by the Home Office for an alleged breach of conditions, such as a prohibition on work, there is no redress at all apart from judicial review. In human trafficking cases, the position as regards appeals was previously incoherent (the tribunal could only go behind the trafficking decision and redetermine factual issues if the initial decision was perverse or irrational), before the Supreme Court ruled that a full right of appeal existed in such cases.[85]

In terms of appeal volumes, Figure 6.1 shows the overall number of appeals and pre-2014 Act appeal rights (managed migration, entry clearance and family visitor appeals) that were curtailed. Figure 6.2 shows the volume of retained appeals (asylum and deportation) and new post-2014 Act appeals (human rights and EEA free movement appeals). Comparing the two figures, it is evident that there has been a significant reduction in appeals owing to the 2014 Act. Figure 6.3 shows the proportion of allowed appeals in the main appeal categories for both pre-2014 Act and retained appeals. Overall, as a mechanism for challenging casework decisions, appeals have been limited and constrained thereby forcing applicants to use judicial review.

Figure 6.1 Pre-2014 Act appeal rights

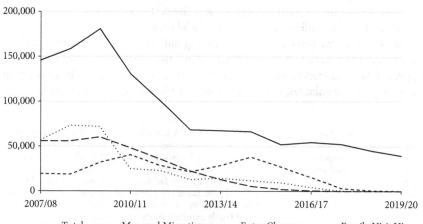

Source: MoJ, 'Tribunal Statistics Quarterly 2020' (TSO, 2020).

---

[84] See *R (AT) v Secretary of State for the Home Department* (n 55) [44]–[45]: 'The clarity of the law would be enhanced if the legislature did not enact commencement orders that seek to amend primary legislation. This is not a good idea and I hope not to have to consider again in my judicial career a commencement order like the short-lived Commencement Order No.3 … There is a further twist to the provisions which make it extremely difficult for a domestic violence victim to navigate even with expert representation, which many such victims do not enjoy' (Kerr J).

[85] *MS (Pakistan) v Secretary of State for the Home Department* [2020] UKSC 9.

Figure 6.2 Retained and post-2014 appeals rights

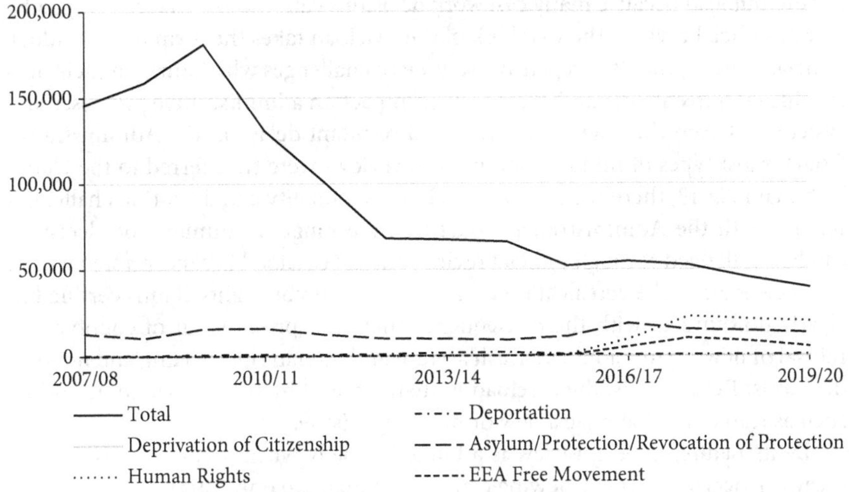

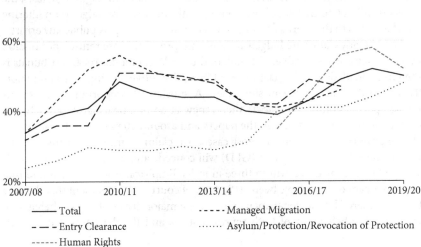

Source: MoJ, 'Tribunal Statistics Quarterly 2020' (TSO, 2020).

Figure 6.3 Proportion of allowed appeals

Source: MoJ, 'Tribunal Statistics Quarterly 2020' (TSO, 2020).

IV. Individual Judicial Reviews

Since the 1980s, immigration has accounted for the majority of all judicial review claims; at times, it has been up to 85 per cent of all judicial reviews.[86] This arises in part because of leakage from the tribunal system to judicial review, but also because many casework decisions can now only be challenged by way of judicial review. The vast bulk of the caseload takes the form of 'individual' judicial reviews, that is, a repetitive volume of challenges which turn on their own specific circumstances and have no wider impact on administrative processes and systems.[87] Given the volume of cases, and resultant delays in the Administrative Court, most types of immigration judicial reviews were transferred to the Upper Tribunal in 2013, thereby being tribunalised. Nationality and detention challenges remain with the Administrative Court. A wide range of immigration decisions can be challenged through judicial review, but the caseload is concentrated within a few categories: the certification of asylum and human rights claims certified as clearly unfounded, with the consequence that any appeal is out of country; the refusal of new submissions as a fresh asylum and human rights claim; and removal decisions. Beyond this, the caseload is characterised by trends that come and go such as lead cases that raise a new or novel legal issue.

By its nature, judicial review is a limited remedy when it comes to correcting casework decisions. The reviewing court or tribunal can only intervene on the relatively limited grounds of public law error. Judicial review is a limited and inferior remedy for resolving what are often factual disputes concerning whether the rules were properly applied. In the majority of claims, the scope for a successful challenge is very narrow. So long as the caseworker has applied the right legal tests, the decision will not be challengeable. Consequently, the focus of judges is on filtering out challenges to the merits of casework decision dressed up as public law errors.

While many claims are lodged, a significant proportion are refused permission because they are unarguable. The bulk of the workload for courts and tribunals is then front-loaded; very few claims result in a substantive hearing. The vast majority are resolved at the permission stage. A substantial proportion of claimants refused permission on the papers then renew at an oral hearing. Around 10 per cent are granted permission on the papers and around 20 per cent of oral renewals are granted permission. In most cases, if a claim is granted permission, the Government Legal Department (GLD) will concede and undertake that the decision will be reconsidered within three months. Empirical studies have found that 20-30 per cent of cases have been settled out of court with agreement that the case be reconsidered by the department. Costs are a major driver of litigant behaviour. However, the behaviour of both representatives and the department can waste

---

[86] For more detailed analysis, see: R Thomas, 'Mapping Immigration Judicial Review Litigation: An Empirical Legal Analysis' [2015] *PL* 652; R Thomas, 'Immigration Judicial Reviews: Resources, Caseload, and System-manageability Efficiency' (2016) 21 *Judicial Review* 209; and R Thomas and J Tomlinson, *Immigration Judicial Reviews: An Empirical Study* (London, Palgrave Macmillan, forthcoming).

[87] 'Individual' judicial review is largely absent from other large-scale systems such as tax and benefits. In contradistinction, more wide-ranging judicial review, in which the higher courts impose wider norms of administrative legality on the department and its operational systems and processes, is considered in ch 8.

scarce judicial resources. For instance, if the department settles a challenge promising to reconsider the decision within three months, but does not then do so, the only remedy is to lodge another judicial review.[88] As the Upper Tribunal has noted, 'this discrete field of activity involves a highly regrettable, frankly deplorable, waste of scarce judicial and administrative resources.'[89]

Figure 6.4 UTIAC judicial reviews

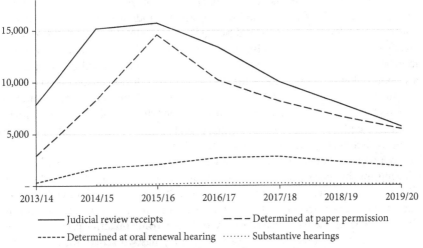

Source: MoJ, 'Tribunal Statistics Quarterly 2020' (TSO, 2020).

There are continuing concerns regarding the poor quality of *some* representatives who lodge template, standard and unparticularised grounds of challenge that mainly rehearse case law without applying it to the facts of the specific case. Using judicial review to buy time to delay the immigration process and exhausting every opportunity to delay irrespective of the merits of the case can ultimately be successful in defeating immigration controls. The higher courts have frequently exercised their inherent jurisdiction to govern proceedings to hold to account representatives whose conduct has fallen below the minimum professional and ethical standards.[90] The Upper Tribunal has increasingly sanctioned

---

[88] *R (MMK) v Secretary of State for the Home Department (consent orders – legal effect – enforcement)* [2017] UKUT 198 (IAC).

[89] ibid [44].

[90] *R (Sathivel) v Secretary of State for the Home Department* [2018] EWHC 913 (Admin) [4]; *Solicitors Regulation Authority (SRA) v Cheng* (Solicitors Disciplinary Tribunal (SDT), 16 June 2020); *SRA v Wasif Ali* (SDT, 10 September 2020).

representatives for lodging vexatious judicial reviews on an industrial scale.[91] At the same time, decent and reputable representatives struggle with funding legal aid funding issues for meritorious cases. Further, such representatives persistently highlight the systemic underlying cause of poor casework decisions. If there were not so many problems with some of the original decisions, then it would not be necessary to go to judicial review.

Judicial review does play an important role in identifying basic casework errors: failing to exercise discretion properly; not applying the relevant immigration rules properly; failing to follow and apply tribunal country guidance; not considering relevant evidence; and not giving the claimant a fair opportunity to clarify concerns. There have also been 'repeat judicial reviews', that is, an initial judicial review that the challenged decision be reconsidered which then leads to a second judicial review because the department's reconsidered decision is almost identical to the initial refusal decision. A common theme of successful judicial reviews has been the department's failure to afford the type of detailed consideration required to make a robust and defensible decision, especially when a case has complex factual, legal and country guidance issues.

In practice, much of the caseload is more akin to satellite litigation over filtering mechanisms (rule 353) and appeal locations (certification) rather than direct human rights adjudication. Under rule 353, a failed asylum claimant can submit new information to the department for consideration on the ground that the fresh evidence is significantly different from material previously been considered; if conditions in the relevant country has worsened, then the claimant may now qualify for asylum.[92] A summary filter process – rule 353 – is used to determine whether to accept such information as a fresh asylum claim; otherwise an unsuccessful claimant could, after having exhausted the in-country appeal process, begin the whole process all over again *ad infinitum*. A rule 353 decision not to accept new information as a fresh asylum claim is not therefore itself appealable, but can be judicially reviewed. Many fresh claim judicial reviews are rejected because the refusal to consider the further submissions was not irrational. There can sometimes be excessive reliance by the Home Office on the findings in past appeal determinations, sometimes beyond their reasonably permissible limits, or a failure to engage with the new information. Practitioners also report claimants often waiting many months for a fresh claim decision, which can then be judicially reviewed – by which stage yet more information may arise in addition to other changes in country conditions. But what is at stake is not a substantive decision on status, but an attempt to generate a right of appeal.

In certification cases, the department's decisions to refuse and certify a claimant's asylum or human rights application as clearly unfounded generates an out-of-country appeal, but the certification decision can be judicially reviewed.

---

[91] See *R (Shrestha) v Secretary of State for the Home Department* (Hamid jurisdiction: nature and purposes) [2018] UKUT 00242 (IAC) amongst many other cases.
[92] Immigration Rules, r 353.

Most challenges are refused because the decision to certify as a claim as clearly unfounded was not irrational. In such cases, an out-of-country appeal is deemed an adequate remedy. The department has sometimes fallen into error by assuming that, because an asylum or human rights has been refused, that it is also clearly unfounded. The two legal tests differ; a refused claim is not necessarily also a *clearly* unfounded one. Again, process affects substance; an in-country appeal is preferable to one out of country, which prompts satellite litigation over appeal location rather than direct adjudication of the claimant's immigration status. Ironically, practitioners report certification judicial reviews taking more time to be decided than that taken by the First-tier Tribunal to decide substantive appeals.

Removal judicial reviews have often been a point of contention with the department. Submitted and heard at speed, the tribunal has to review whether removal is lawful. On the one hand, generic grounds of challenge have been circulated within detention centres, and some representatives have been criticised for lodging abusive claims without merit designed to disrupt the removal process and to buy more time for their clients.[93] On the other hand, some removal challenges succeed.[94] The department has unlawfully removed people and then been ordered to return them.[95] In one case, having rejected an asylum claimant's account and evidence of his ethnicity, the department forcibly removed the man to Sudan. But, the department later accepted, having considered an expert report concerning the man's tribal background, that he was indeed a genuine asylum claimant and had been unlawfully removed.[96] Removals of asylum claimants under safe-third-country Dublin procedures have, on occasion, been halted, for instance, because they would be left there destitute.[97] This line of cases culminated in the *Medical Justice* case concerning whether removes had sufficient opportunity to challenge decisions during the notice period of 72 hours given to them by the department between the setting of removal directions and their actual removal.[98] The Court of Appeal held that this period did not give sufficient opportunity for the individual to challenge any adverse decision relevant to the removal which may have been made or notified during the removal window period itself. The removal policy infringed the right of access to justice as it denied individuals a fair opportunity to present their case. Despite the department's frustration about vexatious claims, removal judicial reviews remain a vital remedy. A likely reform is to introduce

[93] *R (Hamid) v Secretary of State for the Home Department* [2012] EWHC 3070 (Admin); *R (SB (Afghanistan)) v Secretary of State for the Home Department* [2018] EWCA Civ 215.
[94] 'Home Office Admits Mobile Phone Outage in Detention Centres as Deportees Unable to Contact Lawyers' *Independent* (7 February 2020); 'Court Grants Last-minute Reprieve to Dozens of Jamaican Nationals' *Independent* (10 February 2020); 'Home Office Deports Asylum Seekers on Charter Flight to EU Countries Despite Warnings of "Inadequate Access to Justice"' *Independent* (20 February 2020).
[95] See, eg, M. Bulman, '"I Was Terrified": Asylum Seeker Speaks Out After Being Wrongly Deported from UK by Home Office' *Independent* (22 July 2018).
[96] 'Sudanese Asylum Seeker Flown Back to UK After Khartoum Gunfight Delay' *Guardian* (17 January 2020).
[97] 'UK Judge Halts Home Office Flight to Remove Asylum Seekers' *Guardian* (16 September 2020).
[98] *R (FB (Afghanistan)) v Secretary of State for the Home Department* [2020] EWCA Civ 1338.

more expedited form of judicial consideration of priority removal notices with a prior legal aid offer.

As regards substantive judicial scrutiny, the experience of tribunalised judicial reviews contrasts with contemporary accounts of a more expansive approach to judicial review in the Administrative Court and the higher courts. Most of the immigration caseload is fact-specific, highly repetitive, and overwhelmingly takes place at the permission stage and through correspondence between the parties. Standard pro forma grounds of challenge are frequently copied by some practitioners from one case to another and passed around in detention centres. Most challenges fail due to narrowness of public law error, a thin and formalistic legality. The wider shifts inside mainstream judicial review as regards intensity of review, statutory purposes and relevancy are not reflected here. Respected practitioners have highlighted the separation of Upper Tribunal judges from the ethos of mainstream judicial review and the risks of judicial tunnel vision when faced with repetitive cases and poor representation. If a challenge has any merit, the chances are that the GLD will concede to save the time, cost and potentially precedent-setting importance of a substantive hearing. More widely, the disjuncture between mainstream and immigration judicial review is reflected in the mismatch between wider scholarly visions of judicial review and what actually happens. Scholars have argued for more research into lower court (ie Administrative Court) decision-making and taxonomies of grounds of challenge.[99] Yet, this risks a narrow and incomplete account: tribunalised immigration judicial review now accounts for the bulk of all judicial reviews.

Overall, individual judicial review remains an important check on casework decisions. Action against abusive claims and poor-quality representatives is justified and needed. Some judicial reviews are successful, and a fair proportion result in reconsideration. But, overall, it is difficult to conclude that the judicial resources invested in processing these judicial reviews are being used effectively as possible. Individual judicial review has little, if any, discernible impact in terms of addressing the systemic flaws in casework decisions. The underlying problem remains the limits on the department's institutional competence and capacity to make high quality casework decisions in the first place; it is this – in addition to abusive representatives – that largely conditions how the system works in practice.

* * *

The effectiveness of reviews, appeals, and judicial reviews is decidedly mixed. Standing back and considering them together, some common features can be identified. First, they are essentially reactive remedies. It is for affected individuals to decide whether to challenge decisions. Second, the focus is exclusively limited to the specific case. The case-by-case focus means that each error (whether

---

[99] S Nason, *Reconstructing Judicial Review* (Oxford, Hart, 2016).

caseworking or public law error) is seen as a single isolated event and not part of a wider trend. This approach has real limitations. It relies upon individuals consciously deciding to challenge decisions whereas in practice many of them lack the necessary resources, knowledge and assistance to do so, a particular problem in complex administrative law systems affecting vulnerable people and given restricted legal aid.[100] Of course, this has been exacerbated by the variable quality of administrative reviews and limits on appeal rights. Further, when these remedies are used, the outcomes rarely inform organisational learning and improve performance. Judges are deeply reluctant to view individual errors as part of wider trends; they are entirely focused on determining specific disputes and must maintain judicial independence.

There is a related concern that individualised consideration limits transparency. The focus of traditional remedies on individual cases means that there is rarely any systematic analysis of trends across the caseload to identify wider thematic trends and areas for improvement. Important information about such systemic causes is lost in thousands of individual and unreported tribunal determinations and judicial review notices, which are not analysed to provide feedback to casework administration.

At a conceptual level, these remedies reflect a conception of administrative law that views public administration as a bureaucratic machine that makes a huge number of individualised decisions. Any errors in such decisions are viewed as isolated problems limited to the specific decision rather than indications of wider patterns. There is no attention given to the structural underlying causes that produces errors in decision letters and other problems. The following questions then arise. Can new forms of administrative law oversight be developed to fill these gaps? Is it possible to construct a different conception of administrative law, one predicated not solely upon public administration as a machine churning out innumerable individual decisions, but as a performance-based and responsible organisation that needs constantly to supervise and assess its own systems and processes? If so, then how?

V. Responsible Administration: A Proactive Approach to Detecting Errors and Monitoring Administrative Action

A. The Concept of Responsible Administration

The reactive approach toward error-correction of conventional judicial administrative law mechanisms has increasingly been compared with a proactive approach

---

[100] This is a commonly recognised reality beyond immigration. See, eg, *VO v HMRC* (TC) [2017] UKUT 343 (AAC) [3] in which Upper Tribunal Judge Wikeley described the appeal as 'yet another sorry tale of HMRC institutional incompetence and inefficiency which could well have led to injustice, were it not for the persistence of the Appellant'.

toward detecting, correcting and preventing errors.[101] Government agencies make initial individual decisions, but unlike courts and tribunals, they do so as part of a wider project of implementing policy. At a fundamental level, the administrative enterprise involves managing an organisation as an overall system to achieve desired goals. Only in a very simplistic way can administration be understood as an activity undertaken by a single official, such as a caseworker taking an administrative decision. In reality, an administrative institution comprises complex and multiple layers of organisational action in which systems are designed and operated to achieve wider goals and in which different administrative levels – policy staff, managers and operational officials – are interdependent.[102]

This systemic perspective on administration has important implications. To be effective, government must supervise and monitor the degree to which it achieves policy goals. The normative concept of responsible administration requires government agencies to take proactive efforts to identify and remedy systemic problems in their administrative processes, such as decision-making.[103] Consequently, correcting errors should not be understood solely as the function of one-off idiosyncratic factors or framed exclusively in terms of individual fairness to appellants or as an endeavour to be accomplished solely through individualised judicial adjudication. Instead, government agencies should adopt a proactive approach in which they systematically monitor their decisions to identify, diagnose and correct systemic problems that generate errors in front line decisions. Fairness to individuals and implementing policy through accurate decisions overlap. This form of internal supervision includes not just departmental operations, but can – and should – also extend to outsourced private contractors.[104]

A proactive approach is particularly important in the context of large administrative processes, such as immigration. A common feature of mass decision processes is that specific issues are often recurrent: they affect many more people than just the individual challenger. How applications are handled or how a specific provision in the immigration rules is to be interpreted and applied can affect thousands of other applicants. Tribunals and courts can ensure consistency of approach on legal issues by, for instance, issuing guidance and precedent on such issues and by determining issues of statutory interpretation. But this leaves many other systemic issues on which the department's performance could be improved.

---

[101] JL Mashaw, 'The Management Side of Due Process: Some Theoretical and Litigation Notes on the Assurance of the Accuracy, Fairness, and Timeliness in the Adjudication of Social Welfare Claims' (1974) 59 *Cornell Law Review* 772; WH Simon, 'The Organizational Premises of Administrative Law' (2015) 78 *Law and Contemporary Problems* 61; GE Metzger, 'The Constitutional Duty to Supervise' (2015) 124 *Yale Law Journal* 1836.

[102] JD Thompson, *Organizations in Action: Social Science Bases of Administrative Theory* (New Brunswick, NJ, Transaction Publishers, 2006) 147–49.

[103] CF Sabel and WH Simon, 'The Duty of Responsible Administration and the Problem of Police Accountability' (2016) 33 *Yale Journal on Regulation* 165.

[104] See, eg, *R (DMA) v Secretary of State for the Home Department* [2020] EWHC 3416 (Admin) considered in ch 8.

The rate of successful appeals and judicial reviews is unlikely to be the sole consequence of one-off errors by individual caseworkers. It is much more likely to be the result of systemic shortcomings in both decision procedures, substantive decision-making, and the dissemination of knowledge and learning within the department. There is therefore a strong case for an administrative organisation to reframe itself as a responsible agency by taking a proactive approach toward systemic errors. This approach reflects an important shift away from a traditional, almost exclusive, focus on the judicial correction of individual errors toward an administration-centred approach to administrative law based upon organisational performance and effectiveness. This change from conventional administrative law remedies to proactive error detection and monitoring illustrates different underlying organisational premises of administrative law, in particular, the shift from understanding public administration as bureaucracy to a newer approach that views administration as a post-bureaucratic or performance-based organisation. It has also important implications as regards the accountability of administration.

There are two other closely connected aspects. The first is the importance of organisational learning as a means by which administrative bodies can better understand their own operations and performance and how to improve. An organisation can then disseminate that learning through its internal administrative structure and culture.[105] The second aspect concerns the adaptation problem. Given that the wider context of administration is always changing, so too must the focus of responsible administration and proactive monitoring. A government agency must, for instance, monitor and supervise both its current operations and be alert to how future trends in addition to policy and other changes that may potentially increase the prevalence of errors. It is inherent in the notion of responsible administration that monitoring must be responsive to how the administration adapts to its changing context. How a department goes about the task of monitoring, predicting and detecting errors needs fully to accommodate policy, administrative and contextual changes. Indeed, the potential for systemic administrative problems caused by such changes can, if anything, increase the need for proactive monitoring, as Windrush demonstrates.

B. Quality Controls within the Department

A proactive approach has not, generally, comprised part of the department's internal administrative law, although, as discussed in the previous chapter, it has increasingly come to play a role through 'minded to refuse', quality assurance methods, and the Chief Caseworker Unit (CCU). Both the UKVI Central Operations Assurance Team and Home Office Internal Audit have produced thematic reviews

---

[105] R Thomas, 'Administrative Justice, Better Decisions, and Organisational Learning' [2015] *PL* 111; B Burnes, *Managing Change*, 7th edn (Harlow, Pearson, 2017) 165–75.

on operational matters.[106] These systems could and should be developed further to enable better monitoring of decisions and decision processes, better internal communication about casework issues and challenges, and enhanced liaison with external stakeholders. For instance, an unexpected increase in refusal decisions in a specific immigration route could trigger internal monitoring to understand the reasons for it and be followed up by enhanced QA scrutiny. Mechanisms such as quality assurance and the CCU could have a formal statutory framework and reporting requirements to the Chief Inspector and the HAC. The department could publish detailed plans about how it will engage in proactive monitoring, the resulting data, and plans to improve casework.

Such innovations represent important developments, although the lack of transparency concerning internal thematic audit reviews is unfortunate. At the same time, ministerial efforts to limit available remedies have been more common. Overall, proactive monitoring has been lacking. Yet, when the department has failed, it has been subject to detailed critiques by external bodies, and these have been premised upon a proactive and systematic approach to diagnosing errors and the concept of responsible administration. These critiques have, in turn, prompted the department to reconsider its approach.

C. Revisiting Windrush

Let us reconsider Windrush. During the early period in which Windrush cases were initially coming to light, the department ignored warning signs and failed to be proactive by not investigating other possible cases. The subsequent Windrush Review repeatedly highlighted the department's failure to act upon clear warnings signs that there was a wide-scale systemic problem that went far beyond one-off idiosyncratic errors in individual decisions. Systemic and proactive monitoring could have prevented Windrush from escalating into such a crisis that caused people unnecessary harm. For instance, scrutiny of Windrush refusals would have been identified that caseworkers had been incorrectly applying the criminal – as opposed to the civil – standard of proof and that a tick-box approach had led to the substance of cases not being properly considered. The general principle outlined in the Windrush Review is that well-focused and sophisticated early warning systems, in addition to an administrative culture of being aware of risks as opposed to a default defensiveness, were essential in a complex and changing

---

[106] In 2019–20, the UKVI Central Operations Assurance Team completed reports on: El Salvador Asylum Operations; Removals Window; MPs Correspondence; Sponsorship – Pre-licence decision making on applications from Small and Medium sized Enterprises; Administrative Review Decision Quality; and Licence to Operate Baseline. Home Office Internal Audit has produced reports on: Case files and Correspondence Management (KIM), Passports and Visas Overseas Working Processes and Decision Quality; Data Quality– CID and Removals; Effectiveness of Assurance for Overseas Operations: UKVI & HMPO, and Review of Home Office Borders and Immigration Guidance.

operational environment. Such proactive monitoring arrangements, together with senior level accountability and challenge, could have placed the department in a stronger position to identify and resolve problematic issues and errors before they escalated.[107]

To illustrate: when the full scale of the Windrush scandal became clear, the department undertook a limited historical review of the detention and removal of Caribbean nationals and the impact of hostile environment sanctions upon them. However, it refused to extend this review to the circa 160,000 non-Caribbean nationals as recommended by both the NAO and the PAC.[108] The department's view was proactively reviewing the cases of other Commonwealth nationals would be operationally disproportionate.[109] To put matters into context, the department had reviewed Caribbean cases involving 4,629 removals and 7,171 detentions, but it refused to review other Commonwealth cases involving 91,478 removals and 68,213 detentions. This in turn led to a dispute with the NAO about the application of 'Legal Entitlements and Administrative Practices' (LEAP), a longstanding and important piece of cross-government guidance about how government departments should respond when their administrative practices have weakened individuals' legal entitlements.[110] The general LEAP principle is that a legal entitlement, once validly established, must be met, irrespective of the administrative difficulties or costs involved.[111] Further, the onus is on government to use available data to identify those concerned, provide a remedy and publicise the situation for others. The NAO argued that the refusal to extend the historical review to non-Caribbean people undermined LEAP principles.[112] The department's position was that LEAP principles did not apply. Nonetheless, following the Windrush Review, the department belatedly accepted the recommendation to reassure itself that no one from the Windrush generation (Caribbean and non-Caribbean) had been wrongly caught up in the enforcement of immigration law.[113]

One reading of this is that the department's initial response shifted in light of the political context when the full awfulness of Windrush became clear and it had no alternative but to capitulate to the entirely reasonable requirement to investigate non-Caribbean cases. Another reading is that the department was being held to

---

[107] 'Windrush Lessons Learned Review: Independent Review by Wendy Williams' HC 93 (2019–20) 148 ('Windrush Review').

[108] NAO, 'Handling of the Windrush Situation' HC 1622 (2017–2019) [2.11]–[2.14]; PAC, 'Windrush Generation and the Home Office' HC 1518 (2017–19) [17].

[109] HM Treasury, 'Treasury Minutes: Government Response to the Committee of Public Accounts on the Eighty-Second and the Eighty-Sixth to the Ninety-Second Reports from Session 2017–19' (CP 113, 2019), 'Eighty-Second Report of Session 2017–19: The Home Office: Windrush generation and the Home Office' [5.1].

[110] Civil Service Department, 'Legal Entitlements and Administrative Practices: A Report by Officials' (London, HMSO, 1979).

[111] ibid 10.

[112] NAO (n 108) [10].

[113] Windrush Review (n 107).

a different standard of performance and accountability by the NAO, PAC and the Windrush Review. One of the central messages from the Windrush Review was the need for the department to monitor the impact of its policies and procedures, and how the quality of individual casework decisions are affected by a range of wider systems and cultures. The review made various recommendations in this respect. The department needed to revise its governance arrangements for the oversight of its operational performance in order to provide a genuine opportunity to confront and challenge risk and performance issues across its directorates as opposed to within them. The wider picture of siloed operations in which officials did not sufficiently consider an emerging set of circumstances across the whole of the system because their focus was upon their own specific division or directorate was inadequate. By contrast, higher-level oversight and risk assessment mechanisms could have identified the prospect of Windrush arising involved and prompted action to address the potential problems.

Other Windrush Review recommendations included the need to develop a learning culture and to improve operational practice, decision-making and help for people at risk. The importance of proactive monitoring is clearly demonstrated by Windrush. Had Windrush refusal decisions been monitored effectively, the incorrect imposition on claimants of the criminal – as opposed to the civil – standard of proof would have been detected and corrected.[114] That review also made a number of wider recommendations as to how the department should improve its business intelligence and management information.

D. The Potential of Proactive Monitoring

This new standard of accountability developed by audit and scrutiny bodies and ad hoc reviews is clearly premised upon viewing government departments as responsible administrative bodies that are obliged to monitor proactively their own operations and take positive action to identify and correct systemic errors. The underlying assumption is that relying solely on the reactive posture of traditional judicial mechanisms toward correcting errors is inadequate and insufficient. Instead, government must take proactive and affirmative action to seek out systemic problems that arise from its policies and procedures, remedy the problems identified, and monitor and evaluate future operations to reduce the risk of future errors. As Windrush demonstrates, not adopting a proactive and systemic approach toward identifying and correcting errors can not only harms individuals; it also leads to failed implementation of policy and of legal rights.

---

[114] A similar approach can be seen in the review into the unlawful mandating of DNA evidence for immigration purposes, which recommended that the department proactively contact all the people affected and provide them with financial redress. See D Singh, 'Independent Review of the Home Office Response to the Mandating of DNA Evidence for Immigration Purposes' (2019).

From the perspective of a responsible administration, recognised practical constraints on the department's ability to engage in proactive monitoring should not be seen as intractable features of administrative life, but as challenges to be overcome. Take, for instance, the issue of performance and management data. Effective monitoring depends on having the relevant data concerning a range of operational and management issues and also the ability to link up range of different datasets to identify trends. The department's old management information and IT systems have not been sufficiently sophisticated to enable analysis around themes and patterns.[115] Instead, there have been locally managed spreadsheets (ie developed within specific casework teams) that have been incompatible with each other. Further, there has not been any central business intelligence system to allow for effective forecasting, collation of management information, identification of trends and critical issues.[116] There are also the issues of whether there is the cultural willingness and structural administrative vision to engage in proactive monitoring.

The response is that it is for the department to make the appropriate and necessary changes so that it can discharge its responsibilities to monitor proactively its own operations effectively and thereby discharge its duty of responsible administration. The Windrush Review concluded that the department had missed opportunities to anticipate the scandal because its internal information systems, processes and technology lacked the capability to identify and link information across different areas, which would have alerted it to early warning signs and could have led to action to tackle trends as they emerged. It had also been looking at the wrong risks.[117] The review therefore recommended that the department invest in improving data quality, management information and performance measures that focus on results as well as throughput of applicants.[118] Further, senior leaders in the department needed to make and promote the best use of data and improve its capability to anticipate, monitor and identify trends, as well as collate casework data linking performance data to Parliamentary questions, reviews, appeals, judicial reviews, complaints, MP correspondence and other information, including feedback from external agencies, departments and the public. The department also needed to invest in improving its knowledge management and record-keeping.

Accepting the Windrush Review recommendations, the department has moved toward a single digital repository for information, improving its management information to enable it to better identify risks and look for early warning signs, and is developing its skills and resources to capture and manage knowledge.[119] Other relevant changes include a programme of departmental culture change, developing

---

[115] Windrush Review (n 107) 89.
[116] Singh, 'Independent Review' (n 114) [2.21].
[117] Windrush Review (n 107) 147.
[118] ibid.
[119] Home Office, 'The Response to the Windrush Lessons Learned Review: A Comprehensive Improvement Plan' (CP 293, 2020) [140]–[142].

ethical decision standards, improving external understanding and engagement, and revising and clarifying the risk management framework. As regards culture and fragmented structures, the department must undertake substantial changes so that it can improve operations through a system-wide approach, as opposed to the habitual and flawed siloed approach.

The department's 2021 post-Windrush Assurance Strategy may indicate the course of travel.[120] The department now has a wider Early Warnings Working Group and Risk and Integrity Team to identify and manage issues of risk. COAT can make recommendations to identify and alleviate or eradicate causes of concern. Furthermore, if a systematic issue is identified, often relating to policy, systems or processes, or if there no clear ownership of a long-standing issue, then the Chief Caseworker Unit can conduct an early warning review. That unit has the remit to resolve any issues highlighted in its reviews and work across the immigration system to ensure that sustainable improvements are implemented, and to take ownership of cross-cutting issues which have no clear owner. It can also review policies, systems and processes, and link up stakeholders within the department.

A related development has been the broadening of the focus of quality assurance to cover the full range of the department's wider activities beyond casework decision-making (itself large enough). This is the Simplified Management Assurance Framework, which is intended to ensure quality assurance over other areas such as business delivery, policy and Parliament, and financial management. The enormousness of the task is illustrated by the fact that in 27 out of 39 areas of activity, the assurance quality rating was 'unknown'; 'the significant number of activities where assurance levels are unknown or limited presents potential risks'.[121] Another measure has been the development of a strategy by which the department can manage and anticipate different types of risk.[122] There is also external monitoring by the Chief Inspector and NAO. It remains to be seen how things develop. But put together, these trends could represent some movement toward a more proactive monitoring approach. However, much more needs to be done to embed proactive monitoring and organisational learning to improve the quality of casework decisions and associated systems, as complemented by external administrative law remedies such as appeals and judicial review.

VI. Conclusion

This chapter has considered the effectiveness of redress mechanisms and legal challenges against immigration decisions. Given the haphazard, disjointed

---

[120] UKVI, 'Assurance Strategy' (2021).

[121] ibid part 2 – Assurance of Simplified Management Assurance Framework areas. These 39 areas are grouped under the following headings: assurance activities; business delivery; policy and Parliament; financial management; people management; and protective security.

[122] UKVI, 'Risk Management Strategy' (2021).

and policy-driven development of these mechanisms, the overall system lacks coherence and conscious design. Administrative review has a much more limited heritage and history than appeals, let alone judicial review, and has been rightly seen to be inferior. Nonetheless, within a relatively short period of time, the department has somewhat improved the handling of reviews, although many further changes are required, not least restoring appeal rights against credibility-based decisions. Tribunal appeals have been a mainstay and provide the most effective substantive remedy, but their legal framework is unnecessarily confused and their current jurisdiction is too limited. Significant areas of casework decision-making do not currently attract a right of appeal, but should. Individual judicial review remains the migrant's traditional means of legal challenge; it provides an important check, but in many cases it only provides a thin form of legality compared with substantive appellate decision-making.

Overall, conventional judicial remedies are important, particularly from the perspective of aggrieved individuals, but they are insufficient. What is also required is proactive and systemic error-correction through oversight and monitoring – not just to remedy poor decisions, but also to improve organisational performance. This should be developed through enhanced forms of internal proactive monitoring based upon the need to improve substantive decision-making quality through better organisational performance and learning. There is a current framework for doing this through the QA system and the Chief Caseworker Unit. Also required are a culture change around casework, the resources to introduce more extensive proactive monitoring, and the willingness to improve the casework process. The scale of the improvements required are considerable and will require a dedicated focus and resources.

7

Immigration Enforcement

After decisions have been made and outstanding appeals and judicial reviews resolved, the question of enforcement arises. Enforcement is about encouraging, incentivising and compelling people to do things that they would not do voluntarily because they stand to benefit from resisting or evading the rules. Without enforcement, laws are just good advice. Yet, enforcement is, to put it mildly, a challenging endeavour. It raises difficult questions about the most effective means of securing compliance and enforcement of the rules, the lengths to which enforcement should be pursued, its impacts, the trade-offs involved, and how enforcement and compliance activities are organised. While administrative agencies have various powers and means of enforcement, the fundamental issues concern how those powers are used in practice and with what consequences and effects – in terms of both policy goals and affected individuals.

We can then reclaim enforcement as an important topic of administrative law in action. After all, enforcement involves government agencies using their statutory and other powers to enforce the law and deliver policy goals. This suggests an 'implementation model' of administrative law based on the positive functions of the state and the organisation of enforcement activities both internally within the specific administrative institution and externally with other actors. In the immigration context, this model is grounded upon organisational performance, effectiveness and the internal law of administration, as evidenced by administrative practices and behaviours, in addition to critiques of it that are premised upon different ideas as to what administration could and should become. In this context, the critically important issues concern the effectiveness of enforcement action, how internal and external controls motivate and restrain enforcement operations, and how the enforcement agency both is and could be organised. This chapter considers these themes by examining immigration enforcement.

I. Immigration Enforcement and its Challenges

The integrity of the immigration system depends on effective enforcement. If the state is to control its borders, then deterrence, compliance and enforcement naturally constitute essential tools in this endeavour. Enforcement involves the removal of irregular migrants at the end of the in-country immigration process, and pre-entry compliance and preventing irregular entry in the first place. Immigration enforcement is deeply problematic; it involves 'some of the most challenging, controversial, but important jobs across the whole of Government'.[1] The department's major crises have arisen from enforcement – both insufficient (eg foreign national prisoners, 2006) and excessive enforcement (Windrush, 2018). The department is criticised for its heavy-handed enforcement-minded approach. Yet, its enforcement activities are also 'clearly inadequate'; removals are nowhere near the number of irregular migrants.[2]

But what even is the size of the 'illegal population'? In 2006, the department's director of enforcement gave a candid answer: 'I have not the faintest idea'.[3] Nothing has changed since. It is impossible to identify precisely the size of this population. Estimates of the number of irregular migrants range from 240,000 to 1.2 million.[4] But there is neither a generally accepted estimate nor a generally accepted methodology for producing such an estimate. By its nature, the population is unknown and hidden. None of the established methods of government-wide data-collection apply. How is the department to enforce immigration controls against an unknown and unknowable population? The lack of administrative knowledge prompts resignation at the sheer scale of the task.[5]

The size of the challenge can be illustrated by setting the possible size of the 'illegal population' against the department's limited capacity and capabilities. Suppose that there are 800,000 irregular migrants in the country. Such people get by in their lives somehow. They form relationships, have children and try to live their lives as best they can. The longer such people stay in the country without immigration status, the more difficult it becomes to remove them. In 2019, the department forcibly removed 7,354 people while 12,003 people returned voluntarily.[6] On this basis, it would take decades to remove all of those without immigration status – assuming (wholly unrealistically) that there is no increase in the illegal population in the meantime. This is just not going to happen. Almost all officials will candidly accept that there are many people liable to removal that the department will never realistically remove. The same dynamic of enforcement demand exceeding administrative capacity applies to other compliance regimes, such as

---

[1] Immigration Enforcement, 'Our IE – Delivering Our Organisational Priorities' (2019) 3.
[2] HAC, 'Immigration Control' HC 775 (2005–06) [411].
[3] HAC, 'Oral Evidence: Immigration Control', 16 May 2006, HC 775 (2005–06) Q 815 (Dave Roberts, IND Director of Enforcement and Removals).
[4] C Pinkerton, G McLaughlan, and J Salt, 'Sizing the Illegally Resident Population in the UK' (Online Report 58/04, 2004); J Woodbridge, 'Sizing the Unauthorised (Illegal) Migrant Population in the United Kingdom in 2001' (2005); I Gordon, K Scanlon, T Travers and C Whitehead, 'Economic Impact on the London and UK Economy of an Earned Regularisation of Irregular Migrants to the UK' (LSE, 2009); Migration Watch, 'The Illegal Migrant Population in the UK' (Briefing paper, 2010); Office for National Statistics, 'Measuring Illegal Migration: Our Current View – A Report Outlining Our Discussions on the Measurement of Illegal Migration' (2019).
[5] C Boswell and E Badenhoop, '"What isn't in the files, isn't in the world": Understanding State Ignorance of Irregular Migration in Germany and the United Kingdom' (2021) 34 *Governance* 335.
[6] Home Office, 'Immigration Statistics: Returns' (2020).

illegal working. In 2015, it was concluded that if the estimated number of businesses that employ people illegally was set against the department's enforcement capabilities, it would take Immigration Enforcement between 29 and 37 years to visit all the businesses involved.[7]

Another challenge is posed by the nature of the various and changing threats. Organised criminal gangs facilitate the clandestine entry of people into the country. Foreign national offenders may pose harm to the public. There is the need to protect asylum claimants and victims of sex trafficking and human slavery from harm. There are also asylum claimants who have not been deemed eligible for protection, and individuals who have used fraudulent documents to obtain UK residence or mispresent their status on asylum claims, or have entered into sham relationships and marriages. Some employers exploit people without immigration status. At the same time, there are many people without immigration status who pose no threat, but who may, and have been, seen by the department as easy removal targets. An important qualitative study concluded that there is little evidence that immigration enforcement reduces the numbers of irregular immigrants. Instead, it seems to have unintended consequences by increasing human suffering whilst offering opportunities to criminals and giving rise to criminal practices and pushing irregular immigrants further underground.[8]

Immigration enforcement is, of course, politically contested and sensitive territory. Political viewpoints range from total control and the expulsion of everyone without immigration status to total abolition of immigration control, with many granular differences in between. From one perspective, enforcement efforts reflect government failure and incompetence; from another, they reflect the hopeful assumption that, in a globalised world, the state actually possesses the ability to control its borders. From other extremes, the heavy enforcement of controls is necessary to defend society or, alternatively, it represents the reality of state-sanctioned racist violence. There is no hope of reconciling such extremes, although they do not reflect mainstream public opinion.

What, then, of democracy, the purpose of which is to manage political differences? At no stage have the public supported a policy of abandoning immigration controls. The general principle of enforcing immigration law can then be said to have democratic support, but this leaves enormous scope for discussion and disagreement over both the degree and means of such enforcement. These matters are far too detailed and complex to be resolved through the simplistic slogans and campaigns used in general elections. In this context, there are strong political headwinds prompted by individual cases and newspaper headlines. But at the ground level, enforcement will depend on the organisation of enforcement

---

[7] A paper produced in September 2015 for the Cabinet Office's Illegal Working Steering Group quoted in ICIBI, 'An Inspection of the Home Office's Approach to Illegal Working' (2019) [6.1].

[8] F Düvell, M Cherti, and I Lapshyna, 'Does Immigration Enforcement Matter? Irregular Migration and Control Policies in the UK' (Centre on Migration, Policy and Society, 2018).

operations and the resources available. In 2006, the HAC made the hopeful recommendation that the amount resources allocated for enforcement purposes should be determined by the scale of enforcement action required, and not the other way round.[9] But this has never been possible. Indeed, over recent years, the enforcement budget has been reduced. Given limited resources, the department's approach has been to adopt removal targets to focus enforcement action and to regulate its workflow.

Another challenge of enforcement is the scope for adverse consequences for the people concerned. To state the obvious: enforcing immigration controls is never going to reveal the easy-going, soft-natured side of government. Tough policies will, more often than not, be implemented through tough enforcement action that can be punitive and coercive (detention, forced removals), inevitably increasing the risk of harm and unlawful and harsh outcomes for the people concerned.[10] This is also highly contested territory. The deportation of foreign national offenders can have adverse consequences for those affected and their families.[11] On the other hand, the department is required by statute to deport serious offenders who are subject to a scheme of automatic deportation.[12] It is not the purpose here to resolve such matters, but the general point is that part of the challenge for the enforcement agency to ensure that its enforcement actions do not result in harm to those on the receiving end and are lawful.

However, it is not just irregular migrants who are at risk – as Windrush demonstrated. Without being carefully managed, enforcement action becomes simultaneously under- and over-inclusive. How is the department to ensure that in seeking to reduce the harm caused by irregular migrants, it does not itself, in the process, harm people who are present perfectly legally? What happens to enforcement policy post-Windrush? Hostile environment measures have been retained and new internal mechanisms have been introduced to prevent a similar situation, but will they be sufficient to prevent a recurrence, or are they mere window-dressing?

The wider problem is the tension between practicalities and resources on the one hand, and politics and the perceived need of ministers to maintain public confidence on the other. Having rules that cannot be fully enforced creates uncertainty for people with precarious immigration statuses. It also coincides with cases going through successive decision-making processes and sometimes multiple appeals and onward rights of challenge at some cost to the taxpayer and the people involved for little ultimate purpose. Given the remote likelihood of people who ultimately do not have a valid immigration status and the high costs of seeking to enforce the rules, the question of an amnesty or regularisation programme arises.

---

[9] HAC, 'Immigration Control' (n 2) [411].

[10] See ch 9.

[11] See L de Noronha, *Deporting Black Britons: Portraits of Deportation to Jamaica* (Manchester, Manchester University Press, 2020); J Collinson, 'Suspended Deportation Orders: A Proposed Law Reform' (2020) 40 *Oxford Journal of Legal Studies* 291.

[12] UK Borders Act 2007, ss 32–39.

Yet, this has been resisted by ministers on the ground that it would send out the wrong message politically and encourage more illegal migration. But what is the long-term plan for dealing with people who have been resident without immigration status for a long period of time? One strategy was the hostile environment, but its effectiveness has not been demonstrated. The department itself recognises that most irregular migrants pose no harm at all.[13] The policy debate has then returned to the question of whether to introduce an amnesty or regularisation scheme.

This initial look at the challenges of immigration enforcement is only the start of it, as the following discussion demonstrates. But first, what are the means by which the department can seek to enforce the rules?

II. Enforcement Options

Administrative bodies tasked with enforcement can use various means of going about the task. They can: set aside or modify the rules; exhort people to comply with the rules through publicity and persuasion; pursue and punish those who violate the rules; or make it difficult and inconvenient for people to break the rules.[14] Each option has both advantages and disadvantages. The first and second options are softer approaches that have lower administrative costs. The third and fourth options are tougher strategies and require government and others to expend more effort and resources. All these options apply to the immigration department and are identifiable within both the department's legal framework and administrative practice.

(1) Set aside or modify the rules
Abandoning immigration policy altogether because of the difficulties of enforcing it would never be politically acceptable. An alternative is then for the department to engage in limited tokenistic enforcement while recognising internally (but, of course, not publicly) that full or even partial enforcement is just not possible because of the difficulties involved. In 1999, the Immigration Services Union stated that there was a

> long-term view or culture in the immigration and nationality department of immigration control as being too difficult ... We think that the attitude is that it is not possible effectively to maintain immigration control and that the department is attempting to ameliorate the situation, to limit numbers where possible and, if you like, to get illegal immigrants settled in the country as easily as possible. Obviously, that is not what we see immigration control as being about.[15]

---

[13] As recognised by the department: PAC, 'Oral Evidence: Immigration Enforcement', 13 July 2020, HC 407 (2017–19) Q 49 (Tyson Hepple, Director General, Immigration Enforcement, Home Office).

[14] C Hood, *Administrative Analysis: An Introduction to Rules, Enforcement and Organizations* (Brighton, Wheatsheaf, 1986) 51–52.

[15] Special Standing Committee on the Immigration and Asylum Bill 1999 col 455 (22 March 1999) (John Tincey, Immigration Services Union).

Another option is to have an amnesty to regularise the status of irregular migrants, such as those caught up in the asylum backlog who have lived in the UK for many years. As noted above, this has been deemed politically unacceptable and likely to encourage future irregular immigration.[16] Nonetheless, smaller amnesties have occurred through case resolution processes. At the level of individual determination, there is a long-standing provision in the immigration rules for leave to remain on the basis of long-term residence, both lawful and unlawful. Someone who has lived in the country continuously, albeit unlawfully, for 20 years can apply for indefinite leave to remain. The advantage of setting aside the rules is that it reduces pressure on the department and saves resources, but too much of it weakens public confidence and encourages irregular migrants to try their luck.

(2) Use publicity and persuasion to encourage people to comply with the rules
In 2013, the department used much-derided 'go home' vans carrying the message 'In the UK illegally? Go home or face arrest' with a hotline number for illegal migrants to contact for help to return to their home countries. The purpose was to test whether irregular migrants would depart voluntarily if they were made aware there was 'a near and present' danger of being arrested.[17] The department also provides advice to people on how to comply with immigration rules and 'educational visits' to encourage employers to comply.

Another approach is to provide people with incentives to return. The department has, for many years, paid people to leave the country and/or provided them with support. People eligible under the assisted return programme may receive reintegration support of up to £2,000 either as cash or 'in-kind' support. Support can involve helping returnees find somewhere to live and a job, or to start a business in their home country. The attraction of this approach is the lower cost (financial and personal) of encouraging people to comply, but its overall effectiveness can be variable.

(3) Pursue and penalise those who violate the rules
The long-established and traditional means of enforcement is to detain and then forcibly remove people without immigration status. In practice, this includes both the administrative removal and deportation of, respectively, people without leave to remain and foreign national offenders. Enforcement also includes tackling organised criminal gangs that facilitate illegal entry to the country and pre-entry compliance checks to prevent people without adequate documents from boarding flights to the UK. A tough enforcement approach is often the only means of enforcing the rules effectively against those who will evade all other means. It is symbolic of the power of the sovereign state to control its own borders, although it is a complex process.

---

[16] See, eg, HAC (n 2) [471]–[479].
[17] 'May was not opposed to "go home" vans, official accounts suggest' *Guardian* (19 April 2018).

To remove someone forcibly, four or five different immigration enforcement teams need to work together: an intelligence team; a casework team dealing with people in the community; an arrest or detention team; another team to handle casework once the person is detained; and another dealing with the logistics, such as liaising with High Commissions and airlines. Then there are various potential logistical difficulties. The returnee may have no travel documentation. The department may not have a return agreement with the relevant country. The government of that country may not accept the return of its own citizens. Removal escorts may not be unavailable. There might be flight or carrier issues. The returnee may become disruptive or unwell or make a last-minute asylum claim and/or seek judicial review, often raised in the late stages of removal to seek an injunction against removal. The costs of enforced removals are also high.[18]

(4) Make it difficult, inconvenient and uncomfortable for people to break the rules

Another option is then to encourage and incentivise people to leave voluntarily by making staying increasing difficult and uncomfortable. This approach is clearly reflected in hostile environment measures. By preventing irregular migrants from working, accessing healthcare, claiming benefits, opening a bank account, renting, or having a driving licence, the purpose was to encourage them to leave or not enter in the first place. This approach lowered costs by enlisting the involvement of other actors – both governmental and private sectors – as agents in the enforcement process.

Beyond specific hostile environment measures, the department has, over the last two decades, shifted toward greater reliance on other actors – eg employers and universities – to monitor compliance. Categorising certain universities and employers as 'highly trusted' enables the department to focus its attention on riskier organisations. The shift in responsibility has been prompted by reduced budgets. The department has also long sought to reduce the pull factors that are seen as incentivising economic migrants to lodge asylum claims by, for instance, severely restricting asylum-seeker support and preventing asylum claimants from working. But the wider risk is that the involvement of other actors may distort enforcement. Another evident shortcoming, as illustrated by Windrush, is that enforcement becomes over-inclusive. Making life uncomfortable for irregular migrants can and has affected those who are present legally.

* * *

Another approach is to deploy all of these options at the same time, but in different ways. Enforcement is always a question of degree and of selecting the best – or, more realistically, the least worst – approach in the circumstances.

---

[18] 'Home Office spends £13,354 per person on deportation flights' *Guardian* (23 March 2021).

Tough enforcement strategies are likely to be the only effective means of ensuring compliance when those who evade the rules do so opportunistically and will not comply at all unless they are physically compelled to do so. Opportunistic evasion is present, in varying degrees, in all enforcement regimes, although it never accounts for all violations. People may not comply with the immigration rules because of a lack of knowledge, awareness and advice, the inherent complexity of both the rules and system, and the difficulties they experience in trying to interact with the department, and its lack of help and assistance. For non-opportunistic evaders, the mere possibility of being subject to the statistically unlikely event of immigration detention and removal may be sufficient to prevent them from living an ordinary life and to be fearful of any encounter with authority. Inappropriate and excessive enforcement measures can also be counter-productive. Tough enforcement against relatively weak and vulnerable people can undermine public support for enforcement. At the same time, the enforcement agency may have other reasons for using tough enforcement methods, not least the perceived need to reassure public opinion that it can take effective action.[19]

We can now examine how the department seeks to undertake compliance and enforcement in practice.

III. Enforcement Operations

The Immigration Enforcement directorate is responsible for preventing abuse of the immigration system, securing compliance, and encouraging and enforcing the removal of people without immigration status from the UK. Its strategic aim is to reduce the size of the illegal migrant population and minimise the harm caused by foreign nationals in the UK illegally through prevention, compliance, and enforcement.

More specifically, Immigration Enforcement has three operational missions. The first is to prevent illegal migration through greater compliance with immigration law. This involves preventing individuals without an immigration status from physically entering the country. It also involves encouraging compliance by limiting unlawful access to government-funded services, that is, hostile environment measures. The second mission involves dealing with the threats arising from immigration offending. This includes counterterrorism, disrupting criminal gangs and tackling immigration abuse. The third mission involves the physical removal of foreign national offenders and persons without leave to remain to their country of origin. This is achieved through voluntary removals, enforced removals and the deportation of foreign national prisoners. As regards resources, Immigration

---

[19] A Aliverti, 'Making People Criminal: The Role of the Criminal Law in Immigration Enforcement' (2012) 16 *Theoretical Criminology* 417.

Enforcement has a staff of around 5,000 and had a budget of £392 million in 2019–20, which represented an 11 per cent real-terms reduction since 2015–16.[20] Figure 7.1 presents the current internal structure of Immigration Enforcement and its key activities.

Figure 7.1 Immigration Enforcement organisational structure (2021)

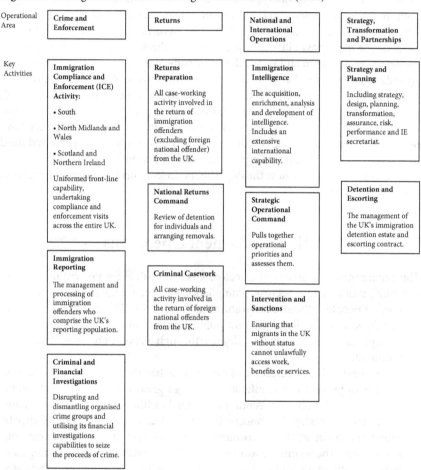

Source: Immigration Enforcement.

In common with UKVI, Immigration Enforcement is a large administrative agency organised into various units and teams, but unlike UKVI, in which caseworkers are ensconced in processing centres, it has more of a frontline on-the-ground presence through enforcement officers and staff at immigration reporting centres.

---

[20] NAO, 'Immigration Enforcement' HC 110 (2019–21) [1.9].

This is accompanied by a variety of law enforcement units which undertake immigration intelligence work, criminal and financial investigations to disrupt organised crime groups, and criminal casework activity required to deport returning foreign national offenders. Alongside UKVI, Immigration Enforcement has also contracted out some of its functions; the management of immigration detention centres and the provision of escort services have been wholly outsourced to private sector contractors. Immigration Enforcement is also an agency under substantial pressure and stress. Furthermore, there is a default tendency toward fragmented and silo-based operations within specific teams in addition to operational difficulties and inefficiencies.

How, then, does enforcement work in practice? Enforcement officers have extensive statutory powers to search premises and arrest persons, seize and retain items and nationality documents.[21] They can detain people in immigration detention indefinitely.[22] They can remove and deport people[23] and arrest people working illegally and impose civil penalties on employers.[24] There are a number of criminal offences with regard to illegal immigration, including illegal entry, deception, illegal working, helping an asylum-seeker to enter the country, and assisting entry in breach of a deportation or an exclusion order, amongst others.[25] There are also the hostile environment measures and other less visible means of securing compliance such as tackling organised criminal gangs and working overseas with airlines to prevent people without visas from travelling to the country.

The critically important issue is one of instrumental rationality, the ability of administration to implement policy effectively by achieving real-world changes. How are these statutory powers, criminal offences, and the hostile environment measures used in practice? What impact do they have in terms of securing compliance with and enforcing immigration controls? What are the consequences of the department's actions? Any inquiry into administrative operations is inextricable from questions of performance.

These questions were largely addressed by the NAO and the PAC in 2020.[26] Overall, they found that the department collected a wide range of management information about its activities and completed tasks, for instance, the number of illegal entrants detected and the number of enforced and voluntary returns. But this information did not enable the department to understand or demonstrate the impact of its activities and performance against its stated missions. It measured its 'success' against activities undertaken rather than outcomes achieved. In other words, the department lacked a detailed understanding of the consequences and impact of its actions. Accordingly, the department's ability to achieve the goal of securing greater compliance with immigration law was largely unevidenced

---

[21] Immigration Act 1971, ss 28A–28I.
[22] Immigration Act 1971, Sch 2, paras 15–25A.
[23] Immigration Rules Pt 13: deportation; UK Borders Act 2007, ss 32–37.
[24] Immigration, Asylum and Nationality Act 2006, ss 15–26; Immigration Act 2016, ss 34–38.
[25] Immigration Act 1971, ss 24–25B.
[26] NAO, 'Immigration Enforcement' (n 20); PAC, 'Immigration Enforcement' HC 407 (2019–21).

and unclear. To consider further, we can examine the department's performance against its three enforcement missions.

A. Mission 1: Preventing Illegal Migration Through Greater Compliance with Immigration Law

This mission seeks to secure greater compliance with immigration law to prevent illegal immigration. The department defines 'compliance' as ensuring people enter and leave the country in accordance with their visa and passport conditions. It seeks to pursue this mission by: reducing the flow of illegal immigration; reducing the incentives to remain in the country illegally through hostile environment policies; and sending decision letters to overstayers.

As regards reducing illegal immigration, the aim is to reduce the number of people entering the country illegally by working with airlines and others to prevent abuse and to ensure passengers have the correct documentation. In the year to the end of October 2019, the department and its partners detected 11,300 clandestine attempts to enter the country at UK ports and 35,600 attempts from overseas. This was an increase from the previous year; in the year to the end of October 2018, these figures were 7,200 and 33,600 respectively. These figures might be taken as an indication of an enhanced performance to reduce illegal immigration. However, the department was unable to explain whether the increase in the number of illegal entrants reflected either a greater proportion of individuals being detected or an increase in the number of individuals seeking to enter the UK illegally.[27] If the former, then this would suggest department's compliance activities were having a greater impact, but this would not be the case if there had been more attempts made to enter illegally.

As regards reducing the incentives for people to remain in the country illegally, hostile environmental measures were intended to make life in the UK uncomfortable for irregular migrants. The department's belief has been that such measures will have an effect in terms of encouraging voluntary removals, compliance and deterring people from remaining in the country when their leave to remain has expired. But this is mere belief, not hard causal evidence. The department has not evaluated these measures. It had no specific evidence on which to base the effectiveness of hostile environment measures in terms of either deterring irregular migrants from entering or encouraging those in the country to leave voluntarily. There is a similar analysis as regards the department's use of penalties and sanctions.[28]

Another means by which the department seeks to secure compliance is to contact people who have overstayed their visas through decision letters informing

---

[27] NAO (n 20) [2.6].
[28] ICIBI, 'An Inspection of the Home Office's Use of Sanctions and Penalties' (2021).

them they no longer have leave to remain and should therefore make prepara-
tions to return to their country of origin. This may lead some people to leave the
country. However, the department was unable to link up such letters with actual
returns. It has been unable to evidence the degree to which its actions actually
prompt overstayers to leave the country.[29] Because the department's data only
described its activity and did not link it up with outcomes, it was unclear whether
its actions provided an effective response to people overstaying.

B. Mission 2: Dealing with the Threats Arising from Immigration Offending

The second enforcement mission involves the department working with the
National Crime Agency and other law enforcement bodies to respond to the
threats posed by immigration offending. This work involves disrupting criminal gangs that enable much of the illegitimate entry into the UK, and tackling
immigration abuse.

Given that organised criminal gangs facilitate a considerable amount of illegal
entry to the country, it is important to disrupt them through criminal investigations, prosecutions and convictions. The type of disruptions of such gangs vary
and include minor, moderate and major disruptions. This in turn raises questions
about the impact of such disruptions on immigration offending. The directorate
has increased the number of minor disruptions from 61 in 2015–16 to 489 in
2019–20. However, it has not increased the number of major disruptions, which
have remained relatively low. In 2015–16, there were 42 major disruptions; in
2019–20, there were 43 major disruptions. The department's position has been
that a greater number of minor disruptions can have a lasting effect on the
activities of criminal gangs, but it has been unable to evidence this assertion.[30]

As regards tackling immigration abuse, the department receives 60,000 pieces
of information per year concerning potential immigration abuse (eg that someone
is working illegally or that an employer is employing people to work illegally).
Enforcement teams will consider such information to assess the potential risk
of harm and whether to act. The traditional method is for enforcement staff to
make visits to, for instance, employers to check that employees are not working
illegally. In practice, operational constraints dictate whether such information is
acted upon. For instance, enforcement teams in London and the south-east are
so over-stretched that they cannot always act upon high-priority tasks let alone
low-priority intelligence. In practice, the department has been unable to assess the
impact of this work on reducing the size of the illegal population because of the
lack of information. It is possible that preventing some people from work illegally
has some effect as regards preventing irregular immigration. On the other hand,

[29] NAO (n 20) [2.12].
[30] ibid [2.16].

it might increase the vulnerability of those people without immigration status and make them more attractive to exploitative employers.[31] What has been absent is the detailed data with which to make evidence-based assessments as to the consequences and impact of the department's actions.

C. Mission 3: Removing Foreign National Offenders and People without Leave to Remain to their Country of Origin

The third enforcement mission involves removing foreign national offenders and irregular migrants. This mission is undertaken through voluntary returns, enforcing returns against those who have refused requests to leave voluntarily, and the deportation of foreign national prisoners. Enforced removals involve the use of detention and charter flights. The priority has been to remove those people who pose the greatest possible risk of harming the public, in particular, foreign national prisoners.

Following the foreign national prisoners crisis of 2006, the statutory framework was changed by creating a presumption in favour of deportation.[32] The department has substantially increased the resourcing of such deportations. Nonetheless, progress in deporting more foreign national prisoners has been slow. Deporting such non-compliant prisoners is inherently difficult because of the range of barriers in play, such as human rights and legal challenges, administrative and documentation difficulties, and the unwillingness of many countries to accept such returns. Nonetheless, the department's performance in deporting foreign national offenders has been poor. In 2015, the PAC concluded that the department was missing too many opportunities to remove foreign national offenders early and wasting resources, through a combination of a lack of focus on early action at the border and police stations, poor joint working in prisons, its own administrative errors, and inefficient caseworking. Overall, when combined with very poor management information and non-existent cost data, the system was failing to deport foreign national prisoners and appeared to be dysfunctional.[33]

As regards other immigrants without leave to remain, the statutory provisions governing removal directions have been amended to reduce complexity, uncertainty, delay and opportunities for challenge. The process used to involve separate decisions concerning a person's immigration status and then further decisions regarding their removal. This segmented decision process has since been replaced by the power to issue a single immigration decision encompassing both immigration status and removability.[34] Yet, enforced removals remain difficult to

---

[31] V Mantouvalou, 'The Right to Non-Exploitative Work' in V Mantouvalou (ed), *The Right to Work* (Oxford, Hart, 2015).

[32] UK Borders Act 2007; Nationality, Immigration and Asylum Act 2002, s 117C(1).

[33] PAC, 'Managing and Removing Foreign National Offenders' HC 708 (2014–15); NAO, 'Managing and Removing Foreign National Offenders' HC 441 (2014–15).

[34] Immigration Act 2014, s 1.

undertake and to complete. Many obstacles – such as documentation problems, other countries not accepting the return of their own citizens, and potential return-ees making last-minute asylum claims or seeking judicial review – are outside the department's control. The long-established tradition has been to view such claims as vexatious and abusive delaying tactics, but the department has not systemati-cally analysed such claims. Voluntary removals are a much more cost-effective and humane method of removing people. Under the Assisted Voluntary Return scheme, returnees receive a financial incentive to return voluntarily.

In recent years, the number of both enforced and voluntary removals has declined. Between 2004 and 2018, the number of enforced returns fell by around two-thirds (see Figure 7.2). The department has attributed this to last-minute vexatious asylum claims. Between 2015 and 2019, the proportion of people released from immigration detention was between 53 per cent and 62 per cent per year – meaning that more people were released from detention than were removed.[35] However, the department has not undertaken any systematic analysis of the reasons for this and has been unable to evidence whether detainees had lodged abusive asylum claims in order to be released from detention. The number of voluntary removals has also reduced since 2015. The department has been unable to explain the reasons for this and the decline in voluntary removals has cast substantial doubt over the effectiveness of hostile environment measures in encouraging irregular migrants to leave voluntarily.

Figure 7.2 Voluntary returns, enforced removals and entry refusals statistics 2004–19[36]

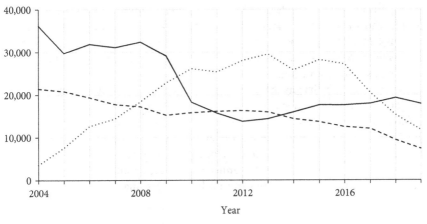

——— Total refused entry at port and subsequently departed

- - - - - Total enforced removals

········· Voluntary removals (including returns from detention)

[35] NAO (n 20) 39.
[36] Source: Home Office, 'Immigration Returns: Statistics' (2020).

IV. Assessing Matters So Far

Pausing here, we can pull together a number of threads. The NAO's overall conclusion in 2020 was that the department was largely unable to demonstrate the individual and cumulative impact of its activities in order to assess its overall success against its missions. It only measured activities undertaken – not results achieved. What the NAO had been looking for from Immigration Enforcement was a theory of change about the causal linkages between activities undertaken and outcomes and results produced. Alternatively, the department could have retrospectively compared its activities against relevant data to understand its past performance and to plan for the future. In the event, the department had done neither.

The PAC was naturally more forthright. The department had 'no idea' of what impact it was achieving; instead, it had relied upon a 'disturbingly weak evidence base to assess the impact of its immigration enforcement activity' and had not been 'sufficiently curious about the impact of its actions'.[37] The need for a robust evidence basis concerns matters of both policy and administration. Take, for instance, the alleged harms and costs caused by illegal migration. It is commonly assumed that irregular immigration causes harm and costs, through the harms caused by foreign national offenders and organised crime, economic harms caused by unscrupulous employers using illegal workers, and the costs to the taxpayer by irregular migrants using public services. However, 'harm' has different meanings from one context to another and the department has not adopted a consistent definition that would enable comparison. Further, there was no data concerning people who are technically irregular migrants, but are themselves victims of harm, such as trafficking victims. As regards the costs imposed by irregular migrants, the department has lacked the detailed analysis required to assess such costs, but instead has made bland generic claims.[38]

In any event, the harms that arise are not caused solely by irregular migration, but also through the department's own actions, in particular over-inclusive enforcement action. This is an established fact. Windrush is the most notorious instance of enforcement action undertaken against people with a legal right to remain. Immigration Enforcement had been the principal directorate that had positively contributed to the unnecessary harm inflicted upon Windrush people. The resulting sensitivities cannot be underestimated. The Home Office's

---

[37] PAC (n 20) 3 and 5.

[38] See, eg, PAC, 'Oral Evidence: Immigration Enforcement' 13 July 2020 HC 407 (2019–21) Q35: Peter Grant MP: 'I have been an elected politician … since 1992 … A lot of the debate has been around the claims and counterclaims about the costs to public services of illegal immigrants being a burden on local authorities and the NHS. Why is it that 25 or 30 years later you are no further forward in being able to identify the scale of that problem?' Tyson Hepple (Director General, Immigration Enforcement): 'I think we are further forward, because we have started a piece of work to do just that – to try to understand the impact that enforcing the immigration laws is having on the economy and society.'

Permanent Secretary later acknowledged that the Windrush Review had only been 'a millimetre or two' away from labelling the department as institutionally racist.[39] The problems are further complicated because immigration status is often fluid. People can slip in and out of having an immigration status; given the factual complexity of individual cases and the legal complexity of the rules, such matters are difficult even for well-experienced experts and judges to determine.

Smarter enforcement and compliance are, then, required. Despite the gaps in the data, the NAO found that the department's preliminary analytical work suggested that compliance activities aimed at preventing irregular migration had a greater impact than enforced removals and deportations.[40] This in turn raises questions as to which types of compliance and enforcement activity are more effective and which are to be preferred. Should more resources be invested in compliance activities that may well be more effective in preventing irregular migrant, although their impact is less visible and certain? Or should the focus be upon more visible and impactful activity of costly enforced removals? From an operational point of view, the assessment would involve a cost-benefit analysis focusing upon matters such resources to be invested which then have to be set against a comparison of the relative effectiveness of the different instruments of compliance and enforcement. But inevitably political considerations come into play, not least the short-term desires of ministers to be seen to be doing something in response to critical media headlines.

A further point concerns the need for performance information – not just to assess the impacts and consequences of the department's interventions, but also to inform its priorities and activities in the first place. Given the complexity and blurring of immigration issues, there is a particular need for the department to proceed on the basis of objective evidence rather than subjective opinion. Again, the PAC has particularly stressed this point: if the department was not setting priorities on the basis of hard evidence, then it risked making them on the basis of 'anecdote, assumption, and prejudice'.[41]

Consider, for instance, the department's belief has been that the increasing proportion of detainees being released from immigration detention prior to removal can be attributed to last-minute abusive asylum claims lodged by detainees playing the system. The problem is that the department had not undertaken the necessary systematic analysis to evidence this belief. As the PAC noted, such last-minute claims could equally be the consequence of other factors, not least other government policies and actions, such as the department's reduction in the financial package of voluntary returns and the lack of good-quality legal advice earlier in the process. The department subsequently accepted that the PAC's point that the lack of early legal advice could influence its ability to make successful returns.

---

[39] ibid Q 71 (Matthew Rycroft, Permanent Secretary, Home Office).
[40] NAO (n 20) [2.32]–[2.33].
[41] PAC, 'Immigration Enforcement' HC 407 (n 26) 3.

In the absence of evidence and analysis, the department had by default ascribed the problem to abuse of the process. Such unsupported claims risked 'inflaming prejudice against legitimate immigrants and bona fide asylum seekers'.[42]

More generally, performance information and a data-driven approach is relevant not solely in terms of understanding activities in terms of securing compliance and enforcement. It is also significant in terms of enabling external accountability, and reassuring immigrants and the public that enforcement action is undertaken in accordance with equality and diversity principles, does not harm innocent people, and is not inadvertently motivated by or inflames prejudices. Again, the PAC highlighted that the department's lack of accurate, timely and good-quality management data makes it very difficult for scrutiny bodies to hold the department to account.[43] Furthermore, the department's failure to identify or evaluate the impact of its enforcement activities on individuals had created a 'risk of harm and distress to innocent people who are here perfectly legally ... we not satisfied that the Department attaches sufficient importance to this risk'.[44]

For all these reasons, the department needed to develop better ways of identifying the impact of its interventions by building a stronger evidence base – rather than just presenting performance information about tasks and activities undertaken. The scale of transformation required is considerable.[45] The PAC recommended that the department develop a detailed improvement plan for the collection, use and analysis of data and a further plan for transforming Immigration Enforcement into a data-led organisation.[46] But before considering the wider question of reform, we need to probe further into how enforcement action has functioned in practice.

V. Organising Enforcement Operations

In the light of the importance of immigration enforcement and the inability of the department to understand fully the impact of its own operations, the fundamental challenge is one of organisation. How then has the department been organised to date? What mechanisms has it used to motivate and coordinate a large-scale system of administrative enforcement comprised of different functions? This section considers three such mechanisms: removal targets; data-sharing; and administrative capacity and coordination. Both this and the next section lay bare

---

[42] ibid 6.

[43] PAC, 'Reforming the UK Border and Immigration System' HC 584 (2014–14) 5.

[44] PAC (n 26) 6.

[45] In 2020, the department stated that it had been developing methods to identify the impact of its interventions and intends to move away from performance assessments that rely heavily on the overall number of returns, although this work was only at the preliminary stages: PAC, 'Oral Evidence: Immigration Enforcement' 13 July 2020 HC 407 (2019–21) Q 77 (Matthew Rycroft, Permanent Secretary, Home Office).

[46] PAC (n 26) 5–6.

the sheer scale of the organisational challenges for enforcement activity, and the risks and consequences of getting things wrong.

A. Removal Targets

The department has, for many years, been set removal targets by ministers to drive its enforcement activities. Such targets have been adopted as a direct political and governmental response to public concern about illegal immigration, to provide a focus for enforcement action, and to measure performance. In 2002, there was a Public Service Agreement to secure 75 per cent more removals in 2004 than in 1998.[47] Subsequent targets were set to achieve year-on-year increases in removals. David Blunkett MP, when Home Secretary (2001–04), set a target of removing 2,500 failed asylum-seekers per month. This target was later abandoned when it became clear that it was massively over-ambitious and unachievable. In 2015–16, there was a target of 40,000 returns to home countries including around 14,000 enforced returns. In 2017–18, the target was to secure 12,800 enforced removals: 230–250 enforced removals a week. Internally, the overall removals target was broken down into detailed operational targets to inform the work of specific regional enforcement teams and local members of staff. The department has had various unpublished targets for removals which have been set at the local regional level within immigration enforcement.

Of course, performance targets are inherently susceptible to gaming and manipulation.[48] Middle-level managers, under pressure to meet those targets, instruct enforcement staff to go looking for the easiest or softest cases for removal, the 'low-hanging fruit' rather than the more difficult cases. The complaint is long-standing. In 2009, an MP noted that to meet its multiplicity of targets, the department often

> aims at the softest targets, when it should be aiming at those who have eluded it for years, who have abused the system, who are in the country unlawfully, who do not comply with the conditions placed on their stay, or who do not observe their reporting restrictions. They are the people on whom the agency should concentrate. They are, of course, the hardest cases.[49]

Windrush highlighted the perversity of the target-led approach to removals which had led enforcement to focus on people, like the Windrush generation, who were easier to detain than more opportunistic rule-evaders.[50]

---

[47] Home Office, 'Confident Communities in a Secure Britain: The Home Office Strategic Plan 2004–08' (Cm 6287, 2004).

[48] C Hood, 'Gaming in Targetworld: The Targets Approach to Managing British Public Services' (2006) 66 *Public Administration Review* 515; C Boswell, *Manufacturing Political Trust: Targets and Performance Measurement in Public Policy* (Cambridge, Cambridge University Press, 2018); J Taylor, 'Public Officials' Gaming of Performance Measures and Targets: The Nexus between Motivation and Opportunity' (2021) 44 *Public Performance & Management Review* 272.

[49] *Hansard* HC, Vol 497, col 1139 (22 October 2009) (Anne Widdicombe MP, Home Office Minister, 1995–97).

[50] Another dysfunction may include the ratchet effect, whereby the setting of targets incrementally year by year prompts managers to restrict performance to well below its limits.

Unsurprisingly, the whole issue of removal targets became toxic in light of Windrush, which confirmed suspicions that enforcement action had been largely driven to game removal targets. MPs scrutinising Windrush removals in 2018 were exasperated by the spectacle of self-parody by seemingly evasive senior officials drawing semantic, Sir Humphrey-esque distinctions between performance goals, key performance indicators, targets, ambitions and the circumstances in which a target is not actually a target.[51] Senior officials could not give straightforward answers to questions about enforcement targets or their impact on operations.[52] But they did highlight the large-scale organisational complexity in which different goals and targets had been set, with some being higher-level overarching goals set by ministers supported by more detailed internal targets agreed at different levels within the organisational structure and hierarchy, first at the higher level of overall command and then cascaded down to the level of individual operational teams and units. Understandably, appreciating the finer points of the means-ends hierarchy and its interplay with goals and targets was hardly a priority for MPs seeking to comprehend the chronic incompetence and dysfunctionality of a government department that had detained and then removed British citizens on the basis that they were irregular immigrants. The HAC also raised its concern about the interaction between targets, bonuses and decision-making, and about the potential for bonuses to create a disincentive for officials to refer back cases they come across which raised concerns or where mistakes may have been made.[53]

Matters were confirmed by the Windrush Review, which found that targets within Immigration Enforcement had led to a search for the cases most likely to result in removals and voluntary departures.[54] Targets had also exerted wider effects upon enforcement behaviour beyond the handling of individual cases. As a former enforcement official explained, 'because of the pressure felt on targets there

---

[51] HAC, 'Oral Evidence: Immigration Detention', 8 May 2018, HC 913 (2017–2019): Q 350 Yvette Cooper MP (Chair) (speaking to senior officials): 'The problem with all of this is that this is basically like you are playing games with us. It is like if we do not use the right word in the question it is okay for you not to give us proper information. If we say "target" but now you call it an "ambition", it is okay for you to basically say, "We do not have to give you that information". ... It all feels really slippery. ... Because of the way you are responding to our questions and because of the way you keep sliding between "targets", "performance goals", "That one is not a target, that one is" it makes it very hard for us to have confidence in any of the information you are giving us and not to just think you might be hiding something because we did not frame the question in the right way.' And Q 351 Stephen Doughty MP: 'What on earth is going on in your Department if we cannot get answers to the most basic questions that have been repeatedly raised with you?'.
[52] HAC, 'The Windrush Generation' HC 990 (2017–19) [59].
[53] ibid [63].
[54] 'Windrush Lessons Learned Review: Independent Review by Wendy Williams' HC 93 (2019–21) 105 ('Windrush Review'). See also NAO, 'Handling of the Windrush Situation' HC 1622 (2017–2019) [3.12]–[3.13] (reasonable to conclude that removals targets influenced how enforcement staff carried out their work; senior officials recognised that targets could lead to staff focusing on enforced removals in cases where a voluntary removal might have been an option; targets also meant staff focusing less on applying a risk-based approach across their work and not removing people from nationalities that were more difficult to remove).

was an *unquestioning attitude* towards hostile environment measures as *anything that put pressure on migrants* was seen as a good thing'.[55] This 'unquestioning attitude' and the reference to 'migrants' without any qualification as to their immigration status are both deeply troubling and illustrative of a profound malaise. Hence, the need for a thorough programme of culture change as recommended by the Windrush Review.

The withdrawal of removal targets post-Windrush significantly changed the operational environment.[56] At an operational level, enforcement officers were unclear about how their performance was being measured; enforcement teams were given conflicting messages about what constituted 'success'. Although there were no longer formal targets, there was still an expectation of removals. As one officer noted,

> the truth is that we don't have the detail about how we are measured. We are told removals are key, but there is no figure attached. We are told safeguarding is key, but no targets are set ... There is a complete lack of direction.[57]

The withdrawal of targets also affected staff recruitment and collaboration between Immigration Enforcement and other government departments and others, who were perceived to be less willing to be associated with the department and hostile environment measures.[58]

The issue again becomes one of how to organise administration and how to motivate officials in one direction without them going too far. Post-Windrush, the department has introduced various internal controls to prevent a similar type of scandal from occurring. These have included: a vulnerability strategy; vulnerability training for staff; more face-to-face interactions between officials and immigrants in reporting centres; reforms to immigration detention; safeguarding measures; and a safety-valve mechanism through which enforcement staff can escalate cases when they feel something is not right.[59] The intention of the safety-valve mechanism is for senior officials to support enforcement teams by: providing advice to officials who feel uncomfortable with the decision that they are making; monitoring trends; and working with policy officials to learn from cases and improve future responses. Such referrals have arisen in the context of frontline enforcement staff encountering people during their work.[60]

---

[55] Windrush Review (ibid).

[56] 'Windrush: Home Office 'to scrap immigration removals targets'' *BBC News* (26 April 2018); HAC, 'Oral Evidence: Windrush Children' 15 May 2018, HC 990 (2017–19) Q 250–251 (Sajid Javid MP, Secretary of State for the Home Department).

[57] ICIBI, 'An Inspection of the Home Office's Approach to Illegal Working' (2019) [8.13].

[58] ibid [3.12].

[59] Immigration Enforcement, 'Our IE' (n 1) 10–12.

[60] Home Office, 'The Response to the Windrush Lessons Learned Review: A Comprehensive Improvement Plan' (2020) [115]–[116].

B. Administrative Capacity and Coordination

Two other dimensions of enforcement concern the capacity of the organisation to do its work and its ability to coordinate different activities. The latter point concerns whether different work units both inside and outside the departmental structure can coordinate their activities effectively so that complex multi-stage processes and tasks can be completed effectively. The experience of the Immigration Enforcement directorate illustrates both how far demand exceeds capacity and the challenges of coordination both within the directorate itself and with other bodies means that the directorate falls short.

Consider Immigration Compliance and Enforcement (ICE) teams. These teams undertake the majority of frontline enforcement work and are regionally organised (Figure 7.1). In their work to detect, arrest, detain or remove people without leave to remain, ICE teams interact with at least 20 internal units and external organisations to undertake the necessary steps to complete compliance and enforcement activities. These include: prioritising and developing intelligence; requesting warrants from the courts; working with local police to use their custody facilities; obtaining travel documents from the relevant consulate; and arranging flights.[61] ICE teams receive tasks from other units. For instance, some units (eg Returns Preparation, Immigration Intelligence, Immigration enforcement threat assessments, Criminal Casework, and UKVI's Third Country Unit) pass information and requests to ICE teams, thereby creating tasks for ICE, which must then make judgements on which work to prioritise and what work will get done. ICE itself shares information concerning whether to impose civil penalties on employers and landlords with Immigration Intelligence and Interventions and Sanctions. ICE teams also coordinate with Detention and Immigration Removal Centres and the National Returns Command as well as the police and the courts to ensure enforcement action and returns can proceed.

The result is that ICE teams are under considerable pressure. The demands placed on them by other units far exceed their capacity. They simply cannot complete all requested tasks. In 2020, the NAO concluded:

> Enforcement teams must manage demand against a set of internal priorities, while also considering logistical and workability factors such as the strength of the intelligence, geographic location, and staff availability. They must balance this against demands for support elsewhere, for example supporting Border Force in its operations.[62] This means different ICE teams may vary in their response to requests from caseworkers, making it more difficult for caseworkers to get a consistent sense of what is required to see their cases actioned. In some cases, ICE teams may not follow the request (for example

---

[61] NAO (n 20) 47.

[62] At busy times of the year (eg holiday periods) ICE staff are temporarily seconded to Border Force to provide support. IE staff have also been moved to deal with migrants using small boats to cross the English Channel.

to undertake an enforcement visit, or to detain an individual for removal when they report at a reporting centre), when they consider the case to be of lower priority than work already planned, or otherwise operationally impractical. Some staff expressed their frustration when they could see ICE teams did not act on a tasking request. A lack of constructive feedback mechanisms means that staff in other parts of the business may lack understanding of pressures on ICE teams.[63]

The challenges are evident in other units. In 2014 the Chief Inspector found inefficiencies in every part of Removals Core Casework.[64] Workflow teams were not allocating cases optimally and cases were not being progressed swiftly. The lack of management information prevented managers from monitoring caseloads and case progression adequately. There was a lack of coordination and cooperation within different teams dealing with removals casework, and compliance and enforcement. The progression of cases was impeded by a lack of communication, the absence of shared targets and inconsistent processes.

Consider also enforcement action against illegal working.[65] It is recognised that illegal working is harmful in terms of attracting irregular immigrants, but also in terms of such people being abused, exploited and mistreated; it can also have adverse effects on legitimate business and tax revenue. Stopping illegal working has long been a focus for immigration enforcement, but its scale far exceeds enforcement capacity. The long-established response is for ICE to deploy teams in response to allegations received from the public against people working illegally – to check the immigration status of employments and then make arrests and removals. This work tends to be focused on restaurants and fast-food outlets, with the consequence that subsequent removals are concentrated on certain nationalities (Bangladeshis, Indians, Pakistanis and Chinese have accounted for almost two-thirds of all illegal working arrests). Other nationals working illegally, especially those not employed in restaurants and takeaways, are much less likely to be arrested for illegal working. Officers have statutory powers of entry to licenced premises (where the department believes a significant proportion of illegal working happens) and can issue civil penalties and closure notices.[66] However, the power to issue closure notices has rarely been used because the resource-intensive process takes officers away from frontline duties.[67] In any event, the effectiveness of such penalties against 'phoenix' firms – businesses that dissolve and reopen under a different name to avoid paying fines – is limited.

The Chief Inspector has also identified coordination problems and 'disconnects' between ICE and other units such as Immigration Intelligence and the Criminal and Financial Investigation unit. Rather than coordination, Immigration Intelligence and ICE teams have criticised each other. ICE teams have been unaware

---

[63] NAO (n 20) 47.

[64] ICIBI, 'An Inspection of Overstayers: How the Home Office Handles the Cases of Individuals with no Right to Stay in the UK' (2014).

[65] ICIBI, 'An Inspection of the Home Office's Approach to Illegal Working' (2019).

[66] Immigration Act 2016, Schs 4 and 6.

[67] ICIBI, 'Illegal Working' (n 65) [3.9].

that Immigration Intelligence was seeking to transform itself by focusing upon middle- and upper-tier intelligence. Further, ICE teams have not acted upon intelligence information passed to it by Immigration Intelligence, which was taking too long to pass on such intelligence so that the information was no longer actionable by the time ICE received it.[68] As regards criminal investigations, ICE lacks a criminal investigation capability whereas the Criminal and Financial Investigation unit focuses on organised immigration crime. The consequence of this has been that lower-level local immigration crime has often fallen between the two.[69]

Drawing upon organisation theory can help us understand the type of interdependencies within the department and the coordination mechanisms required to drive effective action. The interdependencies here are both sequential and reciprocal – and this affects the different types of coordination mechanisms required and their associated costs.[70] Sequential interdependence arises when the outputs from one unit within a system comprise the inputs for other units. This type of interdependency can be coordinated through detailed plans and written agreements about the flow of work. By contrast, reciprocal interdependence arises when the outputs of different units become inputs for other units. This is a more contingent and unpredictable situation because of the variables involved. Accordingly, the most appropriate means of coordination is through feedback or mutual adjustment between the units involved, such as personal contacts and informal agreements between members of those parts of the organisation involved, a more labour-intensive means of coordination.

This analysis brings into sharper focus the challenges facing Immigration Enforcement. The units within this structure are interdependent and require coordination, but the extent to which this happens in practice is clearly significantly limited. There are means of coordination – by plan and mutual adjustment – and they impose costs on administrative time. Yet, Immigration Enforcement lacks capacity as things currently stand and it has a silo-based fragmented structure and culture. More effective administrative action would require more resources in order to coordinate activities between different units. At present, the prospects of this happening seem remote. There has then been a move toward lower-cost digital means of enforcement, but this raises its own challenges.

C. Data-sharing

The implementation of hostile environment measures involves collaboration between the Home Office and other government departments, public bodies and private

---

[68] ibid [3.10].
[69] ibid [3.11].
[70] J March and H Simon, *Organizations*, 2nd edn (Oxford, Blackwell, 1993) 179–82; JD Thompson, *Organizations in Action: Social Science Bases of Administrative Theory* (New Brunswick, NJ, Transaction Publishers, 2006) 54–56.

actors. Decisions about individuals' entitlement to important human activities and essential services – such as working, opening a bank account, renting a property and having a driving licence – are now made by a range of public and private bodies that have been enlisted and compelled to administer hostile environment measures. One key feature of hostile environment measures is the heavy reliance on efficient and effective bulk data-sharing and matching.[71] Such data-sharing takes place on a huge scale with hundreds of thousands of pieces of data being shared.

In 2013, the Intervention and Sanctions Directorate was established to oversee the interventions and sanctions being applied to deny access to services for irregular migrants and to collaborate with public and private sector partners.[72] In this sense, data-sharing is another means of coordinating the implementation of policy. It is external in that it involves collaboration between the department and other government departments and private actors, such as employers and landlords, as regards illegal working and the right to rent scheme.

In such schemes, the correctness of decisions concerning an individual's ability to work, rent and access public services is highly contingent upon the quality of the underlying data. Incorrect data will have very serious consequences for the individuals concerned. Given the department's abysmal reputation for data quality, it is then unsurprising that its systems have often contained unreliable and duplicate data.[73] Incorrect records have meant that people who had fully complied with immigration legislation had been misidentified as overstayers and received notices to leave the country.[74] The Chief Inspector found that 10 per cent of people disqualified from opening a bank account should never have been listed as 'disqualified persons' because of inaccurate data.[75] As regards driving licence checks, some people were incorrectly identified to the DVLA as present in the UK without leave to remain whereas people without leave to remain had been missed. The inspector noted that 'the Home Office did not appear to appreciate the seriousness of such errors for the individuals affected' and recommended that databases be cleansed.[76] The department rejected this recommendation.[77]

---

[71] See also ICIBI, 'An Inspection of Home Office (Borders, Immigration and Citizenship System) Collaborative Working with Other Government Departments and Agencies' (2018).

[72] The existence and purpose of the Interventions and Sanctions Directorate only became public by way of a FOI request.

[73] Poor quality data has been a common theme of many reports: PAC, 'Reforming the UK Border and Immigration System' HC 584 (2014–15); PAC, 'Managing and Removing Foreign National Offenders' HC 708 (2014–15); NAO, 'E-borders and Successor Programmes' HC 608 (2015–16).

[74] ICIBI, 'An Inspection of Overstayers: How the Home Office Handles the Cases of Individuals With no Right to Stay in the UK' (2014) [1.10] and at 2: the inspection found 'a high level of inaccuracy in the classification of Migration Refusal Pool records, with more than a quarter of departures in the sample being incorrectly recorded. … individuals had been wrongly recorded as immigration offenders, which could lead to their being stopped and delayed at the border' and at [8.15]: 'The Home Office had made disappointingly slow progress overall on improving the quality of Migration Refusal Pool data, given the importance of this work and the time available'.

[75] ICIBI, 'An Inspection of the "Hostile Environment" Measures Relating to Driving Licences and Bank Accounts' (2016).

[76] ibid [2.10].

[77] Home Office, 'Response to the Independent Chief Inspector's Report: "An Inspection of the 'Hostile Environment' Measures Relating to Driving Licences and Bank Accounts"' (2016) [11].

Poor data quality has been an important factor both within and beyond Windrush.[78] The PAC has criticised the department for 'making life-changing decisions on people's rights, based on incorrect data from systems that are not fit for purpose'.[79] The Committee found it extremely concerning that the department was not taking issues of data quality seriously, and deeply worrying that senior officials had been unable to provide answers to questions relating to the variable quality of data and whether the incorrect imposition of sanctions on the Windrush generation could have applied to other cohorts of people.

Following Windrush, data-sharing was temporarily paused. The department issued new guidance to other public bodies, employers and landlords, encouraged them to contact the department's checking service and also launched online checking tools, such as a 'right to rent' checking service. The Windrush Review recommended that the department improve the quality of its data.[80] The department itself accepted that there were significant gaps in its data. Its intention is that modernisation programmes will enable better digital evidence of people's immigration status, and it has sought to clean data. The department has been unable to state when its data will be sufficiently robust, but has recognised that improving data quality will be a continuing endeavour.[81] Another option is to enable people to check the veracity of the data held about them.[82]

Overall, there are considerable concerns about the accuracy, scope, scale, governance and oversight of data-sharing and related privacy concerns. The Information Commissioner's Office has criticised the Department for Education for secretly sharing children's personal data with the Home Office potentially for enforcement purposes; the Department for Education had failed to comply fully with its data protection obligations.[83] Concerns over data quality dovetail with the lack of hard evidence needed to understand whether hostile environment measures do in fact secure greater compliance with immigration law.

VI. Improving Enforcement Operations

How, then, is it possible to improve enforcement operations? The NAO concluded that the department did not manage immigration enforcement as an end-to-end

---

[78] NAO, 'Handling of the Windrush Situation' HC 1622 (2017–19) [15]. See also HAC, 'The Windrush Generation' HC 990 (2017–19) [71]–[85].
[79] PAC, 'Windrush Generation and the Home Office' HC 1518 (2017–19) 5.
[80] Windrush Review (n 54) 18.
[81] PAC, 'Oral Evidence: Immigration Enforcement', 13 July 2020 HC 407 (2019–21) Qs 38–39 (Shona Dunn, Second Permanent Secretary, Home Office) and Q 64 (Matthew Rycroft, Permanent Secretary, Home Office).
[82] As regards the right to access data for EU Citizens, see: *R (Open Rights Group and the3million) v Secretary of State for the Home Department* [2021] EWCA Civ 800.
[83] 'Department of Education Criticised for Secretly Sharing Children's Data' *Guardian* (12 November 2019); ICO, 'Department for Education: Data Protection Audit Report' (2020).

system. It did not have, and was currently unable to possess, a full understanding of how its actions impacted upon people throughout each part of the process. Drawing upon the NAO's analysis, this section considers the scope for improving enforcement operations. The NAO highlighted four areas: align strategy and operations; use information to monitor and improve organisational performance; manage and run an end-to-end system by integrating its different parts; and support staff. We examine each in turn.

A. Align Strategy and Operations

This requires an organisation or department to have a clear strategy running throughout its structure and operations, and which it uses to define and inform its activities. There should be a clear link between strategic goals – what the organisation is trying to achieve – and the activities that contribute to those objectives. Further, this link must be clear within the organisation as a whole and the individual units and teams within it. Individual units should map their operational objectives to the overall strategy, and staff should understand their contribution to the organisation's objectives.

What then of the department? Immigration Enforcement has updated its strategic objectives, but has not changed its internal structure accordingly. Individual units contribute across a range of different enforcement priorities and have been allowed to implement their business plans as they have felt to be appropriate. One consequence of this is that officials prioritise the interests of their own unit rather than pursue wider strategic goals and missions, a traditional fragmented, silo-based approach. This has meant that the priorities of some units can have negative consequences for other units. For instance, ICE teams outside London and the south-east accept almost all cases in which an immigration threat is present whereas London and south-east teams only act on information with the highest threat level and may delay their responses, thereby increasing the risk to life for individuals involved in high-risk cases. A fragmented approach also means that staff within units and teams define success as completing the specific task at hand as opposed to contributing to wider and longer-term goals. This suggests that individual units and teams take a greater interest in their own workloads than in contributing to Immigration Enforcement's overall missions and objectives.[84] The NAO recommended that what was needed was a clear rationale of how each unit and team contributed to the directorate's overall missions and objectives and the need to integrate them more fully into an overall coherent system.

[84] NAO (n 20) [3.6].

B. Use Information to Monitor and Improve Organisational Performance

High-performing organisations collect and use management information to raise their performance by looking at their current performance and future needs and by making informed decisions about how to improve. Such data is the basis for informing and evaluating administrative action and performance.

Immigration Enforcement collects data on a number of indicators which largely concern activities undertaken, but the information collected has not enabled senior staff to easily understand the overall health of the system.[85] The department has had few indicators concerning the quality or future scale of work flowing through its processes. It has used management information and metrics that differ from its performance framework and relied heavily upon qualitative information generated through discussions. This incurs obvious risks in terms of the veracity of such information and how representative it is. The NAO concluded that until the department could reliably and consistently collect data that allowed it to assess its performance against its objectives, or define objectives supported by its existing analytical capabilities, then it would struggle to judge its success against its missions through measuring the cumulative impact of its activities.[86]

The department has also been unable to understand how different metrics and indicators link up to outcomes or how they interact with each other. Its established approach has been to view performance in terms of the activities of individual units and teams as opposed to outcomes and its overall performance. Information is only recorded on what happens at the start or end point of individual parts of the system and this prevents understanding what happens to different people throughout the process. The department has not assessed whether the effectiveness of both individual units and teams and the overall system has been improving or reducing and, if so, why. In other words, it lacks the ability to understand and identify causal links between its actions and the outcome of individual cases. For instance, the department has measured the amount of data shared with other government departments to apply hostile environment measures, but is unable to understand the degree to which sanctions imposed on people actually encourage them to leave voluntarily.

Measuring activities rather than outcomes has also meant that the department has been unable to understand how work and cases flow from one unit to another. This is a major gap in its understanding likely to mean that inefficient processes remain undetected. In summary, the department has lacked sufficient information in order properly to understand the effectiveness of its own operations, both in terms of individual units and teams and cumulatively as an overall system.

---

[85] ibid [3.12].
[86] ibid [3.13].

C. Manage and Run an End-to-end System by Integrating its Different Parts

Managing and running the operations of a large administrative process as an end-to-end system is complex and challenging. But it is necessary to ensure that the overall system is efficient, effective and able to manage demand. Manging an end-to-end system is also in the interests of people subject to the process to ensure that they do not experience unnecessary delay and uncertainty.

In reality, the department's capabilities have fallen a long way short of what is required. Both individual officials and units have lacked awareness and visibility of the wider system and their role within it. Completed casework has frequently been passed from other units to enforcement teams irrespective of their capacity and capability to undertake and complete it. Inefficiencies exist both within individual units and across them. Three (unidentified) work areas received significant volumes of cases passed to them that had been sent to the wrong team, contained errors or gaps, or had been wrongly assessed. Some systems and technology have not worked effectively. Staff have not always been able immediately to access necessary information to do their jobs. For instance, officials have experienced difficulties in obtaining warrants and travel documentation within the required time to complete a removal.

Clearly, such problems generate significant scope for inefficiencies, unnecessary duplication and delays. There will also be significant adverse operational consequences. For instance, cases have been rejected for further action and cases planned for removal have been cancelled at late notice – owing to administrative inefficiencies. Staff in the Family Returns Unit have worked on cases knowing that the 'self check-in' process enabled families to abscond, thereby creating work elsewhere within Immigration Enforcement. At the same time, there have been many instances in which enforcement officials have unlawfully removed people.[87] In summary, the department's overall inability to understand and manage immigration enforcement as an end-to-end system has created many systemic inefficiencies and significant negative consequences for those people subject to the process.

Such failures are bad enough, but if the department collected data on the nature and frequency of such problems, then it could understand things better and potentially address them. Yet, this does not happen:

> Immigration Enforcement does not have measures which enable it to understand the quality of work that is being done, or the frequency and impact of any process problems. It also lacks the end-to-end process ownership and feedback loops which will enable issues to be addressed routinely where they cross organisational boundaries. As a result,

---

[87] See, eg, 'Theresa May Rebuked Over Illegally Deported Asylum Seeker' *Guardian* (30 April 2012); 'Nigerian Mother and Son Unlawfully Deported by Home Office Set to Return to the UK' *Independent* (22 April 2015); *R (RA) v Secretary of State for the Home Department*, UTIAC, 20 March 2015 and 13 April 2015 (JR/2277/2015).

process quality issues such as those identified ... will continue to get in the way of staff doing their jobs to the best of their ability, as well as creating additional effort, delays, and costs.[88]

In addition to better understanding the operation of its own processes, the department therefore needed to make greater use of its analytical functions and evaluations to both improve and learn as an organisation. Yet, its evaluations have tended to focus only on process benefits and future risks. For instance, transformation projects, including a new case management system and new technology, such as automated reporting and handheld devices for front-line enforcement staff, have been evaluated. However, the NAO found that evaluations have not assessed whether such changes have actually delivered the expected benefits or their impact on organisational performance. The department had not properly considered such projects against its missions and goals, or how it could improve its delivery in the future.

The department has sought to develop a greater focus on cross-system thinking and working. However, this has been weakened by a lack of information about how the whole system operates and the costs of changing its operations to meet demands. Take the issue of responding to changing operational priorities. Senior officials have responded to pressure points by moving staff from one work area to another, but they have been unable to understand the impact of such moves on routine activities. Yet, given 'the dearth of information' available to such officials about how both enforcement teams and the department as a whole operate, decisions about moving staff resources from one part of the system to another have been made on the basis of judgements, without knowing whether such changes in fact lead to very different unit cost outcomes.[89] Better data and coordination are essential in order to manage the department more effectively as an end-to-end system.

D. Support Staff

This involves senior leaders establishing an environment that supports officials to contribute and apply the principles of good operations to improve organisational performance.

The NAO found that while the department has set up some ways of improving its activities, sharing ideas and best practices did not routinely occur within or between teams. This resulted in inconsistent ways of working as different caseworkers had developed their own ways of working and there was great variability between different teams. ICE teams in different regions had developed their own

---

[88] NAO (n 20) [3.21].

[89] PAC, 'Oral Evidence: Immigration Enforcement', 13 July 2020, HC 407 (2019–21) Q 49 (Shona Dunn, Second Permanent Secretary, Home Office).

performance metrics independently of each other. Different teams undertaking the same functions – such as arranging travel documentation – did so in different ways without collaborating with each other or sharing good practice. Staff did not always have current guidance on how to do perform their tasks. In some instances, casework staff did not use available guidance because either they did not trust it to be current or it was incorrect. There was a considerable time lag between changes in policy and updated guidance being issued accordingly.

Important changes have been made in one part of the Immigration Enforcement directorate without consideration of the implications for other teams. This is illustrated by the change in the role of Immigration Intelligence unit in focusing upon high-priority cases concerning organised criminal gangs while lower-priority cases were passed over to ICE teams. However, this reallocation of functions was implemented without effective coordination. ICE teams had not been given the relevant training. The Chief Inspector identified a disconnect between Immigration Intelligence and ICE which has persisted for some years and may even have become more pronounced.[90]

VII. Competent, Effective and Diverse Administration

We need to take stock. It is clear that the department must improve its management of the enforcement system, respond to its operational inefficiencies, and develop its data and analytical capability. It also needs to do more to support immigrants in navigating its complex systems effectively and humanely, and to understand how its actions affect them.

In its response to the NAO and the PAC, the department recognised the scale of the challenge and that it has plans for transformational change.[91] These include: reaching a better understanding of the illegal population; determining the harms of illegal migration by assessing its economic harms; improved data collection and analysis to support enforcement operations and its policy impacts through re-engineering work processes and cultural change in the way that enforcement uses data; and greater customer insight to inform the design and delivery of the immigration system. The department also explained that it intends to deliver a more joined-up and end-to-end system through digital immigration application processes to improve system coordination and to enhance customer experience including better understanding of people's needs and strengthening its oversight of customer issues. Overall, there is very familiar language of ensuring a 'fairer and firmer' system that deters and prevents illegal migration; delivers more

---

[90] ICIBI, 'Inspection of Illegal Working' (n 65) [3.10].

[91] HM Treasury, 'Treasury Minutes: Government Responses to the Committee of Public Accounts on the Fourteenth to the Seventeenth Reports and the Nineteenth Report from Session 2019–21' (CP 316, 2020) 15–19. See also Home Office, 'New Plan for Immigration: Policy Statement' (CP 412, 2021).

support and a speedy and efficient system for those genuinely fleeing persecution; and enables the swift removal of irregular migrations. As with the Windrush improvement plan, it remains to be seen what will actually happen in practice.

Putting to one side the detail of the specific recommendations and reforms, we can take a step back to consider some wider and underlying points about what is going on here.

A. Administration and Organisational Performance

There are different and competing models of public administration within both current administrative practices and the critique of it advanced by the NAO and PAC. Administrative practice reflects a model of administration as traditional bureaucracy with its division of labour, limited coordination, and a focus on completing the task at hand rather than focusing upon the accomplishment of wider goals. This is to be contrasted with a model of administration as a performance-based organisation. This model stresses organisational performance, managing the organisation as a coherent system, aligning strategy and administrative structure, and internal coordination. It also places considerable priority on evaluating administrative action in terms of achieving policy goals.[92] These different models have clear implications as regards how administration is understood and organised.

The NAO and the PAC have been articulating and imposing an overarching constitutional responsibility on public administration, and more specifically Immigration Enforcement, to understand, analyse and improve its organisational performance. Administration should not merely collect performance information about the exercise of its powers and its actions. It must also collect appropriate data that can then be used to make informed assessments about the consequences and impact of its interventions and actions on the social and economic contexts which it regulates. Administration must exercise its statutory and other powers and undertake its tasks and activities, but it must also evaluate the effectiveness of its programmes and policies and its organisational performance against its stated missions and policy goals.

Viewed in this way, the constitutional framework in which public administration and administrative law operate is not limited solely to constraining and limiting the scope of administrative action. It also includes ensuring that administration is effective in its actions and that its performance is assessed against its goals and functions. This in turn enables administration to acquire a better and more robust understanding of its roles, to align strategy and operations, to better

---

[92] This model is reflected in the NAO's work on managing business operations: 'Managing Business Operations – What Government Needs to Get Right' (NAO, 2015) and 'Improving Operational Delivery in Government: A Good Practice Guide for Senior Leaders' (NAO, 2021).

understand the likely impact of its interventions and its own operations by using information to manage its work more effectively and to learn from this process with a view to adapt to future change.

This is, of course, a highly ambitious and challenging agenda of administrative improvement. The traditional model of a silo-based bureaucracy is now distinctly out of fashion. But moving toward a performance-based model of public adminis-tration involves the hard work of implementing a change programme while at the same time carrying out day-to-day enforcement work. The enormousness of the challenge cannot be understated. It is likely to be a difficult task to be accomplished over the longer-term. There will be strong countervailing forces. On the other hand, there is no alternative but to start to make some progress in this endeavour.

B. Administration and Diversity

There is another dimension which is particularly relevant to the immigration department given its failure, as illustrated by Windrush, to adhere to equality and diversity principles. The department can now be said to be under a constitutional responsibility to prevent another Windrush-style scandal. This has required the introduction of internal controls and support as regards front-line officers.

It is also necessary that the department's workforce itself reflects the diverse nature of contemporary society. This is currently the case as regards rank and file officials. But what of those higher up, the senior officials? These officials work within a very different civil service career structure from that of frontline staff. By their nature, senior officials much are less representative of society as a whole. Yet, the low diversity of such officials is highly relevant given their critically important role in giving policy advice to ministers and also undertaking high-level oversight of administration and issuing instructions.

In 2020, only one member of the Home Office's executive committee had an ethnic minority background. This lack of diversity has attracted critical scrutiny. The Windrush Review highlighted that the need for a more diverse and inclusive approach and for more senior-level representation from ethnic minorities. The PAC has pursued the point: 'the culture and make-up of the Department have left it poorly placed to appreciate the impact of its policies on the people affected'.[93] The significant lack of diversity at senior levels meant that the department had been unable to 'access a sufficiently wide range of perspectives when establish-ing rules and assessing the human impact of its decisions. Professional judgement cannot be relied upon if an organisation has blind spots'.[94]

In other words, greater diversity at the top is required to enable the depart-ment to better understand the impact of its actions upon its diverse clientele. The

---

[93] PAC (n 26) 6.
[94] ibid 3.

department has stated that it is committed to enhancing such diversity, although this is also one of its biggest challenges.[95] At the same time, the department could hardly claim that it has not seen this coming. Over recent years, both Parliament and the judiciary have sought to become more diverse. By contrast, the department's record on the matter, given its role and the interaction between immigration and race, is – not for the first time – behind the times.

The essential and wider point is that a competent and effective administrative institution should now, across all of its levels, include a sufficiently diverse group of officials so that it can draw upon a wide range of perspectives with which to understand, assess and consider the likely impacts of its policies and decisions on society as a whole. More specifically in the context of immigration administration and enforcement, the composition and culture of senior officials must be sufficiently diverse so that they can properly exercise their professional judgement to ensure better decision-making, leadership and governance. This can be defined as a matter of developing an informed administrative culture and of good governance. It also reflects the public sector equality duty on public authorities to have due regard to the need to eliminate discrimination.[96]

VIII. Conclusion

What, then, can be said about immigration enforcement by way of conclusion? On the positive side, the sole point is that there is an institutional structure that seeks to enforce immigration law. Beyond this very basic administrative reality, there is only a long list of negative points concerning the department's inability to measure its performance and impact, to understand its own operations, and to manage compliance and enforcement as an end-to-end system, to evaluate and to learn, and the harms it has imposed upon people subjected to its control. This is on top of failures such as Windrush. Even taking account of the intrinsic challenges of immigration enforcement, the department's lack of even basic information on its organisational performance and its inability to understand the impact and consequences of its activities is striking. The limited capacity of Immigration Enforcement and the challenges of coordinating complex activities again highlights the importance of organisational competence in both enabling administration to deliver policy effectively and in understanding administrative law.

Put together, the NAO and PAC reports comprise a devastating critique. Yet, alongside the Windrush Review, these reports also articulate a different vision of what the immigration department could and should become. It should become an

---

[95] PAC, 'Oral Evidence: Immigration Enforcement', 13 July 2020 HC 407 (2019–21) Q 76 (Matthew Rycroft, Permanent Secretary, Home Office).
[96] Equality Act 2010, s 149.

organisation that is more curious about the impact of its activities. Monitoring the consequences of its actions would enable the department to understand and assess the effectiveness and efficiency of those actions in terms of implementing policy. The department should also become a more diverse organisation. Greater diversity at the higher levels would give the department a wider range of perspectives with which to assess the human impacts of its policies and decisions. This would help prevent another Windrush-style scandal.

More generally, this chapter has highlighted the importance of enforcement as a topic of administrative law, one that is focused on the use of an administrative agency's statutory and non-statutory powers, its organisation, performance, effectiveness and impacts. Enforcement must be investigated from the perspective of both the enforcement agency and those subject to it. Immigration enforcement also highlights the importance of external accountability and its connections with internal operations and monitoring. There is effective, thorough, and independent accountability of enforcement capabilities as demonstrated by the NAO and PAC reports. But the immigration department currently lacks a detailed understanding of the consequences of the various means used to try to seek compliance and enforcement, and ensure that internal supervision and monitoring is adequate. What is then required are internal administrative reforms to deliver an effective end-to-end system that can both assess and understand its own performance and meet the needs of those subject to the process.

8

Judicial Review: Norms and Pragmatism

This chapter analyses the role of wide-ranging and in-depth judicial scrutiny of the immigration department's processes and behaviours.[1] We have previously examined 'individual' judicial review, that is, repetitive case-by-case judicial challenges that solely concern the individual claimant and turn on their own specific facts and circumstances.[2] The focus here is upon those judicial review cases that involve a broader judicial assessment of the systemic and aggregative nature of how the department has been exercising its powers and implementing policy. Such cases typically have impacts far beyond individual cases. Challenges may be brought by public interest campaigning groups, but more often by affected individuals – lead claimants – who are members of a wider class of affected people. Either way, this type of judicial review is very different to the individual checking of whether the rules have been correctly applied in specific casework decisions. Instead, the courts are involved in more wide-ranging 'wholesale' judicial scrutiny of administrative systems behaviours, the interventions of ministers, and the supervision of administrative action. Such cases involve the courts both protecting individual rights and articulating norms of legality, an 'administrative common law' of judicially developed principles that values as to how administration ought to function. In other words, the courts are, to an extent, involved in managing the administrative system. Judicial interventions represent pragmatic responses to administrative and ministerial behaviours that need correcting, and this involves the courts imposing wider norms of administrative legality upon such behaviours.

This chapter considers the character of this form of judicial review, how the courts undertake this role, and its impact upon administration. Whereas some cases raise questions of statutory interpretation, sometimes of excruciating technicality, the focus here will be on the more mainstream common law cases in which the courts have applied general public law principles.[3] It is in these cases

---

[1] P Cane, 'Understanding Judicial Review and Its Impact' in M Hertogh and S Halliday (eds), *Judicial Review and Bureaucratic Impact* (Cambridge, Cambridge University Press, 2004) 18–19 distinguishes between 'bureaucratic' or 'street-level' judicial review, and 'high-profile' judicial review. The distinction is not always binary and is one of degree, but clearly exists.

[2] See ch 6.

[3] Individual human rights challenges are mostly handled through tribunal appeals. For wide-ranging challenges to policies and legislation on human rights grounds, see *R (Baiai) v Secretary of State for the Home Department* [2008] UKHL 53, [2009] 1 AC 287; *R (Quila) v Secretary of State for the*

that judicial control of administration is at its strongest. Most successful individual judicial reviews are settled out of court and typically involve at most retaking a casework decision. Government can also use legislation and other techniques to strike back against rulings with wider effects, but this is mostly confined to reversing judicial interpretations of legislation. By contrast, rulings with wider impacts that apply general norms of legality cannot easily be so reversed.[4] And it is in these cases that the courts do not merely determine the formal legality of administrative action; they also perform an important substantive role in articulating wider legal norms, and managing and supervising administrative behaviour.

I. Judicial Review and Administration

In general terms, judicial review ensures administration according to law. Claimants argue that administration fails to respect legal principles, as demonstrated by its operational failures and a lack of accountability in respect of individual rights. An administrative system that lacks organisational competence will inevitably adversely affect the rights and interests of people who must interact with it. Such failures often affect whole cohorts of similarly situated people. Judicial intervention is based upon normative legal values as to how administration should operate. As Knight has noted, 'while judicial review's immediate role is the policing of administrative legality, it also has an important collateral role in articulating and elaborating the principles of good administration that ministers, public bodies and officials ought to honour'.[5]

How the courts apply these legal principles is heavily conditioned by the context and circumstances of specific cases. Presented with the realities of how administration operates in practice, the courts craft and shape judicial review in response to organisational and political behaviours and their impact upon affected individuals. The perennial issues for the courts are whether something has gone wrong within administration, whether it is the type of problem that judicial review can correct, which legal principle can be used or developed as a basis for intervention, and what degree of judicial intervention is appropriate to correct the problem. Implicit within this approach is that judicial review is a flexible and pragmatic tool shaped to the specific case.[6] It necessarily involves weighing up considerations of

---

Home Department [2011] UKSC 45, [2012] 1 AC 621; *R (Joint Council for the Welfare of Immigrants) v Secretary of State for the Home Department* [2020] EWCA Civ 542, [2021] 1 WLR 1151.

[4] For specific examples, see R Thomas, 'The Impact of Judicial Review on Asylum' [2003] *PL* 479 and, generally, C Harlow and R Rawlings, '"Striking Back" and "Clamping Down": An Alternative Perspective on Judicial Review' in J Bell, M Elliott, JNE Varuhas and P Murray (eds), *Public Law Adjudication in Common Law Systems: Process and Substance* (Oxford, Hart Publishing, 2016).

[5] DR Knight, *Vigilance and Restraint in the Common Law of Judicial Review* (Cambridge, Cambridge University Press, 2018) 32.

[6] cf J Steyn, 'Does Legal Formalism Hold Sway in England?' (1996) 49 *Current Legal Problems* 43, 51: 'Consequentialist arguments and policy factors are the very stuff of decisions in the public law field.'

justice, individual rights, policy factors, consequences and legal values.[7] There is also the underlying issue of relative institutional competence between the courts and the department.[8] The courts' assessment as to whether they are best placed to intervene or whether is the matter best left to the political process is informed by a range of factors such as their own expertise, the nature of the issues raised in a case, and whether there are alternative effective forms of accountability. How these factors play out in practice depends on the individual case and its context.

Seen in this way, the major purpose of judicial review is to exert real-world influence upon administration by bringing its practices and behaviours back into line with how it should operate. Judicial review can correct systemic operational problems that adversely affect individual rights. It can simultaneously guide administration as to what it needs to do to ensure lawful administrative action. In fact, the courts have increasingly drawn upon some of the concepts and ideas already encountered, such as systemic appraisal and improvement of administrative processes, the need for internal supervision and monitoring, and the need to prevent administrative errors and problems from arising in the first place. It has been noted that the 'significant part of judicial review is about "managing governance"'; furthermore, adjudicating upon administrative decisions itself involves administration.[9] If so, then an interesting question concerns the legitimacy and basis of judicial intervention and how far the courts will penetrate into the operation of administrative systems. Another area of judicial intervention concerns politically motivated interventions by ministers into administrative processes. Such interventions are sometimes deliberately designed to weaken the position of certain immigrants seeking to protect their legal rights and/or to enable ministers to escape blame. It is necessary, then, to consider how the courts respond when the focus of judicial review is not the fairness of administrative systems, but ministerial interventions for self-serving political ends.

How the courts exercise judicial review is conditioned by various procedural and substantive factors. In procedural terms, much of the initial stages of litigation involves considerable filtering out of hopeless cases. As the archetypal repeat player, the immigration department sometimes uses tactical concession of legal challenges at the early stages to try to prevent important issues of policy or procedure from being examined by the courts even though – or rather, precisely because – they

---

[7] See generally EW Thomas, *The Judicial Process: Realism, Pragmatism, Practical Reasoning and Principles* (Cambridge, Cambridge University Press, 2005); RA Posner, *How Judges Think* (Cambridge, Mass, Harvard University Press, 2010); R Carnwath, 'From Judicial Outrage to Sliding Scales – Where Next for *Wednesbury*?' (ALBA Annual Lecture, 12 November 2013). For a formalist critique, see C Forsyth, '"Blasphemy Against Basics": Doctrine, Conceptual Reasoning and Certain Decisions of the UK Supreme Court' in Bell et al, *Public Law Adjudication* (2016).

[8] J Jowell, 'Judicial Deference, Servility, Civility or Institutional Capacity?' [2003] *PL* 592.

[9] S Sterett, *Creating Constitutionalism? The Politics of Legal Expertise and Administrative Law in England and Wales* (Ann Arbor, University of Michigan Press, 1997) 130; JDB Mitchell, 'The State of Public Law in the United Kingdom' (1966) 15 *International and Comparative Law Quarterly* 133, 142.

are legally vulnerable.[10] Such practices can be countered by public interest litigation and the ability of the courts to consider hypothetical issues if the public interest requires.[11]

This reinforces the immigration department's distinctive relationship with judicial review. Other government departments tend to experience judicial review as a sporadic intervention, but it is a constant and extensive feature of immigration administration, which attracts the highest proportion of legal challenges across government. This in turn influences the department's approach in various respects.[12] Other departments, such as the Department for Environment, Food and Rural Affairs, design their rules to promote compliance amongst their regulated customer base. By contrast, the immigration department deals with some people who deliberately refuse to comply with the rules. This then results in highly adversarial relationships between the department and migrants and then with the courts. Ministers frequently receive details of upcoming cases, the risks of challenge and of losing cases, and the likely policy impact, which can be controversial and attract media and political attention. As a law-enforcement department, tougher enforcement action is likely to produce more judicial challenges as well as more government losses. From one perspective, if the immigration department is not being challenged, then it is not doing its job properly.

The combined forces of the types of judicial challenges, their volume, and political context also produces an internal mindset that tolerates a higher degree of legal risk when making and implementing policy, sometimes in order to make an issue out of a particular matter. If the department loses a legal challenge, then it can always blame the courts for tying its hands. Immigration has long been a sensitive area in terms of the relationship between ministers and the courts. Both ministers and officials have on occasion sought to push the limits of what is legally acceptable. Indeed, the department has the worst reputation across government for not complying with the rule of law. Alternatively, judicial review can sometimes provide ministers with a politically more palatable, face-saving means of abandoning a policy than discarding it themselves. Judicial review also serves a major role in clarifying the legal framework within which policy and administration can be carried out. In practice, most judicial reviews go in the department's favour, although the department and ministers can find it difficult to stomach adverse decisions.

Viewed in this way, the relationship between the courts and administration is complex, fluid and dynamic. To describe that relationship as one of 'partnership' would be going too far given the tensions that sometimes arise. Yet, judicial review of administrative action is the preeminent form of legal accountability.

[10] R Thomas, 'Mapping Immigration Judicial Review Litigation: An Empirical Legal Analysis' [2015] *PL* 652, 666–67.

[11] *R v Secretary of State for the Home Department, ex parte Salem* [1999] 1 AC 450 (HL) 457 (Lord Slynn).

[12] Institute for Government, 'Judicial review and Policy Making: The Role of Legal Advice in Government' (2021) 9, 12–13,

To investigate further, we now need to consider and evaluate specific cases, their impacts on the department, and the overall contribution of the courts to monitoring and managing the immigration administrative system. We start by considering systemic procedural unfairness.

II. Systemic Procedural Unfairness

A consistent theme throughout 'minded to refuse', administrative reason-giving and legitimate expectations, procedural fairness is fairly uncontroversial at the level of principle, although the outcome in specific cases can be contentious.[13] It has long featured heavily in asylum cases given the importance of the right to seek asylum and the consequences of wrong decisions.[14] The focus here is upon a specific category of procedural review: systemic unfairness, a relatively new judicial development with potentially far-reaching consequences for the scrutiny of administrative systems. Systemic unfairness review has been developed more broadly by the courts and has been applied extensively in the asylum and immigration context. The concept involves the courts reviewing not just individual decisions, but whole systems for making decisions. It therefore illustrates the clear interplay between process and substantive policy and the role of the courts in identifying and repairing structural problems within administrative processes. A key illustration concerns the department's fast-track asylum process.

A. The Detained Asylum Fast-track

In 2003, the department introduced the detained asylum fast-track process to handle straightforward and uncomplicated asylum claims through an expedited

---

[13] Important cases include: *R v Secretary of State for the Home Department, ex p Khan* [1984] 1 WLR 1337 (CA) (legitimate expectations); *R v Secretary of State for the Home Department, ex p Moon* [1997] INLR 165 (HC) (minded to refuse); *R (Q) v Secretary of State for the Home Department* [2003] EWCA Civ 364, [2004] QB 36 (multiple aspects of systemic procedural unfairness in the assessment of asylum support claims); *R (HMSP Forum) v Secretary of State for the Home Department* [2008] EWHC Admin 664 (legitimate expectations); *R (Citizens UK) v Secretary of State for the Home Department* [2018] EWCA Civ 1812 (administrative reason-giving); *R (Balajigari) v Secretary of State for the Home Department* [2019] EWCA Civ 673, [2019] 1 WLR 4647 (minded to refuse). For a divided decision about the application of procedural fairness, see *R (Pathan) v Secretary of State for the Home Department* [2020] UKSC 41.

[14] *Bugdaycay v Secretary of State for the Home Department* [1987] AC 514, 531 (HL) (Lord Bridge): 'the court must be entitled to subject an administrative decision to the more rigorous examination, to ensure that it is in no way flawed, according to the gravity of the issue which the decision determines. The most fundamental of all human rights is the individual's right to life and, when an administrative decision under challenge is said to be one which may put the applicant's life at risk, the basis of the decision must surely call for the most anxious scrutiny'; *R v Secretary of State for the Home Department ex parte Thirukumar* [1989] Imm AR 402, 414 (CA) (Bingham LJ): 'asylum decisions are of such moment that only the highest standards of fairness will suffice'.

process during which claimants were detained – to facilitate removal if refused.[15] Asylum claimants had seven days from the receipt of their initial refusal decision by the Home Office to then prepare and present their appeals. The purpose was to process claims quickly and to ensure that rejected claimants could then be quickly returned to their country of origin, which would be facilitated by claimants being detained throughout. But the operation of this process was both controversial and much criticised. For many years, both practitioners and asylum stakeholder groups had argued that the process was unfair because the timescales involved were too tight. Representatives experienced many difficulties in ensuring that cases were properly prepared for tribunal hearings. Asylum appeals are evidentially, factually and legally complex, and reaching the wrong decision carries not only life-changing, but also potentially life-ending, consequences. In 2004, the Court of Appeal held that the process was not inherently unfair, but stressed that it needed to operate flexibly so that unsuitable cases could be taken out of the system.[16] Nonetheless, concerns continued to be raised.[17]

In 2007, the author spent some weeks at the immigration tribunal in Hatton Cross, west London, undertaking fieldwork for an empirical study of asylum appeals.[18] Many of the tribunal judges there also sat on detained asylum fast-track appeals heard at the nearby Harmondsworth Immigration Removal Centre. The judges explained that the fast-track process was meant to deal quickly with straightforward asylum cases, but in practice the system did not work like that at all. Caseworkers had been routinely putting complex and difficult cases into the fast-track process that should not have been there. Judges said that they sometimes transferred out such cases and there was a general view that the process was being used inappropriately by the department. Further, the physical location of the tribunal within an immigration removal centre brought home how deeply it had become ensconced within the administrative infrastructure of immigration control that anyone could reasonably have assumed it was part of that system rather than an independent and judicial process.

The campaigning group, Detention Action, then mounted an extensive litigation campaign challenging many aspects of the fast-track process based on its

---

[15] There have been two sets of procedure rules: Immigration and Asylum Appeals (Fast Track Procedure) Rules, SI 2003/801; Tribunal Procedure (First-tier Tribunal) (Immigration and Asylum Chamber) Rules, SI 2014/2604, Sch 'The Fast Track Rules'.

[16] *R (Refugee Legal Centre) v Secretary of State for the Home Department* [2004] EWCA Civ 1481, [2005] 1 WLR 2219 (CA).

[17] HMIP and ICIBI, 'The Effectiveness and Impact of Immigration Detention Casework: A Joint Thematic Review by HM Inspectorate of Prisons and the Independent Chief Inspector of Borders and Immigration' (2012); Detention Action, 'Fast Track to Despair: The Unnecessary Detention of Asylum-seekers' (2011); Detention Action, 'Briefing: The Detained Fast Track' (2013).

[18] R Thomas, *Administrative Justice and Asylum Appeals: A Study of Tribunal Adjudication* (Oxford, Hart Publishing, 2011).

experience as to how the process operated.[19] This culminated in the *Detention Action* case, in which the Court of Appeal ruled that the detained fast-track process was systemically unfair and unjust.[20] The time limits involved – the seven-day period between the Home Office's initial asylum refusal decision and the appeal hearing – were so tight that it was impossible for appeals to be heard fairly in a significant number of cases given their complexity, the gravity of the issues raised, and the challenges faced by representatives assisting clients in detention. It was, the Court held, inevitable that a significant number of claimants would be denied a fair opportunity to present their cases on appeal because of the difficulties in preparing cases for tribunal hearings given the expedited timescales and the detention of appellants. The Court fully accepted that the goal of the process – to deal with cases quickly – was entirely appropriate, but the means selected were not. 'Speed and efficiency do not trump justice and fairness. Justice and fairness are paramount.'[21] The nature of the procedural deficiencies and the number of people affected meant that the fast-track process as a whole was systemically unfair. What is notable is the court's focus upon the lack of capacity within the process to ensure fair process.[22] Further, the Court's ruling clearly involved an assessment of ends and means: the detained fast-track scheme was an inappropriate means of ensuring correct asylum tribunal decisions because of its unfairness and the compressed timescales.

B. Other Systemic Unfairness Cases

The courts have applied systemic unfairness in other immigration contexts. In *BF (Eritrea)*, the Court of Appeal held that the department's policy for assessing the age of asylum-seekers who claim to be under 18 years of age did not properly identify the margin of error inherent in such assessments. Consequently, there was a significant risk of children whose age had been incorrectly assessed would be unlawfully detained as adults.[23] *Humnyntskyi* concerned the department's process

---

[19] The litigation started with 'DA1' – *R (Detention Action) v Secretary of State for the Home Department* [2014] EWHC 2245 (Admin), a challenge to the operation of the initial decision-making in the detained fast track; the court held that part of the operation of the system up to the start of the appeal stage was unlawful) – through DAs 2, 3, 4 and 5. See: DA2 [2014] EWHC 2525 (Admin); DA3 [2014] EWCA Civ 1270; DA4 [2014] EWCA Civ 1634; DA5 [2015] EWHC 1689 (Admin).

[20] *Lord Chancellor v Detention Action* [2015] EWCA Civ 840, [2015] 1 WLR 5341 (CA) ('DA6').

[21] ibid [22]. See also DA7 [2017] EWHC 59 (Admin), [2017] 1 WLR 2595.

[22] *Detention Action* (n 20) [27]: 'the core question is whether the system has the *capacity* to react appropriately to ensure fairness' (emphasis added).

[23] *R (BF (Eritrea)) v Secretary of State for the Home Department* [2019] EWCA Civ 872, [2020] 4 WLR 38; overturned by the Supreme Court: [2021] UKSC 38. In *R (Ali) v Secretary of State for the Home Department* [2017] EWCA Civ 138, [2017] 1 WLR 2894, the Court of Appeal held that the Immigration Act 1971, Sch 2, para 18B(2) (as amended by the Immigration Act 2014) prohibited the detention of a person who was eventually determined by a court or tribunal to be a child irrespective of whether it was reasonably believed at the time of detention that they were an adult.

for deciding whether to provide accommodation for detainees given bail (such as foreign national offenders).[24] Detainees were not proactively informed about the process or did not know how to apply for accommodation. In some cases, there was no opportunity to make representations, and representations that were made were not taken into account. Caseworkers did not consider whether to provide accommodation unless the foreign national offender was a high risk to the public, a practice contrary to the published policy and an unlawful fettering of discretion. Furthermore, foreign national offenders were not notified or informed of decisions to refuse accommodation, let alone provided with reasons. The range and depth of such basic procedural defects rendered the process systemically unfair.[25]

In *DMA*, the Administrative Court, in an innovative judgment, adopted a systemic approach in the context of the department's failure to monitor properly the provision of asylum accommodation by its outsourced contractor, thereby resulting in systemic unlawfulness. The department had contracted out the performance of its statutory duty to provide accommodation to destitute and homeless asylum claimants.[26] Nonetheless, the contractor had been responsible for significant and extensive delays in making decisions on whether claimants were entitled to accommodation. This in turn raised the legal duty under Article 3 ECHR not to subject people to inhuman and degrading treatment.[27] As the provision of accommodation had been outsourced, the department monitored the performance of the contractor against key performance indicators. But there were significant shortcomings in the department's monitoring. It did not require full performance and the contractor's failures only resulted in financial penalties. By contrast, the department's duty under Article 3 concerned highly vulnerable destitute people without shelter, food or basic necessities. Further, the department was unaware that the contractor had not been providing accommodation within the required timescales.

The Court concluded that there has been systemic failings and illegality by the department because of its failure to capture the relevant data properly and to then use that data to monitor properly the contractor's performance. Irrespective of the commercial nature of the contract, the department was obliged to perform its legal duty to provide accommodation as appropriate, and the monitoring had to reflect this duty. Consequently, the department had acted unlawfully by failing properly to monitor the provision of accommodation. The Court issued extensive guidance as to how the department was undertake the monitoring and the data it had to collect. The case illustrates how the courts will, in appropriate cases,

---

[24] *R (Humnyntskyi and others) v Secretary of State for the Home Department* [2020] EWHC 1912 (Admin).

[25] See also *R (NB) v Secretary of State for the Home Department* [2021] EWHC 1489 (Admin) (system for safeguarding vulnerable people detained in Napier Barracks during COVID-19 inadequate; a better system required to identify people for whom the accommodation was unsuitable).

[26] Immigration and Asylum Act 1999, s 4.

[27] *R (DMA) v Secretary of State for the Home Department* [2020] EWHC 3416 (Admin).

require affirmative action from the department to ensure systemic legality: judicial review becomes not just a means of controlling government, but of controlling government so that it controls its private contractors.

It has not been all one-way. There have been unsuccessful challenges.[28] Nonetheless, put together, there is clear trend toward greater judicial scrutiny of systems and management of administration. Looking forward, we might expect systemic unfairness review to be the principal litigation vehicle for challenging automated casework decision processes.[29]

C. The Impact of Systemic Unfairness

Given the depth of intervention it entails, systemic unfairness review of administrative decision systems is not to be undertaken lightly. There must be a firm evidential basis and a real risk of unfairness in a significant number of individual decisions.[30] Nonetheless, once underway, this type of judicial scrutiny and intervention illustrates the vanishingly thin line between the court formally declaring what the law is and judicial supervision focused on improving systemic administrative performance by operating a fair system.

This last point is illustrated by considering the impact of *Detention Action*.[31] Following the judgment, the department had wanted introduce a revised fast-track process, but the Tribunal Procedure Committee (TPC) rejected the department's proposals.[32] The TPC reasoned that any revised process would need to include rigorous procedural safeguards – eg early oral case management hearings in appeals – to ensure that unsuitable cases were excluded from the fast-track system. But this would absorb judicial resources with consequent implications for other appeals before the tribunal. Consequently, no form of the detained fast-track was tenable as subset of the wider asylum process. The TPC was clearly acting as a 'judicial' body in terms of its culture and orientation; its intervention was an extension of the de facto judicial process for scrutinising administrative policy implementation.[33]

---

[28] *MR (Pakistan) v Secretary of State for Justice* [2021] EWCA Civ 541 (failure to introduce in the Prison Rules a mechanism equivalent to rr 34 and 35 of the Detention Centre Rules so that healthcare providers in prisons do not inquire whether a detainee is a victim of torture was not systemically unfair).

[29] A Chauhan, 'Towards the Systemic Review of Automated Decision-Making Systems' (2021) *Judicial Review.*

[30] *R (Howard League for Penal Reform) v Lord Chancellor* [2017] EWCA Civ 244, [2017] 4 WLR 92 [48] (Beatson LJ).

[31] On the impact of judicial review in general, see M Hertogh and S Halliday (eds), *Judicial Review and Bureaucratic Impact: International and Interdisciplinary Perspectives* (Cambridge, Cambridge University Press, 2004).

[32] Tribunal Procedure Committee, 'Response to the Consultation on Tribunal Procedure (First-tier Tribunal) (Immigration and Asylum Chamber) Rules 2014 and Tribunal Procedure (Upper Tribunal) Rules 2008 in Relation to Detained Appellants' (MoJ, 2019).

[33] Tribunals, Courts and Enforcement Act 2007, s 22.

The department later attributed the subsequent decrease in removals in part to the impact of *Detention Action*.[34] Yet, any weakening of immigration control must be balanced against the impact of the ruling in terms of securing a systemically fairer process by giving often vulnerable claimants (including victims of torture) and their representatives a procedurally fair opportunity to prepare their appeals concerning life-changing decisions that affected their fundamental rights. The finding inevitably involved a value-judgement by the court about the limited capacity of the department's processes for making good-quality asylum decisions. Overall, *Detention Action* represented an important and positive restructuring of both administrative procedure and policy. In 2021, the department announced that it would introduce a new fast-track appeals process for unfounded or late asylum claims, with safeguards to ensure procedural fairness.[35]

There is another dimension of impact to consider. What of those claimants whose claims had been refused under the fast-track process, which had been found to be systemically unfair? Did all such decisions fall to be void because of this? The Court of Appeal in 2019 concluded that the answer was 'no'.[36] The finding in *Detention Action* that the process was systemically unfair did not entail that each and every case decided under it had been vitiated because of procedural unfairness. The outcome of an individual case would depend upon whether there had in fact been procedural unfairness on the particular facts of the individual case. This reflects the sense in which *Detention Action* was focused on systemic unfairness.

D. The Organisational Basis of Systemic Unfairness

How then are we to understand systemic unfairness review? It involves intensely administrative interventions by the courts in the operation and design of whole decision processes through evaluations of their practical operations and consequences as informed by empirical experience.[37] It functions by 'circumnavigating the constraints of a classical form of procedural review directed at particular decisions, to consider whether the decision-making framework as a whole is inherently loaded against a class or classes of persons'.[38] In contrast to the retrospective nature

---

[34] PAC, 'Oral Evidence: Immigration Enforcement', 13 July 2020 HC 407 (2019–21) Q 80 (Tyson Hepple, Director General, Immigration Enforcement, Home Office). There was no evidential basis for this view, although it cannot be altogether discounted either.

[35] Home Office, 'New Plan for Immigration: Policy Statement' (CP 412, 2021) 28.

[36] *R (TN (Vietnam)) v Secretary of State for the Home Department* [2018] EWCA Civ 2838, [2019] 1 WLR 2647; upheld by the Supreme Court: [2021] UKSC 41.

[37] F Powell, 'Structural Procedural Review: An Emerging Trend in Public Law' [2017] *Judicial Review* 83.

[38] C Harlow and R Rawlings, 'Proceduralism and Automation: Challenges to the Values of Administrative Law' in E Fisher, J King, and AL Young (eds), *The Foundations and Future of Public Law* (Oxford, Oxford University Press, 2020) 290.

of individual procedural review, systemic review embodies a form of prospective quality control to reduce the risk of future procedural errors arising in the first place from a structurally unfair design. While designated as a form of procedural review, it is also demonstrably substantive: aggregate process affects substantive policy by shifting the focus away from individual caseworkers to the policy officials who devise decision systems.

The notion of systemic unfairness is now well-embedded within the case law.[39] It also reflects a deeper structural development in the type of scrutiny over administration embodies different understandings of what administration does. Administration is traditionally framed in terms of single-instance individualised administrative decisions concerning people's entitlements. But the concept has also a systemic character; it also refers to overarching systems and large-scale operations by which administrative agencies implement their policy goals.[40] Such operations in turn require supervision and monitoring, and this oversight itself necessarily has a similarly systemic character. Understood in this way, systemic unfairness review is another manifestation – this time in the judicial sphere – of the wider trend previously highlighted: the move from understanding public administration as a traditional bureaucracy to conceptualising it as a performance-based organisation in need of being subject to systemic forms of monitoring and oversight. This development in turn informs different models of administrative law oversight.[41]

The implications of this seem clear. A model of individual procedural review makes sense when predicated upon an understanding of administration as a traditional bureaucracy taking individualised decisions. By contrast, a performance-based understanding of administration necessarily prompts a more systemic model of judicial scrutiny of procedures. The courts examine and evaluate the operation and performance of the whole decision process. Rather than correcting individual errors one at a time, there is much more value in improving systemic organisational performance. Hence the focus on *systemic* unfairness.[42]

Individual and systemic procedural review also reflect different assumptions about the source of procedural errors. Individual procedural review assumes

---

[39] See *Refugee Legal Centre* (n 16); *R (Q) v Secretary of State for the Home Department* [2003] EWCA Civ 364, [2004] QB 36 (CA) (numerous procedural defects in the process for assessing claims for asylum support under the Nationality, Immigration, and Asylum Act, s 55, under which claimants were not entitled to support if their asylum claim was not made as soon as reasonably practicable after the person's arrival in the UK; the Court issued detailed procedural guidance). See also *R (Osborn) v Parole Board* [2013] UKSC 61, [2014] AC 1115; *R (UNISON) v Lord Chancellor* [2017] UKSC 51, [2017] 3 WLR 409.

[40] G Metzger, 'The Constitutional Duty to Supervise' (2015) 124 *Yale Law Journal* 1836, 1846–47.

[41] WH Simon, 'The Organizational Premises of Administrative Law' (2015) 78 *Law and Contemporary Problems* 61.

[42] Also note the development of own-initiative investigations by ombuds into systemic maladministration/injustice: Public Services Ombudsman Act (Northern Ireland) 2016, s 8(4); Public Services Ombudsman (Wales) Act 2019, s 4(2).

that any decision process is likely to produce aberrant individual mistakes or misjudgements in the specific case by the decision-maker. By contrast, systemic review assumes that errors are often symptomatic of structural deficiencies in the wider process and/or its underlying policy.[43] It is therefore concentrated upon diagnosing the causes of such errors and preventing them from arising in the first place. Where systemic unfairness has been found, it is no answer to say that judicial review is available to correct errors in any single case.[44] Systemic review involves the courts scrutinising the adequacy of whole systems of decision-making and the procedures used. There are inextricable links here between procedure and policy and between different layers of institutional action within the department, that is, between policy-makers and front-line staff.

E. Assessing Systemic Unfairness

What, then, is to be made of systemic unfairness? Some judges have highlighted the risks of excessive judicial intervention.[45] There are limits and it would be mistaken to assume that systemic review is now widely available as a form of global judicial inquiry into administrative decision processes. Only targeted and well-evidenced challenges are likely to succeed.[46] But does systemic unfairness review involve judicial overreach?

The analysis presented here strongly supports the view that systemic judicial review has real strengths in terms of assessing the fairness and effectiveness of administrative systems. It is not merely desirable, but a necessary and legitimate means of judicial control of administration. This is partly because of the importance substantive matters and rights at stake for the individuals concerned. We also need to factor in the department's well-known behavioural traits: its lack of expertise and independence in ensuring its systems are procedurally fair; the variable quality of its operations and the often overburdened or lackadaisical work of officials; the department's defensiveness and unwillingness or inability effectively to scrutinise and evaluate its own systems; the overriding need to please ministers; and the lack of votes in being humane toward migrants.

Arguments in favour of systemic unfairness review include the need for independent judicial expertise and the (in)effectiveness of alternative means of accountability. Through their wide-ranging oversight of the entire legal system, the

---

[43] *R (BF (Eritrea)) v Secretary of State for the Home Department* [2019] EWCA Civ 872, [2020] 4 WLR 38, [63] (Underhill LJ); *R (Humnyntskyi and others) v Secretary of State for the Home Department* [2020] EWHC 1912 (Admin) [272]–[277] (Johnson J). See generally *R (Woolcock) v Secretary of State for Communities and Local Government* [2018] EWHC 17 (Admin), [2018] 4 WLR 49 [49]–[68] (Hickinbottom LJ).

[44] *MR (Pakistan) v Secretary of State for Justice* [2021] EWCA Civ 541 [103] (Dingemans LJ).

[45] *R (S) v Director of Legal Aid Casework* [2016] EWCA Civ 464, [2016] 1 WLR 4733 [18] (Laws LJ).

[46] See J Varuhas, 'Evidence, Facts, and the Changing Nature of Judicial Review' *UK Constitutional Law Blog* (15 June 2020).

higher courts possess incomparably greater expertise and experience in assessing the procedural fairness of decision processes than the department's tunnel vision approach.[47] As regards alternative means of accountability, judicial control has real advantages over political scrutiny when it comes to scrutinising detail and issuing binding rulings. Two years before *Detention Action* the HAC had raised concerns about the fast-track process and recommended changes, but had been rebuffed by the department's standard platitudes about the 'careful scrutiny' given by caseworkers and its intention to 'make every effort' to ensure that only appropriate cases were fast-tracked and then regularly reviewed.[48] In other words, the choice in *Detention Action* was never between the reform of unfair processes by the department or the courts, but only between judicial intervention or continuing with the fast-track process operating unfairly.

Subsequent systemic review cases rulings provide more grist to the Committee's mill given its concerns relating to the poor quality of immigration decisions, administrative unfairness resulting from organisational problems within the department, and limitations on access to justice.[49] In short, given their independence, their in-depth expert scrutiny of procedural systems, and the ability to make legally enforceable rulings, the courts have clear advantages in identifying systemically unfair administration. Judicial intervention also sets a marker for the future.[50]

Overall, systemic unfairness review takes seriously a model of administration as comprising large-scale systems of operational delivery and the need to investigate how those systems operate in practice, their organisational performance, and whether their quality is adversely affected by systemic problems. The courts have intervened when the department has been shown to lack the capability to undertake this type of self-scrutiny itself. By developing systemic review, the courts have framed judicial review on the basis of a more realistic understanding of administration and its systemic nature and thereby significantly enhanced the effectiveness of judicial review in ensuring fair and lawful administration. The shift also reflects

---

[47] In *Detention Action* (n 20) [29] the Court of Appeal justified its expertise as follows: 'the question is whether the Fast-track rules satisfy the requirements of justice and fairness ... The answer to this question does not call for expertise which the court does not possess. The court is well equipped to decide whether an appeal process is fair and just.'

[48] HAC, 'Asylum' HC 71 (2013–14) [64]–[66]; Home Office, 'Government Response to the Seventh Report From the HAC Session 2013–14 HC 71: Asylum' (Cm 769, 2013) 14–15.

[49] See, eg, HAC, 'Home Office Delivery of Brexit: Immigration' HC 421 (2017–19) [54]–[72].

[50] Judicial review can also strengthen the hand of one side of the internal debate within government. A government department thinks privately, although not necessarily with a single mind. There may well be competing viewpoints internally which judicial and other external scrutiny may affirm or weaken. For instance, during the 1970s and 1980s, judicial review of prisons was welcomed by senior Home Office officials because it led to reforms that they favoured but which the Prisons Service had resisted; court decisions had the advantage that prison officers were more ready to accept changes imposed by the courts than if the same reforms had been imposed by prison management. See S Brown, 'The Unaccountability of the Judges: Surely Their Strength not their Weakness' in C Forsyth et al (eds), *Effective Judicial Review: A Cornerstone of Good Governance* (Oxford, Oxford University Press, 2010); D Faulkner, *Servant of the Crown: A Civil Servant's Story of Criminal Justice and Public Service Reform* (Reading, Waterside Press, 2014) 161–62.

the move from an individual redress model of judicial review to one in which the courts supervise and manage administrative governance wholesale. Exposing administrative systems to this form of scrutiny is a valuable discipline in terms of improving the fairness and quality of those processes and protects individual rights.

III. Principles of Legality

We now consider judicial intervention under the general heading of legality. The underlying principles – legality, unlawful administrative action, conspicuous abuse of power, and access to justice, amongst others – are easily stated, but to capture how they take colour from the context, we need to examine how such principles interact with administrative practices and behaviours. In turn, it is clear that judicial interventions are often responses to wider operational problems and improper political manipulation of administration. In the process, the courts have highlighted the importance of internal supervision and monitoring of operations within the department.

A. Applying and Assessing Guidance

Consider, first of all, the judicial response when caseworkers make immigration decisions without applying relevant guidance. Government agencies can adopt policies and guidance which decision-makers should follow and apply, unless there are good reasons for not doing so.[51] To do otherwise would be a failure to apply policy consistently. In *Mandalia*, the Supreme Court held that the failure of a caseworker to take into account the evidential flexibility policy had been unlawful; the caseworker had not invited the applicant to repair the deficit in his evidence as per the evidential flexibility guidance.[52] The case was then returned to the department to make a fresh decision.

Such judicial intervention is non-problematic. It promotes the interests of applicants who have a public law right to have their applications considered under the relevant guidance. From an organisational perspective, the court's intervention also repairs administrative deficiencies in the internal dissemination and communication of such guidance to caseworking teams and/or the simple failure of individual

---

[51] See, eg, *DS Abdi v Secretary of State for the Home Department* [1996] Imm AR 148 (CA); *AG and others v Secretary of State for the Home Department (Policies; executive discretions; Tribunal's powers) Kosovo* [2007] UKAIT 00082; *R (Saadi) v Secretary of State for the Home Department* [2001] EWCA Civ 1512, [2002] 1 WLR 356 [7] (Lord Phillips of Worth Matravers MR); *R (SK (Zimbabwe)) v Secretary of State for the Home Department (Bail for Immigration Detainees intervening)* [2011] UKSC 23, [2011] 1 WLR 1299 [36] (Lord Hope).
[52] *Mandalia v Secretary of State for the Home Department* [2015] UKSC 59, [2015] 1 WLR 4546.

caseworkers to apply guidance. As a form of internal administrative law, guidance is issued within the department to structure administrative action and decisions. It should be applied by officials, but this does not always happen because of weak management practices. Judicial control thereby ensures legal accountability and basic desk-level organisational competence. In a better-organised administrative system, this type of judicial review should, theoretically, prompt the department to improve its internal dissemination processes and/or training for caseworkers. It is inefficient to have to make a second decision when the guidance should have been taken into account first time round, but it is far more inefficient when the department's failures lead to litigation.

Another form of judicial intervention has arisen when the department's guidance has irrationally frustrated the declared purposes of the underlying policy. For instance, in *Limbu*, the Administrative Court held that guidance governing when to grant indefinite leave to remain to Gurkha veterans irrationally excluded important considerations which, in light of the stated purpose of the policy, should have been included.[53] The purpose of the policy had been to recognise the role of Gurkha veterans in protecting the UK. The guidance stated that one factor officials had to consider was the applicant's strength of ties with the UK; had they spent a significant amount of time living in the UK? However, the Court held that requiring physical presence in the UK could not be determinative: long military service on behalf of the UK provided a connection irrespective of where in the world it had taken place. Other parts of the guidance were not rationally connected to its purposes. This type of judicial review is a good illustration of the courts, in essence, applying the substantive standard of instrumental rationality to ensure that the means used to achieve a policy are rationally connected to its goal.

Rashid involved an egregious form of administrative incompetence and is also a more problematic case.[54] The department had adopted a general unpublished policy that it would not refuse asylum to Iraqi nationals on the ground that they could relocate internally to the former Kurdish Autonomous Zone within Iraq from government-controlled areas. The policy was important given the increased numbers of Iraqi asylum claims. However, the policy had not been applied consistently by caseworkers, many of whom had been unaware of it, a situation that the department had allowed to persist for some years. Bizarrely, the department 'never got to the bottom of how some caseworkers knew of the policy and some did not'.[55] Rashid had at the time qualified under the terms of the policy, but had nevertheless been refused, even though his case had been linked with those of similarly situated claimants who had been granted asylum. The Court of Appeal found that this was not a case of a single error, but of systemic failure by the department to ensure that its own policy was properly applied by caseworkers. Inexplicably, the

---

[53] *R (Limbu) v Secretary of State for the Home Department* [2008] EWHC 2261 (Admin).

[54] *R (Rashid) v Secretary of State for the Home Department* [2005] EWCA Civ 744, [2005] Imm AR 608.

[55] ibid [5] (Pill LJ quoting counsel for the department).

department had allowed this state of affairs to continue for a prolonged period of time, which included a considerable number of Iraqi asylum claims in the period 2000–03, and given the situation in Iraq at that time. The Court of Appeal found there that 'serious errors of administration have resulted in conspicuous unfairness to the claimant'; there had 'been flagrant and prolonged incompetence'.[56]

Carnwath LJ later expressed doubts about the weight placed by the Court of Appeal upon the department's conduct; 'the court's proper sphere is illegality, not maladministration'.[57] *Rashid* was also problematic on the issue of the appropriate remedy, which the Supreme Court subsequently overruled.[58] Yet, the department's failure to ensure the policy was properly applied by caseworkers was flawed and resulted in significant unfairness to the claimant.

The legal problems concerning administrative guidance do not end here. What happens when political pressures prompt ministers and senior officials to manipulate guidance for their own short-term political ends? We need to consider the aftermath of the 2006 foreign national prisoners (FNPs) crisis.

B. Secret Guidance and Unlawful Detention

The department's failure to consider for deportation over 1,000 FNPs before releasing them from prison caused a toxic political fall-out. It also presented an immediate political challenge concerning those FNPs who remained in detention. The department's published detention policy guidance included a presumption in favour of release, and this remained in place. But, under intense media and political pressure, ministers and senior officials had adopted very different secret guidance which introduced a near-blanket policy to continue detaining FNPs irrespective of their individual circumstances. Detention caseworkers had been directed to conceal the real reasons when deciding to detain, namely the unpublished policy, but to give other reasons which appeared to conform with the published policy. The obvious purpose was to enable ministers to avoid further media and political blame in the aftermath of the whole crisis.

---

[56] ibid [34] (Pill LJ); [53] (Dyson LJ).

[57] *R (S) v Secretary of State for the Home Department* [2007] EWCA Civ 546, [2007] INLR 450 [41] (Carnwath LJ).

[58] In *Rashid*, the Court of Appeal considered that the unfairness of the department's failure to apply the policy justified a declaration that Rashid was to be granted indefinite leave to remain. However, at the date of the decision, Rashid no longer satisfied the criteria as a result of the invasion of Iraq by coalition forces and the removal of Saddam Hussein's regime. Asylum appeals are determined on the basis of the risk on return at the date of decision (*Ravichandran v Secretary of State for the Home Department* [1996] Imm AR 97 (CA)). See also *MA and AA (Afghanistan) v Secretary of State for the Home Department* [2015] UKSC 40, [2015] WLR 3083 [71] (Lord Toulson): 'In *Rashid* the sloppiness of procedures in the Home Office resulted in the appellant being unfairly denied refugee status when he applied for it; but refugee status is not bound to endure for ever. By the time that his case reached the Court of Appeal the source of persecution in Iraq had been overthrown, and the effect of the court's decision was to give him a right which he did not need for his personal protection'.

In *Lumba*, the Supreme Court held that the unpublished guidance had been unlawful.[59] It contravened the long-established *Hardial Singh* principles that the power to detain could only be exercised reasonably and for the prescribed purpose of facilitating deportation.[60] The secret guidance had also been motivated by an improper political purpose.[61] The detainees had been kept in detention not to facilitate their removal, but to save ministers' skin from media blame. The Court also invoked normative values: the rule of law required a transparent statement by the department as to how it would exercise its statutory powers to detain. The claimants had a basic public law right to have their cases considered under the policy adopted and a correlative right to be informed about that policy so they could know the criteria being applied, make informed and meaningful representations before decisions to detain were made, and be able to challenge an adverse decision.[62] As Lord Walker noted, the 'small army of officials at different levels' who take decisions need guidance to achieve consistent decision-making.[63] Such guidance and policies should be published because those people who will be affected are entitled to know where they stand. Overall, the Court found a serious and deplorable abuse of power.[64]

The department's cynicism had, though, extended beyond merely adopting secret guidance. Having been advised beforehand by Home Office lawyers that the secret guidance was legally vulnerable, ministers and senior officials had proceeded to adopt and apply it anyhow. Avoiding political and media criticism and reputational damage evidently took priority over the need for lawful administration. The department's presentational response to successful judicial challenge had been prefigured in a draft policy submission from senior officials to ministers: 'if we were to lose a test case, we could present any change in FNP detention practice as having been forced on us by the courts'.[65] As the trial judge had noted,

> That may or may not be good politics: but it is deplorable practice, especially when it is seen that almost from day one the new unpublished policy was perceived in virtually all quarters within the department to be at least legally 'vulnerable' and in some quarters positively to be untenable and legally invalid.[66]

Not only was lawful administration dispensable, but the courts were there to be used by the department to absorb the blame to get ministers off the hook.

---

[59] *Lumba v Secretary of State for the Home Department* [2011] UKSC 12, [2012] AC 245.

[60] *R v Governor of Durham Prison, ex p Hardial Singh* [1984] 1 WLR 704 (HC); *R (I) v Secretary of State for the Home Department* [2002] EWCA Civ 888, [2003] INLR 196 [46]. See also A Schymyck, 'The *Hardial Singh* Principles and the Principle of Legality' [2021] *PL* 489.

[61] cf *Padfield v Minister of Agriculture, Fisheries and Food* [1968] AC 997 (HL).

[62] *Lumba* (n 59) [34] (Lord Dyson). The sense of prior judicial movement is evident from *ID v Home Office* [2005] EWCA Civ 38, [2006] 1 WLR 1003 [129]–[131] (Brooke LJ).

[63] *Lumba* (n 59) [190] (Lord Walker).

[64] ibid [175]–[176] (Lord Hope) and [194] (Lord Walker).

[65] ibid [162] (Lord Dyson).

[66] *Abdi and others v Secretary of State for the Home Department* [2008] EWHC 3166 (Admin) [43.12] (Davis J).

Overall, the whole episode illustrates ministers and officials being caught up in problems of their own making. Endemic organisational incompetence had caused enforcement failures, leading to a political crisis, and then ministerial pressures to engage in the systemically unlawfully action of detaining people by applying an unpublished policy. Judicial intervention was essential to prevent ministers from manipulating administrative decision-making concerning personal liberty for their own politically motivated agenda. In particular, the department needed to have transparent and published policies and to act in accordance with them. *Lumba* confirms the value of judicial intervention when ministers and senior officials consciously and deliberately abuse their powers by manipulating internal administrative law for reasons of political self-interest.

C. Arbitrary, Unjust and Unlawful Administrative Conduct

Other cases demonstrate the interconnections between the behaviours of front-line officials, organisational incompetence, the lack of internal controls and supervision by senior officials, the negative consequences on the individuals concerned, and the consequent need for judicial intervention.

Consider *Muuse*.[67] The Court of Appeal here ruled that the unlawful detention by immigration officials of Mr Muuse, a Dutch national born in Somalia, for over three months pending his deportation to Somalia, when there had been no legal right to deport him had not merely been unconstitutional, but also an outrageous and arbitrary exercise of executive power. The illegality had been caused by the manifest incompetence of junior officials handling Mr Muuse's case, but it had been compounded by the lack of supervision of such officials. The facts were extreme. The officials had: ignored Mr Muuse's protests that he was Dutch (partly by their manifest incompetence and partly by their failure to take the most elementary steps to check his documents); disobeyed a court order to release him; not considered the conclusive evidence they held as to his Dutch nationality; and made no enquiries to determine the necessity of his detention pending deportation. Moreover, the officials had: not examined the grounds for deportation; not given reasons for his detention; threatened him with deportation to Somalia; ignored evidence in their possession; not given him adequate time to appeal against the deportation order; refused to revoke that deportation order; and subjected him to racist remarks calculated to degrade and humiliate him.

The behaviour of the officials had clearly been appalling, but the wider institutional failings were also central. The Court of Appeal had been particularly concerned that the power to detain had been entrusted to incompetent and unsupervised junior officers. They had been issued with manuals instructing them how

---

[67] *Muuse v Secretary of State for the Home Department* [2010] EWCA Civ 453.

to exercise their powers lawfully, but no one had examined the competence of the officials given their powers to detain without judicial authority. Indeed, no one of any real seniority had exercised any supervision over them.[68] Further, the junior officials had been able to lead a minister into making an unlawful decision to deport on the basis of a wholly deficient submission. The lack of supervision was also evident from the fact that a junior official had the power to revoke the deportation order, took a month to revoke it and release Mr Muuse, and the minister was not then told that he had made an unlawful decision and advised of the action required to remedy it. The Court was distinctly sceptical about so-called 'improvements' subsequently made to procedures, which, on examination, did nothing

> to remedy the lack of competence of those who make the day to day decisions in respect of persons in the position of Mr Muuse or put in place proper systems of control and supervision over their exercise of powers to deprive persons of their liberty.[69]

In light of the total lack of other forms of Parliamentary or internal scrutiny or accountability, judicial scrutiny was the only means by which the misconduct had been exposed and individual rights protected. Given the absence of Parliamentary accountability for the arbitrary and unlawful detention, the lack of any enquiry, and the paucity of the measures taken to prevent their recurrence, the award of exemplary damages was necessary to deter such conduct and to vindicate the rule of law; 'the award of punitive damages under the common law has a real role in restraining the arbitrary use of executive power and buttressing civil liberties, given the way the United Kingdom's Parliamentary democracy in fact operates'.[70]

In summary, *Muuse* illustrates clearly how organisational incompetence, in particular the lack of effective supervision over junior officials making detention decisions, compelled the need for judicial intervention. The underlying norm relied upon by the Court is quite clear. Effective administrative institutions must have robust internal procedures for monitoring and supervising junior officials performing tasks with important consequences for affected individuals. In the context of making detention decisions, the Court had clearly assumed that such internal controls and supervision have an essential role to play in protecting individual rights and preventing unlawful administration action. Without them, there is no one keeping an eye on officials to tell them when they are stepping out of line and the abuse of power becomes more likely. When such abuse

---

[68] ibid [74] (Lord Thomas LCJ). Also [86] (Sir Scott Baker): 'it is to be hoped that the worrying issues raised by this case have been or will be addressed. Nothing less is acceptable in a true democracy.'

[69] ibid [76] (Lord Thomas LCJ).

[70] ibid [77] (Lord Thomas LCJ). At [79], the court criticised the department's policy of giving the junior officials anonymity and of exempting them from giving an explanation: those who made detention decisions 'should not be permitted to claim anonymity and be shielded from explaining their conduct to a court. It is moreover difficult to see how such a policy is consistent with the rule of law in a democracy'.

occurs, it represents an institutional failure. The absence of internal administrative accountability prompted the court to examine in detail what had been going on within the department and justified the Court's intervention, and the award of exemplary damages.

Anwar provides a similar example.[71] Three immigrants granted to leave to enter as students had enrolled at what they assumed were bona fide colleges. However, the department had then removed the colleges from its register of training and education providers because they had issued bogus qualifications. Having sought advice from the department, the students then transferred to other genuine colleges, but were later shocked to be subject to removal action on the ground of having obtained leave to remain by deception. The allegation of deception had been unfounded; the students had been lawfully pursuing their studies at their own expense. Further, the department had not given them a hearing or advance notice that they had to leave. When making its decision, the Home Office had a choice between using different statutory powers at its disposal. It could have varied the students' leave to remain, a decision route that, at the time, carried an in-country appeal right. But instead, the department had used the deception decision route, which generated the less effective remedy of an out-of-country appeal. The legality of the choice of decision-making routes did not arise for decision, but the Court of Appeal had deep misgivings about the Home Office's 'arbitrary and unjust conduct'; the department's 'effective criminalising and enforced removal of an innocent person without either worthwhile evidence or the opportunity to answer' was arguably a serious abuse of power.[72] The Court also expressed concern that 'the powers of one of the great offices of state appear to have been so misused as to rob the successive administrative decisions of legal authority. We wish this to be brought to the Home Secretary's attention'.[73]

Clearly, there had been a failure of internal supervision and control within the department as to which decision-making powers were appropriate. Again, we see the Court, through the general principle of legality, uncovering and highlighting systemic administrative problems in need of correction that had not been effectively supervised within the department. In common with other types of external scrutiny (the NAO, the PAC, and the Windrush Review), judicial scrutiny has a major role to play in identifying weaknesses within internal monitoring.

D. Access to Justice

Given its controls over immigrants' lives, the department is often able – directly and indirectly – to weaken or altogether undermine their right of access to

---

[71] *Anwar and another v Secretary of State for the Home Department* [2010] EWCA Civ 1275, [2011] 1 WLR 2552.

[72] ibid [6] and [24] (Sedley LJ).

[73] ibid [25] (Sedley LJ).

justice and, in turn, the ability of the courts to apply and enforce the law.[74] This can take place through either the application of administrative routines or intentional undermining of access to justice. Either way, the consequences threaten the integrity of the overall system of public law controls over administration. A cluster of cases then centre upon the constitutional right of access to justice and the department's compliance with and accountability to the law.

Anufrijeva concerned the legality of the department's practice deliberately to delay formally notifying asylum claimants that their asylum claim had been refused.[75] During the delay, the department's practice was to inform the then Benefits Agency of the refusal which would then, without explanation, cease paying benefits to claimants. Claimants were not formally notified of the refusal of their asylum claim, or given the reasons for the refusal, and could not appeal. The House of Lords held that the department's practice entirely ignored the right of access to justice and the rule of law. The need to notify an individual of an administrative decision before it could have legal effect was not a technical rule, but reflected the right of access to justice. Lord Steyn explained:

> A constitutional state must accord to individuals the right to know of a decision before their rights can be adversely affected. The antithesis of such a state was described by Kafka: a state where the rights of individuals are overridden by hole in the corner decisions or knocks on doors in the early hours.[76]

The ruling had implications far beyond the individual case and clearly falls into the wider pattern of the courts using general principles of legality to correct flawed systemic practices.

Other cases have concerned not just access to justice, but also access to appropriate and effective forms of justice, in particular, whether individual challenges are best handled through judicial review or tribunal appeals. The issue has arisen in the context of the department's concerted enforcement action against some 50,000 students alleged to have cheated in their English language tests by cancelling or curtailing their status on the ground of deception.[77] Again, there had been direct ministerial pressure on officials to penalise the students *en masse* by revoking their visas. The department's attitude was that almost all the students had cheated in their English language tests, but many students protested their innocence and highlighted the department's unreliable evidence. As each case turned on personal credibility and its own individual facts, there was an evident need for individualised adjudication, but through which means? The department had responded by selecting an administrative decision-making mechanism within the

---

[74] *UNISON* (n 39).

[75] *R (Anufrijeva) v Secretary of State for the Home Department* [2004] 1 AC 604 (HL).

[76] ibid [28] (Lord Steyn). For other significant access to justice cases in the context of removals, see *R (Medical Justice) v Secretary of State for the Home Department* [2011] EWCA Civ 269, [2011] 1 WLR 2852; *R ((FB) Afghanistan) v Secretary of State for the Home Department* [2020] EWCA Civ 1338.

[77] See generally NUSUK, 'The TOEIC Scandal: An Ongoing Injustice' (2018).

immigration rules that did not attract a right of appeal with judicial review being the only means of challenge. Of course, judicial review is a less effective remedy compared with an appeal. In short, ministerial pressure to crack down on alleged cheats led to administrative action that restricted access to effective and appropriate justice.

In *Mohibullah*, McCloskey J found that the department's handling of the allegations of cheating had been conspicuously unfair and an abuse of power.[78] The department had erred by using decision-making mechanisms that did not generate a right of appeal and also by failing to take into account the relevant consideration that there were distinct differences between tribunal appeals and judicial review when deciding which mechanism to use. The choice was particularly important given McCloskey J's conclusion that the English language test cheating cases had 'demonstrated beyond peradventure that judicial review is an entirely unsatisfactory litigation vehicle for the determination of disputes of this kind', that is, individual fact-specific challenges turning on contested issues of evidence and credibility.[79] By confining Mr Mohibullah to the 'inferior and limited remedy of judicial review' in the context of a fact-sensitive issue, the department had 'acted with singular and manifest unfairness'.[80] The 'dubious conduct' of officials had included firmly taking the view that the claimant had cheated and then exerting 'improper pressure' on the college to withdraw him from his course of study.[81]

Unsurprisingly, McCloskey J rejected the option of allowing students to make post-decision representations as opposed to an appeal – the former was of no value 'given that the Secretary of State's agents were implacably and, in our view, irrevocably committed to the view that the Applicant had practised deception'.[82] An assessment subsequently confirmed that officials, under pressure from ministers, had been using every trick in the book to brand students as fraudsters abusing the process without giving them a fair opportunity to clear their names.[83] Given the number of affected students, the rulings had wider consequences and were

---

[78] *R (Mohibullah) v Secretary of State for the Home Department (TOEIC – ETS – judicial review principles)* [2016] UKUT 00561 (IAC).

[79] *SM and Qadir v Secretary of State for the Home Department (ETS – Evidence – Burden of Proof)* [2016] UKUT 00229 (IAC) [102]. See also *R (Gazi) v Secretary of State for the Home Department (ETS – judicial review) IJR* [2015] UKUT 00327 (IAC) [36]: even an out-of-country First-tier Tribunal appeal was 'a demonstrably superior mechanism' than 'individual' judicial review given the latter's supervisory jurisdiction and the court's inability to hear live oral evidence and to undertake a detailed, forensic examination of both the department's and expert evidence.

[80] ibid [72].

[81] ibid [64].

[82] ibid [80].

[83] NAO, 'Investigation into the Response to Cheating in English Language Tests HC 2144 (2017–19); PAC, English Language Tests For Overseas Students' HC 2039 (2017–19) (criticising the department's 'flawed reaction to a systemic failure' which 'had a detrimental impact on the lives of over 50,000 overseas students'; the department had been 'quick to act on imperfect evidence, but slow in responding to indications that innocent people may have been caught up in its actions').

indeed part of a much larger amount of complex litigation on the same issue. In a subsequent decision, the Court of Appeal issued detailed guidance about the impact on the old and new (post-2014 Act) appeal regimes and when an out-of-country appeal would not be an effective remedy because of the need for the appellant to give oral evidence and the lack of video-link facilities in her home country.[84]

The cases so far have concerned accessing justice and effective remedies. What of administrative non-compliance with judicial decisions? The notion that an administrative department is legally bound to give effect to judicial decisions is an elementary legal principle. Yet, it is precisely this principle that the department has, on occasion, sought to evade.

The notorious case of Afghan hijackers concerned a number of Afghan nationals who had hijacked a plane, landed in the UK and then sought asylum. The case caused media and political uproar. Under intense political and media pressure, the department had refused and resisted the asylum claims throughout. On appeal, a tribunal had found that returning the hijackers would breach Article 3 ECHR. Under the department's own guidance, the successful appellants should have been granted discretionary leave as recognition that they could not be safely returned to Afghanistan. But the department had done nothing to implement the tribunal's determination. The Administrative Court concluded that the department had imposed a deliberate delay in giving effect to the tribunal's determination in order to buy some time before making a revised policy, which could then be used to justify not implementing the tribunal's determination. The Court found it particularly disturbing that the deliberate delay had been authorised, if not initiated, at the highest level, that is, by the Home Secretary personally: 'It is difficult to conceive of a clearer case of "conspicuous unfairness amounting to an abuse of power" by a public authority'.[85] As in *Lumba*, there had been ministerial interference with the administrative process for the improper purpose of seeking to escape media and public criticism.

At the doctrinal level, the concept of the abuse of power has been clearly brought within the traditional grounds of judicial review.[86] The analysis here has focused on the practical effectiveness of the courts in supervising government. In this respect, the courts have used the concept to restrain ministerial attempts to

---

[84] *Ahsan v Secretary of State for the Home Department* [2017] EWCA Civ 2009, [2018] INLR 207. And then extensive litigation on costs, see, eg, *R (Mozumder) v Secretary of State for the Home Department* [2021] EWCA Civ 138.

[85] *R (S) v Secretary of State for the Home Department* [2006] EWCA Admin 1111 [102] (Sullivan J); affirmed by the Court of Appeal: [2006] EWCA Civ 1157.

[86] *R (Gallaher Group Ltd) v Competition and Markets Authority* [2018] UKSC 25, [2019] AC 96 [40]–[41] (Lord Carnwath).

subvert the administrative process for improper purposes and result in substantive unfairness and/or illegality for the individuals concerned.

E. Judicial Control of Rule-making

A final matter concerns judicial review of rule-making. Successful legal challenges to rules and regulations that embody policies are very rare. For obvious reasons, the courts are reluctant to intervene when issues of pure policy are concerned. Nonetheless, the courts have, on occasion, intervened. One particular area of intervention has concerned secondary legislation designating particular countries as being in general safe for asylum purposes, with the consequence that asylum claimants from such countries have restricted appeal rights. In this way, the designation orders are another form of fast-tracking of asylum claims on the basis that such claims from designated countries are presumed to be weak and/or abusive because there is in general no serious risk of persecution in the relevant country. The designation of countries as safe was based upon the department's assessment of the evidence, although there were clearly wider policy considerations such as to ensuring efficiency in the asylum process.

The courts have, though, invalidated regulations that designated Pakistan and Jamaica as safe countries because there was cogent evidence that there was in fact a serious risk of persecution against certain groups (women and Ahmadis in Pakistan and members of the LGBT community in Jamaica).[87] In both cases, the courts based their review on the factual evidence and concluded that the designation of Pakistan and Jamaica had been unlawful and irrational because the evidence did not demonstrate that there was in general no serious risk of persecution in those countries. In asylum cases, the courts adopt an intensive standard of review given the gravity of the issues involved. There is an obvious underlying tension between individual rights and the department being trusted and able to evaluate and frequently review country conditions properly, on the one hand, and ministerial pressures on the other hand to speed up the asylum process. Again, there is a clear link between judicial scrutiny of the means adopted to achieve a policy goal and their appropriateness. Another relevant factor was the relative lack of alternative forms of scrutiny. Given the weakness of parliamentary scrutiny of secondary legislation, judicial review was the only means of evaluating the evidential and legal basis of the designation orders. As in many of the previous cases considered, the impact of such rulings is illustrated by the fact that a general policy was being invalidated which affected a large number of people.

---

[87] *R (Asif Javed) v Secretary of State for the Home Department* [2001] EWCA Civ 789, [2002] QB 129; *R (Brown (Jamaica)) v Secretary of State for the Home Department* [2015] UKSC 8, [2015] WLR 1060.

IV. Conclusion

So, what then are we to make of judicial control? The courts have avoided the two extremes of excessive judicial interference with the department's exercise of its functions on the one hand and complete judicial abstentionism on the other. Instead, they have crafted an effective judicial response to some of the real problems of administration: the use of inappropriate means to achieve policy goals; the lack of effective internal supervision and coordination within administration; the need to protect administrative procedures from improper political interference and pressure from ministers; and the impact of all of these upon affected individuals. Judicial review is often both the result of, and in turn draws to attention to, significant internal organisational weaknesses and shortcomings that require amendment, internal supervision and monitoring. Shortcomings in internal controls and supervision, whether as the result of organisational incompetence or self-serving political game-playing prompts judicial scrutiny and correction.

These features have in turn shaped the approach of the courts when reviewing administration action. The courts have upheld and widened the application of important legal norms of good administration: procedural fairness; transparency; consistency; both access to justice and access to effective and appropriate justice; and administrative compliance with judicial rulings. In doing so, the courts have drawn upon and employed concepts that reflect norms of institutionally competent administration, such as systemic fairness and effective internal norms of administrative accountability such as internal supervision and monitoring. Judicial review has also safeguarded individual rights, restrained ministers, and protected the integrity of administration from improper political interference.

This type of judicial review reveals a different structure from that of conventional understandings of judicial review. The courts are deeply involved in scrutinising how administrative systems operate in practice and the adequacy or otherwise of existing internal means of supervising and monitoring administration. Judging administration itself involves administration. Courts are motivated by a combination of pragmatic administrative and policy considerations and legal norms. More often than many commentators are prepared to recognise, effective judicial review necessarily involves the courts, to some degree, actively managing and supervising administration. This is a legitimate means of imposing legal norms and accountability upon administration. Overall, the deep and wide-ranging scrutiny of the department provided by the courts is an essential means of overseeing and controlling administration.

9

Bureaucratic Oppression

In 2018, Sir David Normington, Permanent Secretary of the Home Office (2001–06), noted that the immigration system he inherited was dogged by ineffective computer systems, with paper files still prevalent, and poor record-keeping practices. 'We slowly tried to put that right. That was still happening as I left and I'm not sure it was completely successful actually.'[1] In 2020, Mr Osman 'Ossie' Bash Taqi finally concluded his 28-year battle to resolve his immigration status owing to the Home Office having lost his passport. Commenting on his experience, Mr Taqi explained, 'I no longer know how sane I am. ... I'm raging against the injustice of all this.'[2] Why does administrative behaviour often result in intense injustice for individuals? And what can be done about it?

The concept of administration is a purposive-rational mechanism that enables the management of large-scale economic and social problems.[3] Through administrative organisation and procedures, resources can be mobilised and political control can be exerted on an unprecedented scale. Administration offers efficiency in the governance of large-scale problems. Yet, administration also creates real dangers for people who must interact with it, often with tragic consequences. People subject to impersonal administrative processes can become imprisoned within an 'escape-proof' metaphorical or real iron cage.[4] The individual is at the whim of the faceless and uncaring Kafka-esque bureaucracy and often without any effective remedy. This chapter examines the problem of bureaucratic oppression in the immigration context, its causes, ways of seeking to counter it, and their effectiveness.

[1] T Rutter, 'No place like the Home Office: former top officials on the department's unique challenges' *Civil Service World* (10 May 2018).

[2] 'Home Office lost passport of man battling for decades to remain in UK' *Guardian* (14 May 2020).

[3] M Weber (eds G Roth and C Wittich), *Economy and Society* (London, University of California Press, 1978) 956–1002.

[4] ibid 1401–03; M Weber, *The Protestant Ethic and the Spirit of Capitalism* (London, Routledge, 2001) 123; R Bruce Douglass, *The Iron Cage Revisited: Max Weber in the Neoliberal Era* (London, Routledge, 2019).

I. Bureaucratic Oppression and Immigration Administration

A. The Nature and Causes of Bureaucratic Oppression

Bureaucratic oppression occurs when government agencies (and their contractors) impose unnecessary and unjustified harm on people who interact with them.[5] It includes unlawful administrative action (and inaction), but the concept extends far beyond a narrow 'legality' model of administrative law. Bureaucratic oppression takes many forms. It includes: delay; lack of sympathy and empathy; inhumane treatment; being forced to wait for hours in long queues; being subject to verbal and physical abuse; being given incorrect advice; being unable to communicate effectively with a government department; having to use phone lines that are not answered or poorly designed websites that do not work properly; and inadequate complaint-handling systems.

To understand bureaucratic oppression, it is necessary identify its causes. Rubin has identified four general sources of bureaucratic oppression: status differences; stranger relations; institutional pathologies; and divergent incentives.[6] The first and second sources – status differences and stranger relations – concern the nature and position of government officials. The third and fourth sources – institutional pathologies and divergent incentives – concern the wider organisational forces that impact upon the behaviours of such officials.

First, status differences. Whenever officials have a higher social or power status than those individuals subject to an administrative process, then such individuals are in a subordinate and hence weak position, and this in turn creates opportunities for bureaucratic oppression. Even if officials have a low social status, their position gives them the power over other individuals. Status differences are reinforced by the monolithic and monopolistic nature of administrative systems. Second, stranger relationships. Officials and individuals are strangers: they do not know each other. Consequently, there are few familial bonds that might reduce the risk of oppression. Instead, the degree of 'otherness' is increased by the high degree of anonymity and the lack of any ongoing relationship. Officials often interact with individuals for a short period of time and have little opportunity to get to know

---

[5] EL Rubin, 'Bureaucratic Oppression: Its Causes and Cures' (2012) 90 *Washington University Law Review* 291, 300. See also VA Thompson, *Without Sympathy or Enthusiasm: The Problem of Administrative Compassion* (University of Alabama Press, 1975). DL Balfour, GB Adams and AE Nickels, *Unmasking Administrative Evil*, 5th edn (London, Routledge, 2019) have articulated the concept of 'administrative evil' as a product of modernity and technical rationality and root it in the Holocaust, but 'bureaucratic oppression' is preferred here: administration can be intentionally used for evil, but it also produces numerous instances of mundane and quotidian oppression which are often the result of unintentional incompetence and oversight rather than deliberate harm.

[6] Rubin (ibid) 296–318.

them and to develop empathetic concern. Instead, given the number of people they must deal with, officials will tend to stereotype individuals thereby reducing their uniqueness.

A third cause of bureaucratic oppression are the institutional pathologies of large and complex administrative organisations. As we have seen, such organisations are, to varying degrees, inherently functional and dysfunctional. Individual officials are just one small part of a large system which in turn heavily conditions their behaviour. Institutional pathologies include: counter-productive targets; political and administrative pressures to respond to certain individuals in a way that causes unnecessary harm; excessively and unnecessarily formalistic and complex rules and regulations that must be followed irrespective of whether they make sense; and administrative procedures that better suit organisational needs than those of the individuals who are subject to the process. A fourth source of bureaucratic oppression are the divergent incentives of officials. Such officials are employed to advance the public good, but they have their own self-interests, such as reducing their workloads, pursuing their personal policy preferences and maintaining group solidarity with other officials. In practice, officials, as human beings, often pursue their own personal self-interests over and above the public interest. One particular feature is that officials who work together in teams are likely to develop and be influenced by an informal organisational culture of group solidarity. By contrast, individuals subject to the administrative process are strangers over whom officials have power and who they either want to get rid of or positively go out of their way to oppress.

Bureaucratic oppression arises because of the role and nature of government agencies and their officials, and the forces that shape and influence their behaviour. It can be intentional, or it can arise from official indifference or as the inevitable result of the uncoordinated operation of large complex systems of rules and administration which often conflict with one another. Such oppression results in unnecessary harm to people, but can also impede policy goals. Further, it is not confined to official behaviour; private contractors increasingly interact with individuals and are also a source of bureaucratic oppression.

B. Bureaucratic Oppression and Immigration

It is difficult to compare empirically the amount and impact of bureaucratic oppression across different areas of government. It is present in every part of government. Nonetheless, there is a strong perception that it is more prevalent in the immigration context than elsewhere. It is necessary to be cautious. It would be incorrect to assume that immigration administration is universally oppressive and that all immigrants are necessarily subject to such behaviour. Yet, oppression occurs frequently within the immigration system. The following list is far from exhaustive: delay resulting in immigrants remaining in administrative limbo; lost passports and documents; routine errors and mistakes; the removal of people lawfully present in the country;[7] providing asylum claimants with substandard and unsafe accommodation;[8] discrimination; applicants being unable to book online free appointments on the new outsourced service with the consequence that they have to travel considerable distances or pay high fees to submit their applications on time;[9] the excessive use of physical restraint on migrants during the removal process; the abuse of immigration detainees; and the failure to provide adequate support and assistance to vulnerable detainees.

The underlying causes of bureaucratic oppression are all accentuated in the immigration context. As regards status differences, it is perilous to underestimate the ability of front-line immigration officials to exercise power arbitrarily. In the context of immigration detention, the source of oppression is not just mere status differences, but the complete imbalance of power between detention centre staff and detainees. It is the case that some migrants can be very difficult for officials to deal with. The archetypal victim of bureaucratic oppression is the uncertain and vulnerable person who is compelled submit to administrative procedures that they do not understand. Many immigrants fall somewhere within this spectrum, but not all of them. Some individuals will resist almost every attempt to comply with the immigration system. This in turn can increase the scope for oppression.

Stranger relations are an indelible feature of the migrant-official relationship and are far more acute than in virtually all other administrative systems, for obvious reasons. Public administration is predominantly a Western construct and has been established as a set of national organisations. To some degree, national administration can generate a degree of solidarity between the official and her fellow nationals while also fostering a degree of substantive indifference to non-national 'others' while operating through ostensibly universal and egalitarian procedures.[10] Many 'unwanted' immigrants are not merely individual strangers; they also come from the global south and from countries with very different cultures with which officials will often be unfamiliar. They will speak different languages, leading to

---

[7] 'Deportation and Child Removal Threats – Just For Living Legally in the UK' *Guardian* (18 September 2017); '"Leave UK Immediately": Scientist is Latest Victim of Home Office Blunder' *Guardian* (26 September 2017). Following the 2016 Brexit referendum and the establishment of the EU Settlement Scheme, the Home Office sent up to 100 removal notices to EU citizens resident in the UK telling them that they were liable to be detained and that they had to leave or face removal action. The Home Office apologised for this 'unfortunate error'. See 'EU Nationals Deportation Letters an "Unfortunate Error"' *Guardian* (23 August 2017).

[8] HAC, 'Asylum Accommodation' HC 637 (2016–17) [68]: 'Some of this accommodation is a disgrace and it is shameful that some very vulnerable people have been placed in such conditions'. See also 'Asylum Seekers Crammed into Rat-infested Rooms' *Guardian* (20 August 2019).

[9] '"He Was Trying to Cobble the Money Together": Vulnerable People Facing "Extortionate" Fees to Apply for Immigration Status' *Independent* (25 June 2019); 'Home Office Outsourcing to "Exploitative" Contractor Must be Reviewed, say MPs and Lawyers' *Independent* (18 August 2019); 'Government "Exploits Migrants for Profit" by Outsourcing Visa Services to Private Firms' *Guardian* (17 November 2019).

[10] M Herzfeld, *The Social Production of Indifference: Exploring the Symbolic Roots of Western Bureaucracy* (New York, Berg, 1992); JM Eckert (ed), *The Bureaucratic Production of Difference: Ethos and Ethics in Migration Administrations* (Bielefeld, Transcript Verlag, 2020).

potential communication difficulties. Even taking account of cultural differences, immigration officials will sometimes struggle to comprehend the position of such individuals. In turn, immigration officials may sometimes view themselves as the last line of defence against a seemingly unlimited number of people wanting to enter. Given the vast gulf between officials and immigrants, there is no sense of cultural familiarity or national solidarity that might reduce the risks of bureaucratic oppression.

Institutional pathologies also seem more severe in the immigration context than elsewhere, as illustrated by political pressures, the hostile environment, the organisational pressures on caseworkers, and removal targets regarding immigration enforcement. Other institutional pathologies include the rigid application of rules that do not cater for the particular circumstances of the individual case, the use of checklists to make casework decisions, and processing targets. Finally, divergent incentives are also acute. The informal working cultures officials develop with their colleagues can, on occasion, induce them to engage in deliberate oppression. By contrast, immigrants subject to the administrative process are strangers over whom officials have power and sometimes want to get rid of or positively go out of their way to oppress in ways that result in intense unfairness. For instance, in 2009, a whistleblower claimed that, in one asylum casework unit, some officials had mistreated, tricked and humiliated asylum claimants; some staff had expressed anti-immigration views and took pride in refusing asylum applications.[11] Immigration enforcement officials can adopt an adversarial approach to their work, resulting in unfair treatment. This tendency is especially prominent when immigrants are detained. Detention centre officials may view requests for assistance from immigrants as attempts to manipulate the system.

C. The Human Costs

Bureaucratic oppression has considerable costs for the people concerned, their families, their employment and their education. At one end of the continuum, there is the inconvenience of having to use poorly functioning websites of outsourced providers for the purposes of making immigration applications which have been characterised by ambiguous application forms, contradictory communications and incorrect specification of documents.[12] At the other end, there is extreme

---

[11] 'UK Border Agency Investigation Finds Cause for "'Significant Concern"' *Guardian* (8 August 2010); UK Border Agency Professional Standards Unit Complaints and Correspondence Standards and Performance Directorate, 'An Investigation Into the Allegations Made by Louise Perrett About Her Experiences Working for the UK Border Agency' (2010).

[12] D Stevenson, 'The Absolute State of the UK Visa Application System' Free movement blog (2 May 2019). See also 'Dozens of Immigration Applicants Forced to Wait in Cold for Hours After Home Office Subcontractor Systems Fail' *Independent* (12 April 2019).

bureaucratic oppression: asylum claimants who have been wrongly returned to their country of origin so that they are placed at risk and suffer the torture and persecution for which they sought asylum; the extreme and avoidable harms imposed of the Windrush scandal; and the verbal and physical abuse of detainees.

Even administrative problems that might at first glance seem relatively anodyne, such as administrative delay, often cause considerable injustice to individuals who are left in administrative limbo and unable to live an ordinary life. Administrative delay itself is inextricably bound up with power relations and is associated with bureaucratic oppression.[13]

The longest recorded case of administrative delay involved Mr Osman Bash Taqi, a teacher from Sierra Leone, who spent 28 years trying to resolve his immigration status, even though he had a legal right to remain from the outset. His key problem was that the department refused him leave to remain because he could not produce his passport, which the department itself had lost in 2010 when he applied for permission to marry. For the next eight years, the department denied possessing Mr Taqi's passport. He applied for leave to remain as a partner of an EU national, but this was refused without a right of appeal on the ground that his passport was missing. This particular decision did not attract a right of appeal following the Upper Tribunal's decision in *Sala*.[14] After *Sala* was overturned, Mr Taqi then appealed.[15] He had sought, without success, to obtain a new passport from the Sierra Leonean Embassy. The Upper Tribunal accepted that his original passport was in the department's possession, but lost in the system. The department's presenting officer provided Mr Taqi with a document explaining how he could apply to the department to retrieve his expired passport in order to improve his chances of replacing it with a new, valid current passport. The Tribunal held that, despite the *Sala* correction, Mr Taqi did not have a right of appeal because he had been unable to produce his passport.[16] However, he could make another application to the Home Office with his passport, once returned, and then, if that was refused, he could seek judicial review of that refusal. Following media coverage of his case, Mr Taqi was later granted leave to remain.[17]

---

[13] A Pérez, 'Emotions of Queuing: A Mirror of Immigrants' Social Condition' in B Sieben and A Wettergren (eds), *Emotionalizing Organizations and Organizing Emotions* (Basingstoke, Palgrave Macmillan, 2010) 166; MBE Griffiths, 'Out of Time: The Temporal Uncertainties of Refused Asylum Seekers and Immigration Detainees (2014) 30 *Journal of Ethnic and Migration Studies* 1991, 1996.

[14] *Sala v Secretary of State for Home Department (EFMs: Right of Appeal)* [2016] UKUT 00411 (IAC).

[15] *Khan v Secretary of State for the Home Department* [2017] EWCA Civ 1755, [2018] 1 WLR 1256.

[16] *Osman Bash Taqi v Secretary of State for the Home Department* (Appeal Number: EA/04398/2016, 14 November 2018) (UTIAC). The relevant regulations provided that a person claiming to be in a durable relationship with an EEA national could not appeal unless he produced a passport: Immigration (European Economic Area) Regulations 2006, SI 1003/2006, reg 26(2A). The Upper Tribunal held that, given its jurisdiction as a statutory tribunal, it could not go behind that provision and create a right of appeal where none existed.

[17] 'Home Office Lost Passport of Man Battling for Decades to Remain in UK' *Guardian* (14 May 2020); 'Home Office Grants Man Leave to Remain After 28-year Battle' *Guardian* (19 May 2020).

This is an extreme case, but not unusual.[18] It is common to encounter immigration cases in which the person has been in the country for years and has experienced considerable difficulties in trying to resolve mistakes and errors that have arisen with their immigration status. Or the person has been caught up in the complex operation of contradictory rules, systems and processes.[19] Or a newly arrived migrant has been badly treated in some way. The scale of bureaucratic oppression in the immigration context is both impossible to calculate and to underestimate. But it is not just the department. Private contractors have increasingly come to perform immigration functions, such as the provision of asylum accommodation, immigration removal escort services, the processing of visa applications, the management of immigration detention centres, and parts of the hostile environment policy.[20]

The causes of bureaucratic oppression are so closely and directly related to the nature and inherent structure of administrative government that effective solutions seem elusive. The nature of particular administrative systems, such as immigration, directly condition the types and forms of bureaucratic oppression that arise and also the effectiveness of solutions to such oppression. Nonetheless, by considering such potential solutions, we can identify their strengths and weaknesses. To this end, we now examine the effectiveness of current solutions: judicial review and tribunal appeals; complaint-handling processes; and independent inspection and monitoring. It is also important to note the role of investigative journalism, which uncovered the Windrush scandal and the abuse of immigration detainees, and then prompted formal investigations and reviews.

II. Tribunals and Courts

The role of traditional administrative law remedies, such as tribunal appeals and judicial review, have various advantages in terms of their legal expertise, judicial independence and ability to issue legally binding remedies.[21] To an extent, they can address some of the structural causes of bureaucratic oppression. When an immigrant challenges an administrative decision before a tribunal or a court, the inherent status differences between officials and the individual disappear, or are

---

[18] For significant delays in the handling of a Windrush compensation case, see: PHSO, 'Final Investigation Report – UK Visas and Immigration' 2020).

[19] See, eg, the case of some Windrush victims who were prevented for years from returning to the UK and did not therefore qualify for British citizenship under the British Nationality Act 1981 because they had not been physically present in the UK for the required five years: 'Windrush victim refused British citizenship despite wrongful passport confiscation' *Guardian* (22 November 2020); 'Windrush victim denied UK citizenship despite Home Office admitting error' *Guardian* (5 March 2021).

[20] See generally T Gammeltoft-Hansen and N Sorensen (eds), *The Migration Industry and the Commercialization of International Migration* (London, Routledge, 2012); R Thomas, 'Does Outsourcing Improve or Weaken Administrative Justice? A Review of the Evidence' [2021] PL 542.

[21] See ch 6.

at least reduced, because the judicial process is designed to restore the balance between the parties and to treat them as equals.

Yet, tribunals and courts have real limitations. The jurisdiction of the immigration tribunal is, in essence, determined by ministers, subject to parliamentary approval. Many people who could win their appeals or judicial reviews do not pursue legal challenges. Tribunals and courts are often unable to resolve the contradictions that arise in the practical operation of complex rules and administration that result in oppressive situations. The role of courts and tribunals in reviewing decisions is clearly important and the volume of legal challenges is large, but is actually quite small compared with the much greater number of informal and everyday interactions between government officials and individuals that lie outside the relatively narrow category of administrative decision-making. And it is in these interactions that most bureaucratic oppression occurs.

Even when assessed on their own terms, tribunals and courts, with their adversarial legalistic procedures, costs and formality, often struggle to provide justice for unrepresented or vulnerable people who lack the requisite resources and cannot reasonably be expected to understand complex legal rules and processes. Further, judicial processes can themselves operate oppressively. For many people, engaging in litigation is difficult, complex and daunting owing to the adversarial nature of the process and the inherent challenges of enforcing individual rights against an experienced, large and comparatively well-resourced government department. There is also the phenomenon by which some immigration appeals were go round and round the system. Such proceedings can be prolonged, sometimes over a period of years, before an individual receives a final decision. In the meantime, the individual is caught up within the process with no resolution of their immigration status. For these reasons, the legality model, upon which tribunals and judicial review are based, can only ever provide a limited solution to the substantial majority of oppressive administrative behaviour. What then of complaint-handling?

III. Complaint-handling Systems

There is a scene in Tony Saint's darkly comic novel on the work of the Immigration Service in which a black British citizen, having returned from overseas, is subjected to prolonged and offensive questioning at passport control by an immigration officer. The individual lodges a written complaint against the immigration officer concerned. The complaint is passed to the chief immigration officer, who looks at it, then crumples it and throws it away: 'Too busy for interference like that ... We're all too busy'.[22] This vignette prompts the following questions: what mechanisms exist for handling complaints against immigration officials? And how effective are they?

---

[22] T Saint, *Refusal Shoes* (London, Serpent's Tail, 2003) 47. For a non-fictional example, see C Mullin, *A View from the Foothills: The Diaries of Chris Mullin* (London, Profile Books, 2009) 264: 'Mike [O'Brien, Minister of State for Immigration, 1997–99] talked about the chaos he discovered at the Immigration and Nationality Department when he was at the Home Office. Once, on a visit to IND, he

A. Internal Complaint-handling

Complaints can be made through two routes: the department's internal complaint-handling systems; and via the complainant's MP. The department defines complaints as 'any expression of dissatisfaction that needs a response about the service we provide, or about the professional conduct of our staff and contractors'.[23] It categorises complaints as follows:

- Service complaints: complaints about the way that the department and/ or its contractors work that relate to the actual service provided and/or the day-to-day operational policies behind them. Examples include: delay; administrative/process errors; poor communication; provision of poor, misleading, inadequate or incorrect advice; lost documents; queues; damage; and poor customer care.

- Minor misconduct complaints: complaints about the professional conduct of staff and/or contractors which are not serious enough to warrant a formal investigation, but if substantiated, would normally lead to discipline. Examples include: incivility; brusqueness; isolated instances of bad language; an officer's refusal to identify themselves when asked; poor attitude, eg being unhelpful, inattentive or obstructive.

- Serious misconduct complaints: complaints against any unprofessional behaviour which, if substantiated, could lead to serious or gross misconduct proceedings. Examples include: criminal assault; sexual assault; theft; fraud or corruption; racism or other discrimination; unfair treatment (eg harassment); or other unprofessional conduct.

Service and minor misconduct complaints are handled by correspondence teams within Border Force, UKVI and Immigration Enforcement. Serious misconduct complaints are investigated separately by the Home Office's Professional Standards Unit (PSU). Figure 9.1 shows the number of complaints made to internal complaint systems. Figure 9.2 shows the proportion of complaints completed within the service standard.[24] Figure 9.3 shows the amount of written correspondence to the department from MPs.[25]

---

opened a cupboard and found it full of unanswered mail, having just been assured there were no more outstanding letters. A hapless junior official was summoned. His explanation? "We put them there so that the Minister wouldn't see them"'.

[23] Home Office, 'Complaints Guidance: For UKVI, HM Passport Office, Immigration Enforcement, and Border Force' (2020).

[24] The service standards are: service complaints: 95% to be completed within 20 working days; minor misconduct complaints: 95% to be completed within 20 working days; serious misconduct complaints: 95% to be completed within 12 weeks.

[25] The service standards for MP correspondence is 95% to be completed within a timescale of 20 working days.

Figure 9.1 Internal complaints received

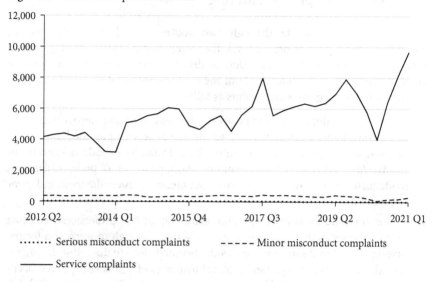

Figure 9.2 Percentage of complaints completed within service standard

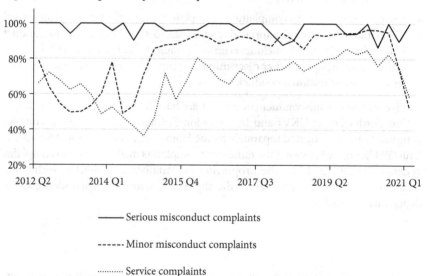

Figure 9.3 Handling of MP correspondence

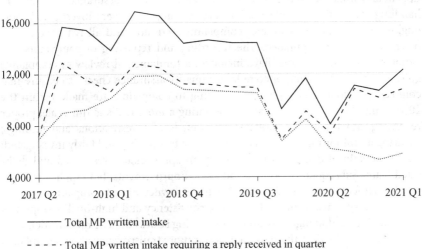

——— Total MP written intake

- - - - - Total MP written intake requiring a reply received in quarter

.... MP written intake completed within service standard timescale

Source: UKVI, 'Transparency data Customer service operations data: Q1 2021'[26]

The department's handling of complaints has long been seen as ineffective.[27] Shortcomings have included: a fragmented and inefficient complaints process; a defensive culture, with complaints being seen as a nuisance; a lack of complaint-handling skills; no agreed standards and effective procedures for complaints; and not using complaints as a basis for improvement.[28] The continual refrain has been the need for improvement.[29] There has been some positive developments. For instance, the consideration of complaints by different units within the department from that which prompted the complaint provides a degree of internal separation. However, complaint-handlers, although separated internally, are likely to be influenced by the department's culture and approach. In 2013, the chief inspector described complaint-handling as 'shockingly poor'.[30]

A 2016 inspection identified various weaknesses.[31] The department had regularly failed to respond to complaints within 20 working days. Written

[26] Available at www.gov.uk/government/publications/customer-service-operations-data-q1-2021.

[27] HAC, 'Immigration and Nationality Department of the Home Office HC 277' (1984–85) [9] (the immigration complaints procedure 'cannot be effective unless it is generally regarded as fair, which is not the case at present').

[28] HAC, 'Immigration Control' HC 775 (2005–06) [506]–[515]; ICIBI, 'Lessons to Learn: The UK Border Agency's Handling of Complaints and MPs' Correspondence' (2010).

[29] See, eg, 'Annual Reports of the Complaints Audit Committee' 2003/04 to 2007/08.

[30] HAC, 'The Work of the UK Border Agency (July–September 2012)' HC 792 (2012–13) [35], quoting the oral evidence of John Vine, Chief Inspector).

[31] ICIBI, 'An Inspection of the Handling of Complaints and MPs' Correspondence' (2016).

responses to complaints often failed to indicate whether the complaint had been upheld and what the complainant could then do. Quality assurance of complaint handling was limited. While Border Service complaints were investigated thoroughly, some minor misconduct complaints were not, and all reasonable lines of enquiry were not pursued. The recording and reporting of complaints was variable. Recommendations have included: a fundamental review of complaints guidance; better handling of complaints; quality assurance checks to ensure that complaints guidance is applied; responding to complaints are made within the 20 working days service standard, or adopting a more realistic timescale; proper recording and tracking complaints and details of investigations and findings; ensuring all minor misconduct complaints are thoroughly and fairly investigated; and ownership of complaint-handling by an appropriately resourced and dedicated team. Subsequent reports found some improvements, but emphasised that the department needed to do better.[32] Clearer 'ownership' of complaints across a fragmented system was needed to ensure consistency and high-quality responses to complaints so that high-risk and cross-cutting issues could be quickly identified and addressed. Further, there was a need for more transparency about complaints received, lessons learned and changes made following complaints.[33] The chief inspector's focus has largely been on procedural aspects of complaint-handling rather than substantive quality.

There are other shortcomings. There is no specific information available about the types of complaints lodged or those upheld. The department's data systems do not automatically record the outcome of complaints.[34] Contemporary thinking about complaint-handling is based on the idea that data about complaint outcomes is fed upwards and used by higher-level boards to assess performance and to drive improvements. But if the department's systems do not even collect the relevant data, outcomes cannot be measured, let alone managed.

Complaints to MPs is another long-standing complaint route. Many enquiries to MPs come from people who need professional advice; some MPs with high immigration caseloads have specialist immigration advisors for this purpose.[35] The department's processes for handling MPs' letters have improved over time, but persistent concerns have been delays in responding to inquiries, unhelpful responses, and an 'overreliance on standard lines', such as 'this case raises complex issues' and is 'not subject to service standards'.[36]

---

[32] ICIBI, 'A Re-inspection of the Complaints Handling Process' (2017); ICIBI, 'An Inspection of the Handling of Complaints and MP's Correspondence by the Home Office Borders, Immigration and Citizenship System (BICS)' (2020).

[33] ibid.

[34] Home Office, 'FOI 61469' (11 January 2021). The only publicly available qualitative information about individual complaints is from PHSO case summaries concerning those complaints which are escalated to the ombudsman.

[35] Young Legal Aid Lawyers, 'Nowhere Else to Turn: The Impact of Legal Aid Cuts on MPs' Ability to Help Their Constituents' (2012) available at www.younglegalaidlawyers.org/sites/default/files/YLAL_Nowhere_else_to_turn.pdf.

[36] HAC, 'MPs' Survey Finds Widespread Dissatisfaction with Home Office over Immigration Case Correspondence' (3 March 2009) (HC 2008–09); ICIBI, 'Handling of Complaints' (n 32) [7.1]–[7.38].

B. External Complaint-handling

Since the late 1960s, administrative law has recognised the need for governmental complaint-handling to be supplemented by independent redress through ombuds. In the 1990s, other large-scale systems – tax and benefits – introduced independent second-tier complaint-handling bodies (respectively, the Adjudicator's Office and the Independent Complaints Examiner). There has not been an equivalent body for immigration complaints.[37] Instead, individuals can complain direct to the Parliamentary and Health Service Ombudsman (PHSO) and other ombuds schemes.[38] In 2015, the PHSO upheld over two-thirds of the 158 complaints investigated about the department, over double the average for other government agencies.[39] In 2016–17, the PHSO upheld 60 per cent of its 163 completed investigations.[40]

The PHSO is, then, an important remedy; it has a major role in championing the principles of good administration. It has also emphasised that the department could do more to resolve complaints properly internally. The ombudsman has identified systemic shortcomings in internal complaint-handling such as: their poor-handling; delays in responding to complaints; not doing enough to put things right; not apologising properly; and accepting that the wrong decision was made, but failing to understand fully the significant impact of the error on the complainant and therefore not doing enough to put matters right. Other themes of complaints about complaint-handling include not thoroughly investigating complaints or responding to the points raised, and not providing clear explanations when responding to complaints.[41] The PHSO has recommended that the department take systemic action to ensure that complaints are part of developing a learning culture and for continuous improvement, as well as providing fair outcomes for complainants.[42] The PHSO's role does not currently extend to advising government agencies of the (in)effectiveness of their complaint

---

[37] The Chief Inspector is specifically prohibited from investigating complaints: UK Borders Act 2007, s 48(4).

[38] The PPO handles complaints from people held in immigration detention whereas NHS England investigates complaints concerning the provision of healthcare in the detention estate in England. The Independent Office for Police Conduct (in England and Wales), the Police Investigations and Review Commissioner (in Scotland), and the Police Ombudsman for Northern Ireland handle referrals of serious complaints or misconduct allegations.

[39] PHSO, 'Complaints About UK Government Departments and Agencies and Some UK Public Organisations 2014–15' (2015) 22–24. Some 95% of complaints against the Home Office concerned immigration matters. See also PHSO, '"Fast and fair?"' A Report by the Parliamentary Ombudsman on the UK Border Agency' HC 329 (2009–10); PHSO, 'Home Office Failures Put a Family in Danger' HC 403 (2013–14).

[40] PHSO, 'Complaints About UK Government Departments and Agencies and Other UK Public Organisations 2016–17' (2017) 23.

[41] Letter from the PHSO to Home Office (12 December 2018).

[42] PHSO, 'An Investigation into UK Visas and Immigration's Handling of Windrush Man's Status' (2021).

processes or requiring them to improve their complaint processes. The fact that the PHSO upholds a high number of complaints represents a double failure: the initial injustice; and then the inability of the department's complaint systems to identify and correct that maladministration. However, the PHSO is limited in various ways. Complainants can only access the ombuds after going through the MP filter. Further, the PHSO in practice only sees a small number of all complaints.

The Windrush Review recommended an urgent review of Home Office complaint procedures and a second-tier independent case examiner to provide independent reviews of initial complaints.[43] In response, the department created a new complaints board to provide consistency and oversight of complaints across the border, immigration and citizenship system. It has also undertaken to appoint a senior officer in each complaint handling team to ensure they resolve complaints within customer service standards. It also intends to publish the lessons learned from complaints as well as changes and improvements made as a result, and to survey MPs on its complaint-handling.[44]

Other long-standing reform issues concern enhancing the role of the PHSO. Removing the MP filter process could make the PHSO more accessible. Another option would be to give the PHSO the power to undertake own-initiative investigations into systemic issues of maladministration even when no one has complained.[45] Both these and the Windrush Review recommendations are likely to enhance complaint processes and oversight by the PHSO of systemic administrative failures.

C. Complaint-handling and Outsourced Functions

It is important to recognise that with increased contracting out, it is not just the department's behaviour in generating and handling complaints that is at issue; the behaviour of its private contractors is also significant. Here, there is another litany of problems and complaints. The outsourcing of visa application services has generated numerous complaints of high fees, poor services, and confusing and problematic online application forms and processes.[46]

---

[43] 'Windrush Lessons Learned Review: Independent Review by Wendy Williams' HC 93 (2019–20) 147 ('Windrush Review').

[44] Home Office, 'The Response to the Windrush Lessons Learned Review: A Comprehensive Improvement Plan' (CP 293, 2020) [174]–[177].

[45] C Gill, 'The Ombud and Own-Initiative Investigation Powers' in R Kirkham and C Gill (eds), *A Manifesto for Ombudsman Reform* (London, Palgrave, 2020).

[46] D Stevenson, 'The Absolute State of the UK Visa Application System' *Free Movement blog* (2 May 2019); 'Private Firms Raking in Millions as People Forced to Pay "Extortionate" Fees to Apply for UK status' *Independent* (16 June 2019).

The outsourced provision of asylum accommodation illustrates the problems. To fulfil its statutory duty to provide accommodation and support to destitute asylum claimants, the department outsourced this service to reduce its costs.[47] Contractors deliberately submitted low-cost bids to win contracts and then provided low-quality accommodation. The contracts resulted in financial losses for the contractors because the number of asylum claimants was significantly higher than forecast.

The major issue with the asylum accommodation contracts has been the substandard, poorly maintained and, sometimes, unsafe accommodation provided by outsourcing companies.[48] Individuals could raise complaints about their accommodation, but complaint systems were found to be wholly inadequate.[49] Complaints could be raised through various means (via the asylum claimant's housing officer, a call centre, or third-sector organisations). Some complainants were passed between landlords, housing officers, private contractor, sub-contractors and the department over the most mundane of issues and without being resolved. Many people were unaware of their rights.[50] Information was only available in English whereas many asylum claimants did not have English as their first language. Some people were reluctant to complain because of a lack of confidence, a cultural predisposition against complaining, or because they feared it would affect the outcome of their asylum application. Those who did complain received slow responses and were treated dismissively or met with disbelief or hostility, or were ignored. Private providers did not consistently record complaints and requests for accommodation maintenance. In response, the department accepted the need for some changes, such as providing information in different languages, but maintained that both it and the providers took complaints seriously, that there were robust complaint procedures in place, and that it had taken steps to improve those mechanisms.[51]

Overall, the deeper concern with outsourcing is that when the department outsources certain services, its mindset is that the contractor is then wholly responsible. Individuals must make their complaints to the private contractor, but their handling of complaints has largely been ineffective and inadequate. The department's role is, then, limited to monitoring the private provider's performance as per the key performance indicators agreed in the outsourcing contract. However, the wider weaknesses are evident from the *DMA* case,

---

[47] Immigration and Asylum Act 1999, s 95.

[48] NAO, 'COMPASS Contracts for the Provision of Accommodation for Asylum Seekers' HC 880 (2013–14); HAC, 'Asylum Accommodation' (n 8); ICIBI, 'An Inspection of the Home Office's Management of Asylum Accommodation Provision' (2018).

[49] HAC (n 8) [74]–[82].

[50] The Committee concluded that the low level of complaints reflected a lack of consistency around how complaints were defined and recorded by outsourced providers.

[51] HAC, 'Asylum Accommodation: Government Response to the Committee's Twelfth Report of Session 2016–17' HC 551 (2017–19) 12.

which concerned the outsourcing of accommodation. There had been a failure by the department to capture properly data on the contractor's provision of accommodation; this failure led to a finding of systemic illegality.[52]

D. Complaints Overall

There is clearly a need to improve the effectiveness of complaint procedures and the substance of complaint-handling. Enhanced and robust complaint systems backed up an expert and independent second-tier complaint-handling body could provide a much more effective process than currently operates. The PHSO has been working with the department amongst others to develop a complaints standards framework, the principal points being the need to enhance leadership of complaints, the training and skills development of complaints-handlers, and to move away from a defensive culture.[53] It remains to be seen how post-Windrush complaints develop, but there is considerable scope for improvement.

In any event, complaint systems have inherent constraints. They are reactive and the impact of successful complaints and of lesson-learning is often limited. Both the department, and the public sector more broadly, suffers from repetitive cycles of problems arising, which are denied initially, then investigated through lengthy complaint procedures, followed by promises of the need to learn appropriate lessons, only for the same or similar problems to recur. Another weakness concerns the fundamental difference between the redress of individual grievances and using the information collected from such complaints to address, or at least ameliorate, the underlying structural causes of such problems in the first place. If complaint-handling is poor, then dealing with their underlying causes is largely non-existent.

Consider administrative delay. This often has wide-ranging consequences for affected individuals, such as leaving people separated from their loved ones, and leaving people in administrative limbo in which their immigration status is uncertain and precarious. Delay can result in people being denied access to education or forced into the informal economy where they can be exploited. To provide an example, consider the case of a teenager who was separated from his mother after she fled her home country.[54] He was able to rejoin his mother in the UK after she was granted asylum, but spent the next 10 years in administrative limbo without legal status waiting for the department to decide his case. While the department decided citizenship applications from his mother and younger sister, it ignored his requests for updates and overlooked his application until his MP sent his case

---

[52] *R (DMA) v Secretary of State for the Home Department* [2020] EWHC 3416 (Admin).

[53] C Gill, 'The Ombud and "Complaint Standard Authority" Powers' in Kirkham and Gill, *A Manifesto* (2020).

[54] PHSO, 'Complaints 2014–15' (n 40) 25.

to the PHSO. The serious delay meant that the complainant was employed in unstable and short-term jobs, did not receive the support other young people receive and could not complete his education.

Delays are an inevitable consequence of backlogs, over-stretched systems, the complexity of individual applications, and lost files and documents. Individual delays combine *en masse* to have important procedural and policy implications. By 2014, the department's Case Resolution Directorate – established in 2007 to deal with the 450,000 asylum outstanding cases – had still not resolved some 29,000 asylum applications.[55] Within this cohort, there have been severe instances of delay. In 2017, 17 people received asylum decisions on claims submitted more than 15 years previously, four of whom had waited more than 20 years for a decision. One individual had waited over 26 years for an initial decision.[56] Destitute asylum claimants often cannot work while their claims are being processed.[57] Asylum backlogs have been exceptional, but there have been significant delays in other routes.

Delay can be challenged through judicial review and complaint processes. Judicial review claims are often lodged just to draw the department's attention to the individual case so that it can be referred to the relevant casework unit. The courts have intervened in particular instances of delay. If an individual has established a right, eg to refugee status, the court will intervene if there has been unreasonable delay in the formal grant of that status.[58] But, the courts have not accepted delay as a general ground of challenge, unless *Wednesbury* unreasonable: moving a claimant to the front of the queue would inevitably push others further down.[59] This would give the green light to satellite litigation that would take up

[55] NAO, 'Reforming the UK Border and Immigration System' HC 445 (2013–14) [2.15]–[2.19].
[56] 'Asylum Seekers' 20-year Wait for Home Office Ruling: Charities Say Making People Wait Two Decades in Abject Poverty is "Utterly Barbaric"' *Guardian* (17 August 2018).
[57] One asylum claimant who waited five years for a decision commented: 'waiting all that time was the worst experience in my life. No one took responsibility to explain why there was such a delay in our case. They have not even apologised for making us live in a limbo for a total of five years. ... Waiting for an answer for five years destroyed my mental and physical health' (ibid).
[58] *R v Secretary of State for the Home Department, ex p Mersin* [2000] INLR 511 (HC). See also *R v Secretary of State for the Home Department, ex p Phansopkar* [1976] 1 QB 606 (CA).
[59] In *FH and others v Secretary of State for the Home Department* [2007] EWHC Admin 1571 [21] and [28], the Administrative Court considered delays in the Case Resolution Directorate's handling of asylum legacy cases: 'The need to deal with so many incomplete claims has arisen as a result of the past incompetence and failures by the Home Office. Concentration on trying to meet the targets for deciding on initial claims has meant that the further necessary action to complete, usually by removal, has not occurred ... past failures do not mean that any delay in dealing with those outstanding claims must be unlawful. The system devised to deal with the situation must recognise that there will be delays which are thoroughly undesirable ... there is a continuing detriment in that individuals whose allegedly fresh claims have not been dealt with are in limbo ... It is not for the court to require greater resources to be put into the exercise, no doubt to the detriment of other matters which must be funded by the government, unless persuaded that the delays are so excessive as to be unreasonable and so unlawful. ... It might be possible to devise a system which may seem better. But that does not mean that the existing one is unlawful, notwithstanding the unsatisfactory and undesirable delays.'

judicial and administrative time and resources dealing with judicial reviews rather than making substantive decisions. In one case, the Upper Tribunal judge refused permission: 'The delay of eight months in processing the applicant's application may be a sign of maladministration but it is not of sufficient length to even arguably constitute unlawfulness'.[60]

The PHSO has upheld a high proportion of complaints of delay. In 2003, the department sought (unsuccessfully) to convince the PHSO that delays should not be held to be maladministration as they arose so frequently because of the pressure of work.[61] Its current position is that delays that occur due to operational constraints and limited resources, ie where a backlog of cases have occurred, are not maladministration.[62] The PHSO would argue that there is, or should be, a direct link between external redress and internal management. It expects departmental boards to use information from investigations when scrutinising the quality of the department's performance and thereby harness learning from complaints. Nonetheless, delays continue to arise.

The basic issue here is that courts and ombuds only provide a limited solution. The underlying problems raise wider problems of internal management, organisation and resourcing – matters over which courts and ombuds have no real influence. The question then arises as to whether a more proactive monitoring function could provide a more effective solution to the problem of bureaucratic oppression.

IV. Independent Inspection and Monitoring

Independent inspection and monitoring oversee the exercise of specific functions through retrospective and prospective accountability and transparency. Such bodies include: the Chief Inspector; HM Chief Inspector of Prisons (HMIP); Independent Monitoring Boards (IMBs); the Charter Flight Monitoring Team (CFMT); and the Independent Monitoring Authority for the Citizens' Rights Agreements (IMA).

The Chief Inspector monitors the efficiency, effectiveness and consistency of border and immigration functions.[63] The Inspector has unfettered access to the

---

[60] UTIAC, Judicial review notice of permission decision (unreported decision, 2016). See also *R (MS) v Secretary of State for the Home Department (excluded persons: Restrictive Leave policy) IJR* [2015] UKUT 00539 (IAC) [139] and [141]: 'Clearly there may be cases when the delays involved are so egregious as to amount to illegality. … We would not regard a six-year delay as being sufficient to amount to illegality on the part of the respondent per se. It is undoubtedly incompetence for such a significant period of delay to occur without any explanation being offered by the respondent in respect of it. However, the incompetence involved does not extend to illegality.'

[61] Public Administration Select Committee, 'Ombudsman Issues' HC 448 (2002–03) [27].

[62] UKVI, 'Ex-Gratia Payments: Financial Redress Guidance' (2019) [1.3.9].

[63] UK Borders Act 2007, s 48(1A).

department, is impartial and expert, and produces evidence-based inspection reports. Inspections have certainly drawn attention to many of the immigration department's shortcomings that result in bureaucratic oppression, such as: poor decision-making; delays; the treatment of vulnerable groups of people; the substandard quality of asylum accommodation; and successive reports on the operation of administrative reviews. Having unfettered access to the department, the Inspector can undertake thorough inspections which are published and frequently relied upon by Parliament and stakeholders. There is little doubt that this informed, expert and high-quality scrutiny has reduced the risk of bureaucratic oppression.

Yet, there are weaknesses. The inspector's mandate is focused upon the efficient and effective performance of immigration functions rather than fairness. The role of the Inspector has been weakened by the department's delays in publishing inspection reports. The department's implementation of and learning from inspection recommendations has not been systematic. It has been more likely to act upon 'process-related' recommendations than 'deeper-rooted' recommendations which require systemic or cultural change, such as the proper evaluation of the impact of policies on different groups of people.[64] Post-Windrush, the department has undertaken to review the Inspector's remit and role with a view to making it more independent, effective and efficient.[65]

Bespoke independent monitoring operates in the context of charter flight removals and detention centres. The latter are subject to external scrutiny by HMIP[66] and IMBs.[67] Both have provided transparency and accountability. For instance, in 2020, HMIP found various failings with the use of Border Force-run short-term holding facilities (STHFs).[68] These facilities are located at airports and seaports to hold individuals and families detained at the border by Border Force officials. HMIP found inadequate oversight of detention practices for children, no access to legal advice for detainees, no management oversight of the length of detention, and poor physical conditions. Senior Border Force managers did not know which ports had STHFs, an 'alarming lack of oversight and accountability'.[69] In turn, officials at STHFs felt forgotten about, lacked guidance or did not sufficiently understand that provided. The officials possessed a poor understanding of the Short-term Holding Facility Rules 2018 or did not realise that the rules applied

---

[64] 'Windrush Review' (n 43) 93.

[65] Home Office, 'Windrush Response' (n 44) [170]–[173].

[66] Prison Act 1952, s 5A(5A) (as amended by the Immigration, Asylum and Nationality Act 2006, s 46). Inspections by HMIP contribute to the UK's responses to its international obligations under the Optional Protocol to the UN Convention against Torture and other Cruel, Inhuman or Degrading Treatment or Punishment.

[67] Immigration and Asylum Act 1999, s 152; Detention Centre Rules, SI 2001/238, Pt VI.

[68] HMIP, 'Report on National Inspection of the Short-term Holding Facilities in the UK Managed by Border Force' (2020).

[69] ibid 6.

to the STHFs they operated.[70] Poor data collection, record-keeping and account-ability meant that the problems had been left largely unmanaged.[71] HMIP has also raised serious concerns concerning the safeguarding of detainees and the legal-ity of detention in the UK's short-term holding facilities in France as part of the 'juxtaposed controls'; Border Force should ensure that children, injured detainees and those held in vehicles are treated safely, decently and in accordance with the law.[72] This prompted an action plan to be developed.[73]

IMBs comprise unpaid volunteers who undertake regular visits to Immigration Removal Centres (IRCs) to 'satisfy themselves as to the state of the detention centre premises, the administration of the detention centre and the treatment of the detained persons'.[74] Immigration detention is considered separately below. Under the rubric of the CFMT, IMB members have since 2011 monitored the use of charter flights to return immigrants to the country of nationality. This non-statutory arrangement is governed by a memorandum of understanding; the CFMT will monitor and report on the conditions and treatment of returnees during charter flights and be afforded the same assistance as to monitoring rights as IMBs. It needs to be borne in mind that some people being involuntarily removed by escorts will be unwilling to comply and may cause disruption so as to prevent their removal, including violence and self-harm. There is a presumption against using restraint equipment during visits to outside facilities and during escort journeys.[75] Any such use, to reduce the risk of a detainee escaping or absconding, self-harming or obstructing their removal, or to prevent harm to others, must be risk-assessed. Restraint equipment must preserve the detainee's dignity, must not breach Articles 2 and 3 ECHR and must not be applied to specific vulnerable indi-viduals. Use of force against non-compliant detainees can only be undertaken by authorised officers and must be reasonable, necessary and proportionate.

---

[70] Until 2018, there were no statutory rules governing the operation of STHFs, even though they are a place of detention. The Short-term Holding Facility Rules, SI 2018/409 made detailed provision for the regulation and management of STHFs, including: the treatment of detained persons and the conduct and duties of officers; the admission and discharge of detained persons; their welfare; food; clothing; accommodation; recreation and religious observance; correspondence and communication; visits; health care; complaints they may make; and the use of security measures such as powers of search.

[71] For instance, there was no comprehensive data on the numbers of detainees, the length of their detention and the types of detainees held.

[72] HMIP accompanied by the Contrôleur Général des Lieux de Privation de Liberté, 'Report on Unannounced Inspections of the UK Short-term Holding Facilities at France-UK Borders' (2020). See also HMIP, 'Report on an Unannounced Inspection of the Detention of Migrants Arriving in Dover in Small Boats Detention Facilities: Tug Haven, Kent Intake Unit, Frontier House, Yarl's Wood, and Lunar House' (2020): wet and cold detainees having arrived on small boats after undertaking sea crossings from Calais spent hours in the open air or in cramped containers and provided with unsuitable facili-ties resembling a building site before being moved to another detention environment.

[73] Home Office, 'UK Short-term Holding facilities at France–UK Borders Action Plan' (2020).

[74] Detention Centre Rules, SI 2001/238, r 61(1).

[75] Home Office Returns Directorate, 'Detention Services Order 07/2016 Use of Restraint(s) for Escorted Moves – All Staff' (2016). Around 10% of attempted Charter and Overseas returns include

While returnees are generally treated fairly, the CFMT has identified areas of unfairness.[76] The use of force and restraint on some returnees by the escort contractor's staff has been excessive. Not all returnees have had access to the Chief Immigration Officer for information or advice during the flight (the sift of potential applicants has been made by the escort contractor's staff). Non-English-speaking returnees have not had access to interpreters at important junctures. Some returnees have been ill-prepared for their removal to the country responsible for dealing with their asylum applications. There has also been weak monitoring by the department of escorting contractors. Inhumane treatment has included a lack of privacy when being searched or changing clothes for the journey, and being confined for hours in coaches. During the COVID-19 pandemic, HMIP found a failure to implement 'safe systems of work' and poor organisation and communication between the department, IRCs and the escort contractor. HMIP recommended that detainees should be referred to in their hearing by name, and not by a number alone.[77]

Recommendations to secure the fair, dignified and humane treatment of returnees have been followed by the recurrence of the same issues. In 2018, the CFMT noted that there had been no Home Office response to its previous report; 'silence suggests official indifference to the important independent role the CFMT plays in monitoring enforced removal by charter. Virtually all the issues identified remain unaddressed'.[78] On the positive side, while recognising the shortcomings, the CFMT and HMIP do, at least, enable a degree of transparency into an otherwise hidden area. Such transparency may exert some preventive role in discouraging officials and contractors from engaging in a greater degree of oppression than is currently the case, but problems remain.

A stronger form of independent monitoring is the new IMA which will, post-Brexit, monitor the UK's implementation and application of the Citizens' Rights Agreements agreed with the European Union.[79] The IMA has been established as a new operationally independent arm's-length body of the Ministry of Justice, not the Home Office. Its purpose is to promote the adequate and effective implementation and application of citizen rights. In doing so, the IMA must have regard to the need to address general or systemic failings and review the adequacy and effectiveness of both administrative actions and the relevant legislative framework. In doing so, the IMA can: (i) investigate complaints lodged by EU citizens who feel their rights have not been properly implemented by UK authorities; (ii) launch an inquiry if a UK authority has failed to implement the citizens' rights agreements; and

---

a use of force incident. A high proportion of such instances include the use of HOMES (Home Office Manual for Escorting Safely) restraint equipment by the contractor. Such equipment includes rigid bar handcuffs, waist restraint belt, leg restraints and/or the use of a mobile chair.

[76] See 'Annual Reports of the Independent Monitoring Boards CFMT 2016–2019'.

[77] HMIP, 'Detainees Under Escort: Inspection of Escort and Removals to Germany and France' (2020).

[78] 'Annual Report of the IMBs' CFMT for reporting year 2017' (2018) [2.1].

[79] European Union (Withdrawal Agreement) Act 2020, s 15 and Sch 2.

(iii) bring judicial review proceedings. The IMA can publish reports and UK authorities must, so far as reasonably practicable, comply with the IMA's request to cooperate. If the IMA finds that there has been a failure, then it can publish its concerns. The IMA is clearly the product of the specific context of Brexit and the position of EEA nationals living in the UK. Its proactive powers should enable it to hold government to account through its monitoring role. However, this does raise the question why such powers should exist only in respective to EEA nationals. All people who interact with the department should be similarly protected irrespective of their national origin. The Windrush Review recommended a Migrants Commissioner as a means of engaging with migrants and communities and for identifying systemic concerns and working to address them, although it remains to be seen what happens.

Overall, independent monitoring has an essential and important role to play. Unlike complaint systems, they are proactive and can adopt a systematic approach. They provide transparency by publishing their reports and recommendations. These permanent bodies have full-time staff that specialise in monitoring functions and develop expertise over time. By comparison, members of IMBs and the CFMT are volunteers, but they can, with guidance and training, provide accountability to further the humane treatment of vulnerable people.[80] Nonetheless, the weakness of independent monitoring arises from the limited action taken by the department to change its practices in response to recommendations. The implementation of recommendations made by monitoring bodies has been very variable. The IMA demonstrates that stronger independent monitoring is possible, although it is limited to EEA nationals.

V. Immigration Detention

We now consider specific contexts of bureaucratic oppression, with particular attention on immigration detention. Processing applications and casework decisions are ordinary administrative functions undertaken by other government agencies. By contrast, immigration detention – administrative detention without trial – is no ordinary governmental function and a quite separate and distinct part of the immigration system. Internationally, immigration detention is regarded as 'one of the most opaque areas of public administration'.[81] By their very nature, 'total institutions', such as IRCs, create the potential for abusive behaviours.[82] In this context, the already accentuated causes of bureaucratic oppression are

---

[80] JA Roffee, 'Accountability and Oversight of State Functions: Use of Volunteers to Monitor Equality and Diversity in Prisons in England and Wales' (2017) *SAGE Open* 1.

[81] Association for the Prevention of Torture/UNHCR, 'Monitoring Immigration Detention: Practical Manual' (2014) 21.

[82] E Goffman, *Asylums: Essays on the Social Situation of Mental Patients and Other Inmates* (London, Penguin Social Sciences, 1991).

heightened further. The inherent prison-like physical structure and authoritarian culture of IRCs reinforce the acute status differences in which detainees are often powerless. While immigration detention is a system of administrative control subject to administrative law controls, in practice it often operates more as a de facto criminal system of penal control, although without established criminal justice protections. Immigrants are detained not because of their involvement in crime, but because of their lack of immigration status, and can feel that they are being punished because of this. In turn, basic values of due process, fairness and equality of treatment and outcome are weakened, if not altogether eroded.[83] Again, it needs to be borne in mind that the department faces particular challenges in managing foreign national offenders and detainees who are often unwilling to comply. At the same time, immigration detention is a site of endemic bureaucratic oppression.

Each year, around 27,000 people are detained for immigration purposes. Since 2000, the department has increasingly outsourced detainee escort services[84] and the operation and management of IRCs.[85] By 2018, nine of the UK's 10 IRCs were contracted out.[86] Immigration officials have statutory powers to detain individuals to examine their immigration status, if there are reasonable grounds to suspect that they can be removed, where the Secretary of State is considering a deportation order against them and where a deportation order is in force.[87] There is no time limit to detention. Under the *Hardial Singh* principles, a person can only be detained for a reasonable period of time; if a detainee cannot be removed within that period, then they should not be detained. Most individuals are detained for short periods of time (for instance, up to seven days), but the *Hardial Singh* principles have often been infringed with some people have been detained for many months and years.[88] Vulnerable detainees with complex needs who have suffered past traumatic experiences often experience mental health issues. The uncertainty and unpredictability about the length of detention inevitably adds to detainees' difficulties, stress and desperation.[89] There are concerns about the provision of

[83] M Bosworth, 'Immigration Detention, Punishment, and the Transformation of Justice' (2019) 28 *Social & Legal Studies* 81; B Bowling and S Westenra, '"A Really Hostile Environment": Adiaphorization, Global Policing and the Crimmigration Control System' (2020) 24 *Theoretical Criminology* 163, 174–75.

[84] ICIBI, 'An Inspection of Home Office Outsourced Contracts for Escorted and Non-Escorted Removals and Cedars Pre-Departure Accommodation' (2016).

[85] Immigration and Asylum Act 1999, s 149. Yarl's Wood IRC has been managed by private contractors since it opened in 2001.

[86] Outsourcing companies such as G4S, Mitie, Serco and the GEO Group have been taking 20% profit on contracts worth £243 million a year: 'Private Contractors Paid Millions to Run UK Detention Centres' *Guardian* (10 October 2018).

[87] Immigration Act 1971, Sch 2, para 16(1)-(2); Sch 3, para 2(2)-(3).

[88] To give some examples amongst many, in 2018, one man was found to have been detained for four and a half years and three other men for over two years each: Independent Monitoring Board, 'National Annual Report for the Immigration Detention Estate 2018' (2019) 7; *Louis v Home Office* [2021] EWHC 288 (QB) (a series of failures going 'very well beyond maladministration' led to a man being unlawfully detained for three and a half years resulting in a depressive disorder).

[89] M Griffiths, 'Living with Uncertainty: Indefinite Immigration Detention' (2013) 1 *Journal of Legal Anthropology* 263; H Grant-Peterkin, H Pickles and C Katona, 'Mental Capacity of Those in Immigration

mental healthcare in detention and that detainees with pre-existing vulnerabilities (eg mental health issues and torture survivors) are at a particular risk of harm if detained.[90]

The strict safeguards in the criminal justice system to ensure independent decision-making and fair processes for detention are largely absent in the immigration context. There is not the same initial access to prompt legal advice, although there are bail hearings before the First-tier Tribunal. There have been many legal challenges for unlawful detention, false imprisonment, and against other aspects of detention.[91] Between 2012 and 2017, the department unlawfully detained over 850 people and paid out compensation of some £21 million.[92] This highlights the lack of rigour in detention decisions and reviews, and the need for independent initial decision-making.[93] The familiar story is of poorly trained and inexperienced officials working with relentless workloads under pressure to make quickly decisions which feature errors and mistakes.[94] In *Hemmati*, the Supreme Court found that the department had unlawfully detained asylum claimants subject to the Dublin third-country process because its guidance was not in accordance with relevant EU law and did not provide an objective framework for assessing whether a person would abscond, or identify criteria for that assessment or set out the limits of decision-making authorities in a manner that was binding and known in advance.[95]

Measures to support vulnerable detainees have largely failed to deliver. The Adults at Risk (AAR) policy was introduced to reduce the detention of vulnerable people, but has been assessed as having either failed to achieve its aim of protecting vulnerable people or had limited effect.[96] The policy contains a presumption that it is inappropriate to detain vulnerable people, but the practice continues.[97] The HAC

Detention in the UK' (2016) 56 *Medicine, Science and the Law* 285; S Turnbull, '"Stuck in the Middle": Waiting and Uncertainty in Immigration Detention' (2016) 25 *Time & Society* 61; M von Werthern, K Robjant, Z Chui, R Schon, L Ottisova, C Mason and C Katona, 'The Impact of Immigration Detention on Mental Health: A Systematic Review' (2018) 18 *BMC Psychiatry* 382.

[90] Royal College of Psychiatrists, 'Detention of People with Mental Disorders in IRCs' (PS02/21, 2021).

[91] G Denholm and R Dunlop, *Detention under the Immigration Acts: Law and Practice* (Oxford, Oxford University Press, 2015); JN Stefanelli, *Judicial Review of Immigration Detention in the UK, US and EU: From Principles to Practice* (Oxford, Hart Publishing, 2020).

[92] Letter from Sir Philip Rutnam (Permanent Secretary of the Home Office) to Yvette Cooper MP, Chair of the HAC (25 June 2018) Annex C.

[93] JCHR, 'Immigration Detention' HC 1484 HL 278 (2017–19).

[94] 'Home Office Chaos and Incompetence Lead to Unlawful Detentions, Claim Whistleblowers' *Guardian* (28 April 2019).

[95] *R (Hemmati) v Secretary of State for the Home Department* [2019] UKSC 56.

[96] Immigration Act 2016, s 59; Home Office, 'Immigration Act 2016: Guidance on Adults at Risk in Immigration Detention' (2018); Bail for Immigration Detainees, 'Adults at Risk: The Ongoing Struggle for Vulnerable Adults in Detention. An Evaluation of the "Adults at Risk" Policy in Practice' (2008); S Shaw, 'Assessment of Government Progress in Implementing the Report on the Welfare in Detention of Vulnerable Persons: A Follow-up Report to the Home Office by Stephen Shaw' (Cm 9661, 2018); HAC, 'Immigration Detention' HC 913 (2017–19) [106]–[121]; ICIBI, 'Annual Inspection of "Adults at Risk in Immigration Detention" (2018–19)' (2020).

[97] '"At risk" Adults Held at Dungavel Immigration Centre' *BBC News* (28 May 2019).

has concluded that the policy was not only failing to protect vulnerable people, but had increased the burden on them to evidence the risk of harm that might make them vulnerable if detained.[98] In 2017, the definition of torture in the AAR policy was held to be unlawful because it was limited to violence perpetrated only by state agents; individuals tortured by non-state agents (eg traffickers, terrorists, individuals committing sexual and gender violence) could therefore be detained under the policy.[99] The amended policy was also criticised.[100] Related initiatives such as the Home Office Detention Gatekeeper, who assesses suitability for detention separately from the caseworker, and Case Progression Panels, which review cases after three months of detention, do not comprise an independent check comparable to those in criminal justice process and have been viewed as ineffective.[101] The Gatekeeper only considers information already held to assess whether a person is vulnerable. There is no proactive screening to identify vulnerabilities that the department may not be aware of before a decision to detain is made. In 2021, the Adults at Risk policy was amended so that the presumption against the detention of potential victims of trafficking and modern-day slavery was removed.[102] This raised concerns that the protections against detention for these groups were being significantly downgraded while increasing the risk of vulnerable individuals being retraumatised in detention.[103]

Rule 35 is another safeguard for vulnerable detainees. Its purpose is to ensure that particularly vulnerable detainees are brought to the attention of officials responsible for authorising, maintaining and reviewing detention. Rule 35 reports relate to a detainee's health concerns, suicide risk, or allegations of torture outside the UK. A medical practitioner will report on whether a detained person's health is likely to be injuriously affected by continued detention.[104] When Rule 35 reports are submitted, the department is obliged to engage with the doctor's concerns and to review detention.[105] However, comparatively few Rule 35 reports are produced and the overwhelming view is that the process does not work in practice. Many medical reports are disregarded by the department as being unsatisfactory because they do not provide independent evidence of torture.[106]

---

[98] HAC (n 96) [118].

[99] *Medical Justice v Secretary of State for the Home Department* [2017] EWHC 2461 (Admin), [2017] 4 WLR 198.

[100] HAC (n 96) [127]–[129].

[101] Home Office, 'Detention Case Progression Panels' (2020); ICIBI, 'Adults at Risk' (n 96) [3.25].

[102] Immigration (Guidance on Detention of Vulnerable Persons) Regulations, SI 2021/184.

[103] *Hansard*, HC Vol 693 cols 89WH–95WH (27 April 2021); *Hansard*, HC Vol 693 cols 429–444 (28 April 2021).

[104] Detention Centre Rules SI 2001/238, r 35.

[105] *R (IS (Bangladesh)) v Secretary of State for the Home Department* [2019] EWHC 2700 (Admin) [91].

[106] S Shaw, 'Review into the Welfare in Detention of Vulnerable Persons: A Report to the Home Office by Stephen Shaw' (Cm 9186, 2016) [4.92]–[4.121]; HMIP, 'Brook House IRC' (2019) 53: 'During the previous six months, the IRC doctors had not submitted any rule 35 reports notifying the Home Office that a detainee may be suffering suicidal ideation. Yet, in our survey 40% of detainees said they had felt suicidal at some time while in the centre. In the previous year almost 100 detainees had been on

Most Rule 35 reports relate to allegations of torture, only a small number of which result in a detainee being released from detention.[107] The result is that Rule 35, which was introduced to safeguard people who have been tortured or whose health will be harmed by continued detention, does not work because of a lack of trust in doctors to give independent advice. Furthermore, some detainees, such as foreign national offenders, are placed in prison and thereby deprived of services available to those in IRCs, such as detention duty advice surgeries and mechanisms to identify vulnerable individuals at risk. In 2021, the Court of Appeal held that the inconsistent treatment of detainees held in prison was irrational.[108]

Each IRC has its own IMB. IMBs have particular duties as regards detainees removed from association, temporarily confined, under special control or restraint, inspecting food for detainees, and to inquire whether a detainee's physical or mental health is likely to be injuriously affected by any conditions of his detention.[109] IMBs have unfettered access to IRCs at any time and can speak to detainees (out of the sight and hearing of officers) and staff.[110] Each IMB produces an annual report. Many reports have highlighted the same concerns as detailed throughout this section.

What, then, of interactions between detention staff and detainees? The sources of bureaucratic oppression within immigration detention can only be understood when situated within the prison-like structure and culture of IRCs and the differential power relationship between detention officers and detainees. There are other features: the ambiguous nature of IRCs (administrative or penal?); the difficulties of providing personalised care to people given the language and cultural barriers; the frustrations and mental health problems of detainees; the precariousness of being a detention officer employed by a private contractor; and their hardened cynicism. Officials can become bitter and hostile toward detainees.[111] The dehumanising nature of immigration detention can lead to detainees being treated by staff as little more than 'a series of biological processes' or as 'objects to be processed', which then makes immoral and oppressive acts possible.[112]

Specific guidance exists for the handling of complaints from detainees.[113] Complaints are managed by the private contractor and overseen by the department's

---

constant watch to prevent self-harm or suicide.' The recommendation that IRC doctors should submit a Rule 35 report to the Home Office on any detainee they suspect of having suicidal ideation simply reflected what had been a legal requirement under Rule 35 since its introduction in 2001.

[107] FOI release (57751) (15 May 2020).

[108] *MR (Pakistan) v Secretary of State for the Home Department* [2021] EWCA Civ 541.

[109] Detention Centre Rules SI 2001/238, r 62.

[110] Detention Centre Rules SI 2001/238, r 63.

[111] M Bosworth, *Inside Immigration Detention* (Oxford, Oxford University Press, 2014); M Bosworth, '"Working in This Place Turns You Racist": Staff, Race and Belonging in Immigration Detention' in M Bosworth, A Parmar and Y Vazquez (eds), *Race, Migration and Criminal Justice: Enforcing the Boundaries of Belonging* (Oxford, Oxford University Press, 2018); M Bosworth, 'Affect and Authority in Immigration Detention' (2019) 21 *Punishment & Society* 542.

[112] A Hall, *Border Watch: Cultures of Immigration, Detention and Control* (London, Pluto Press, 2012) 19.

[113] Home Office, 'Detention Services Order 03/2015: Handling of Complaints' (2017).

Detention Services Customer Service Unit. Complaints have concerned matters such as: lost or damaged property; staff assaulting detainees; staff not responding when one detainee is being assaulted by other detainees; escorts not leaving the room during hospital appointments; inadequate medical treatment; and degrading treatment/verbal and abuse/racism.[114] Yet, the usual shortcomings resurface: excessive delays in considering complaints; inadequate investigations; complainants being disbelieved and not taken seriously; complaint-handlers being biased towards the department's contractors; and responses to complaints that have often not addressed their substance.[115] NGOs, such as Liberty and Medical Justice, have argued that the complaints system is ineffective, as evidenced by very low success rates (only 15 per cent in 2016–17), and the lack of transparency.[116] Detainees have often been reluctant to complain for fear it would adversely affect their immigration case or they have lacked knowledge of or confidence in the complaints system. Their views are not given sufficient weight as compared to those in positions of power. Further, raising informal complaints is often unrealistic given the inherent power imbalance: a classic illustration of how status differences and stranger relations simultaneously generate bureaucratic oppression and silence complaints against it. Internal complaints can be escalated to the PHSO and the PPO, but few are received.[117]

Beyond individual complaint-handling, there have been allegations of assault and sexual abuse by asylum claimants.[118] IRCs and private contractors have used detainees as cheap labour.[119] Vulnerable detainees with complex needs have complained of being treated extremely badly and unable to access mental healthcare.[120] The PPO has found numerous shortcomings including the inability of detention staff to provide emergency responses and to manage the supply of psychoactive substances and the bullying and debt associated with them, and to manage the risks of suicide and self-harm. Despite the need for detainees to be fully informed of the reasons for their detention, the PPO has identified unacceptable

---

[114] Medical Justice, 'Biased and Unjust: The Immigration Detention Complaints Process' (2014); PPO, 'Evidence to the HAC' (3 May 2018).

[115] PHSO, 'Immigration Enforcement Handled Detainee's Complaint About Care and Treatment Poorly' (Summary 86, April 2014); Medical Justice, above n 11.

[116] ICIBI (n 32) [5.31]–[5.33] detailing the submission of Liberty to the ICIBI's investigation; Medical Justice.

[117] For instance, the proportion of complaints received by the PPO as a percentage of the immigration detainee population has been 1.4% compared with 5% of the prison population: PPO (n 114).

[118] Birnberg Peirce & Partners, Medical Justice and the National Coalition of Anti-Deportation Campaigns, 'Outsourcing Abuse: The Use and Misuse of State-sanctioned Force During the Detention and Removal of Asylum Seekers' (2008); 'Capita Staff Used 'Excessive' Restraint on Asylum Seekers' *Guardian* (15 May 2018).

[119] J Burnett and F Chebe, 'Captive Labour: Asylum Seekers, Migrants and Employment in UK Immigration Removal Centres' (2010) 51 *Race & Class* 95; 'Private Firms "Are Using Detained Immigrants as Cheap Labour"' *Guardian* (22 August 2014). The Immigration, Asylum and Nationality Act 2006, s 59 exempts immigration detainees from the national minimum wage.

[120] HMIP, 'Yarl's Wood IRC' (2015); NAO, 'Yarl's Wood IRC' HC 508 (2016–17).

weaknesses in the communication of detention decisions from the Home Office to onsite IRC teams, which has caused detainees considerable frustration and distress. In some cases, the PPO has concluded that inadequate communication appeared to be a key factor in the detainee taking their life. People have died in both detention and the removals process. The most notorious cases involved Joy Gardner (1987) and Jimmy Mubenga (2010), but there have been others.[121] The PPO undertakes fatal incident investigations into the deaths of detainees. In *Lawal*, the UTIAC found that the department had breached its Article 2 ECHR procedural duty to ensure an effective, independent investigation into the loss of life by not halting the removal of a migrant who had witnessed the death of another detainee.[122] The department's policy on deaths in detention was unlawful because it did not require officials actively to identify and secure the evidence of a detainee witness; further, there had to be a policy for caseworkers considering removals requiring them to take account of Article 2 ECHR procedural obligations.

Another egregious episode was the physical and verbal abuse of detainees at Brook House IRC, the management of which had been outsourced to G4S.[123] Subsequent investigations uncovered various issues.[124] Detainees felt dehumanised and were reluctant to complain. There were staff shortages and poor healthcare provision. The outsourcing contract contained 30 performance measures, covering, for example, availability of facilities, substantiated complaints, cleaning, staffing and maintenance. However, the abuses did not themselves amount to a technical breach of the outsourcing contract. Accordingly, the department could not impose any financial penalty on G4S. The abuses came as a shock to both G4S management and the department, confirming a lack of internal monitoring by G4S. The department's oversight had been largely reliant upon performance data collected and supplied by G4S, which was not independently verified. There had also been significant regulatory capture. The Brook House IMB had been unduly sympathetic toward G4S management rather than vigorously holding it to account.[125] Routine contractual monitoring did not communicate the gravity of

---

[121] H Athwal '"I Don't Have a Life to Live": Deaths and UK Detention' (2015) 56 *Race & Class* 50; Medical Justice, *Deaths in Detention 2010–2015* (2016); L Weber and S Pickering, *Globalization and Borders: Death at the Global Frontier* (London, Palgrave Macmillan, 2011).

[122] *R (Lawal) v Secretary of State for the Home Department* [2021] UKAITUR JR006262020 (20 April 2021).

[123] 'Undercover: Britain's Immigration Secrets', *BBC Panorama* (4 September 2017). Previous instances of abuse of detainees had been uncovered at two other IRCs. See PPO, 'Yarl's Wood: Investigation Into Allegations of Racism, Abuse and Violence at Yarl's Wood IRC' (2004); PPO, 'Inquiry into Allegations of Racism and Mistreatment of Detainees at Oakington IRC and While Under Escort' (2005); K Lampard and E Marsden, 'Independent Investigation into Concerns about Yarl's Wood IRC: A Report for the Chief Executive and Board of Serco plc' (Serco, 2016).

[124] K Lampard and E Marsden, 'Independent Investigation into Concerns About Brook House IRC' (G4S plc, 2018); HAC, 'Immigration Detention' HC 913 (2017–19) ch 6; NAO, 'The Home Office's Management of its Contract with G4S to Run Brook House IRC' (2019).

[125] Lampard and Marsden, 'Brook House' (ibid) [1.141].

the abuse suffered by detainees. Given the PPO's inability to compel G4S staff to give evidence for the purposes of an Article 3 ECHR investigation, the High Court ordered an independent public inquiry.[126] The PPO concluded that recruitment, training and whistleblowing systems used by individual contractors, complaint-handling processes, and independent monitoring were all satisfactory so far as they went, but had manifestly failed to prevent the abuse of detainees.[127]

In 2019, the HAC and the JCHR raised a wide number of concerns about immigration detention; the former concluded that the department had 'utterly failed in its responsibilities to oversee and monitor the safe and humane detention of individuals in the UK'.[128] The Committees' recommendations included the following: decisions to detain should be made independently of the Home Office; detention should be limited to 28 days; detainees should have better and more consistent access to legal advice to challenge their detention; more needed to be done to identify vulnerable detainees and treat them appropriately; and improved oversight of IRCs and the detention estate to prevent and correct any ill-treatment or abuse. The department rejected many of the specific proposals.[129] For instance, 'an immigration detention time limit of 28 days would severely constrain the ability to maintain balanced and effective immigration control, potentially incentivise significant abuse of the system, and put the public at risk'.[130] Likewise, independent detention decision-making was rejected. However, the department did accept the need to reduce the use of detention and its length, and to improve the welfare of detainees, increased use of voluntary returns, greater use of alternatives to detention, and to improve the Rule 35 process. Overall, this may reduce somewhat the most extreme instances of bureaucratic oppression in immigration detention, but the department's limited response indicates that the size of the gap that remains.

VI. The Hostile Environment

Hostile environment measures have created scope for new forms of bureaucratic oppression. It is important to recall two aspects of such measures. The first is

---

[126] *R (MA and BB) v Secretary of State for the Home Department* [2019] EWHC Admin 1523; *Hansard* HC Vol 667 col 90WS (5 November 2019) (Priti Patel MP, Secretary of State for the Home Department). G4S subsequently announced its exit from the sector; the department then gave the Brook House contract to Serco: 'Serco: Home Office Hands Private Firm Contract to Run Removal Centres Despite Allegations of Abuse Against Immigrants' *Independent* (20 February 2020).

[127] PPO, 'Assessment of Government Progress in Implementing the Report on the Welfare in Detention of Vulnerable Persons: A Follow-up Report to the Home Office by Stephen Shaw' (Cm 9661, 2018) [13].

[128] HAC (n 124) [270]; JCHR (n 93).

[129] Home Office, 'JCHR Immigration Detention Inquiry Report: Home Office Response to Recommendations' (2019); HAC, 'Immigration Detention: Government Response to the Committee's Fourteenth Report of Session 2017–19' (HC 2602 2017–19).

[130] ibid [10].

restricting access to a range of both public and private services, including medical treatment, residential tenancies, bank accounts, driving licences and employment. The second is the enlistment of other actors (public and private), thereby introducing variations on the causes of bureaucratic oppression. Institutional pathologies and divergent incentives now include those prevalent in other areas, such as the NHS and private actors. For instance, having NHS administrators applying complex regulations about charging for medical treatment raises established NHS tensions, such as those between managerial financial concerns and clinical medical needs. Similarly, requiring private actors, such as landlords, to undertake Right to Rent checks raises the issue of how their financial interests change their behaviour toward potential tenants.

A difference also arises as regards decision procedures and redress mechanisms. Although imperfect, established procedures for challenging immigration decisions are at least informed by basic baseline norms: fair procedures; tribunal independence; and reason-giving. By contrast, the administration of hostile environment policies has been outsourced to a range of different actors who may be unacquainted with such norms, and redress systems may be inadequate. Furthermore, functions have been devolved to private actors such as landlords and employers over which the department has limited any control and without a detailed assessment of the potential risks of such delegation. What, then, happens in practice?

Under the NHS charging regime, people not ordinarily resident in the UK (ie without indefinite leave to remain) will be charged for non-urgent medical treatment, such as secondary (hospital) care and community care services at 150 per cent of the cost.[131] Decisions as to individuals' eligibility for medical treatment are taken by NHS providers and overseen by an overseas visitor manager (OVM). Amidst criticisms that the policy of charging for medical treatment is unfair and harmful to both individual and public health,[132] there are concerns about the scheme's administration.[133]

The complexity of both the charging policy and regulations, and the problems of determining an individual's immigration status, makes it difficult for NHS trusts to make correct eligibility decisions. Medical administrators lack the ability to make informed decisions about people's immigration status. NHS trusts have incorrectly assessed individuals' eligibility resulting in those who are

---

[131] NHS (Charges to Overseas Visitors) Regulations, SI 2015/238 and SI 2017/756; DHSC, 'Guidance on Implementing the Overseas Visitor Charging Regulations' (2020); Immigration Act 2014, s 39(1).

[132] See, eg, A Shahvisi, 'Austerity or Xenophobia? The Causes and Costs of the "Hostile Environment" in the NHS' (2019) 27 *Health Care Analysis* 202.

[133] British Medical Association, 'Delayed, Deterred, and Distressed: The Impact of NHS Overseas Charging Regulations on Patients and the Doctors Who Care For Them' (2019); Maternity Action, 'Duty of Care? The Impact on Midwives of NHS Charging for Maternity Care' (2019); R Feldman, 'NHS Charging for Maternity Care in England: Its Impact on Migrant Women' (2020) 41 *Critical Social Policy* 447; L Murphy et al, 'Healthcare Access for Children and Families on the Move and Migrants' (2020) *BMJ Paediatrics Open* 2020;4:e000588.

eligible being incorrectly charged or having their medical treatment delayed; people unable to pay will forego medical treatment.[134] Many doctors have faced pressure from OVMs when making clinical judgements regarding a patient's need for care, and have raised concerns about non-clinical staff making judgements about the urgency of medical treatment.[135] Charging has deterred some people from seeking medical treatment when they need it, including for non-chargeable medical treatments; delays in accessing care have led to worse health outcomes. Redress mechanisms are highly informal. Individuals deemed ineligible 'should collaborate with the OVM to discuss' their eligibility and 'may want to seek the services of the relevant body's Patient Advice and Liaison Service'.[136] Judicial review is theoretically possible, but unlikely to be effective given its narrow focus and the time and costs involved. The alternative is to create independent and quick appeals process.[137] Patients who have been incorrectly charged can in theory seek reimbursement.[138]

As regards the Right to Rent scheme, landlords undertake checks concerning prospective tenants, but there are concerns of discrimination against legal migrants and UK nationals from ethnic minority backgrounds. There is an online checking service for landlords.[139] A code of practice advises landlords how to avoid unlawful discrimination, but there is no Home Office process by which an individual can raise a race discrimination complaint. While the department can impose civil penalties upon and prosecute landlords and agents who let properties to irregular migrants, it has no role against landlords who racially discriminate against prospective tenants.[140] The only remedy is to bring a race discrimination claim against the landlord in the county court under the Equality Act 2010. This legal remedy is subject to the usual barriers – costs; limited legal aid;[141] the lack of legal advice; and the difficulties of taking a case to court.[142] Its effectiveness has been doubted.[143] It is precisely because of the limitations of individual enforcement that equalities law has long recognised the need for other types of enforcement. Yet, the Equalities and Human Rights Commission's (EHRC) use of its enforcement powers has often been ineffective.[144] Further, the Right to Rent scheme has

---

[134] 'Migrants Wrongly Told to Pay for NHS Care Upfront, Minister Admits' *Guardian* (17 February 2019); 'Asylum Seeker Denied Cancer Treatment by Home Office Dies' *Guardian* (19 September 2019).

[135] British Medical Association (n 133).

[136] DHSC, 'Delayed, Deterred, and Distressed' (n 131) [11.69].

[137] Doctors of the World, 'Delays & Destitution: An Audit of Doctors of the World's Hospital Access Project (July 2018–20)' (2020) 20.

[138] NHS (Charges to Overseas Visitors) Regulations, SI 2015/238, r 5.

[139] *Hansard*, HC Vol 681 col 3WS (29 September 2020) (Chris Philp MP, Parliamentary Under-Secretary of State for the Home Department).

[140] Immigration Act 2014, ss 23, 25, 28, 33A.

[141] EHRC, 'Access to Legal Aid for Discrimination Cases' (2019).

[142] Women and Equalities Committee, 'Enforcing the Equality Act: the Law and the Role of the EHRC' HC 1470 (2017–19) chs 2 and 8. It is not known how many such cases have been either brought or won because the information is not held centrally by the Ministry of Justice.

[143] 'Windrush Review' (n 43) 240.

[144] Women and Equalities Committee, 'Enforcing the Equality Act' (n 142) ch 3.

restricted established aspects of housing law. Unlike ordinary evictions, landlords can evict disqualified tenants without first obtaining a court order.[145]

Other policies, such as restricting the access of irregular migrants to bank accounts and revoking driving licences, rely heavily upon the quality of Home Office data. Bank accounts have been incorrectly closed or frozen and driving licences incorrectly revoked.[146] As regards the latter, there was initially no 'minded to refuse' process, although the department later introduced a 'warning letter' process.[147] Revoked driving licences can be appealed.[148] As regards the illegal working scheme, there is no clear means by which an individual wrongly refused employment or who is dismissed can seek redress.

Overall, the cumulative effect of hostile environment policies vis-à-vis bureaucratic oppression has been threefold. First, it has created new administrative and private sector systems for oppression. Second, these systems rely heavily upon the department's data and the ability of individuals to evidence and demonstrate their legal status. Despite Windrush, people who cannot demonstrate their status or the data regarding them is incorrect are deemed to be illegal even if they are, in objective terms, lawfully present. Third, outsourcing these policies to other public bodies and private actors has 'legally distanced' individuals from the department's own redress systems and into other processes, some of which are substandard, lack the basic norms that inform effective redress systems, or inaccessible.[149] In 2019, the department reviewed redress routes and proposed a simple route to redress, allowing people to rectify errors and, where necessary, signposting routes to establishing status (where certain people face significant difficulties in navigating the system).[150] Redress for driving licence and banking measures were considered sufficient, though in need of better signposting, but redress routes for those affected by private sector-led measures (eg landlords and employers) were less clear.

VII. Ameliorating Bureaucratic Oppression

At this stage of the discussion, it is very difficult to avoid succumbing to fatalism, to the view that the immigration system operates as a colossal, dysfunctional mess

---

[145] Immigration Act 2016, s 40.

[146] ICIBI, 'An Inspection of the 'Hostile Environment' Measures Relating to Driving Licences and Bank Accounts' (2016).

[147] Home Office, 'Sanctions: Vehicle and Licensing' (2019). The process as regards bank accounts is: reject and it is then for individuals to complain: Home Office, 'Guidance: Current Account Closed or Refused Based on Immigration Status', available at www.gov.uk/government/publications/current-account-closed-or-refused-based-on-immigration-status. Freezing orders are made on application to a Magistrates Court: Immigration Act 2014, s 40D.

[148] To a Magistrates' Court: Road Traffic Act 1988, s 100.

[149] S York, 'The "Hostile Environment" – How Home Office Immigration Policies and Practices Create and Perpetuate Illegality' (2018) 32 *Journal of Immigration Asylum and Nationality Law* 363.

[150] Home Office, 'Routes to Redress' (Internal paper, March 2019) cited in 'Windrush Review' (n 43) 254.

that contains myriad ways in which unjustified and unnecessary harms are visited upon people. What then can be done to resolve or, perhaps more realistically, to try to ameliorate, matters?

Even in ordinary circumstances, it is difficult to resolve the problem of bureaucratic oppression because its causes run so deep within administration itself. The power and authority of government agencies and the volume of interactions with people exceed the reach of most of the available solutions. Judicial remedies, complaints, ombudsmen and independent monitoring bodies provide only a partial solution. Even if they worked more effectively, bureaucratic oppression would still arise precisely because it is resistant to strategies designed to reduce it.

These points make any attempt to advance new solutions seem naïve, but improvements are not necessarily impossible. The department has accepted the Windrush Review recommendations to improve internal complaint-handing and create a second-tier complaint-handling body. It has recognised the need to implement major cultural change including understanding 'the unwritten rules and assumptions that characterises' its culture and then designing a programme of culture change.[151] Changing organisational culture is highly challenging task, but not impossible. As regards bureaucratic oppression, what is required are ways of trying to address its underlying structural causes, which are to be found in both attitudes of individual officials and the wider systemic political and organisational forces that influence their behaviour. Both present challenges.

As regards the attitudes of individual officers, it is an inherent feature of immigration administration that many officials develop a hardened cynicism. But there is equally a need for them to become more empathetic toward migrants. Indeed, empathy is probably the single most important ingredient for overcoming status differences and stranger relations, and for creating a more humane and civilised society.[152] It is possible to develop models of administrative empathy.[153] The development of an ethical decision-making model with escalation routes is a step in the right direction.[154] Following Windrush, Immigration Enforcement adopted a vulnerability strategy.[155]

Such empathy is only likely to be generated when officials themselves feel valued. In this respect, it is important to note that officials often view themselves as being trapped within the iron cage of a soulless bureaucracy. The intensity of

---

[151] Home Office, 'Response to the Windrush Review' (n 44) [88]–[90].

[152] S Baron-Cohen, *Zero Degrees of Empathy: A New Theory of Human Cruelty and Kindness* (London, Penguin, 2012); R Krznaric, *Empathy: Why it Matters and How to Get It* (London, Random House, 2014); P Bazalgette, *The Empathy Instinct: How to Create a More Civil Society* (London, John Murray, 2017).

[153] See, eg, M Edlins, 'Developing a Model of Empathy for Public Administration' (2021) 43 *Administrative Theory & Praxis* 22; S Dolamore, 'Detecting Empathy in Public Organizations: Creating a More Relational Public Administration' (2019) 43 *Administrative Theory & Praxis* 58.

[154] Home Office (n 44) [91]–[95].

[155] Home Office, 'Immigration Enforcement Vulnerability Strategy' (2018).

political pressures, micro-management, working to targets, and the sheer scale and complexity of administrative organisation can make officials feel dehumanised and experience internal bureaucratic oppression. Some will feel that they have been discriminated against, bullied or harassed, underpaid, placed under unreasonable workload pressures, constrained by limited resources, unable to contribute their views before decisions affecting them are made, and that organisational change is not well-managed.[156] At the same time, some, if not many, officials are influenced by their own normative orientation as how they should best do their jobs. Many officials aim to do their best. They would also like to enhance the quality of their work and to avoid instances of bureaucratic unfairness so far as possible. Episodes such as Windrush have prompted deep concern for many officials, which indicates the potential for empathy.

Greater empathy by officials would need to be accompanied by attempts to address the wider systemic political and organisational factors that generate bureaucratic oppression. There is are various ways of doing this, but the work is so detailed and voluminous that continuous, dedicated, and expert oversight and monitoring is necessary. What is required is an independent and expert body to investigate bureaucratic oppression and to work in partnership with administrative institutions in order to consider the systemic causes of oppression and injustices. In other words, in addition to the NAO, a National Fair Administration Office is also needed. Alternatively, this monitoring function could be performed by expanding the role of existing monitors. The Chief Inspector could be re-established as a collaborative monitor that could proactively engage with the department with an extended remit to cover the fairness, as well as the effectiveness and efficiency, of the system. The monitoring body would work collaboratively with the department to improve the way that it treats individuals. It could seek to identify root causes of oppression and devise systematic programmes to ameliorate them. It would also report its investigations accompanied by costed recommendations to ministers and Parliament. The PHSO could also have own-initiative investigation powers.

All of this is, of course, easier said than done. However, the type of cultural change required could be assisted in various ways, for instance, by seconding departmental officials to the monitoring body's staff for a period of time who then investigate areas of concern, work up proposals for reform, and then return them to the department to implement specific change programmes. Such programmes would, for instance, include staff training, achieving coordination between different sets of rules and their administration, managing private actors, improving redress and complaints systems and how information collected through complaints is then used to address systemic problems within administrative procedures and cultures, and overseeing a programme for improving immigration detention. The monitoring body would seek to enlist the department's cooperation in generating

---

[156] Home Office, 'People survey 2019: Results for UKVI, Border Force, and Immigration Enforcement', available at www.gov.uk/government/publications/home-office-people-survey-results-2019.

new ways to undertake its tasks while reducing unnecessary harm for individuals. It would seek not to redress individual complaints and instances of unfairness, but to address the underlying organisational systems and culture that engender them. This would be an ongoing process.

The purpose here is not to provide a detailed design as to what type of solution to the problem of bureaucratic oppression would work. Instead, the point is simply to suggest that new and different ways of thinking about the problem will be required if the underlying causes of bureaucratic oppression are to be addressed. Given that the causes are deeply rooted within administration, the solutions are also likely to involve similarly extensive administrative action and culture change.

VIII. Conclusion

Bureaucratic oppression is an endemic feature of immigration administration. Each of the existing mechanisms to reduce such oppression have their own advantages and disadvantages. None of them alone are sufficient. Given the scale and opportunity for such oppression, it is sensible to adopt a redundancy model in which a variety of solutions operate on the basis that it is preferable that some of them are under-utilised than for oppression to go uncorrected. In reality, while external redress mechanisms are important, the nature of the beast requires that the administrative agencies that generate it must also take responsibility for developing and implementing reform programmes to reduce such oppression. This is not a project that can be fully resolved once and for all; it will exist for as long as administration does. Just as administration has to adapt to an ever-changing context, so new forms of bureaucratic oppression will arise. Similarly, the development of administrative law controls reflect a constitutional need to correct instances of abuses of power and bureaucratic oppression; in turn, there is a constitutional need to develop this machinery when required. In this context, the proposals for greater empathy by officials and the new institutional form of a monitoring body that collaboratively works with the department have been advanced as means of addressing the underlying causes.

Political support is required to implement any serious and continuous programme to reduce bureaucratic oppression. This is clearly problematic in such a politically contentious area as immigration, but it is not impossible. On the contrary, it is necessary. Despite the intense harms caused to affected people, injustice is a greater source of harm to those that inflict it. Every instance of bureaucratic oppression represents a further chipping away at the basis of administrative legitimacy. Ultimately, government cannot be based solely upon authority and the top-down imposition of power upon others; it must also be based upon the fair and humane treatment of human beings simply because they are human.

10

Conclusion

The overall aim of this book has been to analyse administrative law in action by examining the operations of the immigration department, how it performs its core functions and, in the process, widen the conversation about what administrative law is. The general approach has been to understand and investigate administrative law as both the law governing the organisation and activities of administration and the law controlling administration. Modern administration is extensive and complex. It regulates society in order to implement policy goals as determined by democratic institutions. This process requires the creation and constant adaptation of large-scale administrative systems, which in turn need to be managed, supervised and controlled. The challenges of administrative law are not just about how to secure individual redress, but also how to organise administration so that it can effectively manage complex social problems.

By drawing upon a wide range of materials and combining legal analysis with that of political science, public administration and organisational studies, this book has analysed a number of policy, institutional and administrative-legal problems often neglected by conventional court-focused scholarship. The preceding chapters have presented different perspectives on administration and how it works in practice, and considered the organisational, policy and legal forces that impact upon it. Having examined administrative operations in detail, this concluding chapter summarises the overall analysis of the immigration department's operations and considers proposals for reforming and improving it. This requires us to consider the challenges of institutional design and the nature of administrative legitimacy. We start by summarising the experience and performance of the immigration department.

I. Administrative Capacity and Performance

It is apparent that the organisational competence of the immigration department is significantly constrained in various ways. The department's substantive policy-making has been deeply flawed, as evidenced by the hostile environment measures, their impact upon the Windrush generation, and the lack of monitoring and evaluation. The department uses immigration rules as a means of making policy, but the rules have, over the years, become unnecessarily complex. The quality of immigration casework is highly variable. It is genuinely difficult for caseworkers initially and for tribunal judges on appeal to make good-quality decisions when the rules being applied are complex and constantly changing. Casework teams and systems also lack significant capacity to perform their tasks to an optimum level. Junior officials often undertake complex casework decisions for which they are not properly equipped. They are subject to relentless pressure to clear a high caseload of decisions quickly with the focus clearly upon processing volume and quantity as opposed to substantive quality. People making immigration applications pay fees that are several times higher than the administrative costs of processing such applications because of UKVI's funding arrangements. Yet, the refusal decisions they receive often contain many errors and inadequate reasoning. This leads to unnecessary administrative reviews, tribunal appeals and judicial reviews. There have been high levels of delay. Huge backlogs of undecided applications have built up at various stages. The department has often struggled to develop effective forms of internal administrative law as a means of motivating and coordinating its operations, as illustrated by the use of performance targets and guidance for caseworkers.

If one of the key components of an effective administrative justice process is that people have confidence in the process and its decisions, then such confidence in immigration casework is often lacking, and this has been exacerbated by the withdrawal of important tribunal appeal rights. The department's efforts to enforce immigration controls have been particularly troubled. Enforcement has been both under- and over-inclusive. The department lacks an informed understanding of the impact and consequences of its enforcement activities. It has been unable to understand which types of compliance and enforcement activities are most effective and which provide the best value for money. It has not sought to manage enforcement as an end-to-end system that is informed by information and effectively coordinated. More generally, the department has often failed to identify the unintended consequences of its policies and not sought to feed back operational matters into policy-making. In terms of legal accountability, the courts have held various actions of the department to have been systemically unfair and unlawful. Further, people who interact with the department experience an enormous amount of bureaucratic oppression that is often beyond the scope of any effective form of judicial or other means of redress.

The department's problems are undoubtedly serious and deep-seated. The immigration system often seems like a complete shambles. Yet, it is not a total disaster either. Every day, immigration officials do their work and much of the time, things work tolerably well. Most casework decisions on immigration applications are processed within customer service standards. Most immigration applications are granted. Over 80 per cent of people who respond to the immigration applicant survey report their satisfaction.[1] The department has increased the

---

[1] UKVI, 'Customer Service Operations: UK Visa & Immigration Transparency Data Q2 2020', tab CS_01: UKVI Applicant satisfaction survey results (27 August 2020).

number of casework decisions made while reducing the unit cost per decision. The department is represented at most tribunal hearings and wins a significant proportion of appeals.[2] Most judicial review challenges against casework decisions are refused permission and the department concedes a substantial number of such challenges to save time and money.

The department has introduced internal systems to address the limits of its organisational competence and capacity. As regards casework, it has developed a QA system and created the Chief Casework Unit. These mechanisms have their shortcomings, but they also have the potential to raise the quality of immigration casework. Although far from perfect, the department's administrative review systems have improved. The process of enforcing immigration controls is never going to be the type of activity that receives a high customer satisfaction response. Yet, Immigration Enforcement has introduced changes following the Windrush scandal, such as a vulnerability strategy and a safety-valve mechanism, which enables staff to raise their concerns when something does not seem right. The department has recognised the need to simplify and rewrite the immigration rules and to improve its guidance. Following the Windrush scandal, the department accepted all the recommendations made by the Windrush Lessons Learned Review and drew up a comprehensive improvement plan. It has also been introducing new casework and IT systems to address long-standing weaknesses in its out-of-date management information and data collection IT systems. Nonetheless, immigration administration remains a deeply troubled and problematic area of government.

In understanding the department's performance, emphasis has been placed upon the wider conditions under which it operates. A major constraint is that the department simply lacks sufficient resources. As the Chief Inspector has explained, the department is 'short of resource generally', meaning everything is under pressure ... its business is bigger than its capacity to manage.'[3] The department lacks the ability to perform all of its tasks to a good enough standard. Ideally, casework decisions would be undertaken by more professional and experienced caseworkers who could foster a culture of quality casework. In reality, casework teams are under-resourced and experience high staff turnover. Likewise, the immigration rules and guidance would be much simpler; guidance would be consistent with the rules and would be communicated effectively to casework and enforcement officers. The department would have a better understanding of the effectiveness of compliance and enforcement actions. Further, the department's casework and enforcement systems would be properly and effectively coordinated with each other. In reality, the department currently lacks the type of knowledge and the ability to understand the consequences and impacts of its activities. There is an unknown number

---

[2] By contrast, the DWP very rarely sends presenting officers to social security tribunal hearings.
[3] 'Home Office outsourcing immigration operations "on the cheap" due to funding shortages and lack of ministerial interest, says chief inspector' *Independent* (15 July 2019).

of people without immigration status who, realistically, are unlikely to leave, and Immigration Enforcement lacks the resources to remove them. The longstanding nature of the internal operational division between the casework and enforcement processes, the different cultures within the department, and its variable organisational competence make the task of better coordinating and linking up these two systems hugely challenging in practice.

The lack of resources has also prompted the department to outsource some of its functions to reduce costs, which in turn has often resulted in substandard services from private contractors while enabling the department to disclaim responsibility. In 2020, the Chief Inspector again noted that the department needed to focus on getting the basics right: creating and maintaining accurate and retrievable records; quality assuring decisions; generating and making use of reliable data and management information to inform policies, priorities and performance; communicating clearly with and listening to its staff and the users of its services; and developing the right tools and IT to support its business.[4]

When set within the wider governmental context, the department's failings are not unique. Almost all administrative institutions with large casework responsibilities struggle and have been repeatedly criticised for the quality of their decisions. Few other government departments evaluate rigorously the impact and effectiveness of their policies and actions. All administrative organisations face real challenges around how they are organised and how to manage their own dysfunctions and weaknesses in their institutional competence. Consider the benefits system, the nearest comparable large-scale process. The DWP has been frequently criticised for the variable quality of its decisions on benefit claims. Other similarities include: the DWP's culture of indifference toward the underpayment of benefits; its failure to act after introducing error-ridden processes; poor engagement with stakeholders, poor communications with claimants; and weak monitoring of its contractors.[5] It is no coincidence that both systems have, over recent years, been at the forefront of a tough environment toward their respective customer base of benefit claimants and immigrants. Further, most large-scale administrative systems – tax, benefits and immigration – have struggled with simplifying their complex rules and processes. Almost all administrative agencies with enforcement powers face enormous challenges. They are simultaneously criticised for both overzealous and lax enforcement.

The prevalence of similar problems and poor administrative performance in other administrative bodies does not in any way normalise them. It does, though, indicate that such problems are often inherent in the nature of the administrative enterprise itself. All administrative organisations experience continual challenges across a range of complex, multi-dimensional issues. Given the scale of

---

[4] ICIBI, 'Annual Report 2019–20' (2020) 4.

[5] PAC, 'Employment and Support Allowance' HC 975 (2017–19); Work and Pensions Committee, 'PIP and ESA Assessments' HC 829 (2017–19).

administration and its changing operational environment, tasks such as aligning operational delivery with policy goals and coordinating different processes and functions into a coherent and well-functioning overall system involve awesome levels of complexity.

Another major – and often dysfunctional – set of factors concern the relationship between the department's operating environment and its political context. There are constant political pressures on ministers, officials and the entirety of the department's operations. These political pressures often become a matter of party politics. Inside the department, such political pressures are a permanent and all-pervasive feature of how officials do their work and how the organisation operates. Indeed, the politics of immigration pervade every aspect of the immigration system. Changes to substantive immigration law and the structure of the immigration department have typically been the immediate response to the latest political crisis rather than conscious attempts to design an effective immigration system and an effective organisation to operate it. All too often, the day-to-day work of ministers and senior officials is taken up by the latest immediate crisis, and keeping the system working and managing the tensions and pressures that arise from it. This inevitably squeezes out the time needed for higher-level more strategic focus and leads to blame games among all concerned. It prompts ministers to require the department to perform tasks for which it lacks capacity. For instance, the number of people without immigration status in the country exceeds the department's capacity and capabilities to remove them, but ministers have been distinctly reluctant to introduce an amnesty programme because of the fear of a negative political backlash.

II. Institutional Design and Administrative Legitimacy

Ultimately, if the immigration department is to enhance its performance, substantial improvement to its administrative capacity and capabilities is required. Having analysed the work of the immigration department, we now consider how it could be improved and reformed. Before doing so, it is necessary to consider two prior and related issues: the fundamental challenge of designing administrative institutions; and their legitimacy. These matters concern how administrative bodies are to be organised, their claims to be acceptable and legitimate institutions, their purpose, and how they are to be held accountable. By examining these wider issues, we can give greater definition to the type of changes that are likely to enhance the performance of the department's operations and its acceptability as a legitimate administrative institution.

We can start by considering what the purpose of the immigration department actually is. Is it there solely in order to respond to public opinion and the latest politically driven ministerial initiative? Or do we want to foster the type of competent and effective administration that requires a degree of insulation from short-term political pressures, whilst retaining some fundamental connection with political and democratic controls? What of administrative efficiency and providing value for money? What of the need for lawful administration and the need to the protect individual rights and to ensure that people subject to an administrative process are not subjugated to oppressive bureaucratic behaviour?

These questions illustrate the complex range of competing demands placed upon administration in general and the immigration department in particular. On the one hand, administration is an essential feature of our governmental system; there is no other means by which government can address complex socioeconomic issues and make and implement policy at scale. On the other hand, no single administrative body could ever fully satisfy all the competing demands placed upon it. Trade-offs between competing demands are inevitable. If greater responsiveness of administration to politics is required, then this tends to weaken long-term administrative effectiveness and rub up against legal controls. Alternatively, efforts to promote more competent and effective administration and better legal controls are likely to frustrate ministers who want quick responses to short-term political pressures.

The problem is more complex, though. Administrative institutions, such as the immigration department, do not serve a single purpose, but several and often contradictory purposes. There is always both internal and external debate about what an organisation is doing, what it should be doing, and the tensions between different visions of its role. Controlling immigration must be balanced against facilitating legitimate immigration. The department must provide a good customer service to people applying for visas and immigration decisions. It must also enforce and ensure compliance with immigration law and prevent harm. It must also seek to maintain the integrity of the process and to prevent abuse. The department must also protect immigrants, such as those in need of asylum and trafficking victims. Any institution would struggle to perform these competing functions while being subject to multiple and competing accountability demands.

A related wider underlying issue concerns administrative legitimacy, that is, what makes administration acceptable.[6] There are competing claims for administrative legitimacy: authority; democracy; expertise; participation; and efficiency. All of these claims are, in some way or other, incomplete and problematic, but for present purposes the focus is the principal legitimacy claim of the immigration department – the ability of elected and politically accountable ministers to direct administration. It is certainly the case that the creation and development of the immigration department reflects a democratic ideal that immigration be managed. This democratic connection supplies much of the department's legitimacy, but far from the whole of it. There are enormous differences of opinion as to how immigration is to

[6] R Barker, *Political Legitimacy and the State* (Oxford, Clarendon Press, 1990) 11 defines legitimacy as 'the belief in the rightfulness of a state, in its authority to issue commands, so that those commands are obeyed not simply out of fear or self-interest, but because they are believed in some sense to have moral authority, because subjects believe that they ought to obey'.

be managed. Further, the vast majority of the department's tasks are too complex and specialist to be resolved solely through public debates and elections. In practice, much of these tasks are undertaken by administrators, not ministers. The legitimacy of administration is then also informed by other values: the institutional competence and capacity of an administrative body; its ability to implement policy goals; and whether it adheres to the principles of fair process, legality, and reasoned and humane administration. People are more likely to accept administrative actions if the administrative institution is itself competent and effective, and acts fairly and lawfully. As we have seen, in the case of the immigration department, organisational competence means the capacity to operate and manage large-scale operations effectively within a changing policy environment. It also includes the ability to ensure fair and lawful treatment for those who interact with the department.

More widely, grounding administrative legitimacy so heavily upon a top-down authority-based model in which ministers exert considerable influence is problematic and can have real dysfunctions. What it often means in practice is that ministers direct officials within their departmental fiefdom for short-term political gains. This model may be justified in terms of ministerial responsibility for policy and operations, but it reflects an assumption that administrative legitimacy centres principally upon officials doing their best to please and not embarrass ministers. Other values, such as fairness and reasoned administration become sidelined. Administrative institutions also need to have regard to the needs of their users irrespective of whether they can vote in elections. Ultimately, a top-down model risks turning administration into a ministerial tool which is heavily shaped by short-term political forces that influence ministers seeking to maintain their personal reputation and that of their government. In turn, this reduces the scope for administrative thoughtfulness and reflection. It also reflects a wider constitutional flaw. The doctrine of ministerial responsibility is not just at odds with the reality of modern administrative government; it can also be dysfunctional in that it enables ministers to intervene in sensitive areas of administration for political ends while simultaneously enabling them to evade responsibility to Parliament for poor operational performance by blaming civil servants.

It is certainly the case that the immigration department will base a considerable amount of its legitimacy on ministerial authority. This is especially the case when it is seeking to ensure compliance with, and the enforcement of, immigration law against irregular migrants who do not see themselves to be under any obligation to comply, but instead seek to evade the department's enforcement activities. However, the perpetual risk is that the department draws more widely upon this authority-based model of legitimacy to the detriment of other important values and principles of good administration, such as: getting decisions right; being open and accountable; acting fairly and proportionately; putting things right; and seeking continuous improvement.[7] The Windrush scandal is a classic example of the

---

[7] PHSO, 'Principles of Good Administration' (2009).

significant erosion of administrative legitimacy that occurs when the department wields its authority in an entirely inappropriate and unlawful way. The development of the hostile environment measures had clearly been driven by the need to please ministers, and in turn, media and public opinion, even though this involved poor-quality policy-making and resulted in ineffective, ill-informed and unlawful casework decisions. This episode of systemic administrative failure irretrievably damaged many people's lives.

It is therefore unsurprising that the Windrush Review recommendations were explicitly premised upon a new institutional design of the immigration department. As the review explained, 'Ministers and senior officials must provide staff with a clear understanding of what effective public administration looks like by establishing an organisational culture and professional development framework that values the department's staff and the communities it serves'.[8] Anything less than this risked not just exposing the department, its staff and leaders to further reputational damage, and harm to individuals and communities, but also further undermining public confidence.

Implicit within this statement is the assumption that an administrative system is not just an administrative system. It is also part of a much wider milieu comprising the political, social, cultural and historical contexts of its substantive mission. As regards immigration, this milieu includes both the UK electorate and the many people who have made the UK their home or have close family and economic ties with them. For many decades, immigrants have not only included people from overseas, but also people living in the UK. Yet, during the Windrush scandal, immigration officials with no understanding of the crucially important development of post-war immigration legislation had taken casework decisions through checklists, applying the criminal standard of proof, and without personal interviews.

An alternative understanding of administrative legitimacy must then accommodate other claims to legitimacy apart from the default 'ministers decide' model. Administration needs political leadership, but excessive political responsiveness to short-term public and media opinion can undermine the need for competent and effective administration. What is needed is a more nuanced approach to the line to be drawn between political and administrative forms of accountability. This is required in order to prevent excessive political interference with administration and to foster effective implementation. Drawing the line between politics and administration is, of course, inherently problematic. At the same time, there is a real need for some degree of separation to enable ministers to be responsible for policy matters and for effective non-politicised scrutiny of administrative operations. Conflating the two leads to more problems than it resolves. If so, then which recommendations are appropriate to this end? And what alternative institutional

---

[8] 'Windrush Lessons Learned Review: Independent Review by Wendy Williams' HC 93 (2019–20) 14.

designs of the immigration department can be devised to provide a more promising basis for competent and effective administration?

III. Reforming Immigration Administration

We now consider recommendations for reforming immigration administration. An initial point concerns the criteria for making recommendations for reform. This book has analysed the real-world behaviours and operations of the immigration department and identified many problems. Recommendations need to promote more competent, effective and humane government. It is necessary to ensure that people who interact with administration are treated with due respect and dignity, and that this is not undermined for reasons of administrative convenience or politics. It is also necessary to ensure that governmental institutions can implement policy effectively. Recommendations should advance these aims. The scope for reform is inevitably conditioned by the real-world pressures and demands of politics and administration. It is then necessary to consider which recommendations are realistically achievable, but without unduly compromising the need for effective administration. There is also the issue of administrative culture. It was once noted that 'existing agencies have congenital characteristics which the most heroic efforts cannot change'.[9] While such characteristics are certainly resistant to change, they are not necessarily fixed in stone for all time either.

The detailed recommendations of the Windrush Review have been considered throughout this book.[10] These recommendations were framed to address the many problematic structural and cultural aspects of the department's operations. The Windrush Review recommended that the department: review the hostile environment; change the culture within the department; improve casework decision-making; enhance its customer service and performance; engage in more robust and inclusive policy-making; become more open to scrutiny; enhance the remit and role of the Chief Inspector; improve the complaints process; and develop a more inclusive workforce.

There is enormous value in the Windrush Review recommendations, the most comprehensive and detailed set of recommendations for improving the immigration department ever published. The recommendations were accepted in full by the department.[11] In some respects, the department stated that it would go beyond the recommendations. It also explained how it would measure its success in implementing the Windrush Review recommendations. If fully implemented,

---

[9] AH Feller, 'Prospectus for the Further Study of Federal Administrative Law' (1938) 47 *Yale Law Journal* 647, 654.

[10] ibid.

[11] Home Office, 'The Response to the Windrush Lessons Learned Review: A Comprehensive Improvement Plan' (CP 293, 2020).

these recommendations would address many of the problems in the department's policy-making and operations.

Yet, given the department's history, it is difficult to be sanguine that it will fully deliver on the substance of the recommendations. Both political and administrative inertia are deep-seated problems. In 2003, the department had been explicitly warned it had an institutional blind spot as regards foreign national prisoners and that it had not been monitoring those foreign national prisoners liable to deportation.[12] Nothing was done. Three years later, the foreign national prisoners crisis occurred. Similarly, the Windrush scandal had been an entirely foreseeable and avoidable crisis waiting to happen. Immigration lawyers had explicitly warned the department that people with the legal right to remain would be harmed unless something was done to prevent it. Again, nothing was done. There have been many other instances in which the department should have taken action but did not, and this resulted in the department failing to perform its tasks properly and/or injustice to affected individuals. To expect the department to change its approach would be a triumph of hope over experience. Nonetheless, change is required.

Another reason for caution is that some of the Windrush Review recommendations set out a long-term agenda. Effectively implementing the full range of the recommendations and embedding them in practice within administrative reality, procedures and culture will require time, determination and concerted effort. Indeed, it will be obviously not a sprint race or even a marathon, but an ongoing endeavour. This inevitably raises the risk that the momentum behind this agenda may well wane over time, that recommendations will be watered down, forgotten about, or implemented only in form, but not in substance. Achieving real long-term change is a difficult endeavour in any area of government and more so in the immigration context. Moreover, the department has a poor reputation when it comes to managing change effectively.

A further feature is that many of the Windrush recommendations involve qualitatively different types of change. They involve structural, systemic and cultural changes within the department to enhance its performance and how it treats people. This type of change is essential. Ultimately, people working within large organisations are highly influenced by the institution's norms and values in which officials are socialised and which they come to internalise as appropriate standards of behaviour.[13] Embedding the right norms and values is more effective than relying solely upon external enforcement mechanisms. We have identified throughout the types of values and norms that need to become deeply embedded within the department: fair process; good quality and ethical decision-making; an internal culture of accountability; humanity; openness; diversity; inclusivity; and

---

[12] HMIP, 'Annual Report for England and Wales 2002/2003' (2003) 24.

[13] cf B Guy Peters, *Institutional Theory in Political Science: The New Institutionalism*, 4th edn (Cheltenham, Edward Elgar, 2019) 35: 'if an institution is effective in influencing the behavior of its members, those members will think more about whether an action conforms to the norms of the organization than about what the consequences will be for themselves'.

evidence-based policy-making and enforcement. The department has been taking action by introducing ethical casework decision-making and implementing a vulnerability strategy as regards enforcement action. Yet, changing administrative culture will always be a long-term and ongoing project. Implementing a reform programme across the entirety of the department's operation is, then, challenging. The degree to which the department is able to change will ultimately be measured over a period of some years.

In light of this, there needs to be a distinct set of institutional arrangements to ensure oversight and scrutiny of the department's progress in implementing the Windrush Review recommendations effectively. These arrangements currently include a subsequent check on the department's progress by the Windrush Review team. The department should also be required to publish an annual report on its progress in implementing the recommendations. This report and the department's progress would then be subject to ongoing scrutiny by the Chief Inspector, the NAO, the PAC and the HAC. The latter, in particular, should scrutinise the department's progress – not just in publishing new formal policies and procedures, but in actually achieving real substantive change. This accountability process would enable transparency and scrutiny of the department's progress in implementing the Windrush Review's recommendations. Giving the PHSO own-initiative powers of investigation would enable detailed scrutiny of the department's casework and enforcement systems.

But even if the Windrush Review recommendations were fully implemented, significant areas for improvement of the department would remain. These areas are: the department's constitutional and legal status and framework; how immigration policy is made and communicated; the constraints placed upon immigration policy by the department's limited capacity and capabilities; and other aspects of improving administrative operations.

A. The Department's Constitutional Framework

A critically important set of issues concern the department's constitutional status, its legal framework, the relationship between ministers and officials, and the accountability of both. In a ministerial department, such as the Home Office, ministers are able to set policy, which is perfectly proper. They are also able to intervene in the minutiae of administrative operations, such as individual casework decisions and enforcement priorities. This flows from the constitutional doctrine of ministerial responsibility: ministers are responsible for all aspects of policy as well as all administrative actions and decisions of their departments. Yet, it has long been recognised that this doctrine is problematic in the context of the scale of contemporary administrative governance. It no longer reflects administrative reality. Instead, ministerial responsibility simultaneously enables ministers to intervene in sensitive areas of administration for political ends while simultaneously evading their responsibility to Parliament for poor operational performance by shifting blame onto their officials. Parliamentarians seeking to hold ministers to account for matters of operational delivery find that the matter becomes politicised in a way that often obscures effective scrutiny.

The consequences of such politically motivated ministerial interventions and the harms they cause are well-recognised. The courts have, on occasion, found that ministers have abused their powers by improperly seeking to undermine administrative processes for political purposes. In other contexts, government and Parliament have recognised the need to establish administrative bodies that are independent from ministers to prevent political interference in casework decisions and thereby maintain public confidence.[14] The closest comparator is HM Revenue and Customs (HMRC), another large casework and process-based organisation that has been reconstituted as a non-ministerial department structurally separate from ministers. The purpose of this was to prevent political interference in operational matters, such as individuals' tax assessments, by ministers.[15] The principal difference between HMRC and the immigration department is that taxpayers are also voters.

What type of institutional framework is appropriate in the immigration context? The dilemma of 'administrative independence v political control' is, of course, long-standing.[16] The real issues concern which values are being prioritised and why. As regards the immigration department, there is a strong argument that it be reconstituted by introducing a similar division in responsibility between policy and operational delivery, especially casework decisions. Given the importance of casework decisions, there should be some separation from direct political control/ interference and/or civil servants internalising and second-guessing ministerial desires. It is difficult to conclude that casework is unaffected by ministerial agendas.

One option is to reconstitute the immigration department as a separate body at an arm's length from ministers. The new agency would then be headed up by a chief executive and an executive board who would be responsible for exercising administrative and operational functions, and who would be separately accountable to Parliament for the agency's performance. This would enable administrative accountability. Ministers would remain politically responsible for setting immigration policy and priorities and would be able to issue general directions that the agency would have to comply with, but they would be unable to intervene in matters of operational delivery. Establishing casework at arm's length from ministers could enable a culture of more professionalised and higher-quality casework to develop. This could promote public confidence that the administration of

---

[14] eg the Financial Conduct Authority, the Food Standards Agency, Ofcom, the Charity Commission and the Competition and Markets Authority.

[15] Commissioners for Revenue and Customs Act 2005.

[16] BLR Smith and DC Hague (eds), *The Dilemma of Accountability in Modern Government: Independence Versus Control* (London, Macmillan, 1971).

immigration policy is not susceptible to political interference. It could also enable the new agency to escape some short-term political pressures, and provide the scope for more effective scrutiny on matters of administration rather than policy.

Legislation would be required to constitute this new arrangement and could draw upon the legislation establishing HMRC. In general terms, administrative legislation concerning the organisation of government agencies has the benefit of being able to provide clarity about roles, functions and responsibility. Providing the new structure with a statutory basis would separate ministers from operational delivery and provide clearer lines of responsibility and accountability for operational delivery and organisational performance. Greater clarity between policy and operations would reduce the risk of self-serving ministerial behaviour. It could also stop the repetitive cycle of politicians making over-inflated promises on immigration in response to short-term pressures, which the department is then unable to deliver in practice. It would also be necessary to introduce new internal coordination structures to improve communications between policy officials and front-line staff.

The legislative framework could also provide an opportunity to place aspects of the new agency's internal structure on a statutory basis. Putting the Chief Caseworker Unit on a statutory basis would give it a degree of permanence and could include an annual reporting requirement. At present, the unit is entirely non-statutory and could be abolished by the immigration minister without any parliamentary scrutiny. Similarly, the statutory framework could impose a reporting requirement on the new agency to publish data on the quality assurance of casework decisions and immigration enforcement and its impact in terms of ensuring compliance with immigration law. Greater transparency would almost certainly be beneficial in terms of enabling both Parliament and the public to have a more realistic understanding of the agency's activities, its organisational competence, and its capacity to control immigration. It would also enable parliamentary scrutiny of the inherent administrative challenges involved and the changes necessary to raise the effectiveness of both casework and the quality assurance process.

B. Developing Immigration Policy

Another area of reform concerns the process by which government develops immigration policy. At present, there is often a lack of transparency about the government's policy objectives on immigration. MPs struggle to discern such policy goals from detailed statements of changes to the immigration rules. This in turn weakens transparency of government policy and parliamentary scrutiny. After all, the role of MPs should be focused on scrutinising matters of higher-level policy – rather than examining the dense and detailed minutiae of the rules. An alternative approach would be for the government collectively to agree the policy objectives and outcomes it wants to achieve on immigration and to set these out in an annual immigration plan laid before Parliament.[17] The annual plan would provide a clear statement of policy goals, how they would be achieved, and how their achievement would be measured. This would provide clear benchmarks by which ministers and Parliament could hold the new agency to account on operational delivery. An annual plan would then provide greater clarity and transparency for both Parliament and the public. This arrangement could also potentially raise public confidence in the government's immigration policy and its delivery. Ideally, the requirement to publish an annual plan would be required by statute in the similar way in which government is required to report its proposals and policies in other policy areas.[18] An annual planning cycle would also provide more certainty for the immigration agency and enable oversight by the HAC. Of course, new institutional arrangements and legislation would take time to resolve in detail and would not solve every problem, although they could provide a clearer framework between policy and operations and greater transparency and certainty.

C. Policy and Administrative Capacity

The process by which government agrees and communicates the specific objectives of immigration policy raises wider questions about the broader relationship between policy and administration. What happens when ministers set policy goals, but administration lacks the capacity to implement them effectively? As noted throughout, instrumental rationality is the substantive standard of administration. In practice, instrumental rationality requires that administration should at least have a reasonable chance of accomplishing a given policy goal.[19] The inherent uncertainties of administrative life – the complex and changing operating environments in which administrative institutions exist and their ability to respond effectively to them – preclude the standard from being set at a higher level. Effective administrative implementation is always a matter of degree.

In many respects, this study of immigration administration demonstrates the centrality of instrumental rationality to administration and law. It also illustrates the organisational competence and capacity required to deliver policy effectively and the consequent problems and failures that arise when these important features of administration are, to a fair extent, lacking. The episode of hostile environment policy-making and Windrush was in part a failure to adopt instrumental rationality because of the department's failure to consider the most effective ways of achieving competing objectives of recognising people's statutory

---

[17] Institute for Government, 'Managing Migration After Brexit' (2019) 25–26.

[18] See, eg, the model of the Climate Change Act 2008 which places duties on government to prepare and report on proposals and policies for meeting carbon budgets (ss 13 and 14) and to produce an annual statement of UK emissions (s 16).

[19] EL Rubin, 'Executive Action: Its History, its Dilemmas, and its Potential Remedies' (2016) 8 *Journal of Legal Analysis* 1, 22–25.

rights and seeking to encourage irregular migrants to leave. There has been an accompanying failure to evaluate hostile environment measures. The analysis of immigration rule-making, casework decisions and appeals, and enforcement are also studies of what happens when administration lacks the necessary organisational competence and capacity to achieve policy goals.

One response to this is to reverse the relationship between policy and administration. Rather than setting policy goals and expecting them to be implemented by an under-resourced administrative system, the alternative is to consider how administrative capacity should frame policy goals. If ministers set a policy goal which an administrative department does not have a reasonable chance of implementing and if more resources are not forthcoming, then the problem is no longer just one of administrative capacity and competence. The problem also concerns the policy goals being set and the mindset of those who make them. If so, then the standard of instrumental rationality would require that policy goals themselves be revised in accordance with what administration can realistically achieve given its available capacity and capabilities. In other words, it is better to pursue a second-best policy that can be implemented rather than a preferred policy cannot be effectively achieved. As a former head of the immigration department has noted, 'it may be controversial, but we need an honest debate on what's possible with our immigration system, rather than what's ideally wanted'.[20]

The problem arises as regards enforcement, perhaps the most problematic policy challenge. Successive ministers have sought to enforce such controls. When irregular migrants pose a potential threat of harm, enforcement action through removals and deportation procedures is necessary. However, the number of removals is significantly lower than the number of irregular migrants present in the country. Is it really realistic to expect the department to enforce such controls against the unknown number of irregular migrants, many of whom have lived in the country for some years and do not pose a threat of harm? Given the inherent challenges involved and absent a major increase in the department's resources and/or willingness to impose significant restrictions on individual rights, it seems virtually impossible to suppose that the department has a reasonable chance of making major headway in removing the majority of irregular migrants. The challenges involved seem insuperable. One option would be to introduce some sort of amnesty or regularisation process, with exceptions for those who pose a threat of harm. Alternatively, if ministers think that enforcing immigration controls against all irregular migrants is a realistic and feasible goal, then they need to produce the detailed implementation plan to demonstrate how they intend to do this and whether there is a reasonable chance of achieving this goal in practice.

Either way, following the Windrush scandal and the department's considerable delay in evaluating the effectiveness of the hostile environment policy, the next

---

[20] Rob Whiteman, UKBA Chief Executive (2011–13), quoted in T Rutter, 'No place like the Home Office: former top officials on the department's unique challenges' *Civil Service World* (10 May 2018).

stage in the development of immigration policy should involve an open and transparent public debate about what policy goals the department does and does not have a reasonable chance of achieving. This is an essential prerequisite for determining which policy goals can reasonably be pursued and the types of enhanced administrative capacities required to deliver them. If ministers, motivated by the need to respond to pressure from the media and public opinion, continue to set unrealistic goals that cannot reasonably be achieved, this will continue the long-established and repetitive cycles of administrative failure, ministerial frustration, troublesome relationships between ministers and civil servants, public distrust, blame-shifting and avoidance, and injustice for affected individuals. It might be objected that it is futile to try to depoliticise the whole area of immigration, but that is not the suggestion being made here. The point is that politicising every aspect of administrative operations has dysfunctional consequences which significantly weakens the effectiveness of administrative action. It also weakens administrative accountability of administration.

The alternative is then for ministers and officials to consider carefully and realistically which policy goals the department can achieve in practice. This can be undertaken through the established procedure of policy analysis, that is, by identifying the policy problem, considering possible solutions, selecting the solution most likely to achieve the goal, implementing it, and then evaluating the effectiveness of such means of implementation in practice, and feeding this back into the policy-making process. It is no doubt difficult for ministers to escape the established pattern of setting policy goals to meet immediate short-term political needs, but which can then fail in practice. However, the idea that policy goals should devised in light of available administrative capacity and resources is an elementary principle of good administration. When ministers set policy goals that the department cannot realistically achieve, then the result is typically dysfunctional, as evidenced by Windrush. It can result in failed administrative implementation, injustice for the individuals concerned, and further loss of public confidence.

D. Improving Administrative Operations

Changing the institutional structure of the agency and reconsidering the relationship between policy and administration are important ways of clarifying roles and responsibilities within the immigration department and for adding some needed reality about which policy goals can realistically be achieved. But they still leave the huge challenge of seeking to improve administrative performance and operations.

As emphasised throughout this book, operationally effective organisations share various features. They plan ahead and devise effective systems. They monitor their work and adhere to the principles of good administration. They are curious about the impacts and consequences – intended and otherwise – of their actions. They measure their performance not just on the basis of activities undertaken, but on outcomes achieved. They feedback what happens within operations back into policy-making. To avoid fragmented siloed structures, such organisations are effectively coordinated both internally and externally with other actors. They set performance goals that aligned through structures and they prioritise overall outcomes rather than the interests of particular unit. They also have effective internal cultures of accountability, are responsive, not defensive, to external challenge and scrutiny, and have high standards of customer service.

As regards immigration operations, four areas in particular stand out. The first concerns the statutory framework of immigration law. There has long been a need for a single comprehensive immigration statute that would provide a simple and comprehensive legal framework for the department. This needs to be accompanied by a simplified and coherent set of immigration rules that are evaluated in terms of their practical effectiveness. Administrative guidance should be consistent and workable, and should be published, unless there are good reasons for not doing so. Second, immigration casework. There is a clear need to improve the capacity of the department's casework systems and the competencies and professional status of caseworkers. Enhanced training and learning should be introduced along with more realistic performance targets that prioritise the quality of decisions rather than processing volumes. There also needs to be a more effective quality assurance process.

Third, immigration enforcement. The department needs to achieve a better understanding of the consequences and effectiveness of its current compliance and enforcement activities. To do this, the department needs to improve its understanding of its own performance and its knowledge of the scale of irregular migration and the barriers in tackling it. Immigration enforcement needs to be managed as a properly coordinated end-to-end system. The department also needs to align its casework and enforcement system; there is a need for an overall integrated system rather than a collection of disparate and uncoordinated parts. A fourth matter is resources. The department is under-resourced. Ministers have, at times, blamed the department for its poor performance, but have not properly funded it. Effective administration needs to be properly resourced if it is to be able to do its job effectively. If resources are not increased in line with the demands placed upon the department, then this reinforces the need to consider which policy goals it can realistically achieve in practice.

IV. Legal Control and Bureaucratic Oppression

Another matter concerns the legal remedies and controls over the immigration department. We have considered challenges against individual administrative decision through tribunal appeals and individual judicial review challenges against immigration casework decisions. We have also examined the exercise of more substantive judicial review by the courts to ensure legal accountability of administration and the remedies available to people whose interaction with administration result in bureaucratic oppression. The overall conclusion from the preceding analysis is that these legal controls are essential and, to a large degree, effective, but they could be enhanced in various ways.

First, there is the availability of appeal rights and administrative review. In the absence of appeals, some individuals resort to individual judicial review, but this is simply a less effective remedy than appeals; it largely provides a thin form of legality compared with a right of appeal. The withdrawal of appeal rights by the Immigration Act 2014 went too far. Administrative review can provide a quick and effective remedy in rule-based decision systems, but when casework decisions involve issues of credibility and judgmental evaluation of the evidence, then a right of appeal is a much more effective remedy. Appeal rights should be reinstated for initial casework decisions that involve complex evidential and judgmental matters that carry adverse consequences if wrong.

A second issue is that tribunal appeals and individual judicial reviews do nothing to address the basic problem of how to promote better quality immigration casework decisions; they are premised upon a reactive rather than a proactive approach to correcting decisional errors. A third weakness is that the scale of the extensive problem of bureaucratic oppression far exceeds the ability of the courts to correct and prevent it. Legal control is largely focused upon the relatively narrow range of administrative action that takes the form of administrative decision-making for which the remedy is an appeal or judicial intervention on judicial review grounds. This focus does not enable the tribunals and the courts to raise the quality of initial casework decisions. Further, beyond the relatively narrow subset of administrative action that falls within administrative decision-making, there are many different types of interactions between immigrants, officials and outsourced providers which result in unjust and oppressive behaviour, but for which there is often no effective remedy.

In both these areas, the most effective solutions are likely to involve the development of new forms of administrative control. In order to improve the quality of casework decisions, the immigration department itself needs to adopt proactive ways of correcting errors and managing the casework process by, for instance, developing being a caseworker into a recognised profession within government and enhancing the department's quality assurance and risk management systems. As regards the extensive scope for bureaucratic oppression of individuals who interact with the department, the most likely effective solutions will include not just more remedies, but also addressing the systemic dysfunctions within the organisation of the immigration system that cause such oppression. This will involve changing the culture of the department by seeking to develop an ethos of administrative empathy and creating an external agency that works collaboratively with the department and its outsourced contractors and widening the role of PHSO.

To some, the use of administration to oversee and improve the work of other administrative agencies may seem unusual and as ineffective when compared with judicial control. However, it is quite a common feature. The NAO, the EHRC, the Chief Inspector and the PHSO are all administrative bodies that oversee administrative operations. The answer then is to create new forms of internal and external administrative oversight to address the very significant and real problems of how to raise the quality of casework decisions and to ameliorate bureaucratic oppression. As regards the task of improving casework, the department is itself is best placed to introduce a more effective quality assurance process based upon the proactive monitoring of casework decisions.

There can be no doubt at all that the task of implementing immigration policy will remain problematic and difficult. Administrative errors and problems will always arise. The perfect administrative system will never exist. The department will need constantly to adapt to the changing nature of its wider environment, immigration flows, and the demands and pressures placed upon it. Nonetheless, if the recommendations and reforms recommended by the Windrush Review and those made here can enhance the department's organisational competence and capacity and its ability to implement policy effectively, then they are likely to improve the operations of the immigration department from its current record or at least ameliorate the difficulties.

V. Studying Administration and Administrative Law

Putting the experience of the immigration department to one side, we can conclude by making some wider points about the study of administration and administrative law. This book has examined the importance of the historical, institutional and policy contexts in which administration operates. It has examined in depth the operational contexts in which a particular administrative department operates, its institutional structure and the organisational challenges it faces, and how the department performs its functions, and the inherent challenges involved. It has taken quite a different approach to the problems of administrative law from that which is usually adopted. This study has approached the problems of administrative law not by focusing principally upon the courts and legal doctrine, but by analysing the policy problems for which administration was created to manage, its functions and goals, and the administrative structures and operations that have been created and developed in order to achieve and implement these policy goals. Whereas court-focused scholarship tends to seek conceptual unity in the law, the underlying aim here has been to examine the effectiveness of administrative governance in performing its tasks and the need for legal control of the problems created by administration.

By widening the study of administrative law beyond the courts, this book has drawn extensively upon different types and sources of administrative law. This has included the positive forms of administrative law such as legislation, and administrative rule-making. It has also included the various forms of internal administrative law such as administrative guidance, administrative structures and operations, how administrative activities are managed and coordinated, and mechanisms such as internal quality assurance systems and administrative review. It has also drawn upon other forms of oversight provided by other administrative bodies which inspect and scrutinise administration and political scrutiny by Parliament and its committees. From this perspective, it has been possible to examine a much wider range of administrative action beyond that which is challenged through judicial review. This approach has highlighted the sheer scale and complexity of administration and enabled analysis of a range of matters that would otherwise be hidden by a focus on the courts. The resulting conceptual structure of administrative law arising from this approach is wider and more complex from that of court-centred scholarship. It concerns the policy-organisational-legal framework in which issues of administrative law are inextricable from the policy and organisation contexts of administration and judicial remedies.

In the wider context of all areas of governmental responsibility, the immigration department is just one department. Further, the problems of administrative law are dynamic rather than static. New challenges will emerge and require fresh study to define their nature and how they might potentially be resolved. There are many other government departments and agencies that are in need of detailed study and investigation. Such studies are likely to require a different approach and structure from that adopted here. Nonetheless, this study has highlighted interrelated concepts that are likely to underpin studies of other administrative agencies and administrative law: instrumental rationality; organisational competence; and internal administrative law.

What these concepts mean and how they operate in practice will be highly contingent upon the specific functions and missions of the specific administrative institution and its organisational and policy context. It is therefore necessary to investigate what these concepts means in other contexts and to analyse critically how they operate in practice. If we are to achieve a more informed and realistic understanding of how administration works, its strengths and weaknesses, how it is controlled, how it can be improved, and how people who interact with government can receive better treatment, then more detailed and contextual studies of administrative law in action are essential. To conclude: the challenge for administrative law scholars is to reassess their priorities by widening their focus to include administrative institutions, how they make and implement policy, their effectiveness, how they are held to account, and what institutional designs of administration are appropriate.

BIBLIOGRAPHY

I. Books and Articles

Adler, M, *Cruel, Inhuman or Degrading Treatment? Benefit Sanctions in the UK* (London, Palgrave Macmillan, 2018).

—— 'Understanding and Analysing Administrative Justice' in M Adler (ed), *Administrative Justice in Context* (Oxford, Hart Publishing, 2010).

Aliverti, A, 'Making People Criminal: The Role of the Criminal Law in Immigration Enforcement' (2012) 16 *Theoretical Criminology* 417.

Athwal, H, '"I Don't Have a Life to Live": Deaths and UK Detention' (2015) 56 *Race & Class* 50.

Bacon, R and Hope, C, *Conundrum: Why Every Government Gets Things Wrong and What We Can Do About It* (London, Biteback, 2013).

Bail for Immigration Detainees, Adults at Risk: The Ongoing Struggle for Vulnerable Adults in Detention. An Evaluation of the "Adults at Risk" Policy in Practice (2008).

Baldwin, J, Wikeley, N and Young R, *Judging Social Security: The Adjudication of Claims for Benefit in Britain* (Oxford, Clarendon Press, 1992).

Balfour, DL, Adams, GB and Nickels, AE, *Unmasking Administrative Evil*, 5th edn (London, Routledge, 2019).

Barker, R, *Political Legitimacy and the State* (Oxford, Clarendon Press, 1990).

Baron-Cohen, S, *Zero Degrees of Empathy: A New Theory of Human Cruelty and Kindness* (London Penguin, 2012).

Bawdon, F, *Chasing Status: The 'Surprised Brits' Who Find They Are Living With Irregular Immigration Status* (London, Legal Action Group, 2014).

Bazalgette, P, *The Empathy Instinct: How to Create a More Civil Society* (London, John Murray, 2017).

Bell, J, *The Anatomy of Administrative Law* (Oxford, Hart Publishing 2020).

Berger, P and Luckmann, T, *The Social Construction of Reality* (London, Penguin, 1967).

Birnberg Peirce & Partners, Medical Justice and the National Coalition of Anti-Deportation Campaigns, 'Outsourcing Abuse: The Use and Misuse of State-sanctioned Force During the Detention and Removal of Asylum Seekers' (2008).

Blau, PM and Meyer, MW, *Bureaucracy in Modern Society*, 3rd edn (New York, McGraw-Hill, 1987).

Boswell, C, *Manufacturing Political Trust: Targets and Performance Measurement in Public Policy* (Cambridge, Cambridge University Press, 2018).

Boswell, C and Badenhoop, E, '"What isn't in the files, isn't in the world": Understanding State Ignorance of Irregular Migration in Germany and the United Kingdom' (2021) 34 *Governance* 335.

Bosworth, M, 'Affect and Authority in Immigration Detention' (2019) 21 *Punishment & Society* 542.

—— 'Immigration Detention, Punishment, and the Transformation of Justice' (2019) 28 *Social & Legal Studies* 81.

—— *Inside Immigration Detention* (Oxford, Oxford University Press, 2014).

—— '"Working in This Place Turns You Racist": Staff, Race and Belonging in Immigration Detention' in M Bosworth, A Parmar and Y Vazquez (eds), *Race, Migration and Criminal Justice: Enforcing the Boundaries of Belonging* (Oxford, Oxford University Press, 2018).

Bourn, J, *Public Sector Auditing: Is It Value For Money?* (Chichester, Wiley, 2006).

Bowling, B and Westenra, S, '"A Really Hostile Environment": Adiaphorization, Global Policing and the Crimmigration Control System' (2020) 24 *Theoretical Criminology* 163.

Bowman, A et al, *What a Waste: Outsourcing and How it Goes Wrong* (Manchester, Manchester University Press, 2015).

Bradley, AW, 'Recent Reform of Social Security Adjudication in Great Britain' (1985) 26 *Les Cahiers de Droit* 403.

British Medical Association, 'Delayed, Deterred, and Distressed: The Impact of NHS Overseas Charging Regulations on Patients and the Doctors Who Care For Them' (2019).

Brown, RGS and Steel, DR, *The Administrative Process in Britain*, 2nd edn (London, Methuen, 1979).

Brown, S, 'The Unaccountability of the Judges: Surely Their Strength not their Weakness' in C Forsyth et al (eds), *Effective Judicial Review: A Cornerstone of Good Governance* (Oxford, Oxford University Press, 2010).

Bruce Douglass, R, *The Iron Cage Revisited: Max Weber in the Neoliberal Era* (London, Routledge, 2019).

Burnes, B, *Managing Change*, 7th edn (Harlow, Pearson, 2017).

Burnett, J and Chebe, F, 'Captive Labour: Asylum Seekers, Migrants and Employment in UK Immigration Removal Centres' (2010) 51 *Race & Class* 95.

Burrows, A, *Thinking About Statutes: Interpretation, Interaction, Improvement* (Cambridge, Cambridge University Press, 2018).

Cane, P, 'Understanding Judicial Review and Its Impact' in M Hertogh and S Halliday (eds), *Judicial Review and Bureaucratic Impact* (Cambridge, Cambridge University Press, 2004).

Carnwath, R, 'From Judicial Outrage to Sliding Scales – Where Next for *Wednesbury*?' (ALBA Annual Lecture, 12 November 2013).

—— 'Tribunal Justice – A New Start' [2009] *PL* 48.

Chauhan, A, 'Towards the Systemic Review of Automated Decision-Making Systems' (2021) *Judicial Review*.

Clarke, C (ed), *The Too Difficult Box: The Big Issues Politicians Can't Crack* (London, Biteback, 2014).

Collinson, J, 'Suspended Deportation Orders: A Proposed Law Reform' (2020) 40 *Oxford Journal of Legal Studies* 291.

Conservative Party, 'Invitation to Join the Government of Britain: The Conservative Manifesto 2010' (2010).

Crozier, M, *The Bureaucratic Phenomenon* (Chicago, University of Chicago Press, 1964).

Czaika, M and de Haas, H, 'The Effectiveness of Immigration Policies' (2013) 39 *Population and Development Review* 487.

Daintith, T and Page, A, *The Executive in the Constitution: Structure, Autonomy, and Internal Control* (Oxford, Oxford University Press, 1999).

Daly, P, 'Plural Public Law' (2020) 51 *Ottawa Law Review* 395.

Day, P and Klein, R, *Accountabilities: Five Public Services* (London, Tavistock, 1987).

de Noronha, L, *Deporting Black Britons: Portraits of Deportation to Jamaica* (Manchester, Manchester University Press, 2020).

Denholm, G and Dunlop, R, *Detention under the Immigration Acts: Law and Practice* (Oxford, Oxford University Press, 2015).

Detention Action, 'Briefing: The Detained Fast Track' (London, Detention Action, 2013).

—— 'Fast Track to Despair: The Unnecessary Detention of Asylum-seekers' (2011).

Doctors of the World, 'Delays & Destitution: An Audit of Doctors of the World's Hospital Access Project (July 2018–20)' (2020).

Dolamore, S, 'Detecting Empathy in Public Organizations: Creating a More Relational Public Administration' (2019) 43 *Administrative Theory & Praxis* 58.

Dunleavey, P, 'Policy Disasters: Explaining the UK's Record' (1995) 10 *Public Policy and Administration* 52.

Dunsire A, *Control in a Bureaucracy* (Oxford, Martin Robinson, 1978).

Düvell, F, Cherti, M and Lapshyna, I, 'Does Immigration Enforcement Matter? Irregular Migration and Control Policies in the UK' (Oxford, Centre on Migration, Policy and Society, 2018).

Eckert, JM (ed), *The Bureaucratic Production of Difference: Ethos and Ethics in Migration Administrations* (Bielefeld, Transcript Verlag, 2020).

Edlins, M, 'Developing a Model of Empathy for Public Administration' (2021) 43 *Administrative Theory & Praxis* 22.

Elliott, M and Thomas, R, *Public Law*, 4th edn (Oxford, Oxford University Press, 2020).

Faulkner, D, *Servant of the Crown: A Civil Servant's Story of Criminal Justice and Public Service Reform* (Reading, Waterside Press, 2014).

Feldman, R, 'NHS Charging for Maternity Care in England: Its Impact on Migrant Women' (2020) 41 *Critical Social Policy* 447.

Feller, AH, 'Prospectus for the Further Study of Federal Administrative Law' (1938) 47 *Yale Law Journal* 647.

Fisher, E and Shapiro, S, *Administrative Competence: Reimagining Administrative Law* (Cambridge, Cambridge University Press, 2020).

Flinders, M, 'MPs and Icebergs: Parliament and Delegated Governance' (2004) 57 *Parliamentary Affairs* 767.

Flinders, M and Kelso, A, 'Mind the Gap: Political Analysis, Public Expectations, and the Parliamentary Decline Thesis' (2011) 13 *British Journal of Politics and International Relations* 249.

Forsyth, C, '"Blasphemy Against Basics": Doctrine, Conceptual Reasoning and Certain Decisions of the UK Supreme Court' in J Bell, M Elliott, JNE Varuhas and P Murray (eds), *Public Law Adjudication in Common Law Systems: Process and Substance* (Oxford, Hart Publishing, 2016).

Foster, M, 'Amber Rudd allies accused of "turning fire" on Home Office staff over her exit' *Civil Service World* (1 May 2018).

Freedom from Torture, 'Beyond Belief: How the Home Office Fails Survivors of Torture at the Asylum Interview' (2020).

—— 'Lessons Not Learned: The Failures of Asylum Decision-making in the UK' (2019).

Gammeltoft-Hansen, T and Sorensen, N (eds), *The Migration Industry and the Commercialization of International Migration* (London, Routledge, 2012).

Garner, JF, *Administrative Law* (London, Butterworths, 1970).

Gellhorn, E and Robinson, GO, 'Perspectives on Administrative Law' (1975) 75 *Columbia Law Review* 771.

Gentleman, A, *The Windrush Betrayal: Exposing the Hostile Environment* (London, Guardian Faber, 2019).

Gill, C, 'The Ombud and "Complaint Standard Authority" Powers' in R Kirkham and C Gill (eds), *A Manifesto for Ombudsman Reform* (London, Palgrave, 2020).

—— 'The Ombud and Own-Initiative Investigation Powers' in R Kirkham and C Gill (eds), *A Manifesto for Ombudsman Reform* (London, Palgrave, 2020).

Gill, N, Rotter, R, Burridge, A, Griffiths, M and Allsopp, J, 'Inconsistency in Asylum Appeal Adjudication' (2015) 50 *Forced Migration Review* 52.

Goffman, E, *Asylums: Essays on the Social Situation of Mental Patients and Other Inmates* (London, Penguin Social Sciences, 1991).

Goldsmith, P, 'Parliament for Lawyers: An Overview of the Legislative Process' (2002) 4 *European Journal of Law Reform* 511.

Goodnow, FJ, *The Principles of the Administrative Law of the United States* (New York, Putnam's, 1905).

Gordon, I, Scanlon, K, Travers, T and Whitehead, C, *Economic Impact on the London and UK Economy of an Earned Regularisation of Irregular Migrants to the UK* (London, LSE, 2009).

Grant-Peterkin, H, Pickles, H and Katona, C, 'Mental Capacity of Those in Immigration Detention in the UK' (2016) 56 *Medicine, Science and the Law* 285.

Griffith, JAG and Street, H, *Principles of Administrative Law*, 4th edn (London, Pitman, 1973).

Griffiths, M, 'Living with Uncertainty: Indefinite Immigration Detention' (2013) 1 *Journal of Legal Anthropology* 263.

Griffiths, M and Yeo, C, 'The UK's Hostile Environment: Deputising Immigration Control' (2021) *Critical Social Policy* (forthcoming).

Griffiths, MBE, 'Out of Time: The Temporal Uncertainties of Refused Asylum Seekers and Immigration Detainees, (2014) 30 *Journal of Ethnic and Migration Studies* 1991.

Guy Peters, B, *Institutional Theory in Political Science: The New Institutionalism*, 4th edn (Cheltenham, Edward Elgar, 2019).

Hall, A, *Border Watch: Cultures of Immigration, Detention and Control* (London, Pluto Press, 2012).

Halpern, D, *Inside the Nudge Unit: How Small Changes Can Make a Big Difference* (London, Allen, 2015).

Harlow, C and Rawlings, R, *Law and Administration*, 5th edn (Cambridge, Cambridge University Press, 2021).

—— 'Proceduralism and Automation: Challenges to the Values of Administrative Law' in E Fisher, J King and AL Young (eds), *The Foundations and Future of Public Law* (Oxford, Oxford University Press, 2020).

—— '"Striking Back" and "Clamping Down": An Alternative Perspective on Judicial Review' in J Bell, M Elliott, JNE Varuhas and P Murray (eds), *Public Law Adjudication in Common Law Systems: Process and Substance* (Oxford, Hart Publishing, 2016).

Harris, N, *Law in a Complex State: Complexity in the Law and Structure of Welfare* (Oxford, Hart, 2013).

Hertogh, M and Halliday, S (eds), *Judicial Review and Bureaucratic Impact: International and Interdisciplinary Perspectives* (Cambridge, Cambridge University Press, 2004).

Herzfeld, M, *The Social Production of Indifference: Exploring the Symbolic Roots of Western Bureaucracy* (New York, Berg, 1992).

Hewitt, G, 'The Windrush Scandal: An Insider's Reflection' (2020) 66 *Caribbean Quarterly* 108.

Hinterleitner, M, *Policy Controversies and Political Blame Games* (Cambridge, Cambridge University Press, 2020).

Hood, CC, *Administrative Analysis: An Introduction to Rules, Enforcement and Organizations* (Brighton, Wheatsheaf, 1986).

—— 'Gaming in Targetworld: The Targets Approach to Managing British Public Services' (2006) 66 *Public Administration Review* 515.

—— *The Blame Game: Spin, Bureaucracy and Self-Preservation in Government* (Princeton, Princeton University Press, 2011).

Hood, CC and Margetts, HZ, *The Tools of Government in the Digital Age* (Basingstoke, Palgrave Macmillan, 2007).

Howlett, M, *Designing Public Policies: Principles and Instruments*, 2nd edn (London, Routledge, 2019).

Ilbert, CP, *Legislative Methods and Forms* (Oxford, Oxford University Press, 1901).

Ingram, H, Schneider, AL and Deleon, P, 'Social Construction and Policy Design' in P Sabatier (ed), *Theories of the Policy Process* (New York, Routledge, 2007).

Institute for Government, 'Judicial review and Policy Making: The Role of Legal Advice in Government' (2021).

—— 'Managing Migration after Brexit' (2019).

—— 'Ministers Reflect: Damian Green' (2015).

—— 'Policy Making in the Real World: Evidence and Analysis' (2011).

Ison, TG, '"Administrative Justice": Is It Such a Good Idea?' in M Harris M and M Partington (eds), *Administrative Justice in the 21st Century* (Oxford, Hart Publishing, 1999).

James, O, *The Executive Agency Revolution in Whitehall: Public Interest versus Bureau-Shaping Perspectives* (London, Palgrave Macmillan, 2003).

James, S, 'The Complexity of Tax Simplification: The UK Experience' in S James, A Sawyer and T Budak (eds), *The Complexity of Tax Simplification: Experiences From Around the World* (London, Palgrave Macmillan, 2016).

Jenkins, K, *Politicians and Public Services: Implementing Change in a Clash of Cultures* (Cheltenham, Edward Elgar, 2008).

Jennings, R, 'Government Scraps Immigration "Streaming Tool" before Judicial Review' *Human Rights Law Blog* (6 August 2020).

Jennings, W, Lodge, M and Ryan, M, 'Comparing Blunders in Government' (2018) 57 *European Journal of Political Research* 238.

John, P, *Analyzing Public Policy* (London, Routledge, 2012).

Jorro, P, 'The Enhanced Non-suspensive Appeals Regime in Immigration Cases' (2016) 30 *Journal of Immigration, Asylum and Nationality Law* 111.

Jowell, J, Judicial Deference, Servility, Civility or Institutional Capacity?' [2003] *PL* 592.

—— 'The Legal Control of Administrative Discretion' [1973] *PL* 178.

JUSTICE, 'Immigration and Asylum Appeals – A Fresh Look' (2017).

Kagan, RA, 'Varieties of Bureaucratic Justice: Building on Mashaw's Typology' in N Parillo (ed), *Administrative Law From the Inside Out* (Cambridge, Cambridge University Press, 2017).

King, A and Crewe, I, *The Blunders of our Governments* (London, Oneworld, 2013).

Knight, DR, *Vigilance and Restraint in the Common Law of Judicial Review* (Cambridge, Cambridge University Press, 2018).

Krznaric, R, *Empathy: Why it Matters and How to Get It* (London, Random House, 2014).

Lipsky, M, *Street-level Bureaucracy: Dilemmas of the Individual in Public Services* (New York, Russell Sage, 1980).

Manning, G and Collinson, J, 'Complexity in the Immigration Rules: Politics or the Outcome of Judicial Review?' (2019) 24 *Judicial Review* 85.

Mantouvalou, V, 'The Right to Non-Exploitative Work' in V Mantouvalou (ed), *The Right to Work* (Oxford, Hart Publishing, 2015).

March, J and Simon, H, *Organizations*, 2nd edn (Oxford, Blackwell, 1993).

Mashaw, JL, 'Between Facts and Norms: Agency Statutory Interpretation as an Autonomous Enterprise' (2005) 55 *University of Toronto Law Journal* 497.

—— *Bureaucratic Justice: Managing Social Security Disability Claims* (New Haven, Yale University Press, 1983).

—— 'Public Reason and Administrative Legitimacy' in J Bell, M Elliott, JNE Varuhas, and P Murray (eds), *Public Law Adjudication in Common Law Systems: Process and Substance: Process and Substance* (Oxford, Hart Publishing, 2016).

—— 'Structuring a "Dense Complexity": Accountability and the Project of Administrative Law' (2005) *Issues in Legal Scholarship*, Article 4.

—— 'The Management Side of Due Process: Some Theoretical and Litigation Notes on the Assurance of the Accuracy, Fairness, and Timeliness in the Adjudication of Social Welfare Claims' (1974) 59 *Cornell Law Review* 772.

Maternity Action, 'Duty of Care? The Impact on Midwives of NHS Charging for Maternity Care' (2019).

McKee, R, 'Home Office Policies' (2006) 20 *Journal of Immigration, Asylum and Nationality Law* 289.

Medical Justice, 'Biased and Unjust: The Immigration Detention Complaints Process' (2014).

—— 'Deaths in Detention 2010–2015' (London, Medical Justice, 2016).

Merton, RK, 'Bureaucratic Structure and Personality' in *Social Theory and Social Structure* (New York, Free Press, 1968).

Metzger, GE, 'The Constitutional Duty to Supervise' (2015) 124 *Yale Law Journal* 1836.

Metzger, GE and Stack, KM, 'Internal Administrative Law' (2017) 115 *Michigan Law Review* 1239.

Meyler, F and Woodhouse, S, 'Changing the Immigration Rules and Withdrawing the "Currency" of Legal Aid: The Impact of LASPO 2012 on Migrants and their Families' (2013) 35 *Journal of Social Welfare and Family Law* 55.

Migrant Rights Network, 'Highly Skilled Migrant Indefinite Leave to Remain Refusals & Covid-19 Realities' (2020).

Migration Watch, 'The Illegal Migrant Population in the UK' (briefing paper, 2010).

Mintzberg, H, *The Structuring of Organizations* (Englewood Cliffs, Prentice-Hall, 1979).

Mitchell, JDB, 'The State of Public Law in the United Kingdom' (1966) 15 *International and Comparative Law Quarterly* 133.

Moran, M, Rein, M and Goodin, RE, (eds), *The Oxford Handbook of Public Policy* (Oxford, Oxford University Press, 2008).

Mulgan, R, *Holding Power to Account: Accountability in Modern Democracies* (Basingstoke, Palgrave Macmillan, 2003).

Mullin, C, *A View from the Foothills: The Diaries of Chris Mullin* (London, Profile Books, 2009).

Murphy, L et al, 'Healthcare Access for Children and Families on the Move and Migrants' (2020) *BMJ Paediatrics Open* 2020;4:e000588.

Nason, S, *Reconstructing Judicial Review* (Oxford, Hart, 2016).

Norton, P, 'Parliament and Legislative Scrutiny: An Overview of Issues in the Legislative Process' in A Brazier (ed), *Parliament, Politics and Law Making: Issues and Developments in the Legislative Process* (London, Hansard Society, 2004).

NUSUK, 'The TOEIC Scandal: An Ongoing Injustice' (2018).

O'Nions, H, '"Fat Cat" Lawyers and "Illegal" Migrants: the Impact of Intersecting Hostilities and Toxic Narratives on Access to Justice" (2020) 42 *Journal of Social Welfare and Family Law* 319.

Oliver, D, 'Improving the Scrutiny of Bills: The Case for Standards and Checklists' [2006] *PL* 219.

Page, EC and Jenkins, B, *Policy Bureaucracy: Government with a Cast of Thousands* (Oxford, Oxford University Press, 2005).

Painter, C, 'A Government Department in Meltdown: Crisis at the Home Office' (2008) 28 *Public Money and Management* 275.

Parillo, NR (ed), *Administrative Law from the Inside Out* (Cambridge, Cambridge University Press, 2018).

Pérez, A, 'Emotions of Queuing: A Mirror of Immigrants' Social Condition' in B Sieben and A Wettergren (eds), *Emotionalizing Organizations and Organizing Emotions* (Basingstoke, Palgrave Macmillan, 2010).

Phillips, M and Phillips, T, *Windrush: The Irresistible Rise of Multi-racial Britain* (London, Harper Collins, 1998).

Pinkerton, C, McLaughlan, G and Salt, J, 'Sizing the Illegally Resident Population in the UK' (Online Report 58/04, 2004).

Port, FJ, *Administrative Law* (London, Longmans, Green and Co, 1929).

Posner, RA, *How Judges Think* (Cambridge, Mass, Harvard University Press, 2010).

Powell, F, 'Structural Procedural Review: An Emerging Trend in Public Law' [2017] *Judicial Review* 83.

Pressman, JL and Wildavsky, A, *Implementation*, 3rd ed (Oakland, University of California Press, 1984).

Rabin, RL, 'Administrative Law in Transition: A Discipline in Search of an Organizing Principle' (1977) 72 *North Western University Law Review* 120.

Rawlings, R, 'Soft Law Never Dies' in M Elliott and D Feldman (eds), *The Cambridge Companion to Public Law* (Cambridge, Cambridge University Press, 2015).

Resodihardjo, SL, *Crises, Inquiries, and the Politics of Blame* (London, Palgrave Macmillan, 2020).

Rhodes, RAW, *Everyday Life in British Government* (Oxford, Oxford University Press, 2011).

Roffee, JA, 'Accountability and Oversight of State Functions: Use of Volunteers to Monitor Equality and Diversity in Prisons in England and Wales' (2017) *SAGE Open* 1.

Rose, R, *Understanding Big Government* (London, Sage, 1984).

Royal College of Psychiatrists, 'Detention of People with Mental Disorders in Immigration Removal Centres' (PS02/21, 2021).

Rubin, EL, *Beyond Camelot: Rethinking Law and Politics for the Modern State* (Princeton, Princeton University Press, 2005).

—— 'Bureaucratic Oppression: Its Causes and Cures' (2012) 90 *Washington University Law Review* 291.

—— 'Executive Action: Its History, its Dilemmas, and its Potential Remedies' (2016) 8 *Journal of Legal Analysis* 1.

—— 'From Coherence to Effectiveness: A Legal Methodology for the Modern World' in R van Gestel, HW Micklitz and EL Rubin (eds) *Rethinking Legal Scholarship: A Transatlantic Dialogue* (Cambridge, Cambridge University Press, 2017).

—— 'Law and Legislation in the Administrative State' (1989) 89 *Columbia Law Review* 369.

Russell, M and Glover, D, *Legislation at Westminster: Parliamentary Actors and Influence in the Making of British Law* (Oxford, Oxford University Press, 2017).

Sabel, CF and Simon, WH, 'The Duty of Responsible Administration and the Problem of Police Accountability' (2016) 33 *Yale Journal on Regulation* 165.

Sainsbury, R, 'Internal Reviews and the Weakening of Social Security Claimants' Rights of Appeal' in G Richardson and H Genn (eds), *Administrative Law & Government Action* (Oxford, Oxford University Press, 1994).

—— 'The Social Security Chief Adjudication Officer: the First Four Years' [1989] *PL* 323.

Saint, T, *Refusal Shoes* (London, Serpent's Tail, 2003).

Schuster, L, 'Fatal flaws in the UK asylum decision-making system: an analysis of Home Office refusal letters' (2020) 46 *Journal of Ethnic and Migration Studies* 1371.

Schymyck, A, 'The *Hardial Singh* Principles and the Principle of Legality' [2021] *PL* 489.

Shahvisi, A, 'Austerity or Xenophobia? The Causes and Costs of the "Hostile Environment" in the NHS' (2019) 27 *Health Care Analysis* 202.

Shapiro, SA, 'Why Administrative Law Misunderstands How Government Works: The Missing Institutional Analysis' (2013) 53 *Washburn Law Journal* 1.

Simon, HA, *Administrative Behavior* 4th edn (New York, Free Press, 1997).

—— *Reason in Human Affairs* (Stanford, Stanford University Press, 1983).

Simon, WH, 'The Organizational Premises of Administrative Law' (2015) 78 *Law and Contemporary Problems* 61.

Smith, BLR and Hague, DC (eds), *The Dilemma of Accountability in Modern Government: Independence Versus Control* (London, Macmillan, 1971).

Stefanelli, JN, *Judicial Review of Immigration Detention in the UK, US and EU: From Principles to Practice* (Oxford, Hart Publishing, 2020).

Sterett, S, *Creating Constitutionalism? The Politics of Legal Expertise and Administrative Law in England and Wales* (Ann Arbor, University of Michigan Press, 1997).

Stevenson, D, 'The Absolute State of the UK Visa Application System' *Free movement blog* (2 May 2019).

Steyn, J, 'Does Legal Formalism Hold Sway in England?' (1996) 49 *Current Legal Problems* 43.

Tamanaha, B, *A Realistic Theory of Law* (Cambridge, Cambridge University Press, 2017).

Taylor, D and Balloch, S (eds), *The Politics of Evaluation: Participation and Policy Implementation* (Bristol, Policy Press 2005).

Taylor, J, 'Public Officials' Gaming of Performance Measures and Targets: The Nexus between Motivation and Opportunity' (2021) 44 *Public Performance & Management Review* 272.

Thaler, R and Sunstein, C, *Nudge* (London, Penguin, 2008).

Thomas, EW, *The Judicial Process: Realism, Pragmatism, Practical Reasoning and Principles* (Cambridge, Cambridge University Press, 2005).

Thomas, R, *Administrative Justice and Asylum Appeals: A Study of Tribunal Adjudication* (Oxford, Hart Publishing, 2011).

—— 'Administrative Justice, Better Decisions, and Organisational Learning' [2015] *PL* 111.

—— 'Immigration and Access to Justice: A Critical Analysis of Recent Restrictions' in E Palmer, T Cornford, A Guinchard and Y Marique (eds), *Access to Justice: Beyond the Policies and Politics of Austerity* (Oxford, Hart Publishing, 2016).

—— 'Immigration Judicial Reviews: Resources, Caseload, and System-manageability Efficiency' (2016) 21 *Judicial Review* 209.

—— 'Mapping Immigration Judicial Review Litigation: An Empirical Legal Analysis' [2015] *PL* 652.

—— 'Refugee Roulette: A UK Perspective' in J Ramji-Nogales, AI Schoenholtz and PG Schrag (eds), *Refugee Roulette: Disparities in Asylum Adjudication and Proposals for Reform* (New York, New York University Press, 2009).

—— 'The Impact of Judicial Review on Asylum' [2003] *PL* 479.

Thomas, R and Tomlinson J, 'A Different Tale of Judicial Power: Administrative Review as a Problematic Response to the Judicialisation of Tribunals' [2019] *PL* 537.

—— 'Does Outsourcing Improve or Weaken Administrative Justice? A Review of the Evidence' [2021] *PL* 542.

—— *Immigration Judicial Reviews: An Empirical Study* (London, Palgrave Macmillan, forthcoming).

Thompson, JD, *Organizations in Action: Social Science Bases of Administrative Theory* (New Brunswick, NJ, Transaction Publishers, 2006).

Thompson, VA, *Without Sympathy or Enthusiasm: The Problem of Administrative Compassion* (University of Alabama Press, 1975).

Turnbull, S, '"Stuck in the Middle": Waiting and Uncertainty in Immigration Detention' (2016) 25 *Time & Society* 61.

Varuhas, J, 'Evidence, Facts, and the Changing Nature of Judicial Review' *UK Constitutional Law Blog* (15 June 2020).

von Werthern, M, Robjant, K, Chui, Z, Schon, R, Ottisova, L, Mason, C and Katona, C, 'The Impact of Immigration Detention on Mental Health: A Systematic Review' (2018) 18 *BMC Psychiatry* 382.

Warren, N, 'The Adjudication Gap – A Discussion Document' (2006) 13 *Journal of Social Security Law* 110.

Weber, L and Pickering, S, *Globalization and Borders: Death at the Global Frontier* (London, Palgrave Macmillan, 2011).

Weber, M (eds G Roth G and C Wittich), *Economy and Society* (London, University of California Press, 1978).

Weiser, PJ, 'Institutional Design, FCC Reform, and the Hidden Side of the Administrative State' (2009) 61 *Administrative Law Review* 675.

White, A and Dunleavy, P, *Making and Breaking Whitehall Departments: A Guide to Machinery of Government Changes* (London, IfG, 2010).

White, RM, 'The Nationality and Immigration Status of the "Windrush Generation" and the Perils of Lawful Presence in a "Hostile Environment"' (2020) 33 *Journal of Immigration, Asylum, and Nationality Law* 218.

Wikeley, N, 'Burying Bell: Managing the Judicialisation of Social Security Tribunals' (2000) 63 *MLR* 475.

Willis, J, 'Canadian Administrative Law in Retrospect' (1974) 24 *University of Toronto Law Journal* 225.

Woodbridge, J, 'Sizing the Unauthorised (Illegal) Migrant Population in the United Kingdom in 2001' (2005).

Wyman, B, *The Principles of the Administrative Law Governing the Relations of Public Officers* (St Paul, Keefe-Davidson, 1906).

York, S, 'The End of Legal Aid in Immigration: a Barrier to Access to Justice for Migrants and a Decline in the Rule of Law' (2013) 27 *Journal of Immigration, Asylum and Nationality Law* 106.

—— 'The "Hostile Environment" – How Home Office Immigration Policies and Practices Create and Perpetuate Illegality' (2018) 32 *Journal of Immigration Asylum and Nationality Law* 363.

Young Legal Aid Lawyers, 'Nowhere Else to Turn: The Impact of Legal Aid Cuts on MPs' Ability to Help Their Constituents' (2012) available at www.younglegalaidlawyers.org/sites/default/files/YLAL_Nowhere_else_to_turn.pdf.

II. Official Publications

Alcock R, 'Internal Review of the Government's Policy on Requirements to Provide DNA in Visa and Asylum Cases' (2018).

Association for the Prevention of Torture/UNHCR, 'Monitoring Immigration Detention: Practical Manual' (Geneva, UNHCR, 2014).

Cabinet Office, 'Capability Review of the Home Office' (2006).

Charter Flight Monitoring Team, 'Annual Report of the IMBs' CFMT for reporting year 2017' (2018).

—— 'Annual Reports of the Independent Monitoring Boards CFMT 2016–2019'.

Civil Service Department, 'Legal Entitlements and Administrative Practices: A Report by Officials' (1979).

Complaints Audit Committee, 'Annual Reports of the Complaints Audit Committee 2003/04 to 2007/08'.

Council on Tribunals, 'Annual Report 1989/90' (1990).

DHSC, 'Guidance on Implementing the Overseas Visitor Charging Regulations' (2020).

DWP, 'Decision Making Standards Committee Annual Report 2009–2010' (2010).
Equality and Human Rights Commission, 'Access to Legal Aid for Discrimination Cases' (2019).
—— 'Public Sector Equality Duty Assessment of Hostile Environment Policies' (2020).
European Commission Joint Research Centre, 'International Migration Drivers: A Quantitative Assessment of the Structural Factors Shaping Migration' (Publications Office of the European Union, 2018).
House of Commons Home Affairs Committee, 'Asylum' HC 71 (2013–14).
—— 'Asylum Accommodation' HC 637 (2016–17).
—— 'Asylum Accommodation: Government Response to the Committee's Twelfth Report of Session 2016–17' HC 551 (2017–19).
—— 'Home Office Delivery of Brexit: Immigration' HC 421 (2017–19).
—— 'Immigration Control' HC 775 (2005–06).
—— 'Immigration Detention' HC 913 (2017–19).
—— 'Immigration Detention: Government Response to the Committee's Fourteenth Report of Session 2017–19' HC 2602 (2017–19).
—— 'MPs' Survey Finds Widespread Dissatisfaction with Home Office over Immigration Case Correspondence (3 March 2009)' (HC 2008–09).
—— 'Sixth Report: Immigration and Nationality Department of the Home Office' HC 277 (1984–85).
—— 'The Windrush Generation' HC 990 (2017–19).
—— 'The Work of the Immigration Directorates (October–December 2013)' HC 237 (2013–14).
—— 'The Work of the Immigration Directorates (Q3 2015)' HC 772 (2015–16).
—— 'The Work of the UK Border Agency' HC 105 (2009–2010).
—— 'The Work of the UK Border Agency (August–December 2011)' HC 1722 (2010–12).
—— 'The Work of the UK Border Agency (July–September 2012)' HC 792 (2012–13).
—— 'UK Border Controls HC 1647' (2010–12).
HM Chief Inspector of Prisons, 'Annual Report of HMIP for England and Wales 2002/2003' (2003).
—— 'Brook House Immigration Removal Centre' (2019).
—— 'Detainees Under Escort: Inspection of Escort and Removals to Germany and France' (2020).
—— 'Report on an Unannounced Inspection of the Detention of Migrants Arriving in Dover in Small Boats Detention Facilities: Tug Haven, Kent Intake Unit, Frontier House, Yarl's Wood, and Lunar House' (2020).
—— 'Report on National Inspection of the Short-term Holding Facilities in the UK Managed by Border Force' (2020).
—— 'Yarl's Wood Immigration Removal Centre' (2015).
HM Chief Inspector of Prisons accompanied by the Contrôleur Général des Lieux de Privation de Liberté, 'Report on Unannounced Inspections of the UK Short-term Holding Facilities at France-UK Borders' (2020).
HM Chief Inspector of Prisons and the ICIBI, 'The Effectiveness and Impact of Immigration Detention Casework: A Joint Thematic Review by HM Inspectorate of Prisons and the Independent Chief Inspector of Borders and Immigration' (2012).
HM Treasury, 'Assurance Frameworks' (2012).
—— 'The Green Book: Central Government Guidance on Appraisal and Evaluation' (2018).
—— 'Treasury Minutes: Government Responses to the Committee of Public Accounts on the Fourteenth to the Seventeenth Reports and the Nineteenth Report from Session 2019–21' (CP 316, 2020).
Home Office, 'A Points-Based System: Making Migration Work for Britain' (Cm 6741, 2006).
—— 'A Report on the Work of the Immigration and Nationality Department' (1984).
—— 'Administrative Review: EU Settlement Scheme' (2020).
—— 'Complaints Guidance: For UKVI, HM Passport Office, Immigration Enforcement, and Border Force' (2020).
—— 'Confident Communities in a Secure Britain: The Home Office Strategic Plan 2004–08' (Cm 6287, 2004).
—— 'Darra Singh's Review of Home Office Response to Mandating of DNA Evidence: Home Office Response' (2019).

—— 'Detention Case Progression Panels' (2020).
—— 'Detention Services Order 03/2015: Handling of Complaints' (2017).
—— 'Educational Testing Service (ETS): Casework Instructions' (2020).
—— 'False Representation: Guidance for Caseworkers' (2019).
—— 'Family Migration: A Consultation' (2011).
—— 'Government Response to the JCHR, Eighth Report of Session 2013–14' (2014).
—— 'Government Response to the Seventh Report From the HAC Session 2013-14 HC 71: Asylum' (Cm 769, 2013).
—— 'Immigration Act 2016: Guidance on Adults at Risk in Immigration Detention' (2018).
—— 'Immigration Bill: ECHR Memorandum' (2013).
—— 'Immigration Bill Factsheet: Appeals' (2013).
—— 'Immigration Enforcement Vulnerability Strategy' (2018).
—— 'Immigration Returns: Statistics' (2020).
—— 'Impact Assessment of Reforming Immigration Appeal Rights' (2013).
—— 'International Group Points Based System Tier 1: An Operational Assessment' (2010).
—— 'JCHR Immigration Detention Inquiry Report: Home Office Response to Recommendations' (2019).
—— 'New Plan for Immigration: Policy Statement' (CP 412, 2021).
—— 'People survey 2019: Results for UKVI, Border Force, and Immigration Enforcement', available at www.gov.uk/government/publications/home-office-people-survey-results-2019.
—— 'Report of the Committee on Immigration Appeals' (Cmnd 3387, 1967).
—— 'Fair, Effective, Transparent and Trusted: Rebuilding Confidence in our Immigration System' (2006).
—— 'Report on Removal of Full Appeal Rights Against Refusal of Entry Clearance Decisions Under the Points-Based System' (2011).
—— 'Response to the ICIBI's Report: An Inspection of the Administrative Review Processes Introduced Following the 2014 Immigration Act' (2016).
—— 'Response to the Independent Chief Inspector of Borders and Immigration's report: An Inspection of Administrative Reviews' (2020).
—— 'Response to the Independent Chief Inspector's Report: An Inspection of the Administrative Review Processes Introduced Following the 2014 Immigration Act' (2016).
—— 'Response to the Independent Chief Inspector's Report: "An Inspection of the 'Hostile Environment' Measures Relating to Driving Licences and Bank Accounts"' (2016).
—— 'Sanctions: Vehicle and Licensing' (2019).
—— 'Simplifying Immigration Law: A New Framework for Immigration Rules' (2009).
—— 'Simplifying Immigration Law: The Draft Bill' (Cm 7666 and Cm 7730, 2009).
—— 'Simplifying the Immigration Rules: A Response to the Law Commission's Report and Recommendations on Simplification of the Immigration Rules' (2020).
—— 'Sir Alex Allan Review: Executive Summary' (2 November 2018).
—— 'Statement of Intent: Administrative Review' (2013).
—— 'The Home Office Response to the Independent Chief Inspector of Border and Immigration, An Inspection of the Review and Removal of Immigration, Refugee and Citizenship 'Status'' (2018).
—— 'The Home Office Response to the Independent Chief Inspector of Borders and Immigration's report: An Inspection of Administrative Reviews' (2020).
—— 'The Response to the Windrush Lessons Learned Review: A Comprehensive Improvement Plan' (CP 293, 2020).
—— 'UK Short-term Holding facilities at France-UK Borders Action Plan' (2020).
House of Commons Constitutional Affairs Committee, 'Asylum and Immigration Appeals' HC 211 (2003–04).
House of Commons Political and Constitutional Reform Committee, 'Ensuring Standards in the Quality of Legislation' HC 85 (2013–14).
House of Commons Public Accounts Committee, 'Employment and Support Allowance' HC 975 (2017–19).

—— 'English Language Tests For Overseas Students' HC 2039 (2017–19).
—— 'Home Office Resource Accounts 2004–05 and Follow-up on Returning Failed Asylum Applicants' HC 1079 (2005–06).
—— 'Immigration Enforcement' HC 407 (2019–21).
—— 'Managing and Removing Foreign National Offenders' HC 708 (2014–15).
—— 'Reforming the UK Border and Immigration System' HC 584 (2014–15).
—— 'Windrush Generation and the Home Office' HC 1518 (2017–19).
Home Office Returns Directorate, 'Detention Services Order 07/2016 Use of Restraint(s) for Escorted Moves – All Staff' (2016).
House of Commons Public Administration Select Committee, 'Ombudsman Issues' HC 448 (2002–03).
House of Commons Women and Equalities Committee, 'Enforcing the Equality Act: the Law and the Role of the Equality and Human Rights Commission' HC 1470 (2017–19).
House of Commons Work and Pensions Committee, 'PIP and ESA Assessments' HC 829 (2017–19).
House of Lords Constitution Committee, 'Immigration Bill' HL 148 (2013–14).
—— 'Parliament and the Legislative Process' HL 173 (2003–04).
House of Lords Secondary Legislation Scrutiny Committee, '33rd Report of Session 2019–21: Statement of Changes in Immigration Rules' HL 161 (2019–21).
Hyde, S, 'A Review of the Failure of the Immigration and Nationality Directorate to Consider Some Foreign National Prisoners for Deportation' (2007).
Independent Chief Inspector of Borders and Immigration, 'A Reinspection into Failed Right of Abode Applications and Referral for Consideration for Enforcement Action' (2019).
—— 'A Re-inspection of the Administrative Review Process' (2017).
—— 'A Re-inspection of the Complaints Handling Process' (2017).
—— 'A Re-inspection of the Family Reunion Process, Focusing on Applications Received at the Amman Entry Clearance Decision Making Centre' (2018).
—— 'A Re-inspection of the Tier 4 Curtailment Process' (2017).
—— 'A Short-Notice Inspection of Decision-making Quality in the Warsaw Visa Section' (2013).
—— 'A Short Notice Inspection of the Tier 4 Curtailment Process' (2016).
—— 'A Thematic Inspection of the Points-Based System: Tier 2 (Skilled Workers)' (2010).
—— 'An Inspection of Administrative Reviews' (2020).
—— 'An Inspection of Asylum Intake and Casework' (2017).
—— 'An Inspection of Family Reunion Applications' (2016).
—— 'An Inspection of Family Reunion Applications' (2020).
—— 'An Inspection of Home Office (Borders, Immigration and Citizenship System) Collaborative Working with Other Government Departments and Agencies' (2018).
—— 'An Inspection of Home Office Outsourced Contracts for Escorted and Non-Escorted Removals and Cedars Pre-Departure Accommodation' (2016).
—— 'An Inspection of Overstayers: How the Home Office Handles the Cases of Individuals with no Right to Stay in the UK' (2014).
—— 'An Inspection of Settlement Casework' (2015).
—— 'An Inspection of the Administrative Review Processes Introduced Following the Immigration Act 2014' (2016).
—— 'An Inspection of the EU Settlement Scheme' (2019).
—— 'An Inspection of the Handling of Complaints and MPs' Correspondence' (2016).
—— 'An Inspection of the Handling of Complaints and MP's Correspondence by the Home Office Borders, Immigration and Citizenship System (BICS)' (2020).
—— 'An Inspection of Tier 4 of the Points Based System (Students)' (2012).
—— 'An Inspection of the Home Office's Approach to Illegal Working' (2019).
—— 'An Inspection of the Home Office's Management of Asylum Accommodation Provision' (2018).
—— 'An Inspection of the Home Office's Network Consolidation Programme and the "Onshoring" of Visa Processing and Decision Making to the UK' (2020).
—— 'An Inspection of the Home Office's Management of Non-Detained Foreign National Offenders' (2017).

—— 'An Inspection of the Home Office's Use of Sanctions and Penalties' (2021).

—— 'An Inspection of the 'Hostile Environment' Measures Relating to Driving Licences and Bank Accounts' (2016).

—— 'An Inspection of the Review and Removal of Immigration, Refugee and Citizenship "Status"' (2018).

—— 'An Inspection of the 'Right to Rent' Scheme' (2018).

—— 'Annual Inspection of "Adults at Risk in Immigration Detention"' (2018–19)' (2020).

—— 'Annual Report 2018–19' (2019).

—— 'Annual Report 2019–20' (2020).

—— 'Entry Clearance Decision-Making: A Global Review December 2010 – June 2011' (2011).

—— 'Lessons to Learn: The UK Border Agency's Handling of Complaints and MPs' Correspondence' (2010).

Immigration Enforcement, 'Our IE – Delivering Our Organisational Priorities' (2019).

Independent Monitor for Entry Clearance Refusals, 'Report for 2005' (2006).

Independent Monitoring Board, 'National Annual Report for the Immigration Detention Estate 2018' (2019).

Information Commissioner's Office, 'Department for Education: Data Protection Audit Report' (2020).

Joint Committee on Human Rights, 'Immigration Detention' HC 1484 HL 278 (2017–19).

—— 'Legislative Scrutiny: Immigration Bill', HL 102 HC 935 (2013–14).

—— 'Windrush Generation Detention' HC 1034 HL 160 (2017–19).

Lampard K and Marsden E, 'Independent Investigation into Concerns About Brook House Immigration Removal Centre' (London, G4S plc, 2018).

—— 'Independent Investigation into Concerns about Yarl's Wood Immigration Removal Centre: A Report for the Chief Executive and Board of Serco plc' (Serco, 2016).

Law Commission, 'Post-Legislative Scrutiny' (Cm 6945, 2006).

—— 'Simplification of the Immigration Rules: Report' HC 14 Law Com No 388 (2019–21).

Ministry of Justice, 'Tribunal Statistics Quarterly 2020' (The Stationary Office, 2020).

Migration Advisory Committee, 'A Points-Based System and Salary Thresholds for Immigration' (2020).

National Audit Office, 'Challenges in Using Data Across Government, HC 2220 (2017–19).

—— 'COMPASS Contracts for the Provision of Accommodation for Asylum Seekers' HC 880 (2013–14).

—— 'E-borders and Successor Programmes' HC 608 (2015–16).

—— 'Handling of the Windrush Situation, HC 1622 (2017–2019).

—— 'Immigration Enforcement' HC 110 (2019–21).

—— 'Immigration: The Points Based System – Work Routes' HC 819 (2010–11).

—— 'Improving Operational Delivery in Government: A Good Practice Guide for Senior Leaders' (2021).

—— 'Improving the Speed and Quality of Asylum Decisions' HC 535 (2003–04).

—— 'Investigation into the Response to Cheating in English Language Tests' HC 2144 (2017–19).

—— 'Investigation into the Windrush Compensation Scheme' HC 65 (2021–22).

—— 'Management of Asylum Applications by the UK Border Agency' HC 124 (2008–09).

—— 'Managing and Removing Foreign National Offenders' HC 441 (2014–15).

—— 'Managing Business Operations – What Government Needs to Get Right' (2015).

—— 'Recent Developments in Government Internal Audit and Assurance' (2013).

—— 'Reforming the UK Border and Immigration System' HC 445 (2013–14).

—— 'Returning Failed Asylum Applicants' HC 76 (2005–06).

—— 'The Home Office's Management of its Contract with G4S to Run Brook House Immigration Removal Centre' (2019).

—— 'The Immigration and Nationality Directorate Integrated Casework Programme' HC 277 (1998–99).

—— 'The UK Border Agency and Border Force: Progress in Cutting Costs and Improving Performance' HC 467 (2012–13).

—— 'Visa Entry to the United Kingdom: The Entry Clearance Operation' HC 367 (2003–2004).

—— 'Yarl's Wood Immigration Removal Centre, HC 508 (2016–17).

Office for National Statistics, 'Measuring Illegal Migration: Our Current View – A Report Outlining Our Discussions on the Measurement of Illegal Migration' (2019).

Office of the Leader of the House of Commons, 'Post-Legislative Scrutiny: The Government's Approach' (Cm 7320, 2008).

Parliamentary and Health Service Ombudsman, 'An Investigation into UK Visas and Immigration's Handling of Windrush Man's Status' (2021).

—— 'Assessment of Government Progress in Implementing the Report on the Welfare in Detention of Vulnerable Persons: A Follow-up Report to the Home Office by Stephen Shaw' (Cm 9661, 2018).

—— 'Complaints About UK Government Departments and Agencies and Other UK Public Organisations 2016–17' (2017).

—— 'Complaints About UK Government Departments and Agencies and Some UK Public Organisations 2014–15' (2015).

—— 'Evidence to the House of Commons HAC' (3 May 2018).

—— '"Fast and fair?" A Report by the Parliamentary Ombudsman on the UK Border Agency' HC 329 (2009–10).

—— 'Final Investigation Report – UK Visas and Immigration' (2020).

—— 'Home Office Failures Put a Family in Danger: A Report by the Parliamentary Ombudsman on an Investigation into a Complaint by Mrs A and Her Family About the Home Office' HC 403 (2013–14).

—— 'Immigration Enforcement Handled Detainee's Complaint About Care and Treatment Poorly' (Summary 86, April 2014).

—— 'Inquiry into Allegations of Racism and Mistreatment of Detainees at Oakington Immigration Reception Centre and While Under Escort' (2005).

—— 'Principles of Good Administration' (2009).

—— Prisons and Probations Ombudsman, 'Yarl's Wood: Investigation Into Allegations of Racism, Abuse and Violence at Yarl's Wood Removal Centre' (2004).

President of the Social Entitlement Chamber of the First-tier Tribunal, 'President's Report: Report by the President of the Social Entitlement Chamber of the First-tier Tribunal on the Standards of Decision-making by the Secretary of State and Child Maintenance and Enforcement Commissioner 2009–10' (2010).

Shaw, S, 'Assessment of Government Progress in Implementing the Report on the Welfare in Detention of Vulnerable Persons: A Follow-up Report to the Home Office by Stephen Shaw' (Cm 9661, 2018).

—— 'Review into the Welfare in Detention of Vulnerable Persons: A Report to the Home Office by Stephen Shaw' (Cm 9186, 2016).

Singh, D, 'Independent Review of the Home Office Response to the Mandating of DNA Evidence for Immigration Purposes' (2019).

Tribunal Procedure Committee, 'Response to the Consultation on Tribunal Procedure (First-tier Tribunal) (Immigration and Asylum Chamber) Rules 2014 and Tribunal Procedure (Upper Tribunal) Rules 2008 in Relation to Detained Appellants' (2019).

UK Border Agency Professional Standards Unit Complaints and Correspondence Standards and Performance Directorate, 'An Investigation Into the Allegations Made by Louise Perrett About Her Experiences Working for the UK Border Agency' (2010).

UKVI, 'Assurance Strategy 2021' (2021).

—— 'Customer Service Operations: UK Visa & Immigration Transparency Data' (27 August 2020).

—— 'Ex-Gratia Payments: Financial Redress Guidance' (2019).

—— 'Operational Assurance Strategy' (2017).

—— 'Risk Management Strategy' (2021).

UNHCR, 'Quality Initiative Project: Key Observations and Recommendations' (2008).

—— 'Statelessness Determination in the UK' (2020).

Upper Tribunal (Immigration and Asylum Chamber), 'Response to Law Commission Consultation on Simplifying the Immigration Rules' (2019).

Williams, W, 'Windrush Lessons Learned Review: Independent Review by Wendy Williams HC 93' (2019–20).

INDEX

CPSIA information can be obtained
at www.ICGtesting.com
Printed in the USA
LVHW080744180722
723743LV00004B/66